SLAVEMASTER PRESIDENT

WILLIAM DUSINBERRE

SLAVEMASTER PRESIDENT

The Double Career of

JAMES POLK

OXFORD

UNIVERSITY PRESS

2003

OXFORD

UNIVERSITY PRESS

Oxford   New York

Auckland   Bangkok   Buenos Aires   Cape Town   Chennai
Dar es Salaam   Delhi   Hong Kong   Istanbul   Karachi   Kolkata
Kuala Lumpur   Madrid   Melbourne   Mexico City   Mumbai
Nairobi   São Paulo   Shanghai   Taipei   Tokyo   Toronto

Copyright © 2003 by William Dusinberre

Published by Oxford University Press, Inc.
198 Madison Avenue, New York, New York 10016

www.oup.com

Oxford is a registered trademark of Oxford University Press

Library of Congress Cataloging-in-Publication Data
Dusinberre, William, 1930–
Slavemaster president : the double career of James Polk / William Dusinberre.
p. cm.
Includes bibliographical references and index.
ISBN 0-19-515735-4
1. Polk, James K. (James Knox), 1795–1849.   2. Presidents—United States—Biography.
3. Polk, James K. (James Knox), 1795–1849—Views on slavery.
4. Polk, James K. (James Knox), 1795–1849—Relations with slaves.   5. Plantation owners—
Tennessee—Biography.   6. Plantation owners—Mississippi—Biography.
7. Slavery—Tennessee—History—19th century.
8. Slavery—Mississippi—History—19th century.   I. Title.
E417.D87 2003
973.6'1'092—dc21
[B]   2002074852

3 5 7 9 8 6 4

Printed in the United States of America
on acid-free paper

To

Edward, Beth, Sam, Martin, and Tomoyo

With love

Acknowledgments

M any of my greatest obligations are to scholars likely to dissent from some interpretations proposed in this book. My debt to Professor Wayne Cutler, director of the Polk Project at the Tennessee Presidents Center at the University of Tennessee, is deep, both for his splendid work in editing *Correspondence of James K. Polk* and for his personal kindness. His colleagues Dr. Jim Rogers and Cindy Rogers have been extraordinarily helpful and hospitable, and they made my stay at Knoxville a delight. Dr. John Holtzapple, director of the Polk Ancestral Home in Columbia, Tennessee, has most generously shared information and ideas about the Polks. Two anonymous readers have kindly saved me from numerous lapses of taste and have judiciously impelled significant amendments to the book's argument.

My debts to readers are profound. Professors James Oakes, James Brewer Stewart, the late Peter Parish, and Christopher Clark; Dr. Robert Cook; and my Oxford University Press editor, Susan Ferber, have all undertaken the arduous task of plowing through the manuscript and have each suggested amendments that surely improve the final version. I am most grateful to all of them for their generous willingness to undertake this thankless task and for the acuteness of their critical remarks. They bear, of course, no responsibility for any mistakes of fact or interpretation that remain.

My obligations to several generations of Polk scholars are great. John Spencer Bassett's 1925 edition of letters written by Polk's overseers made evident the richness of the Polk Papers as a source on slavery. The late Herbert Weaver, Professor Wayne Cutler, and their colleagues have made available to scholars and scrupulously annotated the copious and richly rewarding *Correspondence of James K. Polk*. David Pletcher's *Diplomacy of Annexation,* an extraordinary work of scholarship, may not yet have been quite so widely influential among nonspecialists as it deserves to be. My obligation to Charles Sellers's biography of Polk—an acknowledged masterpiece—will be evident everywhere, especially in chapter 5 and in the second part of this book. On antebellum history and its relation to social history, William Freehling's *Road to Disunion* has been an invaluable guide.

Librarians and archivists have been unfailingly helpful: at the Manuscripts Division of the Library of Congress, the Tennessee State Archives, the Yalobusha (Mississippi) County Courthouse, the North Carolina Office of Archives and History, the Southern Historical Collection of the University of North Carolina, the University of Cambridge Library, the British Library, and the University of Warwick Library. The efficient assistance of these librarians and archivists, and their kindliness, have inspirited many a day far from home.

Generous grants from the Leverhulme Trust and from the University of Warwick proved indispensable to my research trips to the United States. My debt to colleagues in the History Department of the University of Warwick remains, as ever, immense. I am also most grateful, for their hospitality and sympathy, to Dr. John Thompson, Dr. Betty Wood, Professor Tony Badger, Professor Michael O'Brien, Dr. Stephen Tuck, and to the other members of the University of Cambridge's United States history seminar.

Many scholars have offered assistance with the research or with formulation of the book's argument. Among these, and in addition to those already named, I am particularly grateful to Stanley Engerman, Daniel Walker Howe, Winthrop Jordan, and Donald Ratcliffe. Once again I am indebted to Ian Agnew, cartographer of the University of Cambridge's Department of Geography, for his expert drawing of my maps. And Larry O'Brien's warmhearted support has been invaluable.

Excerpts from *The Diary of James K. Polk . . . 1845 to 1849* are quoted by permission of the Chicago Historical Society, where the manuscript is located.

Among my personal obligations, one of the greatest is to Professor William Brock, whose kindness over the years has been for me an inestimable privilege. Professor David Donald has been a lifelong, faithful mentor and friend. Professor Charles Joyner has for years been an unstintingly generous ally. Juliet Dusinberre and Martin Dusinberre were among the manuscript's earliest and most unsparing critics, and their affectionate support has meant more to me than I can say.

Contents

The Polk Family Tree

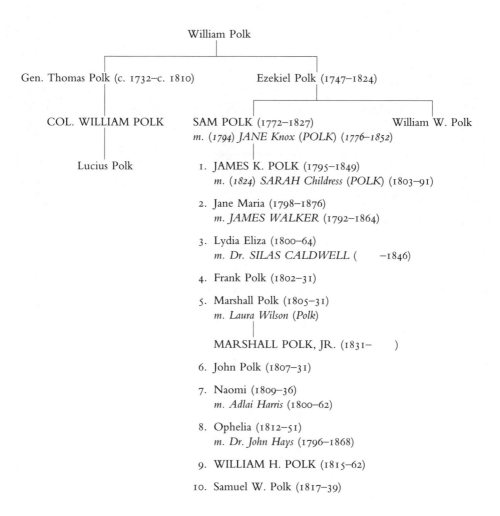

William Polk

Gen. Thomas Polk (c. 1732–c. 1810)   Ezekiel Polk (1747–1824)

COL. WILLIAM POLK   SAM POLK (1772–1827)   William W. Polk
                      m. (1794) JANE Knox (POLK) (1776–1852)

Lucius Polk   1. JAMES K. POLK (1795–1849)
                     m. (1824) SARAH Childress (POLK) (1803–91)

                  2. Jane Maria (1798–1876)
                     m. JAMES WALKER (1792–1864)

                  3. Lydia Eliza (1800–64)
                     m. Dr. SILAS CALDWELL (–1846)

                  4. Frank Polk (1802–31)

                  5. Marshall Polk (1805–31)
                     m. Laura Wilson (Polk)

                     MARSHALL POLK, JR. (1831–   )

                  6. John Polk (1807–31)

                  7. Naomi (1809–36)
                     m. Adlai Harris (1800–62)

                  8. Ophelia (1812–51)
                     m. Dr. John Hays (1796–1868)

                  9. WILLIAM H. POLK (1815–62)

                  10. Samuel W. Polk (1817–39)

Some Polk Slaves

Most of these were still living in 1860, unless a death date is indicated. People whose names are capitalized appear prominently in the text.

Abe (1812–36), blacksmith
Addison (1814–   ), frequent fugitive
Agnes (1833–53), bought 1846
Allen (c. 1794–   ), bought 1839
Alphonso (1827–   )
   m. Maria Davis
BARBARA (1823–   ), removed 1852 by Marshall Polk, Jr.
   m. Billy Nevels
BEN (c. 1808–   ), sold 1834
Billy Nevels (1829–   ), bought 1846
   m. Barbara
Caesar (1806–c. 1841), bought 1831
Calvin (c. 1833–54), bought 1846
CAROLINE CHILDRESS (1830–   ), bought 1845
Caroline Davis (1829–50), bought 1849
Caroline Harris (1828–   ), bought 1849
   m. Garrison
Caroline Henly (1830–48), bought 1846
CAROLINE JOHNSON (1818–c. 1857), daughter of Chunky Jack
   m. J. T. Leigh's driver
Charles (1) (c. 1818–   ), bought 1838, probably sold 1841
Charles (2) (1825–   ), removed 1852 by Marshall Polk, Jr.
   m. Rosetta
Daphney (1828–   ), bought 1839
   m. Giles
Dicey (1817–c. 1841), bought 1834
ELIAS, Tennessee house servant
Elizabeth ("Betsy") (1816–   )
   m. a Leigh slave
Eve (1815–   ), bought 1831
   m. Phil

Garrison (1815?–   ), pygmy
    m. Caroline Harris
GILBERT (1807–   ), Silas Caldwell's; sold 1836 to W. H. Polk and
      1838 to J. K. Polk
    m. "abroad" wife
Giles (1818?–   ), bought 1831
    m. Daphney
HARBERT (1820–   ), probably sold 1856
    m. Mary
Hardy (1808–35)
HARRY, LONG (c. 1800–   ), blacksmith
Henry (1831–   ), son of Mariah; White House servant
HENRY CARTER (1812–52), bought 1834; biggest earner
    m. Mariah
JACK, CHUNKY (c. 1788–   ), fugitive, sold 1834
Jane (1834–   ), bought 1846
    m. Manuel
Jim (c. 1812–   ), sold 1834
Joe (1) (1820?–   ), driver, owned by Jane Polk
Joe (2) (1830–   ), bought 1847, probably sold 1853
Manuel (1824–   ), son of Chunky Jack
    m. Jane
Maria Davis (1831–   ), bought 1847
    m. Alphonso
MARIAH (1814–51?), weaver
    m. Henry Carter
Marina (c. 1817–   ), bought 1838 from W. H. Polk
Matilda (1814–43?), bought 1839
Perry (1818–   ), bought 1838 from W. H. Polk
Phil (1813–   ), bought 1834
    m. Eve
REUBEN (1809–   ), mulatto, removed to Columbia 1836
Rosetta (1833–   ), bought 1849
    m. Charles (2)
Sarah ("Sally") (1834–   ), bought 1846

SLAVEMASTER PRESIDENT

INTRODUCTION

This book explores two aspects of President James Polk's career: his mastery of the slaves on his Mississippi cotton plantation and his stance on the slavery-related political issues of his day. When Polk unexpectedly died of cholera in 1849, only a few months after completing his four-year term as president, he left revealing records about his interaction with his Mississippi slaves.[1] Having moved these slaves in 1835 from a previous plantation in West Tennessee, Polk had established on virgin soil in northern Mississippi a profitable enterprise, which paid him a good return during the years of his presidency and supplied his widow with an ample income after his death. From the Polk records emerges a clear picture of events at this plantation. And Polk's experiences in running his cotton-planting enterprise helped to shape the stand he took on contemporary political issues.

Polk was the product of the slave society of middle Tennessee—the belt of counties in central Tennessee that stretches from north of Nashville down to the Alabama border. His father, a successful land speculator, had emigrated there from North Carolina in 1806. Polk himself, a Democratic Party lawyer-politician, had been a long-time congressman, and he served as governor of Tennessee from 1839 to 1841. He was also a cotton planter. When he was president he looked to his substantial income from this enterprise as the means of his retiring in 1849 (at age 54) to Polk Place—a Nashville mansion that he bought, renamed, and refurbished during his presidential term. He hoped to enjoy there the comfortable life of a gentleman planter.

Because Polk's biographer Charles Sellers did not complete the third volume of his careful scrutiny of Polk's career before the outbreak of the Mexican War, a book is needed to examine the slavery-related elements of Polk's political career and to consider what relation these may have borne to his mastery of his own slaves. Although Polk wrote a four-volume diary, the secretive president kept his cards close to his chest. I think it is nevertheless possible to deduce many of the principles that guided his political policies. In so doing, I believe we can gain considerable insight, not only into the crises of 1845–50—the annexation of Texas, the Mexican War, and the dispute over legalizing slavery in the Mexican Cession—but also into the origins of the American Civil War itself.

This is not a biography of Polk. It does not discuss Polk's role as a congressman in President Andrew Jackson's war against the Bank of the United States. Nor does it portray President Polk's part in securing the Tariff of 1846, nor his diplomacy with Britain, which led to the establishment of the northwestern boundary dividing the United States from Canada. Those stories have been told elsewhere.[2] Instead, this book analyzes only Polk's mastery of his slaves and his stand on slavery-related political issues.

Polk's career offers a remarkable opportunity to explore the connections between social and political history.[3] With the exception of his successor, Zachary Taylor, Polk was the last American who owned slaves while holding the office of president. The suddenness of his death helps explain why the surviving records of his slaveholding activities are even more revealing than those of any other slaveholding president—death gave him no opportunity to select from his papers those items that might have looked most presentable to posterity. Nor did Polk have any children to cull his papers after his demise, to remove items that might have appeared less creditable, the way one supposes that Robert Todd Lincoln did with the papers of Abraham Lincoln. Polk was a meticulous record keeper; and although historians have long known the value of the letters written to him by the overseers on his Mississippi cotton plantation (some of these letters were published as early as 1925), the record has proved even richer than one might have hoped, as well as more full of surprises. So little known have been the facts, even among specialist historians, that an examination of Polk's slavemastership and its relation to his political career is long overdue.[4]

Many vital aspects of the slaves' lives stand forth vividly at the Polk plantation. I hope, therefore, that this book may help us to reach a deeper understanding of the slave system, as well as illuminate the role played by slavery in precipitating the greatest catastrophe of our national existence, the Civil War.

The book's argument emerges from its structure. The earlier chapters examine Polk's plantation, and later chapters focus on his political career.

Antebellum planters often portrayed their involvement with slavery as though it were a burden to them, entailed on them by their ancestors. They projected an image of themselves as paternalists primarily concerned for the welfare of their dependent bondspeople, not as profit-seeking entrepreneurs. When Polk ran for the presidency in 1844, this was the picture of his relation to his dependents—if his ownership of slaves was mentioned at all—that he and his associates presented to the voting public. I seek in my first chapter to determine how many of Polk's slaves were in fact entailed upon him by his ancestors and how many he bought in the slave market to improve his own financial prospects.

No journalist ever asked Polk's slaves what they thought of the conditions imposed on them by their master and by the overseers he appointed to direct their labors. The best surviving evidence on this point lies in the record of flight from the plantation. The number of temporary fugitives was large, and some of these dissident slaves can still be seen with a certain distinctness. Chunky Jack stands out prominently among the dissidents, as do Gilbert (who fled at least ten times), Henry Carter (who engaged an overseer in hand-to-hand combat), and Harbert (whose escape plans resembled those of his famous Maryland contemporary, Frederick Douglass). The experiences of these fugitives throw light not only on the slaves' view of their lives at the Polk plantation but also on James Polk's various methods of dealing with their dissidence. So rich is the evidence that two chapters are devoted to this topic, one focused on flight when the Polk slaves were still in Tennessee and a longer chapter about the fugitives from the Mississippi plantation.

In private correspondence Polk made it clear that his primary object in entering the plantation business was to make a good income for himself and his wife. This was no straightforward task. Polk's first plantation, in West Tennessee, was not as remunerative as he wished it to be, and he soon sold it, moving his slaves to a new plantation in northern Mississippi. His first business partner there quickly became discouraged and left the partnership after only two years. Polk's next partner also left the partnership after a two-year stint. By this time the cotton boom of the mid-1830s was collapsing. Years of low cotton prices ensued, during which time James Polk occasionally thought of reducing his capital investment in his plantation or selling it entirely. But the annexation of Texas was immediately followed by a leap in slave prices; and the price of cotton improved for other reasons, so that Polk's plantation paid him well during his presidency. It paid his widow even better during subsequent years. The records of Polk's financial struggle as a planter-entrepreneur and of his eventual success can help to illuminate our understanding of the whole plantation system.

The spirit that infused the antebellum slave system was vigorously entrepreneurial. This becomes clear from copious evidence in the James Polk Papers and also from the records of Polk's father's first cousin, old Colonel William Polk. A North Carolinian, Colonel Polk was a land speculator on a grand scale and employed James Polk's father, Sam, as his agent in Tennessee. Sam Polk and James Walker (James Polk's brother-in-law) were the two most prominent businessmen in Columbia, the fledgling county seat of Maury County, Tennessee, forty miles south of Nashville. Although James Polk was primarily a lawyer-politician, his own entrepreneurial outlook was shaped by those of his father and his brother-in-law, as well as by the whole expansive atmosphere of the frontier as economic development swept through central Tennessee into West Tennessee and then into northern Mississippi. The Polk records suggest what may be a useful way of characterizing the South's slave society: it was a hybrid, radically different from Northern free-labor society, yet sharing a surprising number of features with the North's economic system.

My longest chapter explores the question, How far did benevolence characterize the Polks' treatment of their slaves? This question of benevolence at Southern plantations is fraught with emotion, both for the descendants of slaves and for the descendants of their masters. Because illustrations of both benevolence and callousness on other plantations can readily be collected from documents scattered all over the South, it is easy for us in a later generation to select evidence to suit our own predisposition. The Polk records can help to clarify this issue. Both benevolence and callousness, of course, are to be found there; but if we examine every piece of relevant evidence and try to assess the strength of the mixed motives involved in particular episodes, we may hope to reach a conclusion—for this group of slavemasters—which is more helpful than a mere bland assertion that both benevolence and callousness coexisted.[5]

Mortality> Taking the antebellum South as a whole, about 46 percent of slave children died before reaching the age of fifteen. This mortality rate was much higher than that for free children in the whole United States (which was about 28 percent) and it was probably a good deal higher than that for free children in the rural South. The child mortality rate at the Polk plantation proves to have been even greater than the norm for slave children elsewhere in the South—at least 51 percent, probably even higher. And the mortality rate for the Polks' young adult slaves (especially the young women) also appears to have been unusually high. Although no clear explanation emerges for this situation, several hypotheses may be suggested.

Probably a *majority* of married slaves at the Polk plantation experienced disruption of their marriages because of actions taken by some member of the Polk clan. The institution of "abroad" marriages (when husbands and wives lived on separate plantations) put a further strain on the slaves' family lives. So did the discontent of many male slaves, which led them to flee the plantation for weeks or months at a time. The young slaves whom Polk purchased were nearly always bought separately from their parents, a fact sure to attenuate even further the slaves' sense of family solidity. And on a frontier plantation the slaves' experience of stable community life was likely—as the Polk records suggest—to be weaker than in longer settled areas.

Beginning as early as 1844 James Polk, unlike most planters, granted his slaves patches of land where they could raise their own cotton in their free time; and after he sold this cotton for them, he put cash into their pockets. He also, for many years, granted his most valuable slave—a blacksmith named Harry—extraordinary independence. The Polk records make it possible to assess how far these grants of privilege may have mitigated the otherwise harsh lives of his slaves.

Once we are aware of how completely slavery and slave management became integral parts of James Polk's life, we may examine the slavery-related elements of his political career with a somewhat altered vision. Not surprisingly, during the years before Polk became president, he sometimes put himself forward as a vigorous defender of what he thought were the interests of the slave South. As early as 1832 he provoked a furious debate in the House of Representatives when—foreshadowing later proponents of the gag rule—he attempted to prevent the House from taking notice of an antislavery petition. In 1839, as governor of Tennessee, he publicly committed himself to the advanced view that Congress had no power over slavery *anywhere*—none, of course, over slavery in the states, but also none over slavery in the federal District of Columbia nor over slavery in the federal territories. This stance helps to explain why John C. Calhoun was delighted when Polk received the Democratic nomination for the presidency in 1844, and it profoundly colored President Polk's response to the efforts by the House of Representatives, from 1846 to 1849, to enact a congressional ban on slavery in the territories conquered from Mexico.

Polk's political strategy, when the 1844 presidential election approached, had been to present himself as a nonsectional candidate. He had persuaded the lieutenants of former President Martin Van Buren that he had remained a firm supporter of Van Buren's candidacy for the 1844 Democratic nomination. Those lieutenants rewarded Polk's apparent loyalty to Van Buren by backing Polk for the presidential nomination when Van Buren failed to secure the required two-thirds majority. Although Polk was supported by Southern Democrats because he advocated the immediate annexation of Texas, he joined to this program a demand that America's northwestern boundary with Canada be fixed far north of the Columbia River (a proposal especially popular with Democrats from the northwestern states). Thus Polk avoided the appearance of seeking only slave-state expansion.

The slave republic of Texas claimed much more territory from Mexico than had been part of the old Mexican province of Texas. Independent Texas's assertion of this claim—which if backed by the United States was likely to embroil the country in a war with Mexico—was a principal reason that it proved almost impossible to get the U.S. Senate to approve annexation as long as Texas persisted in its inflated claim. President-elect Polk seems to have secured a narrow Senate majority for annexation by misleading several senators into supposing he would renegotiate the agreement with Texas if those senators voted for annexation. But Polk's first act as president was to authorize annexation *without* renegotiation. He adopted as his own Texas's demand for an inflated border—even though Polk's secretary of state made clear his conviction that Texas had no legitimate claim to the eastern half of the present state of New Mexico, which the Texans demanded. Polk declined to offer cash to Mexico for this extended boundary line, and his insistence on the Texan border claim was probably the decisive factor in impelling reluctant Mexican leaders finally to enter war with the powerful United States. By the war thus provoked,

7

the United States conquered California and the huge territory lying between Texas and California.

Long before the war's end a bitter controversy erupted—dividing most Southern white people from many Northerners—over legalizing slavery in the western territories. Some antislavery politicians alleged (mistakenly, in my opinion) that the same wish for slave territory that had fueled the annexation of Texas also impelled Polk to seize the lands he conquered in the Mexican War. Contrary to that allegation, I believe (as do most historians) that Polk conquered California and New Mexico because he shared with many of his countrymen a continental vision of American destiny, not because he supposed plantation slavery could be extended to much of that region. But Polk's conquest of the Mexican Cession proved to be as dangerous to the American Union as though the expansion of slavery *had* been his principal motive. That is, Polk—along with most other Southern politicians—insisted that slavemasters' rights must be substantially recognized in these territories, whether or not the extension of plantation slavery there should ever prove to be practicable. Polk's concern was not to extend slavery beyond Texas but to make slavery secure in the states (including Texas) where it already existed. However, he had persuaded himself—in what I believe was a disastrous miscalculation—that slavery could not be secure in the Southern states unless the North made a substantial recognition of slavemasters' rights in the territories too.

Alternative policies concerning slavery were probably available to Southern politicians, and they might have served the interests of Southern white people far better than those pursued by James Polk and his associates in the Southern Democratic Party.

Thus Polk's deep personal involvement in the plantation slavery system—his long struggle from 1831 into the 1840s to make a financial success of his plantation enterprise and to impose order on his often unruly bondspeople—colored his stance on slavery-related issues. Similar experiences may have helped shape the stand that other Southern politicians took toward those same issues.

James Polk's political eminence caused him to hide from public knowledge the fact that, while he was president, he was secretly buying as many slaves as he felt he could afford from his plantation's profits in order to make the plantation more remunerative. A few months before his death, the president quietly drafted a new will, where he expressed the hope that he or his wife might free their slaves—when he and Sarah Polk were both dead. The very next day the president instructed his agent to buy for him, in strictest secrecy, half a dozen more very young slaves. These and other activities of Polk as slavemaster are the focus of the earlier part of this book, after which his political career comes into view.

I

SLAVEMASTER

I

A Market for Labor Power

During James Polk's successful campaign for the presidency in 1844, the question arose of whether he had ever bought and sold slaves. Slavery was a hot subject, for the crucial issue of the presidential campaign was the assertion by Polk and his Democratic Party that the United States should immediately annex the independent republic of Texas; and anti-slavery opponents of annexation alleged that the driving force behind the annexation movement was lust for the profits of extending slavery onto thousands of acres of rich cotton land in Texas. Earlier that year the U.S. Secretary of State, John C. Calhoun, had placed the slavery issue at the center of the annexation controversy. Calhoun declared, in an official document, that in the states where slavery had been abolished "the condition of the African, instead of being improved, has become worse"; that in the slave states, by contrast, the Africans "have improved greatly in every respect"; that "slavery is . . . essential to the peace, safety, and prosperity of those States . . . in which it exists"; and that Texas must be annexed to prevent Britain from pressuring it into abolishing slavery there—a result that would be extremely dangerous "to the adjacent States, and the Union itself."[1] Although these arguments appealed to many Deep South voters, they were no good for James Polk: he could not win the election without substantial support from both the North and the upper South. He must distinguish his own stance from Calhoun's, and he must deny that desire for profits determined his conduct as a slavemaster.

That Polk was a slavemonger was charged by some of his Whig opponents, who printed a fabricated report from a mythical traveler named Roorbach that Polk had once sold forty-three slaves to a slave trader. The newspaper that originally made this charge soon retracted it, and for the rest of the campaign Polk's Democratic Party supporters made as much mileage as they could from the Roorbach forgery. Polk needed to present himself not as a heartless profit-seeker but as a warmhearted paternalist who held slaves only because they were entailed upon him by his parents and siblings—"family" slaves: not ones whom he had acquisitively purchased in the slave market. And it must appear that, if Polk had ever bought or sold a slave, he had done so only from a sense of duty to the slaves themselves. Polk implied to newspaper correspondents that on the rare occasions that he had bought slaves, he had sought only to prevent disruption of their families.[2] His purpose had been to secure the happiness of his bondspeople, not to enrich himself.

Meanwhile Polk's close political ally Gideon Pillow wrote a lengthy defense of the candidate's record: Governor Polk, Pillow averred, "is not . . . a large slaveholder." Calhoun's associate Francis Pickens, governor of South Carolina during the secession crisis of 1860, knew otherwise: Polk "*is* a large Slave holder & plants cotton," Pickens had enthusiastically reported to South Carolinian allies in May 1844—just after Polk's nomination for the presidency—and this was the first of the candidate's several virtues that aroused the Carolinians' delight at the nomination.[3] Polk "inherited some 12 or 15 slaves from his Father," Gideon Pillow's testimonial continued,

> & his wife was the owner of a less number inherited of her father. The Governor inherited some three or four more from a Brother who died without issue & he purchased some 6 or 8 more of another Brother who became embarrassed & was obliged to sell them. These Negros were all Family Negros who had been raised by the Fathers of the Governor or the Lady—were much attached to the Families & would not & could not *without great violence* to their feelings have been sold out of the Family. . . . I never knew [Governor Polk] to sell but two slaves in my life & he sold one of them to myself & another to my Father-in-Law in order that they might not be seperated [*sic*] from their families, when he was about to remove his hands to his present plantation. These two men were two of his best & most valuable servants. I never heard of his buying but one slave, and that was a woman & the wife of a man of his own in order to get them together. The writer of this article is now & has been for many years a near neighbor of Governor Polk . . . & knows *personally* the truth of what he says upon this subject.[4]

This is the comforting image of his relation to his slaves that Polk wished to project, and it is the picture presented by Polk's most authoritative biographer. Gideon Pillow's portrayal of how Polk acquired his slaves was, according to the historian Charles Sellers, "an unadorned statement of the actual facts."[5]

Polk knew, however, that Pillow's picture—and the picture Polk himself projected to journalists—was far from the actual facts; and this helps to explain why later, during his presidency, Polk went to great trouble to hide the fact that he was regularly buying as many new slaves as his plantation revenues permitted. It was, of course, perfectly legal for Polk to buy slaves. But he was eager to buy them because he wanted to increase his income from the plantation; and this strong desire conflicted with the image he sought to project—that he was involved with slavery only because slaves had been willed to him and to his wife and because he felt a paternalist duty to ensure the welfare of those loyal dependents.

Polk preferred youthful laborers for his Mississippi cotton plantation. When his agent purchased in Tennessee a lone slave child aged only twelve, the child was probably torn permanently away from mother, father, siblings, and relatives. (See bill of sale for Jane, figure 1.1.)[6] Yet the president did not repudiate the purchase of young children. Nor did he protest when his agent, having bought two youths from the same estate (perhaps brothers whom the vendors hoped to keep together), frustrated that wish by quickly selling the younger one. Polk confined his advice to stern and repeated warnings that these purchases must be kept utterly secret.

Nine slaves had indeed come down to Polk from his father or from his own deceased brothers, and he had received four more whom his wife had inherited from her father.[7] By 1844 he had also acquired fifteen more slaves—not "6 or 8"—by purchase from members of his family. But his main aim here was to secure laborers for his cotton plantation, not to prevent slave families from being separated.[8] And by 1844—when Pillow wrote the denial—Polk had already bought fourteen other slaves from strangers, only twice to prevent a family separation and nearly always to secure labor for his undeveloped cotton land.[9] Between the election of 1844 and Polk's death in 1849, he secretly bought nineteen more slaves. Although two of these had been owned by other members of his family, Polk's main aim here was to make his cotton plantation more profitable. Polk was caught up in the expansive, entrepreneurial ethic of central Tennessee, and his principal impulses as a slavemaster were acquisitive rather than paternalist.

Polk's father, Sam, who died in 1827, had been a vigorous and successful businessman on the Tennessee frontier. "Business" then in Tennessee meant land speculation, managing slave plantations, selling merchandise, running banks, and developing transportation projects; and Sam engaged in all of these activities. In 1806 Sam emigrated from North Carolina and established a slave plantation in Maury County, Tennessee, where he lived until he moved to the fledgling county seat—Columbia—in 1816. At Columbia (forty miles south of Nashville) Sam Polk became a director of the bank whose president was James Walker, Sam's son-in-law; in Columbia's early days the houses of Sam Polk and Walker were the two biggest in town. Both men lost a great deal of money in an unsuccessful attempt to establish a road and steamboat connection from Columbia to New Orleans. But Sam's speculations in central and West Tennessee lands yielded him an excellent income, and when he died he left title to over 8000 acres of land, as well as about fifty-three slaves, to his widow and his ten surviving children.[10]

Of these children, James Polk (the eldest) was already launched on the political career that led him to become speaker of the U.S. House of Representatives, governor of Tennessee, and president of the United States.

After graduating at the top of his class from the University of North Carolina in 1818, James practiced law in Tennessee. He quickly entered politics and in 1825, at the age of twenty-nine, was elected to the national House of Representatives as a supporter of Andrew Jackson.[11] He served fourteen successive years in the House before being elected governor in 1839. But politics was risky, and Polk needed an income if he should lose office. His law practice had been good—he had grossed about $3000 during the last year of his practice before he went to Washington[12]—but he felt that a steady income from a cotton plantation would make his finances more secure. Therefore in 1831 he sent slaves to clear plantation land left him by his father in southwestern Tennessee—near Somerville, thirty-five miles east of Memphis and a few miles north of the Mississippi border.[13] He would become an absentee planter, visiting his plantation for a few days once or twice a year but leaving its daily direction to an overseer. He might have rented the Somerville land to a farmer and drawn an income from it that way, as he continued to do from hundreds of other acres of West Tennessee property bequeathed by his father, but he thought he could do better by establishing his own plantation. Since he then owned only about seven slaves suited to field work, he had to "stock" his plantation with more laborers. Some of these—like a slave named Chunky Jack—he rented from members of his own family. Others he acquired in 1831 by investing $1870 in young, able-bodied slaves. In separate transactions, mainly in Kentucky, he purchased five bondspeople, including four males:

Peter	about 11
Giles	about 13
Eve	about 16
Reuben	about 22
Caesar	about 25.[14]

Because older children fetched a better price than younger ones, vendors had an interest in lying about the ages of children: Peter may have been only nine or ten when he was thus taken, forcibly and forever, from his Kentucky home.

The Somerville plantation proved to be only moderately profitable, and after three years Polk's eyes turned southward. The Choctaw Nation had recently been dispossessed of its lands in northern Mississippi, the price of cotton was buoyant, and Polk joined the rush to buy fertile soil where he could get a better return on his capital investment. He therefore sold the Somerville plantation (for $6000) and entered into a partnership with his brother-in-law Silas Caldwell: they bought (for $9200) 920 acres of uncleared land a few miles southwest of Coffeeville, Mississippi. Situated thirty-five miles south of Oxford, the plantation lay east of the fertile Yazoo delta, but the land was nevertheless better than in western Tennessee and its proximity to the Yalobusha River—a tributary of the Yazoo—offered relatively cheap access to the New Orleans market. Even before finding the new plantation, Polk avowed his motive to his wife: "I am resolved to send my hands to the South, [and] have given money to [an agent] to buy a place. . . . I am determined to make more money or loose [lose] more." A minor consideration was that several of Polk's slaves had tried to flee the Somerville plantation, Chunky Jack even reaching the Arkansas territory before being captured. Polk realized that fugitives would be less likely to escape permanently if he moved them farther south. "The negroes have no idea that they are going to be sent to the South," he confided to his wife in Columbia, "and I do not wish them to know it, and therefore it would be best to say nothing about it at home, for it might be conveyed back to them."[15] Polk demonstrated here the secretiveness that was one of his most marked characteristics as a politician.

Polk's big new Mississippi plantation needed to be stocked, and once again he entered the market for labor. For $2250 he bought in 1834–35—in five separate transactions—three young laborers, a house servant, and the servant's grandchild:

Dicey	about 17
Phil	about 21
Henry Carter	22
Nancy	35–37
Henrietta	2

In addition his partner, Silas Caldwell, supplied as many slaves as did Polk, bringing the total to about thirty "full hands."[16]

But Caldwell quickly became discouraged by the difficulties of establishing the new plantation. The terms of the brother-in-laws' agreement seemed financially disadvantageous to Caldwell, and he dissolved the partnership after two years—thus ensuring for himself a good speculative profit by selling his share of the Mississippi land at a much higher price than he had paid for it.[17] Polk entered a new arrangement late in 1836 with his much younger brother William, who had just come of age and could supply slaves and cash to replace Caldwell's. William viewed the plantation in entrepreneurial terms: returning from his first visit there, he assured James Polk that "nothing [is] required but a moderate share of attention to make [the plantation] very profitable." At first William's youthful enthusiasm seemed to bring new vigor to the enterprise, and William could have relieved Polk—who was by then speaker of the House of Representatives—from close attention to plantation affairs. But the young man soon lost interest. The plantation's revenues, though substantial, could not support William in the style to which he aspired; moreover, he disliked having his imperious elder brother looking over his shoulder, and he bought a farm of his own near Columbia, terminating the Mississippi partnership at the end of 1838.[18]

To sustain the numbers working on the plantation—or old enough soon to become full hands—James Polk now invested another $5600, buying eight of William's slaves. Three were young adults, and the others were part of a family that William had inherited from Sam Polk:[19]

Perry	about 20
Marina	about 21
Gilbert	about 30
Cloe	about 50
Caroline	about 20
Manuel	about 14
Fan	about 10
Eliza	about 8

This parcel did not include Cloe's husband, Chunky Jack, because Jack—discontented with life at James Polk's Somerville plantation—had repeatedly fled, and in 1834 Polk had sold him. Like nearly every other slavemaster, James Polk thought it acceptable to sell a slave, permanently separating husband from wife and child from parent if he believed this necessary to maintain plantation discipline. What Chunky Jack's boy Manuel, just ten years old in 1834, may have thought of his father's sale will appear below.[20]

Polk spent nearly $3000 in 1838 and 1839 on five more slaves.[21] But the expenses of campaigning twice more for the governorship (he was defeated in 1841 and 1843) and of running for president in 1844 prevented any big further investment until mid-1846.[22] Then—looking to his retirement from the presidency—he reasoned that buying more slaves and clearing the rest of his Mississippi plantation would be his best route to financial security. He had no intention of toiling again as a lawyer, and he and his wife had no children to support them in their old age. He fancied purchasing a mansion in Nashville and living the comfortable life of a gentleman farmer, perhaps in emulation of his mentor Andrew Jackson, who had famously retired to his own "Hermitage" not far from Nashville. Slavery, that is, a productive cotton plantation in Mississippi, was the route to securing for himself and his wife all of these blessings.

His plantation income was, he alleged in 1845, his "main reliance to pay my [campaign] debts"; more to the point, it was the reason he already hoped he would be able "to retire with something to subsist upon at the end of his [four-year presidential] term." In 1846 he claimed that it was his slave plantation to which "I *must* look for my future support." Although Polk here invoked necessity, he knew that in fact other forms of investment were possible. His brother-in-law and business adviser, James Walker, had at least once discussed this matter of investments with Polk. If one had a spare $15,000, Walker then averred, one might buy bank stocks or, much more safely, invest in 6 percent state bonds. But Walker thought that "a still better & more secure investment could be made, and the money and interest undoubtedly secured, by being upon land and negroes to double the amount." Polk, too, believed that investment in slaves was the best way of increasing one's income, and this was what, in August 1846, he advised his newly widowed sister to do. Instead of buying a house of her own in Columbia, she ought—he urged—to move into her mother's house: she could then "apply [the money she had saved] to an increase of your [slave] force on your plantation, so as to enlarge your yearly income." Exactly these economic considerations—not a paternalist attitude to slaves—impelled President Polk to try to increase the "force" on his own plantation; and he was so successful that, when three years later he lay on his death bed, he could assure his wife that (although he could not be certain) he had done his best to guarantee "that the plantation in Mississippi would support her."[23]

In 1846, however, when Polk was making these plans for his retirement, there were a couple of problems. In the previous year, Polk, by effecting the rapid annexation of Texas, had vastly expanded slavery's domain. And in 1846 he launched against Mexico a war, one of whose aims—if certain vociferous critics of that war were to be believed—was to extend still further the empire of slavery. Polk had spare cash for the first time in years, and he was keen to buy as many slaves as he could afford. But would it be helpful for the public to know that, at this time of intense controversy about the extension of slavery, the president himself was again expanding his own slave holdings—and all in contradiction to what he himself had implied to newspaper correspondents and contrary to the words that Polk's friend Gideon Pillow had inscribed during the election campaign? Pillow had been one of the principal engineers of Polk's nomination at the deadlocked Democratic Party convention of 1844, and for this (as well as for services such as writing the denial that Polk traded in slaves) Pillow's reward was a generalship in the Mexican War, where he gained the reputation of being the most incompetent and factious of all American military leaders in that conflict.[24] Polk also paid Pillow $1436 for three slaves in 1846. On May 10—the Sunday when Polk was frantically drafting his war message to Congress—the president made time to write a detailed letter instructing his agent to buy Pillow's slaves; and the settlement of the price for these slaves was contained in a subsequent letter, the same one in which Polk offered Pillow a military command.[25]

Polk bought Pillow's slave Harbert (and Harbert's wife and her child) partly because of pressure from Polk's wife, Sarah. When Sarah had married in 1824, the bride had inherited the three-year-old slave boy (Harbert) along with his mother and his elder sister, and the Polks still owned the two women. But Polk had sold Harbert to Pillow in 1840, partly because he then needed the cash but principally because Harbert—like Chunky Jack—was discontented with being a slave and was "unruly." Although Sarah Polk had reluctantly consented to Harbert's sale, she had always hoped he might be purchased again after a proper period of punishment; and more than five years having elapsed, she pushed Polk into buying him back from Pillow.[26]

Polk was willing to be persuaded by his wife because his $25,000 annual presidential salary was much larger than his current expenses. With his campaign debts having been repaid, he was now free to plow back his plantation profits into further investment in enslaved labor.[27] Within three months of paying Pillow $1436, Polk spent nearly $3000 more for six young slaves, two of them not yet even teenagers (see also figures 1.1 and 1.2):

Jane	about 12
Sally	about 12
Agnes	13
Calvin	probably about 13
Caroline Henly	16
William	about 17

The president bought all of these young people separately from their parents, and each was sold separately from any siblings. The one probable exception was William, who was sold at the same estate sale as the twelve-year-old Jim, who may have been William's younger brother. But Polk's agent, after buying the two boys together, nine weeks later sold the younger one away from even the comfort of accompanying his older brother (or perhaps acquaintance). Polk profited from this transaction: after buying the twelve-year-old for $392, the president's agent was able to sell him for $450, the difference going into Polk's pocket.[28]

These purchases took place just before and soon after the introduction into Congress of the Wilmot Proviso, which—had it been enacted—would have barred the extension of slavery into any new territory acquired from Mexico. The president uttered dire warnings that his purchases must be kept secret. No one must learn that he was buying slaves. Polk's knowledge of the law assured him that nothing required the slaves to be registered in his name, even though his agents (who ostensibly bought the slaves for themselves) immediately made them over to Polk. The president had discussed his plans with his brother-in-law John Childress in March 1846, and he soon spelled out the legal niceties: "You can take the title in your own name and make a quit-claim conveyance without warranty to me." That summer Childress employed Polk's cousin Robert Campbell as Polk's agent; and five days after the House of Representatives had adopted the Wilmot Proviso, Polk reminded Campbell of the injunction to secrecy. Childress had explained to Campbell, Polk warned, "the reasons why, it should not be known to any one but him and yourself that you are making the purchases for me. There is nothing wrong [in] it, but still the public have no interest in knowing it, and in my situation it is better they should not."[29]

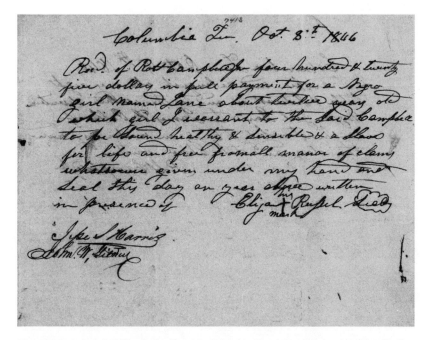

Figure 1.1   Jane's bill of sale (front.) *Columbia Ten. Oct. 8th 1846 Recd. of Robt Campbell Jr four hundres & twenty five dollars in full payment for a Negro girl named Jane about twelve years old which girl I warrant to the said Campbell to be sound healthy & sensible & a slave for life and free from all manner of claims whatsover given under my hand and seal this day on year above written in presence of Jake S. Harris John W. Gilder [?] . . . Elija Russell (his mark) Seal [?].* Reproduced from the Collections of the Library of Congress.

The next year, as American armies prepared an amphibious invasion of central Mexico, Polk spent another $1675 on three more slaves. Like a speculator in a bullish stock market, he urged his agent to act speedily, "as I think it probable that such property [slaves] will continue to rise in price for several months to come." And, with double emphasis, he repeated "my former request, that as my *private business* does not concern the public you will keep it to yourself. There is a great disposition with many persons to parade everything connected with the President although *private* . . . before the public."[30]

Because Polk did not sell his 1847 cotton crop until early 1849, he deferred authorizing further investment in slaves until the last fortnight of his presidency.[31] He then ventured another $3275 on half a dozen young bondspeople. Polk's agent heeded the president's instructions not to buy slaves over twenty-one; but he judged (correctly) that Polk would not reprimand him for acquiring half the slaves under the specified age limit of twelve:

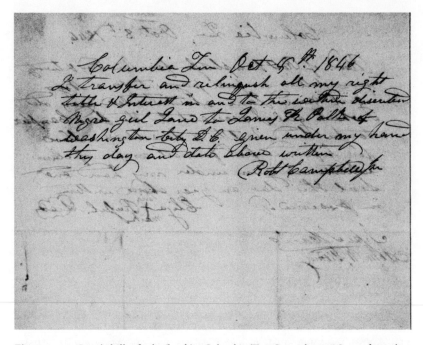

Figure 1.2 Jane's bill of sale (back). *Columbia Ten Oct. 8th 1846 I transfer and relinquish all my right title & interest in and to the within described Negro girl Jane to James K Polk of Washington City D.C. given under my hand this day and date above written . . . Robt Campbell Jr.* Reproduced from the Collections of the Library of Congress.

Jerry	10 years old
Anderson	11
Jason	11
Rosetta	16
Caroline Davis	19
Caroline Harris	20[32]

As in his earlier clandestine forays into the slave market, President Polk insisted that these purchases must be kept secret. "This letter is for yourself alone," he inscribed on the missive authorizing his agent "to buy me some property [aged between twelve and twenty-one] for my Yalobusha plantation." And to another agent he wrote, "For the reasons stated in my [previous] correspondence with you . . . it will be unnecessary that you should make it known that you are purchasing for me. You can take the title in your own name and transfer it to me as you did in a former case."[33] The president's specification that the new purchases were to be aged between twelve and twenty-one made certain that each of these children would arrive at Polk's plantation separated from the child's parents.

Were these children orphans, who had already lost their parents? No evidence suggests that this was the case. Of the nineteen slaves Polk bought during his presidency, one was ten years old, two were eleven, two were twelve, two were thirteen, two were fifteen, two were sixteen, and two were seventeen. Each of these children was bought apart from his or her parents and from every sibling. One or two of these thirteen children may possibly have been orphans, but it would strain credulity to suggest that many of them were.

Evidently other considerations were more important to the president than acquiring laborers with family ties. Perhaps he felt, as did his contemporary Bennet Barrow (a Louisiana cotton planter), that very young bondspeople could be more readily converted into well-disciplined workers than older slaves, who might prove incorrigibly uncooperative. "I will never [again] buy grown negroes from V[irgini]a— or [the] upper Country—," Barrow had written with exasperation in 1840: "Small boys and girls may do, but grown ones are not worth as much—by at least one third as our creoles."[34]

The small boys and girls purchased by President Polk had probably been separated from their parents by the children's vendors, not by the president's purchasing agents. Vendors had a financial interest in dividing children from their parents: they could make more money by selling the children separately than by offering them in a parcel that included the older slaves. But the reason for the relatively high price for children who were sold separately was that there were many other planters, like President Polk, who specified that he wanted to buy only property aged between twelve and twenty-one.

Why Polk sought to keep secret his purchases of these children remains uncertain. He acknowledged that slaves were human beings,[35] and he knew some people believed that "all men are created equal . . . , endowed by their Creator with certain unalienable Rights." Hence he probably felt that slavery could not be justified merely by an appeal to the property rights of slavemasters. Instead, slavemasters must be presented as benevolent paternalists, whose conduct was determined by their obligation to take good care of their dependents. The public had better not know, therefore, that their president was buying slave children away from their families—contrary to a paternalist's putative duty to respect his slaves' family ties—to increase their purchaser's profits from his Mississippi cotton plantation. And it was particularly important to hide the president's slave purchases during a period of controversy over slavery, when he sought to present himself as a representative of national interests, not a sectional partisan.[36]

That Polk felt squeamish about these purchases is suggested by the fact that, although he bought slaves with his plantation revenues, he never used his presidential salary for that purpose. He used his savings from his salary to pay campaign debts, to buy and refurbish a mansion in Nashville, and to buy U.S. Treasury certificates, but never to buy slaves. Evidently he distinguished his private income—from the plantation—from the public salary he received from government revenues. Thus, if the public had ever learned of his buying young slaves, he could always have truthfully denied that he had spent his presidential salary for that purpose.

In 1977, the historian Richard Marsh reported the secrecy in which Polk had shrouded these transactions, but the facts seem not to have been widely disseminated.[37] Thus for a century and a half Polk concealed from public knowledge the frequency with which he had bought slaves—often very young ones—from strangers in order to expand his cherished plantation enterprise. Commercial success, not a paternalistic sense of duty to "family negroes," was the driving force behind Polk's forays into the market for enslaved labor power.[38]

2

⊶ ⊰◈⊱ ⊷

Flight (I)
Tennessee

Chunky Jack was by no means the only bondsman to flee Polk's plantation. Indeed, the most striking feature of James Polk's cotton business was the frequency with which slaves absented themselves. The
records are incomplete because from 1845 onward Polk—and then his
widow—employed an overseer who was peculiarly reticent about plantation events. When this overseer bothered to write, he was brief and
tended toward the formulaic ("Your servants are all well"), and only later
might one discover that in fact a slave had been hiding in the woods at
that very moment.[1] Copious evidence nevertheless remains of the extent to which the Polks' slaves undertook their risky, usually dangerous
flights from captivity.

Their wanderings from the plantation took four forms. (1) Sometimes
slaves left the masters' supervision briefly—perhaps only for a few hours at
night—without permission to do so. Such absences, though probably frequent, were seldom reported by an overseer unless they led to a more
serious breach of discipline. (2) A surprising number of slaves fled to a white
patron—perhaps a brother-in-law of James Polk or a local agent whom
Polk had deputed to look over his overseer's shoulder—seeking the patron's
intercession to protect them from a threatened calamity or from what they
regarded as unjust abuse. (3) Often slaves fled for weeks or even months at
a time, yet with little prospect of permanent escape. These seem to have
been by far the most common recorded flights. (4) Much less often, a
determined slave sought permanent freedom. There is no record of a Polk
slave ever having succeeded in this endeavor. Yet for one or another of
these reasons, slaves frequently fled dozens or even hundreds of miles in
search of relief.

Polk wavered in his response to these flights. When he had owned
only a few slaves in central Tennessee (before he established his West
Tennessee cotton plantation in 1831), he may have been an "indulgent"
master; and during the three years of the West Tennessee plantation's
operation he betrayed indecision about how best to impose discipline upon
the slaves. But near the end of 1834, Polk determined to sell the most recalcitrant fugitive to a slave trader (separating that man permanently from
his wife and children). The desire to make the cotton-planting enterprise

23

financially successful impelled Polk to tighten discipline, and he concluded that the best way to achieve this purpose at the new Mississippi plantation was to back the overseer who had caused Polk's slaves distress on his West Tennessee plantation.

The first flights of James Polk's slaves had occurred (before he moved his slaves to West Tennessee) when—as so often in the South—the death of a white person sent panic through the slave quarters that slave families would be shattered because the estate would be divided among the heirs. In both of the following two cases the slaves fled *toward* Columbia, Tennessee, which suggested that they liked being with the Polks there better than coming under the control of some new master. Indeed, the first case was one of those flights best called absence without leave.

James Polk had married Sarah Childress at her home near Murfreesboro, Tennessee (forty miles east of Columbia) in 1824. The bride's dowry seemed to include ten slaves she had inherited from her father, Joel Childress. Polk's law practice being in Columbia, the young couple settled there, apparently bringing with them most of Sarah's slaves (including a girl named Mariah, who perhaps served as Sarah's maid). A lawsuit was pending, which eventually resulted in Polk's losing title to six of these slaves (including Mariah) to help pay Joel Childress's debts. When Sarah Polk returned to Columbia after visiting Murfreesboro in December 1825, she ordered the teenage Mariah to stay in Murfreesboro. Mariah—perhaps fearing the outcome of the pending court case (which later temporarily separated her from her mother and her sister)—disobeyed orders and "started immediately after you [Sarah Polk], to Maury County. The negroes here," Sarah's brother continued, "say that she threatened some time ago, to follow you when you should go, and that if you did not start soon she would take a horse and go alone." Mariah's cross-country trip did not much alarm the Childresses, for they understood that she expected to turn up at a Christmas dance held by other Polk slaves near Columbia, where she may have had a boyfriend. This was not a real flight but a mere disobeying of orders. Mariah's insubordination did her no lasting harm; indeed her apparent desire to stay near Sarah Polk benefited her. When the legal case was settled, James Polk paid $350 to buy Mariah from a creditor of Joel Childress, thus enabling Mariah to stay with her mother and sister.[2] These three were among the slaves Polk sent in 1831 to his new plantation in western Tennessee. Mariah quickly entered an "abroad marriage" with a young man named Henry Carter from a nearby plantation. Abroad marriages—very common among slaves in the United States—were between partners owned by two different planters. The male slave might be obliged to walk anything from half a mile to twenty miles to visit his wife and children, usually once a week, sometimes twice, sometimes less often.

When Polk sold the Tennessee plantation in 1834 to establish a new plantation in Mississippi, he needed more laborers, and he bought Henry

Carter, thus preventing Mariah's marriage from being broken. This was an act of considerable benevolence, and it richly rewarded Polk for Henry Carter was soon regarded as the most valuable of Polk's plantation hands. Mariah, who suffered some ill health, became a seamstress and weaver in Mississippi, where she proudly notified Sarah Polk that she had increased her monetary worth to Sarah by learning new weaving skills. James Polk selected Mariah's son—named Henry after his father—to be a house servant in Tennessee; and this young Henry was the only slave President Polk took with him to Washington to work, along with free blacks whom Polk hired there, as a servant in the White House.[3] Mariah's absence without leave—her determination not to be separated from her family, her friends, and her white mistress—appears, rather than alienating the Polks, to have won Mariah their favor.

· The next recorded flight was a much more serious affair. James Polk's younger brother Marshall, a lawyer in Charlotte, North Carolina, died suddenly in April 1831, and the will he hastily signed on his deathbed authorized his executors "to dispose of [seven of his slaves] at sale, for the benefit of my family." This was paternalism for the benefit of Marshall Polk's family, not the slaves. The next year these seven slaves were sent to the auction block.[4] But eighteen-year-old Wally and his older brother Gabriel, fearing that this would be their fate too, had already (in July 1831) fled toward Tennessee (see map 2.1 and its inset).

The young men had been reared near Columbia, Tennessee, and their mother, father, and three younger siblings still lived there (as did Wally's friend, Martha), from all of whom they had been separated when Marshall Polk deported them to North Carolina a year or two earlier. Columbia was some 400 miles west of Charlotte, North Carolina, and the two daring young men had already traversed half this distance, across the Appalachian Mountains, when they were caught and jailed at Knoxville. For weeks they hid their identity, but the jailer's advertisements eventually came to the notice of the Polks, and James Polk paid the hefty fees—$30 to the man who had caught the fugitives and another $57 to the jailer for incarcerating them for seventy-two days. Polk's practice on such an occasion was probably to whip a slave, for in a Washington speech the previous year he had told the House of Representatives that imprisonment was an inadequate restraint upon bondspeople. "A slave," Polk then declared—with just a touch of circumlocution—"dreads the punishment of stripes more than he does imprisonment, and that description of punishment has, besides, a beneficial effect upon his fellow-slaves."[5]

Yet the fugitive Wally probably felt that his dangerous trek across the mountains, the long incarceration, and any subsequent flogging had been worthwhile; he was not sold to strangers. Instead Polk sent him to labor on Polk's new Somerville plantation, not far from where Wally's friend Martha was a slave (at the plantation of Polk's brother-in-law Silas Caldwell). Polk's overseer, doubtless having been warned that Wally might

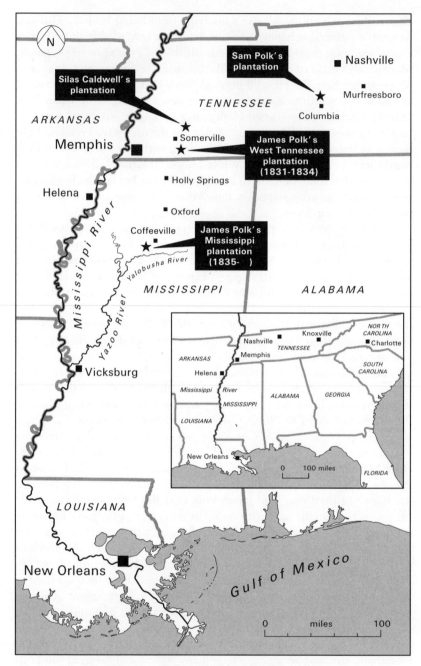

Map 2.1 Polk (and Caldwell) Plantations

flee again, soon reported with surprise that Wally "has behaved himself very well and I think will make me a first rate hand."[6] Wally and Martha soon entered an abroad marriage, where Wally's being able to spend Saturday nights and Sundays with Martha depended on the overseer's willingness to let Wally leave the plantation regularly.

When Polk moved his slaves from central Tennessee to his new plantation in West Tennessee, he disturbed the marriages of two of the young slaves, Ben and Jim. Ben had an abroad marriage to a slave near Columbia, and Jim was married to a bondswoman near Columbia. Apparently when Polk first deported Ben and Jim, he let them come back from West Tennessee to stay with their wives once a year for a five-week visit in midwinter, after the harvest was in; this did not seem to the master an unreasonable arrangement. Ben thought otherwise. He was a "family negro" and had been promised that he would never be sold out of the Polk family; when James Polk had most recently visited Somerville, Ben seems to have extracted a further promise: that Polk would move him back to Maury County, where he could see his wife more often.[7] These circumstances help to clarify the events at the Somerville plantation in 1833–34.

In central Tennessee the discipline over the Polk slaves had probably been relatively relaxed. Even after Polk deported the slaves to his new cotton plantation in West Tennessee, his first overseer, Herbert Biles, governed them comparatively mildly. But Biles became ill in 1833, and when toward the end of that year Polk replaced him with a new man, Ephraim Beanland, a struggle to impose tight discipline quickly ensued. Beanland thought Biles had not made the slaves work hard enough, nor had Biles required the slaves to get a pass from him, authorizing them to leave the plantation. Certain local whites had encouraged Polk's slaves to trade with them, and Beanland was convinced that the Polk slaves were "spoiled" altogether. "Your boys," he lamented,

> has traded so much with white people and bin let run so loose reined that I am compeled to not let won of them [offen] the plantation with out he askes my leave and then if I think he ought to go I let him go and if not I ceep him at home.
>
> . . .
>
> Your negroes has . . . bin let run at so lose rained [reined] that I must be verry close with them.

Beanland also felt that the plantation was shorthanded—the work force then comprising just nine adult males (one of whom was chronically ill), along with four or five adult females—and Beanland pushed them hard.[8]

One November night in 1833, after they had worked the cotton press until 11:00 P.M., the overseer forced the slaves to shuck corn before going to bed. Later that night a grocery shop five miles away was broken into, and flour, sugar, tobacco, and whiskey were stolen. Beanland believed he had proof that Chunky Jack was responsible, and he whipped him severely—reportedly 200 lashes interspersed with four or five saltings of the lacerations to intensify the pain. Under this torture Jack "confessed" to the burglary. Ben—the aforementioned bondsman, who was in his twenties—also incurred Beanland's wrath. Allegedly Ben lied about why some stolen flour had been found in his possession, and for this supposed offense Beanland inflicted 100 lashes. That evening the two slaves fled, Jack to Memphis and Ben to seek protection at Columbia, Tennessee, nearly 150 miles away.[9]

Three weeks after Ben and Chunky Jack had fled and once the crop had been sent to market, Beanland despatched his best worker—the aforesaid Jim, now twenty-one years old—to Columbia, where first he might enjoy a visit with his wife and then was to drive a herd of pigs back to the plantation. While at Columbia, Jim reported on plantation affairs to Polk's brothers-in-law. Meanwhile Ben turned himself in at Columbia and showed the scars on his back as proof of Beanland's severity. Thus both slaves contributed to a discussion among the brothers-in-law—which lasted for two months—about how order could best be imposed on Polk's plantation. "Jim says that Beanland is very severe," wrote one brother-in-law, "that he gives them no encouragement—that if they exert themselves to please him they get nothing but curses for it." Another brother-in-law, Silas Caldwell (who sometimes stayed at his own West Tennessee plantation), went from there to Polk's plantation and found that "your negroes here are very much dissatisfied. . . . Some others [besides Ben and Chunky Jack] spoke of running away. . . . I think if Beanland would be more mild with the negroes he would get along with them better." Even the tough-minded James Walker expressed puzzlement: "It is strange that Beanland would tie up your negroes, whip them most unmercifully, then let them run away. He makes no exertions to recover them. . . . I shall advise Caldwell to get another overseer for you. . . . Beanland has not got sense enough, and it is likely he too drinks too much."[10]

The first matter to be settled was Chunky Jack's future. A man of about forty-five, he worked at Polk's plantation with eight other male slaves all in their twenties, and Beanland considered the older man (Jack) to have been the dissidents' leader. Jack had fled to Memphis where he had had the misfortune of falling into the hands of two white kidnappers, who chained him and carried him in a skiff 150 miles down the Mississippi River, bound for the Mexican province of Texas, which was exempted by Mexico from the ban on slavery applied to every other Mexican province. The kidnappers could count on selling him there to an American emigrant greedy to acquire unpaid labor. But a sort of vigilante-entrepreneur who called himself Hughes—probably the man later responsible for capturing the notorious slave kidnapper John Murrell—apprehended Jack's captors at a hut beside the Mississippi River and, for a $100 fee, including $50 "expenssis," enabled Beanland and Silas Caldwell's overseer, George

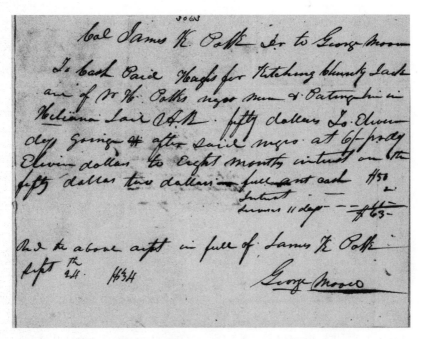

Figure 2.1 Receipt for catching Chunky Jack. Reproduced from the Collections of the Library of Congress.

Moore, to fetch Jack from an Arkansas jail (see figure 2.1). By the time the Polks had paid another $47 for their agents' stagecoach, ferrying, and steamboat fares; Chunky Jack's $12 jail fee; $11 to Moore for his eleven-day search; $11 accommodation and food; $7 for hiring horses, mules, and a yawl; and a bit more for the interest on the tardily paid bills, the total cost was $195. Recovering Jack, whose monetary value can scarcely have been as much as $400, from this first of his flights was expensive.[11]

Polk's brother-in-law and future business partner, Silas Caldwell, wanted to sell Jack or else to work him on his own West Tennessee plantation, for he presciently thought Jack would escape again if returned to Beanland's supervision. James Walker was of similar persuasion. But Beanland was determined to have Jack back in order to teach the other slaves a lesson: "I want them boath [Jack and Ben] brought back. If they aint they rest will leave me also." Polk's instincts sometimes were for strictness. (For example, a decade later, as Polk prepared for the Mexican War, he instructed the secretary of the navy to court-martial any naval officer "guilty of unreasonable delay" in executing orders: "It was necessary," the president declared, that military officers used to a comfortable life "should be taught their duty by enforcing the most rigid discipline.") Polk placed Jack again under Beanland, even though every report suggested that the overseer was a heartless brute.[12] No doubt Beanland then inflicted condign punishment on the captured fugitive.

Ben, however, presented a different case, for he was a "family negro" and might therefore receive special consideration. Ben—having fled to Columbia and turned himself in voluntarily to Polk's rich brother-in-law, Adlai Harris—made his feelings plain. "Ben will not go back [to Beanland]," Harris reported to Polk. "He says he relys on your promise of keeping him here, of selling him or hireing him in this county. He is afraid if he goes back of being whipd for running away and says that he cannot live with Mr. Beanland." Harris sympathized with Ben and hired him out, at an annual rent of $100, to work in a nearby iron mill. The other brothers-in-law offered divided counsel. Although Silas Caldwell thought Beanland too severe, he didn't like Ben either—"Ben is a bad boy"—and at one point he ordered Ben to be put in irons and sent back to Beanland. James Walker, however, favored selling Ben to a local businessman who would continue the arrangement of hiring him out to the local ironworks. Polk at first tried to sell Ben, but Beanland's vehement protest temporarily dissuaded him. Beanland "swears he will have Ben," Walker reported, "or leave the plantation [himself], and have his wages." In plantation management as in domestic politics, Polk was to some degree a compromiser. In this instance he decided to send Ben to the plantation so that Beanland could show the other slaves that fugitives would be hauled back and punished; but before the year was out Polk sold Ben to Gideon Pillow (or to Pillow's father-in-law). Although Polk reneged on his earlier desire that Ben "should never be sold out of the family," he honored his promise to Ben not to sell him away from the county. Indeed, he sold Ben to the owner of Ben's wife, so that the couple could live together again.[13]

While Ben's fate was being decided, unrest spread among Polk's other slaves. Jim, who had been sent temporarily to work for James Walker's overseer at Walker's West Tennessee plantation, fled from that overseer, afraid of getting a whipping for allegedly not working hard enough; he ran back to the Polk plantation. Another slave, Hardy, recently entrusted to go on his own to Memphis with a wagon load of Polk's cotton, now fled the plantation after having been threatened by Beanland for not working properly. Although Hardy was caught within a week, his exposure to the elements in midwinter was the possible cause of his later developing a "very violent cough" from which he died at the age of twenty-six. Perhaps Beanland punished Hardy so severely that it provoked two of Hardy's friends into an act of defiant solidarity. Whatever the reason, these two slaves (the aforesaid Jim and the young Wally, who had fled across the Appalachians in 1831) now disappeared into the woods. "I had not struck them [Jim and Wally] a lick nor thretened to do it," Beanland exclaimed in self-justification, naming in passing two of the most common provocations of a slave's flight. Beanland had now achieved the distinction of driving off five of his nine adult male laborers within an eleven-week period. One of the four who had remained on the plantation, Austin, who was dying of tuberculosis, was too ill to run away.[14]

Although Wally, the slave who fled with Jim, was caught after a fortnight's absence, he benefited from having a slightly sheltered position: James Polk (having only rented him from the executor of Marshall Polk's estate) did not wield ultimate authority over Wally. Two days after the slave's capture, James Walker (who was the Tennessee executor of Marshall Polk's estate) decided—instead of leaving Wally under Beanland's control—to sell him to a Maury County businessman who would hire him out to the local ironworks. Another of James Polk's brothers-in-law, Dr. Silas Caldwell, then intervened. He owned Wally's wife, Martha, and he bought Wally from the Columbia businessman to be united with Martha on Caldwell's West Tennessee plantation. Caldwell had genuine sympathy for Wally, and he acted upon it.[15]

Like Wally, the fugitive Jim also benefited from his flight. To be sure, as Jim approached Columbia, after a five-week trek, he was caught by a white man; James Polk probably then treated Jim as he had handled Ben, by sending him briefly back to Beanland to be whipped for the sake of its influence on the other slaves. But Polk then sold Jim to the Maury County planter who owned Jim's wife. By fleeing, Jim had succeeded in getting back to his wife and to his home territory in central Tennessee. Probably Polk made this concession to him because Jim had been willed to Polk's wife, and she did not want Jim to be forced permanently away from his wife and his boyhood region.[16]

Before Jim's fate was determined, Chunky Jack fled again. Beanland had overheard Jack telling other slaves "that he would not stay and the next time he left that he would not be so easy caught." On March 30, Beanland started to whip Jack, whereupon—in Beanland's vivid report—Jack

> curste me verry much and run alf before my face which in runinge 2 hundred yards I caught him and I did not [k]now that he had a stick in his hande and he broke it over my head the 3 lick which I stabed him 2 [licks] with my nife and I brought him backe to the house and chainde him and I have him in chaines yet.

The doctor pronounced Jack's wounds not life threatening. Jack, unbowed, "swares [Beanland announced] that he will at never stay with the Polke family any more." Five months later the indomitable man was off yet again—"without any known reason," Polk attempted to reassure his wife. Jack got across the Mississippi River into the territory of Arkansas. Beanland pursued him across the river, but hearing that Jack was in Shawnee Town, the overseer returned empty-handed: "I was advised to not go" to Shawnee Town, he explained, "for they is A den of thieves." Although Beanland feared that Jack would never be captured, in fact he was caught (probably by an Arkansas sheriff) and jailed eighty miles south of Memphis.[17] It is likely that the Polks incurred yet another big bill for getting Jack back from Arkansas. The masters distinguished temporary flight from an effort, such as Jack's, to escape permanently; and Beanland had long since read out to the slaves a letter from James Walker threatening (on Polk's behalf) any of them who tried "to get entirely away" with sale to "a regular negro trader who would take them to the lower country." This appears to have been the fate that Polk—with Beanland's assent—now meted out to the valiant Jack. Jack never saw his wife, Cloe, and their children again.[18]

Thus, by late 1834 when Polk was set to move his slaves from Tennessee to his new plantation in Mississippi, the master had been pressed—by his slaves' dissidence—into selling three of the nine adult males on his Somerville plantation; the executor of Marshall Polk's estate had been pressed into selling a fourth slave; the fifth dissident, Hardy, was too ill from his fatal chest infection to make the trip to Mississippi (he soon died in Tennessee); and a sixth man had died of tuberculosis. But Polk was not yet willing to fire the overseer who had caused his slaves so much of this distress.

Polk had had little managerial experience before establishing his West Tennessee plantation in 1831. He was a Democratic congressman devoted to promoting the interests of President Andrew Jackson in Washington, and Polk's first three years of plantation management betrayed inexperience, indecision, and reluctance to cause his slaves what he regarded as undue hardship. When Polk bought slaves, it sometimes helped to prevent family disruption—as when he had originally bought Mariah and when he later bought Mariah's husband, Henry Carter. Polk sometimes sold slaves (like the "family negro" Ben and Sarah Polk's slave Jim) to avoid disrupting their marriages further than he had already done by moving those two men to West Tennessee. Yet Polk threatened to sell to a slave trader—for distant sale—any slave who sought permanent escape; and he fulfilled this threat in the case of Chunky Jack. Having lost one overseer because of ill health, Polk hesitated to remove his second one, Ephraim Beanland, just because Polk's brothers-in-law thought that Beanland was a brutal tyrant. When Polk moved his slaves to Mississippi at the end of 1834, he sought a better return on his capital investment than he had achieved in West Tennessee, and he needed an overseer who could impose the discipline on his slaves that had previously seemed to be lacking. In deciding to back Beanland, Polk displayed some of the same obstinacy with which he pursued his war against Mexico a dozen years later. Tight discipline must finally be imposed on the plantation, and Polk seemed to have concluded that the overseer's authority must be upheld if Polk was to make a financial success of his plantation business.

3

※◆※

Flight (II)
The Mississippi Plantation

Although the flight of slaves from Polk's plantation owed a good deal to the tyranny of a particularly harsh overseer, Ephraim Beanland, that is not the whole story. When Polk's partner, Silas Caldwell, finally dismissed Beanland—a year after Polk had reemployed him during the year 1835—that did not put an end to the slaves' dissidence. More than half of the Polks' adult male workers fled at one time or another *after* Beanland was dismissed: there were certainly thirteen fugitives—probably more—among the group of twenty-five male slaves old enough to venture flight during the period 1838 to 1856, when overseers' letters are extant. Most of these men—eight of the thirteen—fled more than once: indeed, the persistence of some fugitives was remarkable. One man fled at least ten times, another seven times (until he was sold), others for three, four, and five times. The total number of flights by these men was at least forty during a nineteen-year period.[1] This average of more than two flights per year almost certainly underestimates this type of dissidence because many of the overseers' letters have not been preserved; also, an overseer was likely to avoid mentioning that a slave was missing until he or she had been away a long time and might never return.[2]

Flight was extremely dangerous. A fugitive sleeping out of doors without shelter might become ill; he might be shot or stabbed by a pursuer; he might be kidnapped by some avaricious slave trader; he was likely to be severely whipped when caught; and he might be sold away from family and friends, never to see them again. As every one of these fates befell one or another of Polk's male fugitives, we need to try to understand why—despite these formidable deterrents—slaves continued to flee year after year.[3]

No doubt the character of an overseer like Beanland was an important provocation to flight. Some blend of harshness with occasional kindliness and indecision in Polk's regime may also have encouraged slaves to flee. A slave's circumstances might be decisive: thus, a newly purchased slave sold away from his wife might try to get back to her; and a slave who had little to lose might be more likely to flee than one more deeply rooted in the slave community. Yet each of these explanations seems insufficient. More general causes were at work.

33

L ate in 1834, Polk—preparing to move his slaves to the new Mississippi plantation—rehired his overseer Beanland, presumably because he wanted strict discipline to be imposed from the outset.[4] Life was extraordinarily harsh that first winter, and Polk's partner, Silas Caldwell, acknowledged that the slaves were "only tolerable well satisfied." He seemed to imply that they were *not* contented. The labor of clearing the timber was severe; the low-lying land struck Caldwell, a doctor, as very unhealthy; Caldwell distrusted Beanland; and before the harvest was completed, Beanland had—in Caldwell's words—"run off" the slave Gilbert, as well as two others. The fees for recovering these three fugitives amounted to some $55.[5] By this time Caldwell had dismissed Beanland, replacing him with an overseer named Mayo.

Caldwell gained among the slaves the reputation of a master to whom they could appeal against an overseer's tyranny. Unlike Polk, Caldwell had a long experience of plantation management, and he had apparently learned the value of not pushing the slaves too hard. His medical training was likely to have bred into him a greater concern for health conditions and for the slaves' welfare than that felt by the average slavemaster. Through long personal contact, Caldwell knew many of the slaves better than did Polk. Caldwell may have had more self-assurance than Polk and thus felt less need to make demonstrations of authority. He may also have had a more kindly nature, as illustrated by his purchase of Wally. The slaves remembered that it was Caldwell who fired Beanland; and after Caldwell left his partnership with Polk (at the end of 1836) and resided on his own West Tennessee plantation, slaves more than once fled from Polk's Mississippi plantation to Caldwell's in Tennessee in order to seek his protection.

However, Mayo's brief, one-year tenure was proving unsatisfactory to the masters because cotton production was smaller than expected and probably because Mayo relaxed plantation discipline further than they wished. Polk's local agent later complained that Polk's slaves "were no doubt spoiled by the inefficient and trifling" Mayo; when a new overseer, George Bratton, was installed in 1837, he had an uphill battle to govern the slaves. Bratton had been in charge for more than a year when Polk's agent acknowledged, with his own underscoring, that Bratton "seems to have the negroes completely under his control <u>now</u>." The restoration of discipline provoked the slave Gilbert, during the 1838 harvest, into his second flight. Bratton advised that when Gilbert was caught, he must not be sold (as had happened to four slaves who had fled from Beanland in Tennessee) because if flight led to the easy option of sale, Gilbert's friend— the slave Henry Carter—"will be sirten to foller."[6] Bratton's version of the domino theory impelled him to favor severe whipping as the surest means for suppressing insurgency.

Yet the punishment that Polk's overseer meted out to Gilbert in 1838 did not deter that intrepid slave from fleeing the plantation eight more times during the next thirteen years. Overseer Bratton did not live to witness this test of the efficacy of whipping, for he died during a dysentery epidemic in 1839.[7] His replacement, John Garner, soon experienced a bout of slave dissidence when at least six slaves fled within a year. Polk had by this time moved from Congress to the governor's mansion in Nashville, Tennessee, and he cannot have relished the reports of Garner's maladministration.

In the perpetual struggle between slaves and their masters, slaves often tested the mettle of a new overseer. "When I came here," Garner reported to Polk soon after arriving at the plantation, "there was some three or fore [slaves] lying up with out a cause." Garner took a strong line against these supposed malingerers, boasting that "I have not bin pestered cence." Garner's stance impressed one of Polk's agents, who reported that the new overseer "commenced in the right way, and has the negroes under fine command."[8]

But Garner had hidden from this observer the fact that one of Polk's slaves had already fled the plantation. This was Charles, permanently separated from his wife when his Tennessee master had put him up for sale and the buyer, James Polk, had sent him to Mississippi. Perhaps when Polk had bought Charles he did not know that the slave was married, and perhaps Polk had not ascertained this fact from Charles before deporting him to Mississippi. Overseer Garner denied that yearning for one's wife offered a black man cause for discontent; Charles, the overseer complained, "run a way some fore weks a gow withe out any cause what ever. I think he has gaun back to tennessee where his wife is."[9]

Garner was also "pestered" by the conduct of a twenty-two-year-old slave woman, Marina, "strolling over the contery [country]." At the least her offense was leaving the plantation without a pass; more likely, she was fleeing from time to time, returning after a day or two, then departing again. Garner whipped her. As often occurred when the owner of a plantation lived hundreds of miles away, Polk had appointed a local businessman—A. T. McNeal—to represent his interests in cases of urgency, and Marina went to this agent for protection. Garner chafed at finding his authority limited.[10]

Although Charles returned voluntarily to the plantation when the weather turned cold in December—after nine weeks of harried freedom in the woods—Garner's equanimity was soon thereafter disturbed by the flight of the twenty-five-year-old Addison.[11] The overseer's problems came to a head later in 1840 in a confrontation between himself and the plantation's best worker, Gilbert's friend Henry Carter.

Polk had purchased Henry six years earlier, when he moved his plantation slaves—including Henry's wife, Mariah—from western Tennessee to Mississippi. Mariah (a member of a favored slave family inherited by Polk's wife) had an abroad marriage in western Tennessee with Henry Carter. Henry's master, Archibald Carter, owed Polk money for land previously purchased from him. In buying Henry, Polk was achieving multiple purposes. He was glad to avoid breaking up a slave's marriage, especially if this gratified his own wife. He needed more workers for the Mississippi plantation, and he was at this moment acquiring other slaves as well. Polk was pleased to get what promised to be an excellent worker at a bargain price—for Archibald Carter would probably never have sold Henry, and certainly not for just $600, if Carter, too, had not been glad to prevent his own slave's marriage from being destroyed. And Polk was happy—by giving no cash but only Carter's IOUs, as full payment for Henry—to secure the payment of the debt that Carter owed him.[12] In the slave South a huge proportion of commercial transactions were effected on credit, and Polk constantly had to sue his debtors to try to get them to pay up; by taking a slave in payment of a debt, Polk ensured that at least he would never have to take Archibald Carter to court.

When a mistress or master saved a slave's marriage by buying an abroad partner, the slave would sometimes become tractable out of gratitude.[13] But Henry Carter did not become docile. No doubt he was proud of being the plantation's best worker, and overseer Garner seems to have offended his pride. Apparently Henry then protested by slowing down. Garner retaliated by making Henry take off all his clothes and submit to a whipping. Enraged, Henry took his life into his own hands by daring to fight a white man. Fortunately for him, Garner—unlike Beanland at a similar juncture—was not armed with a knife and could not defeat Henry in man-to-man fighting. When the overseer called on nearby slaves to seize Henry, their refusal signaled a profound challenge to Garner's authority. "Henry has become so indifernt a bout his duty," Garner expostulated to Polk,

> I was compelled to correct him. He resisted and fought mee. I awdered Charls to take hold of him, being the nearst but [he] refused. . . . After Henry and my self [had been] cumbatting some time he got loose from mee and got in to the swamp. Wile I was pursuing him Gilbert, Charls and Perry was runing the other wey. The onley reson was because they did not take holt of the other boy when awderd.[14]

Expecting that the naked Henry would creep back to the plantation after nightfall to collect some clothes, Garner enlisted two white neighbors, armed with shotguns, to await his return. When a black man came into view, they told him to give himself up; and when he ran instead, a shotgun put birdshot into his thigh, bringing him down. But it was not Henry. His ally Perry had dared to come back to fetch clothes for Henry. "While watching for him," Garner explained with satisfaction, "Pery was slipping up and was awderd to stand but he broke and he shot him in the legs with smawl shot sow I got him, and he is at work."[15]

Henry, somehow obtaining clothes to wear and probably traveling only at night, walked during a week and a half the 110 miles, as the crow flies, to Silas Caldwell's plantation in western Tennessee, where he sought protection with Polk's brother-in-law and former partner. Henry, as Caldwell reported, "says the Overseer thretened to shoot him, he says for nothing." Henry told Caldwell that Polk's neighbor Leigh had—in league with Garner—shot Perry in the thigh, disabling him from work; and because Henry "says he is afraid to go back," Caldwell let him stay in Tennessee until he heard from Polk.[16]

Polk promptly fired Garner. The overseer's offense was *not* having authorized the slave to be shot, for Polk continued to be friendly with his Mississippi neighbor Leigh, whose son Randolph was probably the "Mr. Leigh" who had gunned down Perry. Garner's offense was losing control (and failing to report the event promptly). It is chilling to think that if Garner had been more of a "man," had armed himself with a knife and had stabbed Henry—as Beanland had stabbed Chunky Jack—he could have captured Henry without calling for the aid of the other slaves.[17] Perry, Charles, and Gilbert would not then have fled, and Polk would probably have hired Garner for another year, as he had done with Beanland after Beanland had stabbed Chunky Jack.

Polk turned instead, once again, to a new man. This was Isaac Dismukes. Dismukes proved, by the standards of Mississippi's taciturn overseers, to be almost loquacious in theorizing about how Polk's slaves were to be brought under control. He suggested, indeed, that Polk himself was not enough of a man. "You noe," Dismukes reasoned scientifically, "that you have had . . . [overseers] hear of different ages and sizes and the [slaves] runaway from all." The problem, therefore, was not in the overseers but in their employer. "You wil have to bea the man that wil have to stop that amoungst your negroes," the overseer boldly affirmed; and the key to success would be Polk's permitting his overseer to inflict whippings so horrific as to terrify the slaves into submission.[18]

The background to Dismukes's outburst is quickly sketched. Three months earlier the overseer had inflicted a savage whipping on Addison—twenty-six years old and always owned by the Polk family—who had been one of the few males not to flee from overseer Beanland in 1833–34 (Addison's first recorded flight was from overseer Garner in 1840). Like several other Polk slaves, Addison felt that Polk's brother-in-law Silas Caldwell was relatively sympathetic; and after Dismukes's whipping, Addison set out on the 110-mile trip from Mississippi to Caldwell's plantation in West Tennessee. After a four-week journey he turned himself in to Caldwell. "From the wounds that are on [Addison's] neck & arms," Caldwell informed Polk, "it appears that the Overseer intended to kill Him."[19]

Slaves knew that only a thin line divided those whippings that masters approved of from savagery that—even to the masters—was beyond the pale. Three years earlier Polk and his slaves had learned that, on the West Tennessee plantation of Polk's brother-in-law James Walker, Walker's overseer had overstepped the line. This overseer, a Mr. Gee, had killed Jack Long, one of the Polk family's slaves, just before Jack was to have been sent to work on James Polk's Mississippi plantation. We do not know why Gee killed the slave, only that Gee fled to avoid prosecution (for manslaughter? for murder?). The overseer and his family agreed to pay the Polks unusually high compensation—$1000—for the dead slave, and that appears to have settled the matter as far as the white community was concerned. The Gees seemed to feel (correctly?) that a big payment would reduce the chance that James Walker and the Polks would demand criminal prosecution of the killer.[20] Although laws theoretically banned the killing of a slave except in self-defense (or if the slave happened to die when "under moderate correction"), this episode offered the slaves further confirmation that their lives were precarious and that such laws offered them little real protection.[21] Caldwell's report—that Dismukes appeared to have intended to kill Addison—may not have been wholly hyperbolic. During Addison's four-week flight from Dismukes, his wounds had healed enough so that he could work again; but "he says the overseer says he will kill him and [he] is afraid to stay there." Caldwell therefore hired out Addison to work in Tennessee while awaiting Polk's instructions.[22]

By this time thirty-four-year-old Gilbert had also fled from Dismukes, and he, too, set out for West Tennessee. But three weeks later Gilbert was captured near Polk's former Tennessee plantation and jailed in Somerville. Seeking Caldwell's protection, Gilbert lied: he alleged that Caldwell owned him, though in fact Caldwell had sold him to the Polks almost five years earlier. Caldwell arranged for Gilbert to be brought the nineteen miles from Somerville to Caldwell's plantation, where both slaves accused Dismukes of mismanagement and of drinking too much. Mrs. Caldwell (James Polk's sister) wrote to Sarah Polk, recommending that they fire Dismukes; she named another man who she thought would make a better overseer.[23]

Polk's local agent, William Bobbitt, advised selling Addison. But Polk persuaded himself that he could suppress flight by whipping "the offenders in every instance . . . instead of selling." And Polk's esteemed, gentlemanly, Virginia-bred neighbor, John T. Leigh, approved, saying that "no other course will correct the evil."[24] Polk, however, feared that Dismukes would incapacitate or even kill Addison or Gilbert, and he therefore insisted that Bobbitt should witness Dismukes's whippings. After Caldwell sent the two slaves back to Mississippi, it took a couple of days to get Bobbitt out to the plantation, and this gave Gilbert time to flee yet again. This time he eluded capture for a month. Dismukes angrily wrote that he would have whipped the two slaves immediately after they had arrived "had it not bin of your request that mr Bobit should bin preasent." And he would have whipped them so hard that "I think that . . . Gilburt would not of run away again soon." But, he protested, he would not have whipped them so badly "as to disenable them from work." Caldwell had owned Gilbert before 1834, and Gilbert told the other slaves that Caldwell wanted to buy him again. This aroused Dismukes. "Doo not sell him," the overseer implored Polk:

> If you whish to brake them from running away for they had reather bea sould twice than to bea whip once. [Dismukes wanted Gilbert to be sent back to the plantation in irons.] I wil not inger him by whiping him. I beleave that they balieve that tennessee is a place of parridise and the[y] all want to gow back to tennessee.[25]

This, then, was the background to Dismukes's exhortation that Polk must "bea the man." Although Polk was "very much perplext" over how to handle the situation, he finally decided, as previously with Beanland, to back his overseer. Gilbert was captured some seventy miles northeast of the plantation and jailed at Holly Springs until Dismukes was able to bring him back for his whipping. Polk did not sell either slave. Although Polk distrusted Dismukes's financial management (banning him from buying plantation supplies on credit), the crops were good, and Polk rehired Dismukes each year for the next three years. Addison fled again for a fortnight in 1842; he had feared another whipping after Dismukes accused him of killing a young hog. This flight apparently engendered in Addison a prolonged illness. Gilbert also fled again to seek Caldwell's protection late in 1844. The absence of the overseer's letters after January 1843 prevents one from learning how many other fugitives there may have been during this period. But when Polk's local agents finally sacked Dismukes at the end of 1844, evidently they did so not because Polk disapproved of the overseer's disciplinary measures but because Dismukes neglected his duties (e.g., he failed to pay the plantation's taxes), he kept "to[o] much company," and he probably left the plantation too often.[26] Perhaps Dismukes's criticism had left in Polk's mind a festering irritation, which overcame any reluctance Polk might have felt about parting with his undeferential subaltern.

The new overseer, John Mairs, who took over in 1845 when Polk became president, served Polk and later Polk's widow for fifteen years, until she sold a half share of the plantation in 1860—an extraordinary record in a job in which dissatisfied employers often dismissed the overseers after only a year or two. Polk's neighbor Leigh considered Mairs "an excellent manager . . . very attentive, stays constantly at home [unlike Dismukes], appears to be a good judge of work, and [the decisive virtue] certainly has a great deal of it done." Polk's agents Robert Campbell and Daniel Graham joined in a chorus of approval, and as late as 1852 Sarah Polk's New Orleans factor attributed to Mairs's skill the unusually high price her cotton fetched: "Your overseer," the factor enthused, "deserves much praise for the beautiful manner he has prepared it for the market." Moreover, Mairs was a good self-publicist, always beginning his reports in an upbeat tone and only later tacking on any, to him, minor qualification. The death of a young slave was, to Mairs, insignificant; thus in 1855 he informed Sarah Polk, "Your people are all well. Jane lost her child by the name of Patson."[27]

Although only one slave seems to have run away during the first three years of Mairs's tenure, thereafter bondsmen fled from this overseer as regularly as from his predecessors. During the thirteen years (including the three years just mentioned) for which a fair number of Mairs's letters have been preserved, at least ten male slaves ran away from the plantation; on average each of these fled almost three times, so the total number of flights was at least twenty-eight. The first recorded fugitive was Joe, a youth whom Polk's agent Robert Campbell bought for himself in Tennessee and then sold to Polk at a moderate price in January 1847. Joe had scarcely arrived at the Mississippi plantation before he fled, but he was promptly jailed in nearby Coffeeville. In July 1847 he ran away again and remained away long enough to steal many hogs. After he had been absent for six and one-half weeks, Campbell tried to reassure Polk that "since he [is] only 17 years old (but large) I cannot [think] he will stay out long." Joe's third flight, beginning in February 1848, lasted more than two months and disturbed even the impassive John Mairs: Joe "behaves bad," the overseer acknowledged to the president. "It appears he [won't] stay at hand. I have [taken] him out of jale 3 times. I will keep him inside [i.e., indoors at the plantation] until I hear from you. It will not prevent him from work." Three and a half weeks later, before Polk had replied, Joe managed to escape yet again. The president concluded that Joe "will do me no good," and he authorized John Leigh to sell him; but—as Leigh became mortally ill—this had not yet occurred when Polk himself died in 1849.[28]

During the next few years Joe ran away at least three more times, and Mairs attributed to him a malign influence ("Joe will ruin your young men"). Apparently he was then sold because whippings had not tamed his spirit. "I dough not think chastising him will dough him eny good," Mairs finally lamented in 1853, just before Joe disappears from the record.[29]

Meanwhile, other slaves were fleeing. The next known fugitive was the familiar Addison, who in 1848 once again made the long trek to Silas Caldwell's West Tennessee plantation. Caldwell, however, had died. His widow (James Polk's sister) was less sympathetic to the slaves than Caldwell had been, and she determined to dispatch Addison immediately to Mississippi for a whipping. The president instructed Mairs that it not be too severe: "I do not wish you to treat [Addison] harshly," Polk requested, repeating the promise he had just made to his sister. "As [the slave] has received no countenance at Mrs. Caldwell's he will not be apt to repeat this visit." Polk claimed to disbelieve Addison's account of Mairs's ill treatment of the slaves: "Addison's story is probably made up to excuse himself for leaving." Yet, self-contradictorily, the president acknowledged that the slaves might have just grounds for complaint. He said that next year, when he intended to visit the plantation for the first time since 1844, he would "put all right which may be necessary." Since Mairs had become the overseer, Polk ruminated, Addison's was "the first instance of any of my people running back to Tennessee . . . and I was hoping they had abandoned or forgotten their old tricks."[30]

Addison turned out to be so ill that Mrs. Caldwell could not, for five weeks, fulfill her intention to send him back to Mississippi. Addison's serious illness surely was not faked; he would have slept badly and without shelter during the several weeks of his flight from Mississippi, and he could scarcely have deceived Mrs. Caldwell's doctor during the long period of his illness. Addison's ill health did not, however, win him good will from Polk's sister. And once Addison had been safely returned to Mississippi, Mairs whipped him—mildly, Mrs. Caldwell alleged—yet (inconsistently) so much as to deter any repetition of the offense: "I had Addison . . . Ironed and Chained every Night," she assured the president: "The Overseer [Mairs] was very moderate with him. He corrected him but not bad. . . . I showed Addison no [favoring?] nor did I allow him after your letter to ever speak to me. [My agent] Mr. Short says he will never try it again." Addison's flight cost Polk, in addition to the lost labor, $105 for the ill slave's care at Mrs. Caldwell's and for the hire of someone to escort him back to Mississippi. Within a few weeks of Addison's return to the plantation, the veteran fugitive Gilbert fled, in midwinter, and tasted eleven weeks of relative freedom. Mairs conjectured that he, too, had set off for Tennessee, but in fact he was eventually incarcerated at Oxford, Mississippi.[31] This was the first of four times that Gilbert ran away from Mairs during a period of two and one-half years.

After James Polk died in June 1849, his Mississippi plantation served—as he had intended—as the principal support for his widow, Sarah. She retained Mairs as overseer during the next decade, expecting him to report to her from time to time; and she also depended on her brother, on Polk's cousin Robert Campbell, or on one of Polk's executors to keep tabs on Mairs. By examining events during the years after Polk's death, we can follow the lives of individual slaves from one decade to the next in a way rarely possible for historians of slavery. We must understand, of course, that James Polk was no longer responsible for what happened after his widow assumed proprietorship. He had been accustomed, however, to engage his strong-minded wife in the details of his political campaigning and in selecting political reading matter for him from newspapers, and he surely had discussed plantation affairs with her as well. She had sometimes visited the plantation with him before 1845, and she was substantially prepared to undertake her new role.[32]

Slaves continued to flee from the plantation as regularly as or even more so than they had done during earlier years. "Some of [the slaves] have behaved vary badly," Mairs complained in January 1851. "Some of them are in the woods." One of these was Gilbert, who eluded Mairs for three months. When Gilbert was finally captured, he succeeded in escaping again, the very next day, for another five or six weeks of quasi free-dom. Meanwhile Joe was also absent, probably for six weeks or longer. While both Gilbert and Joe were gone, Pompey—a man in his midforties who seems to have been a brother of Jack Long (the man killed by over-seer Gee)—also fled. And that winter a slave named Wilson (younger brother of the Henry whom Polk took to the White House as a personal servant) made the first of at least three flights from the plantation.[33]

In 1853 three more slaves—none previously recorded as fugitives from Polk's plantation—joined the long list of those who dared to run away. The first was Billy Nevels, the bondsman bought by Robert Campbell at an estate sale in 1846 (when Billy was seventeen) and separated from a younger companion. Early in 1852 Billy had suffered a heartrending sepa-ration. His wife, Barbara, was torn from his arms and sent to Tennessee, as was their baby. Barbara had been willed in 1831 to James Polk's nephew Marshall Polk, Jr. (whom James Polk as president appointed a cadet at West Point), on condition that Marshall not take possession until James Polk's mother died. Old Mrs. Polk was scarcely in her grave, in 1852, when the young cadet—eager to make as much money as he could and unwilling to accept another slave in place of Barbara so that she could remain with her husband—had Barbara deported to Tennessee. Marshall uttered pieties about how he "would much prefer purchasing . . . the husband of the woman," and his agent, reporting Barbara's distress at her separation from her husband, "hope[d] we may be able to accommodate [Barbara's] wish" (that Marshall would buy Billy Nevels). But nothing was done.[34]

Thus Billy Nevels lost not only his wife but also his infant, Marthy, for a slave child was the property of its mother's owner, and Marthy there-fore belonged to Marshall Polk. A year later Billy Nevels fled the planta-tion (in the company of the frequent fugitive Joe), probably trying to see Barbara and Marthy again. But in the previous autumn Billy had become "very sick" during an epidemic, and within a few days of leaving the plan-tation he fell ill again—perhaps a recurrence of erysipelas of the internal organs, which had killed the plantation's best worker, Henry Carter, in the previous epidemic. To save Billy's life, Joe brought him back to the plantation, where they both turned themselves in. Billy probably never saw his wife and child again.[35]

Then at harvest time, Phil, one of the ablest and most versatile work-ers, fled. He was a good hewer of wood, a good shoemaker (sometimes earning cash by working at this trade in the evenings), and a "rite smarte blacksmith." Polk had been able to buy him in 1834 because he was then in jail (in West Tennessee) after a failed attempt to escape from his previ-ous master. This had been Phil's second flight from that owner, Parson Reeves, and Reeves consequently was willing to sell Phil below his nor-mal market value. Overseer Ephraim Beanland had strongly urged Polk to make the purchase. Everyone knew that slaves often tried to escape, and this was after all only "the 2 time that [the twenty-two-year-old Phil] ever run away in his life." In any case, Phil was not (in Beanland's view) wholly responsible for his action because he had been cajoled into this second venture by the inveterate fugitive Chunky Jack. Moreover, Beanland was confident—with a menace—that Phil "can be broke from runninge away." These arguments (and Phil's comparatively low price) had persuaded Polk to undertake the risk of buying him, and for nearly twenty years Phil apparently did not run away from the Polk plantation. Perhaps one reason was that he had soon married a young wife, Eve, by whom he had many children. Four of these children had already died young, however, and although Ananias, Phil's youngest child, was born on August 18, 1853, Phil's discontent was such that he fled when this infant was only a few weeks old. Phil (by now forty-one) escaped in the company of Manuel, the twenty-nine-year-old son of that Chunky Jack with whom Phil had made his earlier, abortive escape attempt. Chunky Jack had then sought permanent freedom by crossing the Mississippi River into the Arkansas territory, and one may therefore presume that Phil in 1834, and again in 1853, was also hoping for a permanent escape, as was Manuel. Manuel had been only ten years old when his father, Chunky Jack, was captured and sold, and no doubt Phil had often told the young man about his father's determination to be free. Manuel, like Phil, left a wife in this bid for freedom. But his and Phil's hopes were shattered, for they were quickly captured.[36]

By the mid-1850s Mairs's most persistent fugitive was Harbert, a privileged slave of Sarah Polk whose demands for special treatment discomfited the Polks for twenty years. Harbert's parents, Coy and Matilda, were to have been bequeathed to Sarah Polk by her father, but debts against the estate had led in 1828 to Coy's being allotted to Sarah Polk's sister, while Matilda and her children became the property of James and Sarah Polk. Polk—perhaps influenced by the allegation that Coy had already found a new wife—refused to buy Coy, and Matilda's marriage came to an end.[37] After becoming ill on Polk's West Tennessee plantation in 1832, she was made a house servant in Columbia, Tennessee, where she and her son Harbert lived in Polk's mother's house. (This is the "Ancestral Home of James K. Polk"—the only Polk residence that has survived for the inspection of modern visitors.) Harbert, when a young teenager, apparently served James Polk as a body servant for seven or eight months of each year and was rented out to local townspeople during the months when the congressman was away in Washington.[38]

Town life offered the young bondsman enough freedom of movement for him to flout discipline. "Harbert has been acting badly for some time past," James Walker had reported to Polk in 1836. Polk's brother William had "hired him to Mrs. Frazer. He was seldom there, generally at the grocery places where he ought not to have been." Dr. Silas Caldwell—still alive in 1836—agreed that Harbert, then fifteen, "is doing very badly. He is stealing, drinking and doing as bad as he can." Caldwell determined to send Harbert to West Tennessee for a dose of plantation discipline, but Caldwell's intentions became known: "Harbert & Matilda [James Walker reported] eluded the Dr. and he could not be found" until after Caldwell's overseer—who was to have taken Harbert back to West Tennessee—had departed. A few weeks later Caldwell locked the youth "in his room up-stairs at [James Polk's] mothers, planning to send him to [West Tennessee with another agent]; but Harbert jumped out of the window and cleared himself. It is strange he did not cripple himself." (And when one views the height of the second-story window in the Polk Ancestral Home, one wonders how indeed Harbert could have avoided injuring himself with any such leap; could a confederate have unlocked the room long enough to let him out?) Despite Jane Polk's urgings, Caldwell now washed his hands of any further attempt to transfer Harbert to his West Tennessee planta-tion, and Mrs. Polk rented Harbert to a local brickmaker. Harbert and his mother objected to the youth's having to labor in a brickyard, and Harbert set off in a stagecoach to Nashville to appeal to Polk's younger brother William. James Walker had the stagecoach overtaken, and he jailed Harbert until extracting from "him & Matilda . . . such fair promises that I . . . hired him to [the brickmaker again] at $5 per mo[nth]."[39]

Harbert remained unslavish. Polk rented him for a stint with a local blacksmith, but Harbert took to this trade no better than to brickmaking. Soon after Polk became governor in 1839, he brought Harbert with him to Nashville and rented him for a year to an important political ally (the editor of the *Nashville Union*), who perhaps employed the nineteen-year-old bondsman to run errands. Polk was already thinking of ridding him-self of Harbert; and as the young man continued to be unsubmissive, the governor resolved upon speedy action. Normally Polk would have con-sidered that sending a town slave to his plantation would be sufficient chastisement, but he knew Harbert was unlikely to become more docile in the country than in town. In any case, Polk needed money to pay debts incurred during the 1839 gubernatorial campaign, so he decided to con-vert his recalcitrant bondsman into cash. "My boy Harbert is getting into base habits here," Governor Polk wrote to William Polk from Nashville,

> and is not behaving well. I fear he will do me but little good on the plantation, and I am anxious to sell him. I will take consider-ably less for him than I have been asking. Will you let me know whether you can sell him for me at Columbia and what can be got for him. . . . If I can get a fair price I am resolved to sell him.[40]

Polk's Tennessee political ally Gideon Pillow—who, like Polk, had an absentee plantation in Mississippi—now paid Polk $650 for Harbert and deported him to Mississippi, some 250 miles away from his mother, Matilda. After Harbert had been punished for five and one-half years in this way, President Polk (perhaps at his wife's urging, and now no longer financially pressed) bought Harbert back. "Harbert is a family servant and I own his mother and therefore desired to procure him," Polk explained, employing paternalist language in a note (on the back of the receipt) that the president presumably didn't need as a reminder to himself and, therefore, may have written for posterity. Harbert by this time had a wife, and Polk bought her and her eight-year-old son, too. Polk was now seeking to expand his plantation labor force again; and here—as in his earlier purchase of Mariah's husband, Henry Carter—he gladly killed two birds with one stone, helping to preserve the marriage of a favored slave and increasing the number of laborers on his plantation.[41]

This mixture of punishment with "indulgence" (as masters denominated the grant of favor to a privileged slave) did not convert Harbert into an obedient bondsman. Indeed, by the 1850s he had become the biggest thorn in overseer John Mairs's flesh. Harbert's most daring exploit led Mairs to admit that he had not reported the slave's previous flights. Only after getting Harbert back from the Memphis jail did Mairs acknowledge to Sarah Polk, "I dyed not rit you word that he had left the plas. He has left wons or twis before but dyed not stay out long. Come in himself." Harbert, dissatisfied with these two brief sojourns in the local woods, had this time aimed at permanent freedom. Memphis was the magnet for a fugitive like Chunky Jack or Harbert who sought a real escape. Harbert's plan resembled Frederick Douglass's now-famous flight from Baltimore in that it required the use of another black man's papers. Also, Harbert had by now graduated from horse-drawn stagecoach to mechanized travel: "Some negro give Harbard a pass [Mairs reported] and he went a part of the way [to Memphis] on the ral cars and exspected to git a bote at Memphis." After recovering the fugitive from the Memphis jail and whipping him, Mairs confined him in irons for more than three months; but this did not terminate Harbert's influence over other discontented slaves. Wilson, who had already fled once, ran away again a few weeks after Harbert's capture. "I suppose [Wilson] has taken the same Rout that Harbard tuck," Mairs speculated. "I exspect Harbard got him of[f]." Although Wilson was back at the plantation later that spring, he joined Harbert later that year in a venture that cast light on Mairs's conception of good order. "The servants has behaved well," Mairs reported to Sarah Polk in upbeat fashion:

> All but Harbard, Manuel, and Fonser, and Wilson. Harbard left on 9th [September] and has taken thes boys [aged thirty-two, twenty-nine, and twenty-eight] along with him. And some of the negros say he tryed to get 2 others along with him. Told them he cold of got away before but he thort he wold stay with Mr. Sam Walker [Polk's nephew and business agent in Memphis]. I think his a[i]m is to git to Memphis thinking you may sel him thar. He liks to be in a sity.

But the barriers between a Mississippi slave and permanent freedom were virtually insurmountable. Sensing this, Manuel and Alphonso immediately got cold feet and returned voluntarily to the plantation with Harbert, cooking up an imaginative lie that gave Mairs an excuse not to incapacitate them from work, even temporarily, by flogging them: "Manuel and Fonser sa[y] Harbard was agoing to take them to Memphis to sey there oncle," Mairs reported with a straight face. "But the got afird and come home. I have not whipped nary wone of them. I will try them sey if the will dough without it. The wether is warm and I want to git the coten out." Mairs's leniency this time may have also encouraged Wilson to return promptly to rejoin the cotton pickers. Yet within a few weeks Mairs admitted that "some of the boys have behaved badly" (usually a euphemism for running to the woods); and a few months later Alphonso ("Fonser") certainly fled again, seeking temporary respite.[42] Probably the dauntless Harbert was one of those who continued to "behave badly," and there is every reason to suppose that he was soon sold to a slave trader.[43]

This record suggests how the Polk slaves felt about their lives in bondage. So dreary was the routine, so harsh the regimen, so constricted the opportunities for relief, and so wholly lacking in prospect of improvement that discontented slaves dared the elements and human persecutors, year after year, in their bids for temporary surcease. Lacking any other clear way of expressing their opinions about the circumstances of their lives, these disfranchised human beings voted with their feet. The message was unambiguous. They wanted relief, and they wanted it so badly that they defied—in desperately seeking some brief measure of freedom—the near certainty that they would never be permanently free. Time after time slaves were captured, returned to the plantation, and flogged. Yet time after time they or their comrades fled again, seeking at least temporary respite from the conditions to which they were subjected by an owner who—if Gideon Pillow was to be believed—was "a kind and humane master to his servants & they are all much devoted to him. No man in the country treats his slaves with more *tenderness* and *regard* than does Governor Polk."[44]

Did this remarkable record of the slaves' dissidence issue from circumstances peculiar to the Polks' plantation? To a limited extent the answer must be yes. When overseer Isaac Dismukes declared that at Polk's plantation slaves "runaway from all" overseers (regardless of whether the overseer was young or old, large or small), he was contrasting Polk's plantation with others, where flight was not quite so common. One of Polk's problems was that his wife—a strong-minded woman with genuine loyalty to bondspeople she had inherited, like Jim, and Harbert's mother, Matilda—sometimes pressed Polk to give these slaves special treatment. An even more important influence was exerted by Polk's three brothers-in-law, especially by Silas Caldwell. Although Caldwell was nearly as quick as his peers to call an adult slave like Ben a "bad boy" and although his judgment may sometimes have been mercurial, he showed genuine feeling for some of the slaves—as when he purchased Wally (uniting him with his wife, Martha) or when he hired out Addison in West Tennessee instead of sending him back immediately to be whipped by Dismukes. Slaves in the American South often sought relief from one white man's tyranny by discovering another white person who might act as protector; and testimony to the desperation of Polk's slaves appears in the month-long flight of Jim to seek (at Columbia) the aid of Polk's brother-in-law Adlai Harris, as well as the long flights of Henry Carter, Addison (twice), and Gilbert (two or even three times) to seek out Silas Caldwell, even though his plantation was well over 100 miles from Polk's Mississippi establishment. Like other oppressed people, slaves sought relief from present tribulation by constructing the image of some past golden age, and by 1841 Tennessee had become, to Polk's Mississippi slaves, "a place of parridise."[45]

Historians have debated which were the masters' most powerful weapons in enforcing plantation discipline. Kenneth Stampp pointed to the whip— "To Make Them Stand in Fear"—whereas more recent attention has been directed to the threat of sale (with consequent separation from family and community) as the "most effective long-term mechanism of control."[46] Polk's overseers, seeking short-term results, vigorously propounded Stampp's view. One overseer after another—Beanland, Bratton, Dismukes, Mairs—urged that the Polks *not* sell a recalcitrant slave, Beanland even threatening to quit and demand his wages if Polk sold Ben. "They had reather bea sould twice than to bea whip once," Dismukes aphoristically pleaded. But this rule had to be modified in the case of certain exceptional slaves, whom even the most savage whippings could not "break." Beanland finally accepted the sale of Chunky Jack, and Mairs eventually concluded—after Joe's seventh flight— that whipping would not do "eny good" in curbing this man's spirit.[47] The nature of a sale also affected its power to terrify: threat of sale to a long-distance slave trader was obviously a greater deterrent than sale within the slave's familiar neighborhood. To Polk's overseers, a major problem was that Polk (because of his wife's pressure or because of his sense of responsibility to a slave like Ben, whom he himself had inherited) had sold the slaves Jim and Ben within their old central Tennessee homeland and to the owners of their wives, instead of exiling them to the deeper South.

President Polk, perhaps thinking of posterity, once wrote a letter suggesting, in considerate tones, that the frequent fugitive Joe "may be better satisfied" to be owned by someone other than Polk.[48] Yet Polk's actions usually spoke louder than these soft words. If his plantation was to be profitable, his slaves must submit to discipline. A lax overseer like Mayo was quickly dismissed, whereas harsh overseers like Beanland and Dismukes received Polk's backing when slaves fled; and Polk's agents later dismissed them for other reasons, not because Polk believed they were heartless despots.

Yet Polk's experiences with fugitive slaves were not unique. Although there probably were even more fugitives from the Polks' than from most other plantations, flight was common elsewhere too. During the 1850s nearly eighty fugitives were lodged *annually* in the Savannah, Georgia jail,[49] and these surely made up only a small proportion of the low-country slaves who fled in this region, most of the others eventually returning voluntarily to their plantations or being captured and sent back without incarceration. The historians John Hope Franklin and Loren Schweninger have shown how common fugitives were all over the South. They believe that more than half of Southern planters (those with over nineteen slaves) had at least one runaway a year.[50] Thus, although the number of fugitives from the Polk plantation probably was larger than normal (as the overseer Isaac Dismukes implied when advising Polk that greater severity was required), it probably was not greatly so.

Overseers' letters are the most revealing evidence on this point. Whereas an overseer like John Mairs might conceal from his employer the brief flight of a slave to the local woods, he felt obliged to report long-term fugitives who might disappear permanently. The problem for us today is that the vast majority of overseers' letters—relatively free as they were from a propagandist's purpose—have been destroyed. The two best collections of overseers' letters appear to be those from the Polks' cotton plantation and those from Charles Manigault's Savannah River rice plantation. It is remarkable that in both cases these letters prove that fugitives were even more numerous than historians had previously supposed.[51] Evidence from other sources—especially travelers' reports, jailers' records, advertisements for fugitive slaves, petitions to county courts and state legislatures, and interviews with elderly former slaves—suggest that flight was the most important overt form of slaves' dissidence all over the South.[52]

How could it have been otherwise? For a slave to raise his hand against a white man was to invite death. Jack Long was killed by an overseer even when he did *not* "resist." When Chunky Jack hit Beanland with a stick, he was lucky that the knife wounds Beanland inflicted on him were not fatal. And when Henry Carter engaged in hand-to-hand combat with overseer Garner, he was fortunate that Garner was unarmed. These are the only two cases of a slave's physically resisting a white man in all of the Polk records; and Chunky Jack's first act was to flee, not to fight (he fought only when Beanland tried to stop his flight). Henry Carter did indeed fight in order to terminate what he believed was an unjust whipping. But Henry was dealing with a probably unimposing overseer, and Henry himself was a proud, privileged slave. Few slaves would risk their lives, as Henry did, by fighting. Far more common was flight to the local woods, where one could cool off for a few weeks before being captured or before voluntarily exchanging the perils of life in the woods for the more predictable ones of the plantation. A few hardy souls—Chunky Jack; probably his son, Manuel; his companion, Phil; and the town-bred Harbert—attempted permanent flight, but Mississippi was too far from free territory for them to have much chance of success. Flight to the woods, however dangerous, remained the best temporary alternative to the constricted existence of a captive on a cotton plantation.

4

✦

Profit

Dreadful though a slave's existence might be, the life of a cotton planter obviously was not entirely trouble-free either. Polk accepted his troubles and—when he felt he could afford it—bought more slaves because he hoped to make money. How far did he succeed?

The Mississippi plantation's first two years (1835–36) looked so unpromising to Polk's partner—his brother-in-law Silas Caldwell—that Caldwell quickly withdrew from the partnership. Caldwell had injudiciously entered the arrangement on terms highly favorable to James Polk, and Polk actually did very well financially during these first two years, even when the plantation was not yet producing much cotton. The reason was that, at this time, the new Mississippi plantation was being run as part of a joint enterprise that also included Caldwell's own, relatively long-established cotton plantation in West Tennessee; and Polk's revenues included a half-share of the proceeds of Caldwell's Tennessee plantation, as well as a half-share of those from their new Mississippi plantation (see Map 2.1). Thus Caldwell's Tennessee plantation subsidized the new Mississippi venture during its first year, when little land had yet been cleared, and the subsidy continued (on a smaller scale) even during the second year. In effect Caldwell gave Polk eleven and one-half bales of the 1835 cotton crop (worth about $675 at the high price then prevailing) and another seven bales of the 1836 crop (worth about $305 at the next year's lower prices).[1] Thus Polk, who in 1835 would barely have covered costs on the Mississippi plantation's revenues alone, ended that year with a 5 percent cash profit on his capital investment. And in 1836—augmented again by Caldwell's subsidy—Polk's cash profit was 10 percent [see table 4.1, column (a)]. These figures, moreover, did not include the capital gains on the value of his slaves during the price inflation of the mid-1830s.[2]

Overoptimism had induced Caldwell to make this bad bargain with his brother-in-law. Cotton prices were rising to bonanza levels in 1834; Caldwell had supposed that the land would be quickly cleared and that the new plantation—if it produced a bale for every acre planted in cotton—would (helped by Caldwell's own Tennessee plantation) yield enough cash to cover the big payments due for the new plantation at the end of 1835 and 1836. But most of the land first cleared had to be planted in corn

Table 4.1
Profit Rates from the Polks' Share of the Mississippi Plantation, 1835–57
(estimated, as percent of capital investment)

Year of Crop	(a) Rate of Cash Profit (percent)	(b) Rate of Profit from Undistributed Capital Gains★ (percent)	(c) Rate of Total Profit [(a) + (b)] (percent)
1835	5.3	4.6	9.9
1836	10.1	4.1	14.2
1837	6.2	4.0	10.2
1838	6.9	−7.8	−0.9
1839	6.5	−0.6	5.9
1840	3.8	—	3.8
1841	5.5	−0.6	4.9
1842	9.6	−2.4	7.2
1843	?	—	?
1844	5.0	—	5.0
1845	8.3	0.5	8.8
1846	12.1	1.1	13.2
1847	6.5	−0.1	6.4
1848	5.9	1.2	7.1
1849	13.4	—	13.4
1850	11.1	0.6	11.7
1851	9.2	0.8	10.0
1852	12.6	5.9	18.5
1853	3.1	8.1	11.2
1854	2.1	7.3	9.4
1855	8.5	1.1	9.6
1856	11.1	1.5	12.6
1857	9.2	1.1	10.3
Average Annual Rate of Profit			
1835–44 (excluding 1843)	6.5	−0.8	5.7
1845–57	8.7	2.2	10.9
1835–57 (excluding 1843)	7.8	1.4	9.2

★Column (b) refers to the Polks' gains (or losses) from the increasing (or decreasing) value of their capital investment in land and slaves. Land values increased when the virgin land was cleared and when the cotton boom of the 1850s caused an inflation of land prices. The value of the Polks' slaves increased when there was an inflation of slave prices and when there was a natural increase in the slave population. See chapter 5 and Appendix B.

Sources: Columns (a) and (c) are transcribed from Table C1 in Appendix C, columns (j) and (k). Column (b) is calculated from table C1; columns (e)–(g) are divided by that table's column (a).

to feed the slaves; the cotton land produced much less than a bale to the acre; and even with the subsidy, profits from the joint enterprise barely covered half of the land payment due at the first year's end.[3] Caldwell blamed overseer Beanland for low production, high expenses, and mistreatment of the slaves, and he fired him at the end of 1835. A year later Caldwell concluded that Beanland's replacement—a young man named Mayo—had not gotten enough work out of the slaves, nor had he raised sufficient corn, and he too was fired. Meanwhile, Caldwell (a doctor) had become anxious that the land—which he himself had selected—was too low-lying and wet for the slaves' health. (Four years later the slaves' cabins were finally moved to the other side of a little hill in hopes that this would reduce the incidence of illness.)[4] Discouraged by the difficulties of establishing a new plantation, too impatient to be satisfied with the gradual appreciation of the plantation's worth as land was cleared, and eager to profit by disposing of his land at the high prices then prevailing, Caldwell (at the end of 1836) greatly improved his fortunes by selling his share in the partnership to James Polk's much younger brother William H. Polk. William, having just come of age, had come into possession of some slaves and other assets, which he wished to put to profitable use.[5]

This young man entered zestfully into plantation affairs, and under a new overseer the plantation for the first time produced a substantial cotton crop (eighty-eight bales) in 1837. But that year William Polk spent wildly on overpriced mules, overpriced pork, and the like, and the plantation's recurrent expenses were so much higher than in any subsequent year that the rate of cash profit was just 6 percent.[6] Moreover, when the crop was sold in New Orleans, the young man got his hands on James Polk's share of the profits too, so that James had nothing to show for the 1837 crop except some IOUs from his brother.[7] The younger Polk then lost interest in Mississippi planting; bought instead a farm near Columbia, Tennessee, where he settled with a bride; and soon got into a fracas with a local lawyer, whom (after a public dinner) he horsewhipped outside the lawyer's office. Everyone knew the lawyer would want to avenge this affront to his honor, and three days later 100 witnesses were discussing the dispute outside Columbia's shops when the two antagonists confronted each other again, with pistols drawn. William killed his assailant with grapeshot; a divided grand jury acquitted him of murder, indicting him instead only for assault (i.e., the horsewhipping). He eventually paid a $750 fine and spent a comfortable six weeks in the local jail, where his bride was permitted to stay each night to console him for this brief interruption to the usual pleasant course of his life. This was middle Tennessee, where business enterprise coexisted with the ethic of Southern honor.[8]

James Polk—twenty years older than his errant younger brother and always more like a father than a sibling to the young man—could see long before the shooting episode that William was neglecting their Mississippi plantation, and in the autumn of 1838 James tried half-heartedly to sell it.

Unable to get the price he wanted, Polk concluded that he must buy half of his brother's land and slaves and become sole proprietor; within a year he plunged $14,000 into the enterprise, doubling his plantation investment.[9] The price of cotton was high in 1838, and no doubt Polk calculated that— with a good deal of land now cleared and with his young brother no longer wasting money at the plantation—he would soon be able to realize a good cash return. But the 1838 crop was disappointingly small, cotton prices collapsed for the 1839 crop, and in only one of the subsequent years before 1845 did cash profits exceed 6 percent [see table 4.1, column (a)]. Meanwhile slave prices plummeted, erasing Polk's capital gains of the mid-1830s and replacing them by 1842 with substantial capital losses.[10] Polk wavered during the early 1840s about whether to alter his investment strategy. Short of money after his second unsuccessful attempt to win reelection as Tennessee's governor, Polk tried in 1843 to persuade a nephew or one of his brothers-in-law to buy half of the plantation. Polk's wife didn't want him to sell any slaves, and one of his proposals was that the nephew buy half of the land and work it with some of Polk's slaves, whom Polk would rent to him. These ideas came to naught.[11]

When Polk was elected to the presidency, however, his financial prospects changed dramatically. The president's annual salary of $25,000 dwarfed the mere $2,000 Polk had received during each of his two years as Tennessee's governor. Although Polk had incurred debts of over $16,000 by the end of the 1844 presidential campaign and although his expenses in the White House were bound to be substantial, he could hope—by keeping an eye on those expenses—to pay his debts and soon to have a surplus.[12] Within a month of learning of his election, Polk had bought from his brother William the last quarter of the plantation land. In September 1845, President Polk eagerly anticipated the shipment of his cotton crop to New Orleans: "By the last accounts from Liverpool," he wrote to his nephew (a factor's agent in Memphis), "there is every reason to believe that the price this year will be better . . . than it was last year. I hope it may be so, for after all I find it must be my main reliance to pay my debts. I find that my present position is no money-making affair."[13]

These doleful comments were at best economical with the truth. In fact, Polk's total expenses ($54,000) during four years in the White House consumed scarcely more than half of his total presidential salary ($100,000 over four years). The remainder of that salary supplied him with funds to pay off his $16,000 debt; to invest $11,000 in U.S. Treasury certificates; and to spend approximately $19,000 on buying, repairing, and extending a mansion in Nashville, where he planned to retire after leaving the White House.[14]

Polk could therefore plow back his plantation profits into buying more slaves in order to secure a good income when he retired. From 1845 through 1848, the plantation's cash profits averaged $2,700 each year, and (as we have seen) Polk poured almost every penny of this money—a total of nearly

$10,000—into purchasing nineteen new slaves to work on the plantation.[15] In January 1846 he rebuffed his agent Robert Campbell's offer to buy the plantation, for the president now was wholly committed to expanding his own cotton business. "My plantation," he exclaimed to Campbell,

> may be my only source of income at the end of my time [in the presidency] when I shall retire to private life. . . . I desire to apply the proceeds of my present year's crop, and also of the next two years, to the increase of my force. If I can do this, I will have a respectable force by the end of my time. This is my private intention and therefore I decline to sell.[16]

Although the president was fully committed to cotton planting, this did not mean he was necessarily committed to his lands in Yalobusha County, Mississippi. Later in 1846 and again in 1847, he asked another agent to try to find him "a good cotton plantation well improved and in a healthy location," to which Polk probably hoped to shift his Yalobusha slaves.[17] Doubtless he had noticed that, whereas other cotton planters could reckon on a steady 2 percent annual increase in the size of their slave force—through an excess of births over deaths—his own force was scarcely growing at all, except by purchase of new slaves. But this agent, as well as others, failed to discover a suitable alternative plantation, and Polk had to continue focusing his hopes for a high retirement income on the Yalobusha enterprise.

Happily for him and for every other substantial slaveholder, the market value of their slaves began to rise in 1845, as soon as President John Tyler, his Secretary of State John Calhoun, and President-elect James Polk pushed the immediate annexation of Texas through a bitterly divided Senate. By 1846 slave prices had leaped 30 percent, for everyone knew that the market value of slaves must rise once it was certain that hundreds of thousands of acres of virgin soil (given away virtually free by the Texas legislature) would be available for exploitation by American slavemasters. Although political upheaval in Europe caused the price of the 1847 and 1848 cotton crops to crash, and although the American political crisis surrounding the slavery issue (in 1849–50) created further uncertainty, slave prices were still as high in 1850 as they had been in 1846, and after the "Armistice of 1850" was devised, a sustained boom set in. The world's demand for cotton seemed insatiable, and from 1849 on the best cotton from the Polk plantation fetched at least 9 cents a pound, reaching 12½ cents in 1856 and 1857. By 1857 slave prices were double the amount when Polk was elected president, and they leapfrogged even further in 1858 and 1859.[18] The consequences resembled those of a boom in the stock market or housing market of a later century: everyone who owned a parcel of slaves felt prosperous.[19] The capital gains each year—when the market value of slaves increased—were part of a plantation's total rate of profit. In the thirteen years after Polk was elected president, the capital gains on his slaves, because of the inflation of prices, were nearly $9,000 during years when the total cash profit was about $56,000. Thus, during these years, inflation in slave prices increased the Polks' total profits (including these capital gains) by nearly 16 percent.[20] Sarah Polk turned half of these capital gains (and of those of 1858 and 1859) into cash when, in 1860, she sold—at a price reflecting the capital gains—a half-share of the plantation.[21]

When Polk was on his deathbed in 1849, he had assured his wife that he had done everything he could to secure for her a good income from the Mississippi plantation. This promise was splendidly fulfilled. The plantation's rate of total profit had exceeded 13 percent in 1846, and it reached another peak of nearly 13½ percent in 1849. During most subsequent years, the profits—including capital gains on slaves and on newly cleared land—averaged nearly 12 percent. The only disappointments were in 1853 (when more than half the Polk crop was lost to boll worms and excessive rain) and in 1854 (when a fire at the Yalobusha River warehouse destroyed two-thirds of the crop, which turned out not to be insured at this one point on its long passage to the New Orleans market). Yet even during these two disastrous years the plantation returned—including capital gains from higher slave prices—about a 10 percent profit. Thus Polk, by persevering during the years of low cotton prices, had made for himself and his wife an investment that brought in every year, for the thirteen years beginning in 1845—and even including the two disastrous years of 1853 and 1854—a total annual profit of virtually 11 percent.[22] This certainly beat U.S. Treasury certificates, at only 6 percent. Considerable discretion was required, however. Polk felt he must keep quiet about the nineteen slaves bought since the election—necessary, the president thought, if he was to secure a good retirement income. And there was also the problem that the slaves kept running away, often "withe out any cause what ever," Polk's agents insisted.

5

The Nature of the Regime

For years controversy has simmered among historians about how to de-
nominate the slave society of which Polk was so prominent a representative. Some writers have seen the South as noncapitalist and paternalist. Others have regarded the South as a capitalist society, resembling that
of the North. Although a compromise position has emerged—that Southern society was a hybrid—agreement has not yet been reached about how
this hybrid may best be characterized. These may seem mere semantic quar-
rels, but real issues are at stake, and James Polk's experiences can help to
resolve them.

Many social historians have followed the thinking of Eugene Genovese
as it has evolved since 1965. Originally Genovese saw the South as pre-
capitalist. Although more recently he and Elizabeth Fox-Genovese have
spoken of the South as a hybrid, they have held fast to the central tenet of
the earlier formulation, even when declaring that

> in essential respects the slaveholders of the Old South had much
> more in common with northern Americans of all classes than they
> did with, say, Russian boyars or Prussian Junkers. But [the South]
> did not have a market society. At the root of . . . the absence of a
> market society lay the absence of a market in labor-power.
>
> · · ·
>
> The social relations of slavery yielded an essentially noncapitalist
> ruling class and created a hybrid society in but not of the world-
> wide capitalist mode of production.

The core of this belief is that the social relations of production determine
whether a society is capitalist: if there is a "market in labor-power," the
system is capitalist, and if not, the system is not capitalist.[1]

This distinction has been adopted in the influential work of Peter
Kolchin, who, like the Genoveses, acknowledges that the antebellum South
participated fully in a burgeoning system of commercial capitalism. Modern transportation, banking, and mercantile systems ensured that the South's
staple crops reached their markets in New York, Liverpool, or wherever
the best prices could be found. But to Kolchin, as to the Genoveses, the
most important institutions were not the systems of distribution (which of

course were capitalist), but the systems of production. In the antebellum South, Kolchin avers, a "market . . . for labor power (i.e., labor hire) was largely lacking. . . . [Thus the South's economy was] based on non-capitalist productive relations."[2]

The phrases "market for labor power" or "market in labor-power" are used by these writers in a limited sense. These terms mean only, as Kolchin makes explicit, a "market . . . for . . . labor hire," where the laborer hires his or her labor power to an employer. As most Southern blacks could not sell their own labor power, the South did—in this constricted sense of the term—largely lack a "market for labor power."

In a wider sense of the term, however, the Southern economy depended crucially on such a market—the vigorous domestic slave trade. During the 1850s alone this trade sent perhaps 188,000 bondspeople from the slave-exporting states, like Virginia and Kentucky, to the slave-importing states, such as Mississippi and Louisiana (in addition to perhaps 120,000 other slaves who migrated with their masters).[3] This market for labor power was indispensable to the functioning of the South's economy: it supplied the labor needed by Louisiana and Mississippi planters, like James Polk, if they were to maximize profits from the plantation lands they had acquired; and it supplemented the revenues of slavemasters in the slave-exporting states, whose farmlands were no longer so profitable as they had once been. This was a market for labor power, too, although the seller was another slavemaster, not a laborer.

The market for slaves was very different from the market for one day of labor power (paid by a daily wage) or for the annual hire of an agricultural worker. But all of these were markets for labor power, each with its own peculiar characteristics.[4] In contrast to the Northern purchaser of a day's labor power, the Southern buyer of a male slave was purchasing the capitalized value of this slave's *lifetime* labor. The buyer of a female slave got not only her own labor but also the discounted value of the future labor of all her surviving children and of her daughters' descendants.[5]

The differences between the South's slave society and the North's free-labor society were immense. Every page of the preceding chapters points toward those differences. Most slavemasters, like James Polk, had a large capital investment in their ownership of slaves' labor power, whereas Northern employers merely paid a wage for a relatively small parcel of it. In a slave society, young children were frequently separated from their parents (as when President Polk bought thirteen children, aged ten to seventeen, separate from their parents). Slavery also witnessed considerable numbers of involuntary separations of wives and husbands, such as the breakups of Barbara's marriage to Billy Nevels, and (as will be seen) of her brother Charles's marriage to Rosetta.[6] If a slave disappeared from the workplace (as Chunky Jack did), the slavemaster often incurred heavy expenses (as James Polk did) in dragging the laborer back to work. A Northern employer, by contrast, could simply hire another laborer. The

South's system depended on an array of physically coercive instruments—the whips with which each of Polk's overseers sought to enforce discipline, the knife with which Ephraim Beanland stabbed the fleeing Chunky Jack, and the gun with which Henry Carter's ally Perry was shot—none of which was normally arrayed against a Northern laborer. Slavery also depended on an apparatus of state power, including a patrol system and jails (such as those in Memphis, Somerville, Oxford, Holly Springs, and Coffeeville, which temporarily lodged Chunky Jack, Gilbert, Joe, and Harbert). Educating slaves was illegal, though there was no such ban on the literacy of Northern laborers. Slavery also involved a system of advertisements (such as the one by which the Oxford jailer in 1849 notified the Polks that the fugitive Gilbert was jailed, awaiting collection) and of vigilant white neighbors (such as the Mr. Leigh who put the buckshot into Perry's thigh). Although state power in the North was also used—especially if there was a strike—to strengthen the employers' hands in the contractual bargaining process with their laborers, there were no close Northern analogues to these Southern means of bolstering the slavemasters' power.

This list of differences between Southern slave society and Northern free-labor society is easily extended. Because the South's enslaved labor force was more oppressed than were Northern free laborers, Southern white people were more anxious than were Northerners that the laborers would rebel or become unruly, and they were more intolerant of any criticism that they felt might encourage their laborers to be unruly. The rigid caste distinction between free whites and enslaved blacks made white people of all classes more touchy about defending their "honor" than was true in the North. Wealth was more heavily concentrated in the South than in the North. European immigration was much lighter in the South (except to certain cities like New Orleans and St. Louis), and urbanization and the development of small towns moved more slowly there. Southern industrialization was less rapid than in the North; and railway building in the South proceeded less quickly and connected different types of regions than in the North. Slavemasters' interest in the capitalized value of their labor force gave them a very different set of economic motives from those that impelled Northern landowners to boost the capitalized value of their land.

After specifying all of these differences between a slave society and a free-labor society, one might seem rash to suggest that the South nevertheless had a partially capitalist economy, which bore important resemblances to that of the North. But Orlando Patterson has suggested that slavery should be seen not as an economic system (as some Marxists have done) but as a social system that could be combined with any number of different economic systems. During the nineteenth century, slavery could be combined in West Africa with a traditional economy, whereas in the United States it was combined with a capitalist economy.[7]

If one pursues this line of reasoning, one might call the antebellum South a semicapitalist slave society. This socioeconomic system was indeed a hybrid, very different (as has just been pointed out) from the capitalist free-labor society of the North. But the South was capitalist not only in its system of distribution but also, to a considerable degree, in its system of production. The South had booming markets for the distribution of its staple crops, as well as for the factors of production—markets for land, for (enslaved) labor power, and for cotton gins, cotton presses, rice mills, sugar-refining machinery, and mules. This productive system functioned very differently from a seigniorial system based on serfdom, where serfs were tied to the land and were not usually sold away from the other serfs and from the land attached to their village. The South's market for slave labor gave James Polk far more flexibility than he could have had with serfdom, for slaves could readily be bought or sold unencumbered by land, one at a time, and with remarkable speed; and he could move them wherever he pleased in order to develop his plantation rapidly. Thus a slave-based economic system could become much more adaptable to considerations of profit and loss than a seigniorial system.[8] In a word, it could become more "capitalist" (if by that term one means a flexible system of capital investments operated with a fine eye for maximizing their returns).[9] Moreover, the ethos of the slavemasters was, in substantial measure, entrepreneurial. This mixture of a highly capitalist system of distribution, a partially capitalist system of production, and a vigorous entrepreneurial spirit resulted in the antebellum South's modernizing itself in some ways much more rapidly than occurred in the contemporary seigniorial society of Russia[10] or in the free-labor but landlord-ridden societies of southern Italy and Sicily.[11]

"Capitalism"—as, for example, the term "democracy"—may perhaps best be seen as made up of several different elements, breaking with the Genovese and Kolchin approach, which specifies a *single* criterion: the dominance of a free-labor system. Contrary to this focus on just one element, we may define capitalism as a complex mixture of private ownership, capital investment in the means of distribution, capital investment in the means of production, the existence of vigorous markets in the factors of production, the existence of a free-labor market, and the burgeoning of an entrepreneurial ethos (to mention only some of its elements); and any particular economic system may be considered to be more or less capitalist as it combines more or fewer of these elements. The South was less capitalist than the North because of the South's relatively small free-labor market. But compared with mid-nineteenth-century Russia, the South does seem to have been a semicapitalist slave society.[12]

The experiences of James Polk and his family help to test this way of viewing Southern society. Everywhere in the Polk Papers there is evidence of the entrepreneurial spirit that suffused the slave society of middle Tennessee. Polk's father-in-law, Joel Childress, was a wealthy merchant, land speculator, and medium-sized planter. Polk's own father, Sam Polk—like Joel Childress—combined agrarian with other entrepreneurial pursuits;

although for eleven years he farmed a small plantation near Columbia, Tennessee, he made his fortune as a land speculator. He was a principal Tennessee agent for the great North Carolina land speculator Colonel William Polk (Sam Polk's first cousin). The ledger book of Colonel William Polk—listing, say, for 1833 some one hundred individuals who owed money for Tennessee lands they had bought or rented from him—makes plain that this was a large capitalist enterprise; and at Sam Polk's death in 1827, his own land business (though on a smaller scale) involved more than forty tracts of West Tennessee lands, totaling more than 8000 acres. James Polk's biographer Charles Sellers is perfectly clear about the entrepreneurial ethos that infused Sam Polk's activities: "Sam was ostensibly a farmer, but . . . gradually the land business came to be his main interest." The inscription on Sam Polk's tomb "proclaimed with singular aptness the central motif" of his life: "Men of enterprise, here Moulder the Mortal Remains of a kindred Spirit."[13] Benjamin Franklin himself could scarcely have proclaimed with less sense of irony the virtue of energetically seeking to improve one's material condition.

Land speculation and plantation slave businesses went hand in hand. In the 1820s Colonel William Polk exported at least eighty slaves from North Carolina—many of them evidently recently purchased there—to work a cotton plantation near Columbia, Tennessee, and his son Lucius (James Polk's second cousin) was manager of the enterprise. When Lucius proposed in 1827 to diversify the production by raising some hemp, old Colonel Polk looked at the scheme with a businessman's sharp eye for deploying the labor of his slaves (including children) to maximum financial advantage. "The expense of erecting the [hemp] houses and works, being only equal to about $200," he wrote to Lucius,

> is so far encouraging; and presuming upon your having made a thorough examination and investigation of the business in all its parts; that it will be a profitable [one] and carried on by the weaker and younger portion of the Negroes, I have concluded to embark on the plan, on the terms stated . . . out of which I promise myself an income of greater extent, than the planting *entirely* cotton.[14]

James Polk's father, Sam, was (as Tennessee agent for Colonel Polk) enmeshed in the web of capitalist transactions that surrounded plantation slavery. The fates of bondspeople depended on the outcomes of these transactions, for slaves might be mortgaged to secure the debts of planter-entrepreneurs; then, if a plantation's profits were insufficient to pay the debt, the mortgaged slaves might be put on the auction block and torn away from family, friends, and familiar locale. For example, sometime before 1820 Colonel William Polk had lent money to an Alabama planter, Thomas Childress (probably an uncle of James Polk's future bride), with Childress's slaves as security, and in 1820 Childress begged Colonel Polk not to foreclose. "If you will renew the mortgage for twelve months longer," he pleaded,

> I can keep my hands and make another crop. If you must have it all I shall have to go down the River with my Cotton and a part of my hands to raise the money [by selling not only the cotton but also the slaves]. I am in hope that in case you must have it all you will direct your agent Major S. Polk [James Polk's father] not to advertize the sale of my mortgaged negroes till I return.

Two years later Childress acknowledged a financial defeat that would disrupt the lives of many of his bondspeople. "You can sacrifice twenty of my negroes, if you think proper," he wrote to old Colonel Polk, "by ordering a sale."[15]

James Polk's father, Sam, the agent in these transactions for old Colonel Polk, had moved from his farm into town in 1816. As befitted a successful entrepreneur, he built one of Columbia's two largest residences—the brick Polk Ancestral Home, which can still be visited there—and he became deeply involved with his son-in-law James Walker in transportation and banking ventures. Walker (James Polk's brother-in-law) became Columbia's biggest capitalist, and in 1832 he presided over a statewide banking convention that secured the creation of the Union Bank of Tennessee. The bank's Columbia branch fell under Walker's control, and another of James Polk's brothers-in-law, the prosperous merchant Adlai Harris, was its cashier. James Polk, who was becoming President Andrew Jackson's principal subaltern in the U.S. House of Representatives, can scarcely have objected when the Jackson administration—embroiled in the famous Bank War—decided in 1833 to begin to transfer federal deposits from the Bank of the United States to (eventually) ninety-one "pet banks," including the Union Bank of Tennessee. Indeed, years ago the economic historian Bray Hammond argued that the most powerful enemies of the Bank of the United States were the avaricious state bankers who sought their own profit from the overthrow of the national bank. At the forefront of these capitalists in Tennessee was Polk's brother-in-law James Walker.[16]

In addition to the Union Bank of Tennessee, another of Walker's principal ventures depended on national patronage. This was his stagecoach business, delivering the U.S. mail from Nashville to as far as Natchez, Mississippi (on its way to New Orleans). Polk's biographer Charles Sellers is scathing about how Walker sought to wield his political influence with Polk in order to promote his own financial interest. "With the easygoing Major Barry in charge of the [federal] Post Office Department," Sellers avers,

> it was not hard to circumvent the requirement for competitive bidding on mail routes, and political influence was the determin-

ing factor in awarding the more lucrative contracts. . . . [In January 1834 James Walker] proposed a corrupt arrangement whereby these routes would be surrendered to a dummy for [Walker's competitor, John] Donly at the high bid, provided that Donly would pay Walker's associates a bonus of $4,000 a year, or $16,000 for the four-year term of the contract. Donly seems to have rebuffed this proposal, but the upshot of the matter was that the Walker-Caruthers combination finally got the whole contract . . . at the handsome compensation of $27,500 a year.

Two years later, as the presidential election of 1836 approached, Walker threatened to shut down a Van Buren-Polk newspaper that he controlled unless Polk got him extra money from the postmaster general for carrying the mails.[17]

Polk depended on this capitalist businessman not only for political support but also for assistance with family affairs. Walker was named Tennessee executor for the estate of one of Polk's younger brothers, Marshall Polk, who died in 1831; he helped manage James Polk's mother's finances, when Polk was in Washington; and it was to Walker that Polk turned in 1838 when Polk's younger brother William killed a young lawyer outside of the Columbia courthouse and seemed in danger of being indicted for murder. "It is of the first importance that you should be at home when the Court meets," Polk (who was then speaker of the U.S. House of Representatives) wrote anxiously to Walker, "No one else can be so safe an adviser." An unfavorable verdict in young William Polk's case might have damped the chances of James Polk's being nominated and elected governor a few months later.[18]

In addition to Walker's other enterprises, he owned a cotton plantation in western Tennessee (where, in that same year of 1838, Walker's overseer, Mr. Gee, killed the Polk slave Jack Long). Walker ran his planting business, with its slave labor, in the same entrepreneurial spirit with which he conducted his banking and stagecoach businesses. In 1835 cotton prices were so high that Walker projected opening a second plantation in Arkansas, and he dangled in front of James Polk's nose the prospect of a share in the new venture. Even Walker's language was that of a capitalist entering the markets for land and for labor power. He intended, he declared, to put all of his western Tennessee

> lands in the market except my [West Tennessee] plantation. . . .
> [With the proceeds I intend] to make investments in Arkansaw
> lands & to make a plantation on the Miss river on the Arkansaw
> side. . . . I think it a very fine cotton region, and am disposed . . .
> to make investments there. I think it likely we will make up a
> company to have 20 or $25000 invested. I will write you on this
> subject.

Because Walker viewed a plantation as an "investment," it was unsurprising that, when he discussed James Polk's initial planting venture in western Tennessee, he used the unsentimental language of a calculating business-man. "The worst feature I see in your concern," he wrote in 1833, "is the great complaint of sickness among your negroes." A year later he prom-ised Polk that, as soon as he could, he would go to Somerville, Tennessee, to "see that your business and my own there is in such condition, that we can make reasonable calculations of fair crops &c."[19]

Another of Walker's business schemes was the Columbia Central Turnpike Co., which he got the legislature to incorporate in 1837 and which eventually constructed a turnpike that connected the seventy miles between Columbia and the Tennessee River. Here again everything de-pended on the market for (enslaved) labor power, and once again political influence was indispensable. Walker and his nine business associates got the legislature to grant them $150,000, which they intended to use for building materials, while the businessmen invested their own money—apparently $150,000—in buying the slaves who would build the turnpike. Walker calculated carefully whether, after the panic of 1837, he might be able to buy the slaves cheaper in the Mississippi market than in Virginia. The businessmen's hope was that after the turnpike was completed their profit would include their ownership of the slaves, whom they could then convert into cash in the best available market for this form of labor power.[20]

Like James Walker, Polk's other male relatives and in-laws looked on slavery as a field for business enterprise. Thus Polk's brother-in-law John Childress complained in 1843 that "I am making nothing [on my plantation here in Tennessee] and am determined to remove [to Mississippi]." Feeling that he could not, however, afford to invest in a Mississippi plantation until he had first sold his Tennessee land, Childress explained his dilemma in re-vealing language: if he bought a Mississippi plantation, he would need im-mediately to move all of his slaves there and would be left "with a *dead capital* of $10,000 in land [in Tennessee], which would yield me nothing."[21]

Polk's first cousin Robert Campbell (to whom he entrusted his plan-tation's management from 1845 to 1847) avowed openly that in the upper South he had, for $625, "bought [a young male slave] for the purpose of speculation and could [in the Deep South] have got $700 in gold for him." Polk's younger brother William understood that what Polk wanted out of his Mississippi plantation was a good rate of return; and, as we have seen, William was at first convinced that "there is nothing required but a modest share of attention to make it very profitable." Similarly, Polk's brother-in-law Silas Caldwell assured Polk in 1834 (when Polk was not earning a good return from the slaves on his West Tennessee plantation) that "I can arrange things in such a way as to make your negroes profitable to you." Later that year Polk acknowledged that his motive in shifting from Ten-nessee to the Mississippi plantation was to "make more money or loose [*sic*] more."[22]

James Polk brought to plantation management the same keen business eye as his relative Colonel William Polk, and he attempted to sharpen the vision of his own younger brother William. In 1836 James Polk's business partner, Silas Caldwell, had ordered $500 worth of corn for their Mississippi plantation, to be delivered on New Year's Day 1837 but conditional upon the payment that day of the last $350 of the price. James Polk instructed his young brother to be sure to collect this money from their Columbia bank so that he would have the cash on the appointed day. "As I have no doubt [the corn] will rise in value before that time," Polk wrote in late November, "you must be punctual to apply for it [the corn] by the day, and be prepared to pay for it [in cash], otherwise you may not get it." This same letter was suffused with the entrepreneurial spirit of a true son of the land-speculator Sam Polk. James Polk had bought his Mississippi plantation in 1834 at $10 per acre, and he hoped that the boom of the mid-1830s might enable him to sell it—scarcely more than two years later— at a 200 percent profit. Westward expansion into the territory of Arkansas (where Polk already had staked some land claims) fired the congressman's imagination, and he had already instructed an agent to "procure for us a first rate cotton plantation in Arkansas this winter." He would buy on credit, then would authorize another agent "to sell the [Arkansas] lands [the agent] has already [claimed], if it can be done on handsome profit, and apply the proceeds to the payment [of] the cotton farm. . . . Write me whether our [Mississippi] plantation can be sold for $30 per acre. If it can, it may be our interest to remove our hands to Arkansas."[23] Although the panic of 1837 temporarily punctured the land bubble, this letter may help explain the renewed excitement in 1844—when the panic was over—about the potential profitability of westward expansion, when James Polk and the whole Southern Democratic Party sought the immediate annexation of Texas.

These events suggest that cotton planting was a speculative, semicapitalist business, and Polk's overseers referred to it as just that: a "bisiness." Polk's Mississippi agent characterized a new overseer—with complete approbation—as "an Energetic, business man." And when Polk in turn addressed his overseer, he told him that he wanted from him a monthly letter "to learn how my business is getting on." The hoary distinction between agriculture and capitalism, between Southern planters and Northeastern capitalists—which goes back at least as far as the influential historians Charles and Mary Beard—serves rather to obscure than to illuminate James Polk's world. Cotton planting was an enterprise conducted in a spirit similar to that of other capitalist enterprises but with a labor system vastly different from that of the North.[24]

The sale of James and Sarah Polk's cotton depended on an advanced form of commercial capitalism—embracing the transportation, banking, and mercantile systems that forwarded their cotton to its buyers—as is evident from every page of their business correspondence. The cotton must be got to market, and once the slaves had carted it the few miles from the Coffeeville plantation to the Yalobusha River, this required the following:

1. A warehouse at Troy, Mississippi, to store the crop until the river rose high enough for a boat to fetch it
2. A keelboat to carry the cotton twenty miles down the shallow Yalobusha River to Williams Landing, Mississippi
3. A warehouse at Williams Landing, where the cotton waited for transshipment
4. A steamboat to carry the cotton down the Yazoo River and to New Orleans[25]
5. A factor to hold the cotton in New Orleans until Polk—calculating that prices were high enough to maximize his return—authorized the factor to sell it to the agent of a New York, Liverpool, or Barcelona importer
6. Crop insurance for each of the previous five stages of the journey
7. A banking system, such that the New Orleans factor could write a banker's draft that would be paid, without too heavy a discount, by a bank in Tennessee or Washington (resembling a modern foreign exchange transaction between, say, dollars and European currency, with constantly changing rates of exchange, and a banker's commission to be deducted).

Getting the cotton to market was a remarkably risky business. In 1837 nearly half of Polk's crop was destroyed by a fire in New Orleans, but happily the cotton was insured at a reasonable price. A decade later Polk decided to hold back his 1847 crop until prices rose again after the European revolutions of 1848, and he ended up paying his factor a year's warehousing and insurance charges in New Orleans before he finally decided to sell. One-fifth of the 1850 crop got wet when the river rose at Troy and could only be sold for two-thirds of the current price. About 10 percent of the next year's crop was temporarily lost at Troy, and one of these bales did not turn up until more than a year later. Twenty percent of the 1852 crop was destroyed by a fire in New Orleans, and this time the insurance paid only 65 percent of the cotton's actual value.[26] In 1854 three disasters struck. Low water on the Yalobusha River prevented boats from coming upstream, and while the cotton languished in the Troy warehouse, two-thirds of the crop was burned in what may have been a fire set by a slave who lived near Troy. Then a keelboat carrying the remainder of the crop sank on the Yalobusha River; fortunately the cotton, though damaged, was saved. But then a steamboat burned on the Yazoo River, destroying this ill-fated third of the crop (this cotton was well insured). It turned out, however, that no insurance had covered the fire at the Troy warehouse, and Polk's widow thus lost two-thirds of the expected annual revenues. The next year, another fire on a

Yazoo steamboat destroyed one-third of the crop, but this time it was fully insured.[27]

The uncertainties of river transport may explain why Yalobusha planters persuaded the county's voters in 1853 to authorize a 200 percent tax raise to subsidize construction of a railway connection to Memphis.[28] Yet, although keelboats and steamboats on a shallow river had proved risky, the river transportation system was far cheaper than overland transport could have been before the railway, and insurance offered protection if one could get one's agents to insure for every step of the route and for the full value of the crop.

Not only the distribution but also the production of cotton was pursued along capitalist lines. The key factor in the cotton boom was one Southern agricultural entrepreneurs understood toward the end of the eighteenth century: if producing short-staple cotton was to be profitable, they needed an improved mechanical device to separate the cotton from the cotton seed. It was relatively speedy for slaves to separate by hand long-staple cotton from its seed, but long-staple cotton could be grown only in the limited area near the Atlantic Coast. The short-staple cotton suited to the vast Southern interior clung tenaciously to its seed and could be separated manually only very slowly, at immense cost of labor power. What was needed was an efficient machine to speed up this process. The need was strongly felt, and the basic idea (two adjacent cylinders spinning in opposite directions) was an ancient one. The famous improvements patented by Eli Whitney in 1794 were quickly improved upon by local blacksmiths, and almost overnight profitable cotton planting became feasible throughout the Deep South. This quintessentially capitalist, technological development lay at the heart of the whole production process.[29]

When James Polk established his Mississippi plantation, he quickly installed his own cotton gin, and one of his overseer's essential tasks was to ensure that the gin and the cotton press were in working order at harvest time. By 1842 overseer Dismukes complained that "the gin dos not doo good work. It draws too many motes through. I am trying to have it altered." In 1844 it seemed rational to replace this cotton gin by a better one, and Polk—during the heat of the presidential election campaign—made this technological improvement with a businessman's shrewd eye to minimizing costs. He must, of course, try out the new gin—supplied by a Memphis manufacturer—at his plantation, and the seller expected Polk to pay interest on the gin's capital value while Polk was testing it; but Polk threatened to buy elsewhere if the seller insisted upon his paying anything at all during the testing period. When making a new capital investment in his system of production, Polk was a businessman, keen to get the most for his money.[30]

Besides a gin and a press, Polk had to invest in plows and mules and in pigs, cattle, and sheep to feed and clothe his labor force. But, as can be seen in table 5.1, column (b), less than 10 percent of his initial $14,150 investment was in animals and equipment. A cotton planter must put a much larger sum into land (c). Into his half-share of the 920-acre plantation, Polk invested $4,600; four years later he bought from his younger brother William another 230 acres of the land (over half of which had already been cleared); in December 1844, when he knew he could count on a princely presidential salary ($25,000 per annum), he bought from William the last quarter of the original tract (probably uncleared land); in 1847 he acquired forty acres more, and in 1854 his widow purchased another 155 acres from their overseer John Mairs (who may have inherited this woodland from a relative). Thus the Polks' total capital investment in land was over $11,000.[31]

Except for 140 acres bought from William Polk in 1838, this was virgin land: it had to be cleared. A start was made in 1835 and 1836, and more land was cleared in almost every subsequent year. Even when he was president, Polk kept his eye on this form of capital development. Thus, in 1846 he ensured that his slaves would not relax during the broiling summer month after the cotton no longer needed to be hoed and before the harvest would begin: "When the crop is made and laid by," Polk instructed his agent, "I wish some more land cleared."[32] By the time of Polk's death in 1849, 508 acres were being planted; but the collapse of land prices after the boom of the 1830s canceled the monetary value of clearing the land, so that at Polk's death his plantation land was still worth no more than the $11,000 he had paid for it. Column (e) of table 5.1 makes plain that it was only during the 1850s—when Polk's widow had another 190 acres cleared and when the cotton boom inflated land prices again—that the monetary value of the plantation lands increased to $15,000.[33]

The other principal capital investment was in the labor power of slaves. Column (d) of the table shows that initially Polk invested over $8,000 in this way, and by purchasing thirty-two more slaves, he (by the time of his death in 1849) more than trebled this investment. Furthermore, there was available to the Polks—and to all other planters—a form of capital gain unmatched in Northern free-labor capitalism: the increased value of one's investment in labor power, when the price of slaves increased. Because of the annexation of Texas, prices rapidly recovered from the nadir they had reached between 1842 and 1844.[34] Then the worldwide demand that fueled the cotton boom of the 1850s caused prices to leap upward after 1851.[35] Thus, during the 1850s, over $16,000 was added to the capital value of the Polks' slaves (f). The modest natural increase in the number of their slaves added over $1000 more (g), bringing by 1860 the total value of their capital investment in labor power to nearly $42,000. The total value of James Polk's plantation was, at his death in June 1849, almost three times that of his initial investment; and its total value had increased another $18,000 by 1860.

Further elements in this semicapitalist mode of production were the running costs Polk incurred every year. He must, of course, pay his overseer an annual salary, which was kept as low as possible—ranging from $325 (for the ineffectual young Mayo in 1836) up to the $550 that Sarah Polk paid in 1851 once John Mairs had proven himself.[36] Polk also had to pay his New Orleans factor every winter about $300 for plantation supplies: rope, twine, and bagging for packing the cotton; blacksmith materials for shoeing the mules and keeping the gin in order; shoes, hats, blankets, salt, and sometimes extra pork for his slaves.[37] In addition, Polk paid several hundred dollars annually for taxes, doctors' bills, and local supplies such as corn if the plantation had failed to produce enough.[38] One of the overseer's important duties was to minimize this last type of expense; and even when Polk was president he kept a vigilant eye on the plantation's food production. "In view of the probability of some increase of force next year," he wrote his agent early in 1846 (when already planning the purchase of nine more slaves), "it has struck me, that it would be well to put some 20 or 30 acres more in corn this year than Mr. Mairs has planted." Polk had learned from sad experience that profits were woefully reduced if the plantation was not fully self-sufficient in corn and pork. One of Mairs's virtues as an overseer proved to be that he not only usually produced enough food to supply the plantation but also in some years raised sufficient pork and corn to sell a surplus in the local market, adding to the plantation's revenues.[39]

Of course, cotton production depended heavily on the weather and other natural conditions. Sarah Polk catastrophically lost more than half the 1853 crop to boll worms and heavy rains. Smaller natural disasters struck frequently, and overseer John Mairs was as sharp as any Yankee businessman in seeking to deceive customers about the quality of defective produce. When caught once, Mairs confessed, "It is true thar ware more yellow coten this last yeare than usual. . . . I mix some white with the [yellow] to try to make it sample well." Mairs put this problem down to bad springtime weather, which had obliged him to replant some of the crop, which then had not matured well. What could a man do except mix good cotton with bad and hope the New Orleans factor would not notice? Mairs had persisted in this practice even after having been discovered in a previous deception. He had fooled the New Orleans factor about the 1846 crop, and a sale had been consummated at a high price. But the wily buyer had unpacked President Polk's produce and found that ten or fifteen bales were "mixed in the packing, having good cotton on the side & . . . inferior put in the middle of the bale." The angry buyer had then thrown up the sale, and the factor had had to resell the whole lot at a lower price. President Polk had not, however, dismissed his overseer for hiding his production of faulty goods; and the offense was repeated.[40]

Thus Polk's cotton business was capitalist both in the distribution of its produce and in most aspects of production itself. The main difference from the productive process of any large Northern concern was that the markets for labor power were different. In the North that market was for

Table 5.1
Capital Investment in the Polks' Share of Mississippi Plantation, 1835–1860 (dollars)

Year	(a) Risk Capital at Beginning of Year [= (h) of Preceding Year]	(b) Animals and Equipment	(c) Land	(d) Slaves	(e) Undistributed Capital Gains: Polks' share of Value Added/Lost — To Land by Clearing or Price Inflation	(f) To Slaves by Price Inflation/Deflation	(g) To Slaves by Natural Growth of Population	(h) Risk Capital at End of Year [total of columns (a) − (g)]
1834		$1330	$4600	$8220				$14,150
1835	$14,150			−600		$650★		14,800
1836	14,800					600		14,800
1837	14,800					600		15,400
1838	15,400	1500	4050	6350		−1200		26,100
1839	26,100			2110		−150		28,060
1840	28,060			−750				27,310
1841	27,310			−450		−150		26,710
1842	26,710			1950		−650		28,010
1843	28,010							28,010
1844	28,010		2000					30,010
1845	30,010	200		450		150		30,810
1846	30,810	200		4270		350		35,630
1847	35,630	200	350	1680		−150		37,810
1848	37,810	200				450		38,460
1849	38,460	200		3270			$100	41,930
Subtotal 1834–1849		3830	11,000	26,500		500	100	41,930

Year								
1850	41,930	−50			$250			42,130
1851	42,130	−50			300			42,380
1852	42,380	−50		−1500	400	2100		43,330
1853	43,330	−50			500	3000		46,080
1854	46,080	−50	200	−700	400	3000		49,630
1855	49,630	−50			350		200	50,130
1856	50,130	−50		−600	350		400	50,230
1857	50,230	−50			350		200	50,730
1858	50,730	−50			350	2100	200	53,330
1859	53,330	−50			550	5970	200	60,000
Jan. 1860	60,000							
Total 1834–1860		3330	11,200	23,700	3800	16,670	1300	60,000

*Includes $500 for increased value of slaves when moved to Mississippi, as well as $150 for the inflation of slave prices that year. See appendix B for sources.

the daily wage of a laborer (or sometimes for the annual wage of an agricultural worker), whereas in the South the market was for the capitalized value of enslaved labor power. When slave prices rose or when there was a natural increase in the slave population, as occurred on most cotton plantations, the planter capitalist could add to cash profits the capital gains in the value of the labor force. The spirit in which Polk and his close associates, like James Walker, conducted their businesses was thoroughly capitalist. President James Polk, it might be suggested, was the representative of at least a semicapitalist slave society.

The material interests of Southern planter-entrepreneurs did not, of course, predetermine their political allegiances. Some planters voted Democratic, whereas others supported Whigs; and indeed, the more securely established planters tended to favor the Whigs. However, Southern Democrats like James Polk offered a program that could appeal at once to substantial planters, to would-be planters, and to farmers relatively distant from the market economy. The Democrats' states' rights doctrine promised to protect slavemasters from any Northern antislavery influence that might otherwise have been exerted through the federal government. The Democrats' doctrine of unconstrained economic individualism fostered the slavemasters' belief that their management of their planting enterprises was their own private business, into which the public had no right to intrude. And the Democrats' advocacy of territorial expansion into Texas promised Southern entrepreneurs and would-be entrepreneurs hundreds of thousands of acres of cheap land with which to enrich themselves. In the 1840s President James Polk proved to be the most effective national exponent of these Democratic doctrines because he could promote the short-term interests of Southern planter-entrepreneurs while also appealing to a national constituency. These matters will be examined when Polk's political career comes to center stage.

6

The Spirit of Governance

I n the South's semicapitalist slave society, how far was the masters' conduct toward their slaves paternalist? By that term I mean "benevolent, as
a person conscious of superior power and rank might act benevolently toward someone of inferior power and rank." In this sense, a "capitalist" might
act in a "paternalist" manner since these two words are not antonyms.[1]

"Paternalism" has often been used in a different way: to denote a system of dependency, where masters constantly intruded into the lives of
their enslaved dependents. When the term has been employed simultaneously in this sense and *also* to mean "benevolent," confusion has arisen
about the answer to the important question, "How benevolent were the
masters?"[2] One way of clarifying the matter—though not necessarily the
only way—would be to apply the term "paternalist" to a master's conduct
only when there proves to be evidence of the master's benevolent intent.
This is what I shall do. Whenever possible, however, I shall avoid the word
entirely, employing instead the terms "benevolent" or "humane." Perhaps historians' use of this confusingly ambiguous term—though it will
never die—will gradually fade away, except when strictly confined to
phrases like "paternalist ideology" and "paternalist code" (where it serves
a clear and useful function).

Striking the balance between indications of benevolence and evidence
of callousness must, of course, be difficult. Both benevolence and callousness toward slaves abounded in the antebellum South, and historians may
naturally be tempted to select evidence to suit their own predilections.
This problem is compounded because many slavemasters saw themselves
in the light of paternalist ideology. When they thought about it, planters
often sought to present themselves as conforming to the image of a kindly
paterfamilias. Paternalist ideology suggested that masters sought, above all
else, the welfare of their dependent slaves, just as fathers sought the welfare of their dependent children. The master's household was supposed to
resemble that of a family (where the paterfamilias put the welfare of his
dependents above his own selfish financial interest), not that of a business
enterprise (whose proprietor was primarily concerned with his own financial success). Masters were supposed to care for their dependents, supplying them with food, shelter, clothing, and release from care. These were

comforts with which, in the absence of this paternalist tutelage, black people were alleged to be incapable of supplying themselves. (It was claimed that if blacks were freed, their condition would degenerate and they would be likely, eventually, to die out.) According to paternalist ideology, masters tried to keep slave families together, often sacrificing their own financial interest to achieve this goal. Masters were supposed to treat with particular consideration their "family negroes"—the ones they had inherited from their own parents. The burden of slavery, according to paternalist ideology, rested not on the slaves but on the shoulders of their kindly masters, who exhausted themselves in caring for their often faithful (but sometimes exasperatingly ungrateful) dependents.

Because masters often presented themselves as acting in consonance with this paternalist ideology, we principally need to see what slavemasters did rather than being beguiled by what they said. And when examining what they said, we need to apprehend the tone in which they spoke. Perhaps we can modify and refine the picture of the complex relation between masters and slaves by concentrating on a small group for whom extensive records are available.

One of the strongest indications of benevolence in the Polk Papers involved John Catron, a Nashville friend of James Polk. Catron was an associate justice of the U.S. Supreme Court, to which President Andrew Jackson had appointed him, and a confidant of Polk. Contrary to the principle that a Supreme Court judge ought not to engage in partisan politics, Catron lent money to Polk to help pay the expenses of his 1844 presidential campaign.[3] In 1857 Catron was up to his neck in disreputable secret negotiations between members of the Supreme Court and president-elect James Buchanan, preceding the Court's issuance of the notorious *Dred Scott* ruling. Yet by remaining a stanch Unionist during the Civil War, Catron avoided the odium attached to the author of *Dred Scott*, Chief Justice Roger Taney. Catron, though certainly no saint, performed in 1844 a small but remarkable act of genuine benevolence toward a slave of James Polk named Elias.

When Elias was a child in 1824, Sam Polk had given him to James Polk as a wedding present; in James Polk's first will he named Elias one of his three most favored slaves, who was never to be sold out of the family. Polk kept Elias with him as a reliable personal servant in Tennessee, or sometimes in Washington, or hired him out as a house-yard servant in Columbia, but he never sent Elias to work at the Mississippi plantation. During the 1844 presidential campaign, this slave was entrusted to ride horseback the forty miles between Columbia and Nashville, carrying messages quickly and confidentially for Polk. Unhappily, Elias stumbled and lamed Polk's horse and had to leave it to recuperate at Judge Catron's house in Nashville. Some days later Catron sent Polk a message intended for Elias's ears: "The horse is better recovered than any horse so foundered I have ever known. . . . This, especially for Elias's comfort." These simple words show genuine concern to assuage the mortification Elias must have felt after the horse stumbled, and Catron's words stand forth boldly in the Polk Papers because of the rarity, within Polk's male entourage, of any real feeling for a black person.[4]

Next after Judge Catron, Silas Caldwell was the most benevolent of Polk's male associates. Having criticized overseer Ephraim Beanland for ill treating Polk's slaves, Caldwell finally fired him in 1835. Although Caldwell was scarcely indulgent and was as quick as any other slavemaster to term a dissident adult slave like Ben "a bad boy," he nevertheless won from Polk's slaves the reputation of a man who might protect them from a brutal overseer. On at least five occasions, Polk's fugitives attempted the long trek from Mississippi to Caldwell's Tennessee plantation in hopes of gaining succor from him.[5] No doubt they remembered that Caldwell had purchased Wally after his flight from Ephraim Beanland. Caldwell's benevolence complicated James Polk's efforts to impose strict discipline in Mississippi, and Polk obviously was relieved when, after Caldwell's death, he felt he could rely on his sister (Caldwell's widow) to turn a deaf ear to the slaves' complaints. Yet even Caldwell's humanity should not be exaggerated. His report to Polk of one slave's death betrayed no more benevolent feeling than if a mule had expired—simply a wish to sort out the business aspects of the event: "Your boy Hardy [aged 26] died [of respiratory illness] . . . which leaves not Enough of hand to Cultivate the farm in Haywood. It will be necessary for you to Buy another hand as soon as you can." Similarly, when one of Caldwell's own slaves died, what he lamented was the destruction of his own property: "I have lost a negro boy about eight years old, Sophas oldest boy."[6]

At the other end of the spectrum that ranged from benevolence to callousness was Polk's younger brother William, agent for a still younger brother who owned the slave Jack Long. William Polk—having hired out Jack Long to James Walker to work on Walker's plantation during 1838—intended to move Jack at the year's end to Mississippi to labor on James Polk's plantation. When the slave's death intervened, William Polk briskly arranged for a substitute to be sent so that James Polk's business concerns would not be disturbed. William's announcement of the slave's death was markedly laconic. "Jack Long is dead," he reported to his brother, "killed by Mr. Gee, [Walker's] overseer. . . . [I have therefore asked Mr. Walker to send another slave in place of Jack.] This I thought best for you, and the loss of Jack would make no material change in your arrangements." What seemed important to William was that James Polk should not be discommoded; William could count on James Walker to make Gee's family pay a sum of money large enough to compensate the Polks for their loss of a dead slave.[7]

A couple of years later, William Polk conceived of running for the Tennessee State legislature, and he permitted no paternalistic sense of duty to his slaves to deflect him from this quest. Although his finances were in a mess, William persuaded himself that he could straighten everything out: first, he would sell his western Tennessee lands; and then, "by selling my surplus negroes," he continued (underlining the two key words), "I will be entirely easy." To William, becoming "easy" meant getting out from under his debts, and evidently paternalistic scruples caused him no uneasiness about selling off "surplus negroes."[8]

Another young man almost wholly devoid of benevolent impulses was James Polk's nephew Marshall Polk, Jr., whom the childless James had treated something like a son. This West Point cadet seized the first possible moment to tear his newly inherited slave Barbara away from her husband, Billy Nevels, and bring her to his own Tennessee lands.[9] His motives were purely economic: in this transaction the young man acquired a share in the labor power of the twenty-eight-year-old Barbara and of her twenty-six-year-old brother Charles. Marshall Polk thus smashed two slave marriages: in addition to wrecking Barbara's union, he seized Charles away from Charles's young wife, Rosetta, after they had been married less than three years. Marshall Polk's parcel of three slaves included Barbara's infant daughter, Marthy, who, if she survived, might eventually (like Barbara herself) produce more babies to enrich the grasping young man.[10]

Although the words of the white people associated with these transactions often seemed to express concern for the slaves' feelings, self-interest largely determined their actions. As early as 1849 James Walker had (in his own words) "made some discoveries worth a few hundred dollars to Marshall Polk." Only after old Jane Polk died in 1852 did Sarah Polk become aware that her slave Billy Nevels was married to Marshall Polk's slave Barbara (even though Billy's marriage to Barbara was recorded in the 1849 inventory of James Polk's slaves); and Sarah Polk immediately then betrayed her (well-founded) anxiety that Billy Nevels might cause her trouble if his wife was deported. Self-interest breathed from every syllable of Sarah Polk's lament: "I do not wish to produce discontent with my own [slaves] that might result to my injury. I learn that the woman is married to one of my most valuable men."[11] Sarah promptly suggested sending two of her unmarried slaves instead of Barbara and Charles, but Marshall Polk stalled: "It would be improper [for me] to part with [Barbara and Charles] while I am perfectly ignorant of the negroes themselves & of the ones offered for them." Marshall's next words accorded with a paternalist code but proved to be veneer over his calculations of his own financial interest: "I would much prefer purchasing the wife [Rosetta] of the man [Charles] & the husband [Billy Nevels] of the woman [Barbara]," Marshall insisted before reaching the disabling clause, "if . . . my finances will allow."[12]

Marshall Polk and his guardian, John Bills, doubted whether it would be financially prudent for Marshall to buy the two slaves, but each white man passed the buck to the other about making the decision that would destroy the slaves' marriages. Apparently the two slave couples hoped that

Marshall would indeed buy Billy Nevels and Rosetta, which would have preserved their marriages, as well as getting them back to Tennessee and away from the Mississippi plantation and its overseer, John Mairs. They intimated as much to a slave named Bob, who was being sent from the Mississippi plantation to West Tennessee.[13] Marshall Polk's guardian in West Tennessee then asked the newly arrived Bob what Barbara and Charles wanted, selecting from Bob's message those elements that suited his own purposes: Bob, the guardian wrote, "says the people [Barbara and Charles] prefer to come to Tennessee." The guardian ordered them sent as soon as possible, separate from their spouses. A few weeks later Sarah Polk's brother delivered Barbara (with her infant, Marthy) and Charles to Tennessee but left their spouses behind. Even Marshall Polk's guardian acknowledged "the apparent distress of these people for having parted with their family and friends." More fair words were therefore in order: "I hope we may be able to accommodate their wishes," John Bills suggested to Sarah Polk, "when my ward returns from West Point." Nothing happened, and nine months later Marshall Polk (now a commissioned army officer) was still uttering soothing words (coupled, as ever, with disqualifying clauses): "Aunt Sarah I think will sell me the negroes connected with mine," the young officer speculated (while placing responsibility for action on his guardian), "so when you judge it prudent for me to buy, let me know and I will make the necessary agreements with her."[14]

Part of Barbara's economic attraction to Marshall Polk was that she had proved to be fertile, and Marshall reckoned that she was likely to produce more children by some other man, even if her husband were never restored to her. Marshall therefore tried to buy the share of Barbara's legal title held by Marshall's young stepsiblings so that he himself could enjoy maximum profit from any future children Barbara might produce. When this negotiation failed, Marshall—to express his disappointment—employed the language of an unhappy investor: "I am sorry you could not purchase the [stepsiblings'] share of the negroes," Marshall wrote to his guardian, "for if the woman [Barbara] still increases I suppose they [his stepsiblings] will have a portion of said increase. Write me if anything can be done." Nothing could be done, nor apparently did Marshall's guardian ever think it "prudent" to buy Barbara's husband or Charles's wife. And as Sarah Polk's plantation was still shorthanded, she cannot have been keen to part with two more slaves (Billy Nevels, "one of my most valuable men," and Rosetta) after having already been deprived of Barbara and Charles. Marshall Polk's imagination soon became filled with other ways of using his money than by trying to buy Billy Nevels and Rosetta. These two slaves were still at Sarah Polk's Mississippi plantation in 1860, and they probably never saw their spouses again—unless they were able to do so after emancipation in 1865.[15]

Meanwhile Marshall Polk thrashed around, wondering how to secure the best return on a capital investment. Writing from California in 1853, he thought perhaps he could get Sarah Polk to lend him $5000, which he could use for land speculation or moneylending there. "All one wants in this country [California] is capital," he wrote, "& if he has that he is sure to make, if not a fortune, at least good interest on his money. Money can be invested in California at two percent per month at the lowest calcula-tion. . . . I have written to my aunt telling her that I should probably apply to her for assistance." A few months later the young officer wrote from New York City, "Capital is worth a great deal at present, & I can get two percent per month for money in this city." If Marshall could not become a moneylender, he toyed with the idea of a mercantile career, but he was reluctant to sell his Tennessee land and his slaves and wondered whether he might do best by resigning his army commission and settling on his Tennessee farm. Whatever he should decide, he must keep an eagle eye on his enslaved capital: "Has their [sic] been any division of Grandma's [Jane Polk's] property?" he inquired in 1854. "If so which negroes are mine?"[16]

Somewhere between these two poles—between Judge Catron's be-nevolence and the callousness of William and Marshall Polk, but perhaps closer to the latter end of this spectrum—lay the conduct of the capitalist slavemaster par excellence, James Walker. Walker was married to a sister of James Polk; thus Polk's mother, the elderly Jane Polk, was Walker's mother-in-law. In one notable instance Walker allowed his actions to be influenced by Jane Polk's intervention on behalf of a favored female house servant. In 1847 the old white woman was worried about the fate of a slave woman named Dolly, the daughter of Jane Polk's slave Violet. The prob-lem arose because James Polk's father—in a violation of paternalistic pre-cepts that occurred whenever planters tried to leave more or less equal numbers of slaves to each of their legatees—had separated Violet from her daughter Dolly: Violet had been bequeathed to Jane Polk, but Dolly was willed to James Polk's younger brother Samuel, who died in 1839. Dolly had then somehow come into the possession of a Mrs. Dickinson, who in 1847 proposed to sell Dolly (and Dolly's children) in the Nashville slave market, separating Dolly's eldest boy from his mother in order to fetch the highest price for him. Apparently the boy's grandmother Violet then appealed to Jane Polk to intervene, and Jane Polk persuaded James Walker to use her funds to buy Dolly and her children, even though Walker thought them overpriced. Walker believed Dolly's family was worth only $1200, but Mrs. Dickinson (after trying first for $1500) held out for $1400. "You know how such a state of things would operate on the old lady's [Jane Polk's] feelings and nerves," Walker reported to the president. "I con-cluded to settle the matter at once, believing a few hundred dollars was of no consequence, compared to your mother's peace of mind."[17] The peace of mind of Jane Polk—not that of Violet nor of Dolly nor of Dolly's young boy—was what principally concerned Walker, and the extra $200 was Jane Polk's, not Walker's. Yet if a privileged slave like Violet could get a white woman like Jane Polk to intercede, benevolent considerations might induce James Walker to mitigate the harshness of Nashville's market for labor power. Here, as so often, the beneficiary of a white person's benevolence was one of those slaves whom white people regarded as elevated above the mass of field hands, a house servant in this case; the "family negro" Ben whom James Polk had eventually sold to the master of Ben's wife; a mulatto such as Reuben; or a skilled artisan like blacksmith Harry.

Were white women like Jane Polk more likely to act benevolently than males like James Walker? This case suggests no clear answer, for one white woman, Mrs. Dickinson, was the most ruthlessly self-interested of anyone involved in the episode. James Polk's wife, Sarah, presents a more complex case. Nothing in white women's "nature" made them more humane than white males; but insofar as the social roles played by women differed from those of men, the pressures exerted by such roles might help shape the women's conduct. Thus when, after James Polk's death, Sarah Polk assumed financial responsibility for the Mississippi plantation, her evident reluctance to sell a valuable field hand like Billy Nevels was greater than it might have been when Sarah Polk had been simply a politician's wife. And old Jane Polk's role as an elderly widow in close daily contact with the house servant Violet was likely to make her more sympathetic to Violet's distress than was the more distant role of a businessman-slavemaster like James Walker.

In a macho society like that of the antebellum South, a white man with benevolent feelings toward slaves might sometimes have been tempted to dissemble—to attribute his own benevolent action to the influence of a "weak" woman rather than to assume responsibility himself for doing something that to an outsider might seem weak-minded, such as paying $1400 for two slaves worth only $1200. Although James Walker did indeed attribute this action to "the old lady's feelings" rather than to his own, he may possibly have had humane impulses, which he sought to disguise. Alternatively, the seventy-year-old Jane Polk and her daughter Maria (Polk) Walker[18]—James Walker's wife—may have made such a "fuss" about the impending sale of Dolly and her son that James Walker acted to placate the white women, who perhaps cracked the whip more than Walker cared to acknowledge. These are speculations, however. There is nothing in the rest of Walker's career—for example, in his conduct of the Columbia Central Turnpike Co. or in his failure to prosecute his overseer Mr. Gee for killing the slave Jack Long—that suggests much benevolent feeling toward the slaves.

Like Walker, James Polk sometimes—but more often than Walker—permitted humane (and other nonfinancial) considerations to deflect him from treating slaves according to purely economic criteria. A significant piece of evidence is the new will that President Polk signed on February 28, 1849, just a few days before he left the White House. Polk expressed here an intention (if nothing unexpected should interpose) to free every one of his slaves once both he and his wife were dead: "Should I survive [my wife]," Polk's new will declared, "unless influenced by circumstances which I do not now foresee, it is my intention to emancipate all my Slaves, and I have full confidence that if, at her death, she shall deem it proper she will emancipate them."[19] With the single exception of George Washington, Polk was the only American president whose will suggested an intention to authorize a general emancipation of his bondspeople. Even Thomas Jefferson freed only about 3 percent of his slaves, whereas Polk expressed the wish that all of his be emancipated.

This wish seemed to have been of recent origin. His 1831 will had contained no such emancipating clause. And although Polk may have written another will sometime before leaving Tennessee for the White House in 1845,[20] no such will has survived; and there certainly is no hint that an emancipating clause was included.

If Polk had had children of his own to provide for, he probably would not have contemplated freeing his slaves. But, like George Washington, Polk was childless. Although he was guardian to his nephew Marshall Polk, Jr., the young man was sure to inherit several slaves when James Polk's elderly mother finally died (as she did in 1852). Furthermore, the president had already provided for Marshall by appointing him to a cadetship at West Point, and he bequeathed to Marshall all the lands he owned in Arkansas.[21] No further provision seemed necessary.

Polk's wife, however, must be provided for. and the Mississippi plantation was intended to be her principal support as long as she lived.[22] Polk did not expect any of his slaves to be freed until Sarah died. She did so in 1891, forty-two years after her husband, by which date the great majority of Polk's adult slaves surely would have died too. Thus (in the absence of the general emancipation of 1865) the president's hope that Sarah would emancipate their slaves would not have benefited most of them, although it might have freed those of their children and grandchildren who were still alive in 1891.

Polk had made the situation of his slaves profoundly different from that of George Washington's. Polk, unlike Washington, gave his widow discretion about whether or not to free his slaves. Washington, by contrast, did not leave in the hands of his widow the decision of whether or not to free his 150 slaves; Washington's slaves were *definitely* to be freed when his widow died. (And in fact Martha Washington decided in December 1800, just a year after her husband's death, to free immediately all the slaves owned by her husband—though not the 170 "dower" slaves, of whom she was proprietor in her own right).[23] Sarah Polk, unlike Martha Washington, was not independently wealthy: Sarah had brought only four Childress slaves to her marriage, and no doubt she felt she could not afford to free the Polk slaves right away. Indeed, the Polks' cotton plantation was paying very well during the 1850s, and there is no indication that

Sarah Polk would ever have renounced her plantation income in order to free James Polk's slaves sooner. Her husband did not expect her to do so.

The prospects for Polk's slaves, however, were even more parlous. In 1860 Sarah Polk sold a half-interest in the plantation and in fifty of its fifty-six slaves to the husband of one of her nieces.[24] Sarah thus put into her own pocket about $28,500,[25] and she vacated sole authority to decide the future of most of James Polk's slaves—or at least of those in whom her new business partner had a half-share. It is scarcely credible that this man paid Sarah Polk $28,500 with the intention of emancipating *his* half-share of the slaves. And whether Sarah Polk, having sold one half-share in fifty of the slaves, would ever have freed the slaves in her other half-share of the plantation must remain moot. Perhaps in due course her new business partner would have persuaded her to sell him the other half-share, too, in an enterprise of which she had already converted most of the first half into cash.[26]

If, then, James Polk's expressed wish to free his slaves was likely to have proved of very little benefit, or of none at all, to most of them, why did he write the emancipating clause? No doubt part of the answer lies in miscalculation: the president could not have known that his wife would live to nearly the age of eighty-eight. Nor perhaps did he suppose that she would sell a half-interest in the slaves to someone else.

Another part of the answer may lie in Polk's wish to look well to posterity. His political strategy had depended on his presenting himself as a nonsectional candidate. Thus in 1844, when the Democratic Party was choosing its presidential nominee, Polk projected the image of being a loyal supporter of the New York candidate Martin Van Buren, at the very moment when some of Polk's Tennessee associates were conspiring to prevent Van Buren's nomination by joining others in requiring that no one be nominated at the Democratic convention without a two-thirds majority. Had Van Buren been nominated for the presidency, Polk had hoped to be selected for the vice-presidential slot; but when Van Buren could not obtain the stipulated two-thirds majority, Polk's ostensible loyalty to Van Buren gained him enough support from Van Burenites—like the Massachusetts historian and politician George Bancroft and the chairman of the New York delegation, Benjamin Butler—that Polk secured the presidential nomination itself.[27] His campaign pledge to achieve the speedy annexation of Texas was coupled with a second pledge: to acquire a huge Oregon territory. Thus Polk sought to remove the imputation that he would pursue only the interests of slavery expansionists. And when Polk as president then captured New Mexico and California, he asserted that he acted as a national statesman, not as a sectional partisan: "Slavery has no possible connection with the Mexican War," he inscribed in his diary, which he wrote with an eye over his shoulder for the judgment of future generations. By the time the president drafted his new will in February 1849, furious debates over the Wilmot Proviso—passed again by the House of Representatives in February 1847 and December 1848—had made plain that Polk had opened the Pandora's box of the territorial slave issue, which already threatened to lead to civil war. What better way to indicate to posterity that he had always been a national statesman, never a slavery partisan, than to write an emancipating clause into his will while instructing his agent to buy secretly half a dozen additional slaves?[28]

Nevertheless, humane feeling probably was also an important factor in his writing the emancipating clause. I believe Polk thought he would be doing his slaves a good turn by freeing them. Yet this sentiment was curiously mixed with others. Did the president suppose, if the eleven-year-old slave boy Jason was going to be sold anyway (separated from father, mother, and every sibling), that he could best show benevolence toward Jason by buying him (as Polk's agent did on March 22, 1849, twenty-two days after Polk had signed his new will), working him on the Mississippi plantation for twenty or thirty (or forty-two) years, and then freeing him, once neither James nor Sarah Polk was still alive to benefit further from the income they would secure from Jason's unpaid labor?[29]

Although the president's new will supplies only a modicum of firm evidence of benevolence, there is clear proof elsewhere that humane feelings sometimes influenced Polk's treatment of his slaves. This was especially true in the early 1830s, when Polk was still finding his feet as a plantation manager. Benevolent impulses were most likely to affect Polk's conduct when they blended with, or at least did not conflict with, his own self-interest. They were most likely to make themselves felt when a white woman—especially Polk's mother or his wife—pushed him in that direction.

The interplay of these forces became evident during an episode in 1832–33. James Polk—as Sam Polk's eldest son (and the only one of Sam's four elder sons to survive past 1831)—assumed the main responsibility for his mother's welfare after she was widowed in 1827. He also tried to keep the peace among his four married sisters. The youngest of these, Mrs. Ophelia Hays—a high-tempered twenty-year-old who drove her family to distraction—quarreled fiercely in 1832 with her thirty-year-old domestic slave Silvy. Ophelia's husband, Dr. John Hays, seeking to terminate the endless ructions, got Ophelia's consent to sell Silvy and her three young children to James Polk, who punished Silvy by sending this house servant and her children for a year's exile on Polk's new West Tennessee plantation, where doubtless she was demoted to hard field labor. Separating Silvy from the father of her children, Polk gave her a harsh lesson in the perils of quarreling with a white woman. He then let Silvy return with her children to Columbia, where he installed her as a house servant to his mother. By this transaction Polk helped his brother-in-law to remove a trouble spot at home and helped to "discipline" Silvy, yet he satisfied his mother's desire that Silvy not be sold out of the family. Polk also secured for himself at his shorthanded Somerville plantation the labor of Silvy for a year (and thereafter the labor of one of his mother's other slaves, sent there in exchange for Silvy).[30] Polk did well for himself out of these transactions; yet his wish to aid his brother-in-law and his mother, without selling Silvy away from the family, had shaped Polk's actions somewhat differently than if he had acted solely to secure labor for his cotton plantation.

Clearer evidence of Polk's benevolent actions (usually with other motives interwoven) is familiar from earlier chapters. By 1832 Polk had deported Ben and Jim to his West Tennessee plantation, from where they would seldom be able to visit their wives, 150 miles away in central Tennessee. After both men fled back to central Tennessee, Polk relented—Ben being a privileged "family negro" and Jim being a Childress slave for whom Sarah Childress Polk probably intervened. Polk (after letting Beanland whip them) sold these two men to the planters who owned their wives, in an act surely shaped by some benevolent feeling.[31]

In 1834, having thus sold Ben and Jim (and knowing that he might never see the fugitive Chunky Jack again), Polk was especially keen to buy other slaves to stock his new Mississippi plantation. When he deported his slave Mariah to Mississippi, he purchased her husband, Henry Carter, to accompany her, both for humane reasons and because Henry was an excellent worker sold at a bargain price; in addition, Henry's owner owed Polk money, and this was a splendid way to ensure that the debt was promptly paid.[32] Polk also tried to buy from the same Tennessee master the wife and child of Polk's slave Caesar (to accompany Caesar to Mississippi), but she became, or pretended to be, ill and would not hear of changing masters. Her owner, Archibald Carter—who seems to have been a man of genuinely humane feeling—listened to the slave woman's wishes and refused to offer her for sale. Perhaps she did not greatly love Caesar, for slaves sometimes got sick of their spouses, just as other people sometimes do, and she may have been glad to be parted from him. But her calculation was probably more complex. Some slaves followed the maxim, "If you have good master, stick with him even if that means splitting up with your husband or wife."[33] Caesar's wife knew the reputation of Polk's overseer, Ephraim Beanland. If she were offered only the package deal of staying with Caesar on the condition that she accept the dominion of the brutal Beanland, she probably decided that she would do better to stay with Archibald Carter. It is unlikely that Caesar ever saw his wife and child again. By moving him to Mississippi, Polk destroyed this family, though he had tried to avoid doing so.

But Polk had not tried very hard. A person of strong humanitarian feeling would have offered to exchange Caesar for Henry Carter, which would have saved both men's marriages. Then Caesar's wife could have stayed with her husband without placing herself under Beanland's power. Polk's primary object in this transaction, however, was to secure more laborers in Mississippi, not to safeguard his slaves' marriages; and an exchange of Caesar for Henry Carter would have left Polk shorthanded in

Mississippi. It would also have meant that he had not secured the payment of the debt Archibald Carter owed him.

A more convincing case of Polk's benevolence in trying to avoid destroying a slave family occurred at about the same time. A slave he bought late in 1834 was the house servant Nancy (about thirty-six years old). She soon told Polk that she had been separated from her two-year-old mulatto granddaughter, Henrietta, and she urged Polk to try to buy Henrietta too. Polk's younger sister Naomi seems to have interceded on the slave woman's behalf. Henrietta's Nashville owner put her up for sale and gave Polk first preference; Polk bought her for $150. Henrietta's father was almost surely a white man. Possibly Henrietta's young mother had died, or possibly her white owners wished to sell the infant to remove daily evidence that one of their white men had produced this child. The story is not salubrious, but at least James Polk did what he could to respect his sister Naomi's wish—and that of the slave woman Nancy—that the two-year-old child not be sold away from every one of her relatives.[34]

It was common for light-skinned mulatto slaves to be singled out for special treatment of one sort or another. This was true, eventually, of the seventeen-year-old "yellow boy" Reuben, whom old Sam Polk, when he died in 1827, had bequeathed to his widow on condition that she pass him on to her children. James Polk bought Reuben in 1831 and dispatched him to his West Tennessee plantation, where he was the third-best cotton picker. Then Polk sent Reuben to Mississippi when he founded his new plantation. But Reuben was constantly ill there from malaria (which for genetic reasons tended to afflict mulattoes even more often than it did blacks); Polk, after two years, granted Reuben the inestimable privilege of leaving the cotton fields and returning to town life in Columbia, where he was hired out—at exceptionally high rates—to various local shopkeepers and businessmen. One of these shopkeepers was willing to let Reuben hire out some of his own time, a smaller version of the concession granted to the mulatto Frederick Douglass in Baltimore in about the same year. When Governor Polk (badly short of money) sold Reuben to his younger brother William Polk in 1840, Reuben fetched the unusually high price of $1000. William Polk doubtless let Reuben continue his life as a privileged town slave, far from the dull routine of the Mississippi cotton fields. Humane motives had undoubtedly helped impel James Polk to offer this special treatment to one of his most privileged "family negroes." The fact that this slave was a mulatto—possibly a cousin or some other blood relation of James and William Polk—helped account for the preferential treatment they accorded him once he was brought back to central Tennessee. Yet for even this privileged slave, the decisive factor in his recall from the Mississippi plantation was Polk's financial interest, as Polk's own words suggest. Reuben "has been sick and is willing to return to Tennessee," Polk wrote in November 1836, at the moment he was making the crucial decision: "Every time I have heard from the plantation, since my negroes went down [in January 1835], he has been reported as sick, and I fear if he remains I may lose him. He is the most valuable boy I own."[35]

Even more valuable than Reuben—indeed, by far the most valuable of the Polk family's slaves—was the blacksmith Long Harry, who was given special privilege not because of the color of his skin but because of his artisanal skill. James Polk granted him extraordinary license. Harry had been bequeathed by old Sam Polk to his youngest son (Samuel W. Polk), who died in 1839 just after attaining his majority: thus James Polk, as executor of his father's estate, controlled Harry's destiny even before he finally became his legal owner. Polk might permit a town slave like Reuben to hire his own time to local shopkeepers, but blacksmith Harry, after being moved for several years from Columbia to West Tennessee, was accorded the remarkable privilege of being allowed to migrate on his own to Carroll County, Mississippi (the next county south of Yalobusha County), where for seven years he was hired out annually to employers in or near Carrollton, the county seat. This move to Carroll County allowed Harry (presumably after several years of being kept away from her) to rejoin his wife, who evidently had been deported by her owner from central Tennessee to Mississippi. The enslaved couple eventually had eleven children. Polk let Harry stay near his wife until she died in 1845. He even let Harry stay at Carrollton, near his younger children and his second wife, until 1848.

Here, as usual, Polk's motives were mixed. In a slave society, when a male slave had an abroad marriage, as Harry did, he must expect to lose his wife and children if their owner decides to move them (as the owner of Harry's first wife had done); by the very low standards of a slave society, James Polk's permitting Harry to follow her ranked as one of the most genuinely benevolent acts of Polk's life. But it was also economically sensible because blacksmiths were in greater demand in Mississippi than in Tennessee. Harry was by far the highest earner for Polk of any of his slaves. Harry's annual hiring fee (which peaked at $412 in 1841) was then large enough (or nearly large enough) to pay the annual salary of Polk's Mississippi overseer (which was probably $400 in 1841). Benevolence sometimes paid.

Yet even toward Harry, Polk's benevolence was not without limits. Sending Harry from central to western Tennessee during the late 1830s had probably disrupted his marriage for several years (just as sending Ben and Jim to West Tennessee had temporarily disrupted *their* marriages). And although Polk had then permitted Harry to join his first wife—who had been deported to Mississippi—and to stay near her until she died in 1845, Polk permanently wrecked Harry's second marriage by removing the blacksmith from Carroll County in January 1848.[36]

The slaves to whom Polk accorded special treatment tended to be very valuable ones (like blacksmith Harry), mulattoes (like Reuben), and especially those for whom some other member of Polk's family interceded. Among the last was the slave Harbert. As has been seen, Governor Polk in

1840 had lost patience with this town-bred, freedom-loving bondsman and had sold him—at what Polk regarded as a relatively low price—to his political ally Gideon Pillow. Polk retained ownership of Harbert's mother, Matilda; and he probably promised Sarah Polk (who had inherited Matilda and Harbert from her father) that after Harbert had been sufficiently punished, Polk would buy him back. Five and a half years later (in 1846), Polk's large presidential salary had enabled him to pay his debts, and he was now keen once again to expand his plantation labor force. Although he may have felt unsure of whether Harbert would prove a tractable field hand, Polk fulfilled his promise to Sarah by buying him, and he also bought the woman Harbert had married on Gideon Pillow's plantation, along with her eight-year-old son. Here again—as when in 1834 Polk had bought Henry Carter, the husband of Mariah (another of the slaves Sarah Polk had inherited)—Polk acquired for himself much-needed laborers, and he did so without destroying the marriages of the slaves whom he intended to send to his Mississippi plantation. (But apparently Sarah Polk herself finally decided, in about 1856, to dismantle Harbert's marriage by selling him after he had repeatedly tried to escape from the plantation.[37])

The language of benevolent paternalism was sometimes invoked in transactions that in fact betrayed little of its spirit. Thus, a year before President Polk bought Harbert, he had purchased a young slave woman from Sarah Polk's mother, who claimed she was selling out of consideration for the slave. Mrs. Childress wanted to get rid of Caroline, a fifteen-year-old girl (raised as a privileged seamstress and house servant), because Caroline was accused of prostituting herself to a white man. By selling her to Polk, Mrs. Childress could soothe her conscience, affirming that she was not selling the girl out of the family. Mrs. Childress persuaded the president (who was no longer short of cash) to buy Caroline and deport her to his Mississippi plantation. This seemed at first blush a simple case, in which Polk got himself a new laborer and simultaneously helped Mrs. Childress to punish a female slave without transgressing the code that "family negroes" ought not to be sold out of the family.

But the matter was more complex than at first appeared, for the Childress white women were divided on the issue. Sarah Polk's niece believed that old Mrs. Childress had punished the wrong slave. According to the niece, Caroline had been forced into an impossible situation by a slave named Paul; and it was Paul, not Caroline, who should have been sent away:

> The girl was hired to do the act by Paul. She did not do it herself. Paul is the one that ought to have been sent [to Mississippi] for ruin[in]g the girl. . . . [Caroline's mother and father are terribly upset at Caroline's being deported:] It has nearly taken the other servants' life, and Nat is very much afraid the girl will be used bad at your farm.

Sarah Polk's niece offered to buy Caroline so that she could return to her distressed parents. And Polk's cousin Robert Campbell also felt anxious about sending a house-bred young girl who had never done field work to labor under the supervision of Polk's overseer, John Mairs. Campbell proposed to the president an exchange, whereby Campbell would send to Mississippi (in Caroline's place) a strong, twenty-year-old slave woman inured to heavy field labor, and Campbell would bring the relatively delicate Caroline back to Tennessee to wait on Campbell's own daughters. Mairs, however, had already put Caroline to picking cotton and reported that she "does vary well considering she has Bin all hir time in the house." President Polk, rejecting these two offers to restore Caroline to the neighborhood of her own family, put the responsibility for this decision on old Mrs. Childress, who had made it a condition of selling Caroline to Polk that she be deported. Polk employed paternalistic logic to justify keeping Caroline from her own family: Mrs. Childress "desired to send her out of the state," the president reasoned, "but as she was a family negro, and she [old Mrs. Childress] had raised her in her own family, she disliked to sell her to a stranger. She is young and had been guilty of some indiscretion which induced the old lady to think this step necessary. I feel bound under the circumstances to keep her at the plantation." At the plantation Caroline remained. Presumably she never saw her parents again, unless they were still alive in 1865.[38]

A few months later the president again invoked the language of benevolent paternalism to discuss the future of another of his slaves, also named Caroline. In 1846 Polk's esteemed Mississippi neighbor John Leigh offered to buy Polk's twenty-eight-year-old slave woman Caroline Johnson. The president put aside preoccupation with the war against Mexico to consider Leigh's offer: "My foreman," Leigh beguilingly explained,

> has a wife at your place (Caroline) who has no children. She is I understand only an ordinary hand and as she does not have children no prospect of being more valuable to you. It is a matter of some importance to me that my foreman should *be always at home* particularly as hereafter I shall keep no overseer (my son Randolph managing entirely . . .). Can you let me have Caroline. I know you do not wish to part with any of your negroes, nor [Leigh flatteringly added, ignoring the number of fugitives from Polk's plantation] do I think any of them would be willing to leave you (I have said nothing about buying her) but in consideration of her being with her husband who is a favourite negroe of mine and her having no children possibly you might be induced . . . to let me have her. Of course I am willing to pay any reasonable price for her.

Leigh's motives were mixed. By purchasing Caroline he would increase both her comfort and that of her husband by enabling them to be together every night. The purchase also would diminish their anxiety that their marriage might one day be destroyed if Polk should move his slaves to Arkansas (as he several times contemplated doing) or if Leigh should re-move his own slaves from Yalobusha County. Yet self-interest principally impelled Leigh to make the offer. He depended heavily on Caroline's enslaved husband, his plantation's driver ("foreman"), to impose discipline on his other slaves, and it was not in Leigh's interest to have the driver leaving his plantation to make unauthorized nocturnal visits to Caroline. Nor would it suit Leigh (once he dispensed with an overseer) to have the driver leaving the other slaves unsupervised every Sunday.[39]

Leigh understood that the master of a fertile slave woman would be reluctant to sell her for fear of losing the ownership of her progeny. But as Caroline was not fertile, Leigh supposed that benevolent impulses might lead Polk to accede to Caroline's sale. Leigh understood, to be sure, that Polk did "not wish to part with any of [his] negroes"; but Leigh failed to reckon with the strength of Polk's aversion to selling a slave to the owner of the slave's spouse.

In 1834 Polk had sold Ben and Jim to the owners of those men's wives in central Tennessee, and the consequence—it must have appeared to the president—had been to undermine discipline on the Mississippi planta-tion. Polk's slaves kept running away, as Ben and Jim had done. Several of them now, like Caroline (and previously Ben and Jim), were married to slaves not owned by Polk. If Polk should sell Caroline to Leigh, all his other slaves with abroad marriages might hope that they too could escape the discipline on Polk's plantation by being sold to the owners of their spouses. And the new slaves whom President Polk was buying might ac-quire the idea that they could also escape strict discipline by entering an abroad marriage, which could lead to their being sold away from Polk's plantation. The rot must not be allowed to set in.

Against Leigh's seemingly humane concern, Polk therefore arrayed his own apparently altruistic arguments. "It would give me sincere plea-sure to accommodate you," Polk began, with a Southern gentleman's courteous flourish:

> But as *Caroline* is a family servant, I would feel great reluctance in parting with her. And if not [i.e., even if Caroline were not a family servant] all of her relatives are in our family—and nothing would induce me to dispose of her unless it would be to keep her with her husband. As your plantation and mine are only a mile or two apart, I will promise you never to move her so as to separate her from her husband. I fully appreciate the considerable *motive* which induces you to desire to purchase, and I am sure you will appre-ciate the considerations which induce me to prefer not to sepa-rate her from her family relations.

Polk's anxiety not to separate Caroline from her family relations had not always been so strong as it now appeared to be. When Caroline Johnson was sixteen she had witnessed the breakup of her own parents' marriage: James Polk (acting no doubt with the consent of his younger brother William Polk, who had inherited Caroline's family) had sold her father—the indomitable fugitive Chunky Jack—away from Caroline's mother and their children. Because William Polk had four years later sold Caroline, Caroline's mother, and Caroline's three siblings to James Polk, the president now adduced these family connections as arguments against letting Caroline join her husband on the Leigh estate. Polk had no thought of asking Caroline herself whether she wished to follow the injunction—in many Christian marriage ceremonies—to leave her natal family (those of them who were still left) to join her husband. Instead the master was to make this decision for her, according to what he alleged was her own best interest.[40]

This was an instance of intrusive, domineering interference in a slave's life by a nearly omnipotent master—"paternalism" in a different meaning of that word; but one may question whether or not these two masters acted very benevolently. What Leigh wanted above all else was to keep good discipline on his plantation by preventing his black driver from leaving home in order to sleep with Caroline at Polk's plantation. Leigh did not realize that Polk had a strong reason to keep his hands on even an unfertile slave woman. Polk wanted to discourage his slaves from believing that, by some subterfuge (such as entering an abroad marriage), they could get out from under his thumb, for this might undermine plantation discipline. Selling a slave to a nearby plantation was not, to Polk, an attractive option. Thus both gentlemen had employed deceptively paternalist language; but Polk never sold Caroline to Leigh, and in neither Leigh's offer nor in Polk's response can one detect much genuine benevolence of spirit.

If Polk invoked his wife's sense of responsibility to the Childress and Polk family slaves, he was not always sincere. Thus in 1843, when the costs of his failed campaigns to be reelected governor of Tennessee had impelled him to seek a partner to pour new capital into his Mississippi enterprise, he had threatened Sarah that he might have to sell the whole plantation, along with its slaves. By contrast with any such drastic step, his merely selling a half interest in the plantation might then seem a concession to Sarah Polk's scruples: "I think the slaves on that [half of my land] I will sell to [a prospective buyer]," Polk had notified Sarah. "If I do I will retain the other half & still continue the farm. This I know will suit your views better than to sell the whole plantation." Sarah's sense of obligation to her slaves was thus a force—if another were needed—toward keeping the Polks deeply involved in the plantation slavery system.[41]

The language of benevolent paternalism might also be employed as a means of boosting a slavemaster's self-image. When in 1848 President Polk wrote to his Mississippi neighbor John Leigh—who, as we have seen, was himself a master of paternalist usage—that the frequent fugitive Joe "may be better satisfied" with a different owner, Polk was assuring himself, as well as Leigh (and posterity), that his motives were kindly. Leigh was one of those Virginia-bred gentlemen who liked to talk about "my family . . . white as well as black." Yet this same gentleman (or probably his son Randolph) was the Mr. Leigh who fired buckshot into the legs of Polk's slave Perry to prevent his escape in 1840; and Leigh was adamant that the only other way to deter Polk's slaves from fleeing was with the whip.[42]

It is a mixed record. Polk was conscious that there existed a paternalist code that was supposed to govern how gentlemen treated their slaves, especially their "family negroes." This consciousness sometimes affected his actions in important ways, and it often influenced how he presented himself. The secrecy within which the president shrouded his purchase of slaves was a product of his wish to avoid appearing to be a hard-headed businessman, anxious to increase the profits that accrued from his capital investment in Mississippi cotton lands. He was most likely to act benevolently—as he did to blacksmith Harry—when the consequence was a substantial addition to his own income. He was more likely to act the paternalist in dealing with a "family negro" (like Ben or Reuben) than with an ordinary hand. Under his wife's prompting, he accorded special treatment to some of the Childress slaves, like Jim and Harbert, and (probably urged on by his sister Naomi) he even bought the two-year-old mulatto granddaughter of the house servant Nancy. In 1847 (a dozen years after he had founded his Mississippi plantation), President Polk benevolently, if belatedly, contributed toward building a church that his slaves could attend. Requiring overseer Dismukes to postpone a whipping until Polk's agent could monitor its severity might also be regarded as a slightly benevolent act.[43]

Yet, like his neighbor John Leigh, Polk placed the imposition of discipline at the top of his plantation agenda, even though this conflicted with an image of kindliness. He instructed the House of Representatives that slaves must be whipped because imprisonment was an insufficient deterrent. He briefly sent the fugitive slave Ben, who had voluntarily given himself up, back to the plantation to be whipped by Beanland, even after James Walker had suggested dismissing that overseer. Polk continued to employ Beanland even after Beanland had stabbed Chunky Jack. Polk backed his overseer Isaac Dismukes in whipping, rather than selling, slaves who escaped temporarily. But—distinguishing local flight from an attempt to escape permanently—he threatened the latter type of fugitive with sale to the Deep South; and he fulfilled that threat against Chunky Jack, separating him permanently from his wife, his daughter Caroline Johnson, his son Manuel, and his other two children. Polk also authorized the sale of the fugitive Joe.[44]

The frequency with which Polk purchased very young slaves, unaccompanied by either parents or siblings, suggests how little he cared for the family ties of these children. His instruction to one agent that he wanted property between the ages of twelve and twenty-one made it impossible for the agent to buy any slave not separated from the child's parents. Polk's slaves demonstrated by the regularity of their flights how little benevolent they judged his regime to be.

The shallowness of Polk's concern for some of his chattels was reflected in his inscription on the envelope of a letter, dated November 8, 1848, in which overseer Mairs mentioned to the president the death of a slave named Caroline Henly. Mairs claimed that the doctor had thought Caroline recovered from an old complaint, but the doctor had been wrong, and she—forced to work by Mairs when she was ill?—had died. The methodical Polk usually wrote on a letter's envelope a brief summary of its contents, but benevolent feelings did not impel him to write Caroline Henly's name. Instead he carefully recorded there what most interested him—the exact weights, which Mairs had sent to him, for each bale of his cotton.[45] Perhaps the president preferred not to remind himself that he—by buying this girl in 1846 and placing her under the dominion of John Mairs (who "certainly has a great deal of [work] done")—might bear some responsibility for her death in the Mississippi cotton fields.[46]

Aware that slavery was becoming condemned by much of the world, well-bred Southern slavemasters turned naturally to paternalist ideology to create for themselves a satisfactory self-image. This was not entirely hypocritical, for the influences of Jeffersonian natural-rights philosophy, evangelical religion, and even humanitarianism created in some of them genuinely benevolent feelings. But in a semicapitalist slave society, humane practice was bound to be weak. A slavemaster like James Polk mixed one part of benevolence with perhaps a dozen parts of indifference or callousness. Benevolent feelings did indeed influence Polk's conduct toward a family slave like Ben or toward a slave like Harbert, partially sheltered by Sarah Polk and by Jane Polk. But far more powerful was Polk's wish to maintain his own authority, reinforced as that motive was by the drive to make a good profit, and therefore to govern the slaves firmly.

This impression of the Polks' relative indifference toward their slaves' welfare may be augmented by the evidence of ill health at the plantation. It is also corroborated by the records of family disruption there.

7

Births and Deaths

When slavery in the United States is compared to that in the Caribbean, a striking contrast appears. Slaves in the Caribbean died at a
faster rate than they were born, and their masters therefore had to import
new slaves from Africa if they were to maintain or expand their plantation
operations. But in the United States, slaves were born at a considerably
faster rate than they died. When the African slave trade to the United States
was banned in 1808, this did not throttle the expansion of slavery into
Alabama, Tennessee, Mississippi, and further west. On the contrary, the
South's slave population grew rapidly, increasing on average 27 percent
during each antebellum decade. This fact indicated that health conditions
for Caribbean slaves were worse than for those in the American South;
and it *might* have seemed to show that health conditions for American slaves
were actually not bad at all by nineteenth-century standards. Indeed, an
apologist for American slavery, the famous British geologist Charles Lyell,
used population figures to argue in 1849 that American slaves were well
treated. Up-country slaves, Lyell exclaimed,

> are healthier than those in rice plantations, and multiply [even]
> faster, although the rice grounds [of the low country] are salubri-
> ous to the negroes as compared to the whites. In this lower re-
> gion [coastal Georgia] the increase of the slaves is rapid, for they
> are well fed, fitted for a southern climate, and free from care. . . .
> Such advantages, however, would be of no avail, in rendering them
> prolific, if they were overworked and harshly treated.[1]

Two questions thus suggest themselves about James Polk's plantation: was
there a natural growth of the slave population at his plantation compa-
rable to the Southern norm? Do the Polk records imply that health conditions there were relatively salubrious for the slaves?

To both questions, the answer is no. Polk's new Mississippi enterprise witnessed only a 2 percent natural population increase between 1835
and 1849. Although the records are fragmentary, it appears that by 1849
Polk had stocked the plantation with fifty-five slaves. Although about nineteen babies had been born, eighteen slaves had died.[2]

Several causes for this surprisingly small population growth spring to mind. There was a shortage of young women of childbearing age since Polk had at first sent more males than females to clear his virgin land. Although he soon started sending women in equal numbers, a remarkably large proportion of the young women at the plantation—one-third or even more[3]—died young, nearly always while they were still in their twenties or even younger. For these reasons—and because at least one of the married couples was infertile and another became so—the birthrate was very low. In addition, the child mortality rate (to age fifteen) exceeded 50 percent.[4]

The dozen young adult slaves whom Polk assigned in January 1835 to his new Mississippi enterprise included four females. One of these women, Dicey, became ill early in 1837; she was very weak and "unable to do anything" by December, and although she seems to have recovered for a time, apparently she died a few years later, childless, at about the age of twenty-six.[5] Of the remaining women, Eve was the most fertile. Polk's agent had bought her in Kentucky in 1831, aged sixteen and separated from every member of her family. Five years later Polk permanently separated her from the father of her first two children when he sent her from Tennessee to the Mississippi plantation.[6] Eve married Polk's slave Phil, to whom she bore at least ten more children, including twins in 1850. But neither twin survived more than a few months; another infant, Ananias, lasted less than a year and three others scarcely longer. Thus, six of Eve's twelve known children perished. Overseer John Mairs sought to blame Eve herself for her misfortunes. "It appears that she cant rase no children," he complained in 1854, just after the sixth death; "I have them well nursed [i.e., presumably an old woman cared for them while Eve toiled in the fields] and medical ade." Yet, despite multiple sorrows, Eve proved in fact to be the most successful "breeder" of all of Polk's slaves, with six children who survived—at least to 1860, when the record ends.[7]

Among the early arrivals at the plantation, the next most fertile woman after Eve was Elizabeth, who succeeded in keeping slightly more than half of her children alive. Elizabeth had been a slave of Polk's father-in-law, Joel Childress, and in 1828 Polk bought her—then twelve years old—from Childress's creditor. In 1832, soon after Polk sent her to work on his West Tennessee plantation, Elizabeth—now sixteen—entered an abroad marriage with a local man, and their child was born twelve months later. It died of crib death within two weeks. Elizabeth "smothered it somehow," Dr. Caldwell reported. "No person knew it was dead until this morning." Polk dismantled Elizabeth's abroad marriage a year later, when he deported her to Mississippi. Meanwhile she suffered recurrent medical problems: she temporarily lost the use of an arm in 1833, she seems to have had congestive fever in 1834, and an illness during her first year in Mississippi (just after she was taken away from her husband) nearly killed her.

Like several other slaves, she had severe dysentery in 1838, and she had another lengthy illness in 1841—all before she had reached her twenty-sixth birthday. In Mississippi she again entered an abroad marriage, which produced at least six more children, of whom four outlived childhood.[8]

The last of the original group of female slaves was Elizabeth's older sister Mariah. In 1834 this twenty-year-old woman already had had two young children by her husband Henry Carter, whom Polk then bought from a Tennessee neighbor to accompany Mariah to Mississippi. It was a privileged family, the first listed in the inventory of Polk's estate in 1849; and one of Mariah's children, Henry, was selected by President Polk to go with him to the White House as a personal servant. Meanwhile, Mariah (who, once owned by Joel Childress, continued to think of herself as a slave of Sarah Childress Polk) had taken pride in learning to weave. She defined her own value in monetary terms: in 1841 Mariah got Polk's agent "to inform her mistress that she is worth at least $30 more than when she left Tennessee. She can spool, warp, and *weave* and with a little more practice thinks she will make a first rate weaver." Within a few months Mariah was weaving seven yards of cloth per day; she made up the slaves' summer suits, as well as weaving the material for their winter garments. But she seems never to have had any more children after the age of twenty, presumably because of gynecological problems. Mariah "has spells onste a month very bad," overseer Garner reported in 1840. She is "in a very bad condition every thre or fore weks. So very bad onst this spring she was throne into fits of spasms in which I had to have the Doct with her." Although Mariah recovered from these attacks, the condition was chronic and she appears to have died when only about thirty-seven years old.[9]

Thus the four young women whom Polk first dispatched to Mississippi bore twelve children still alive in 1860 (although three of these children were then still so young that they may not have survived to adulthood). Eve had seen six of her children die, Elizabeth lost three, Dicey perished young, and Mariah became sterile after two successful pregnancies; yet these four women had nevertheless borne enough surviving children to produce a steady population growth if Polk's other female slaves could have been equally "fortunate."

But most of them were not. Of the seventeen other young women at the plantation, five died within a few years of their arrival. Matilda, apparently in poor health when Polk bought her in 1839, probably succumbed to dropsy about four years later, aged twenty-nine. Eliza, a daughter of the indomitable fugitive Chunky Jack, was already classified as a "hand" (at age fifteen in September 1845) when she died after a ten-day spell of "the feaver" (presumably malaria). Caroline Henly, purchased in 1846 at age sixteen, had "a spell of fever" later that summer, and she perished at the plantation two years later. Caroline Davis, bought for Polk in 1849 by his nephew, was diseased, the overseer alleged, when she arrived at the plantation, and within a year she died of pneumonia, aged twenty. Agnes, purchased at age thirteen, died at just nineteen, five days after the birth of a stillborn child.[10] Thus, including the previously mentioned deaths of Dicey and Mariah, seven of the twenty-one young women at the Polks' plantation died young, usually within a few years of their arrival. Indeed, the mortality rate among relatively young women was probably even higher than 33 percent—for I have omitted from these deaths the probable demise of Caroline Johnson at about age thirty-nine, and one or two of the other women, still in their early twenties in 1860, may well have died before reaching the age of forty.

Although young males did not die quite so quickly, they, too, perished at a surprisingly high rate. Six of the twenty-eight young adult males whom the Polks assigned to their Mississippi enterprise succumbed while still young. These were Hardy, a twenty-six-year-old wagoner and plowman, who may have contracted his fatal respiratory illness when fleeing from overseer Beanland the previous winter; Abe, a twenty-three-year-old blacksmith fatally thrown against a tree by a mule; Chunky Jack's son Fan, who probably died when about fifteen; Caesar, who appears to have been about thirty-five when he died; forty-year-old Henry Carter, who perished of pneumonia during an erysipelas epidemic; and Calvin, who succumbed to typhoid fever aged about twenty.[11] This 21 percent mortality rate among relatively young males—grim though it may appear—was substantially exceeded by the 33 percent mortality rate among the young women. And these women's average age at death (twenty-three) was even lower than the corresponding men's average age when they died (twenty-six).[12]

This information may suggest an answer to a puzzle: why could female field hands always be bought for a lower price than male field hands? Male hands, of course, were on average bigger and stronger. But many female slaves, inured to hard labor, also became strong and tough; and the price of a female slave was substantially increased if she was supposed to be a good "breeder"[13] because the buyer would also become the owner of all of her future children and of all of her daughters' offspring, too. In determining the women's prices, why did not this potential breeding capacity offset their relatively lesser physical strength? The Polks' experience points to one possible explanation: perhaps young slave women all over the South were substantially more likely to die prematurely than were young males and at an earlier age. The U.S. censuses of 1850 and 1860 support this hypothesis, for they suggest that everywhere in the South female slaves were about 24 percent more likely to die young than were male slaves.[14] The vicissitudes of childbearing, combined with hard field labor and with the effects of chronic malaria, took a heavy toll on the lives of female slaves. Thus the probability that a young female field hand would die sooner than a young male may have kept the prices of female field hands relatively low.

The seven Polk slave women who died young bore altogether only three children who probably survived to adulthood.[15] Therefore, if the slave population of Polk's plantation was to reproduce itself or to grow, everything depended on the fourteen women who managed to stay alive. One of them was infertile; there is no record that two others ever had children when Polk owned them, and Marshall Polk removed his slave Barbara from the plantation as soon as he was able to do so.[16] The chances of augmenting the labor force therefore depended on ten women. Polk bought most of them in 1846 and 1849, too late for them to bear many children before he died. Thus, during the plantation's first fifteen years, the total number of births had only exceeded the number of deaths by one (see table 7.1).

By 1855 the young women recently bought by Polk began to bear enough surviving children to alter the dreary record of the previous years. During the 1850s births exceeded deaths by six, leading to a natural population growth of 12 percent.[17] Although this figure may have heartened Sarah Polk, it still remained substantially lower than the 23½ percent increase witnessed elsewhere in the South during that decade.[18]

Over half of the slave children born from 1835 at the plantation died before reaching age fifteen.[19] Consequently a Polk slave woman was unlikely to raise as many as three children to maturity.[20] Four of Daphney's children died young, only three of her seven known infants surviving until 1860. Similarly, only three of Jane's five known babies survived until 1860. Yet Daphney and Jane were fortunate compared to most of the Polk women, as may be seen in table 7.2. Column (d) shows that of the seven Polk women who died early, only Mariah Carter and Agnes left children still alive in 1860; and the other fourteen Polk women had produced only twenty-eight children still alive in 1860, an average of only two surviving children for each of these women.[21]

Of the twenty-one women named in the table, only Eve, Elizabeth, Daphney, and Jane seem to have borne as many as three children still alive

Table 7.1
Estimated Number of Births and Deaths
at the Polk Plantation, 1835–59

| | (a) | (b) | (c) |
| | | | Population Growth |
Years	Births	Deaths	[(a) − (b)]
1835–49	19	18	1
1850–59	36	30	6
Total	55	48*	7

*Of these deaths, 28 were of children born at the plantation from 1835.
Sources: tables A1, A2, and A3 in appendix A.

Table 7.2
Size of Twenty-one Families, Polk Plantation, 1835-59

Names of Women	(a) Woman's Year of Birth	(b) Woman's Year of Death	(c) Number of Known Live Births	(d) Number of Children Still Alive in 1860
Seven Women Who Died Young				
Dicey	1817	1841?	—	—
Mariah Carter	1814	1851?	2	2
Matilda	1814	1843?	2	0
Eliza 1	1830	1845	—	—
Caroline Henly	1830	1848	—	—
Caroline Davis	1829	1850	—	—
Agnes	1833	1853	1	1
Fourteen Women Who Did Not Die Young				
Eve	1815	—	12	6
Elizabeth (Betsy)	1816	—	7	4
Daphney	1828	—	7	3
Jane	1834	—	5	3
Marina	1817	—	3?	2?
Maria Davis	1831	—	4	2
Mary	1818	—	1	1
Caroline Harris	1828	—	1	1
Sally	1834	—	3	1
Caroline Johnson	1818	1857?	—	—
Rosetta	1832	—	—	—
Caroline Childress	1830	—	2?	2?
Barbara	1823	—	2	1?
Malinda	1836	—	2?	2?
Subtotal			54	31
Unrecorded births, to these 21 women, of Children who died unrecorded (est.)			7	0
Total			61	31
Of whom, born before 1835 or before Polk owned the mother★			−6	−4
Total born at plantation after January 1, 1835			55	27

★The children born before 1835 included both of Mariah Carter's children, one of Eve's children, and one of Elizabeth's children; Mary's child and one of Matilda's children were born before Polk bought their mothers.
Source: table A1 in Appendix A.

by 1860. Perhaps nine of these women had other children later, but (because seven of the other women had already died, and many of the remainder were by 1860 relatively old for childbearing)[22] the total number of their future children will not have been huge. Everything points to the difficulty these slave women had in keeping their children alive.

Clues that point to why the health record on the Polks' plantation was so dismal are scarce. A central factor was that (as everywhere in the South) child mortality among the slaves was, by the standards of nineteenth-century America, appalling. Among free children, child mortality (to age fifteen) in the antebellum years was about 28 percent. This figure is for the whole United States—urban and rural, Northern and Southern. Thus it offers only limited guidance about the child mortality rate among Southern rural free people (a group that might serve best for comparison with the mortality rate of slaves). We know that among slaves during antebellum years the child mortality rate (to age fifteen) reached some 46 percent[23]—far higher than among free children in the whole United States and probably even much higher than among Southern rural free children. At the Polk plantation the record of slave child mortality was even worse—surely 51 percent, almost certainly even higher.[24] Evidently the mortality rate among Polk's slave women of childbearing age was also very high.

The experience of the slaves at Polk's West Tennessee plantation had warned him of health problems encountered whenever slaves had to work in cold, wet conditions and with drinking water of doubtful purity. The worst feature of Polk's West Tennessee business, James Walker had reported in midwinter 1833, "is the great complaint of sickness among your negroes. 5 of them were sick when I was at your plantation, and [the overseer] says there is frequently 10 or 11 sick at a time, generally with colds." The next year overseer Beanland implied that the water supply at the Tennessee plantation had been unsatisfactory: "I wold like for you to by a place that has good warter if posiable," Beanland had urged Polk, when the Mississippi plantation was about to be purchased. In the late autumn of 1835 a large fraction of the field workers at the new plantation were ill. Elizabeth, whose abroad marriage Polk had disrupted when he deported her at age eighteen from Tennessee, nearly died (from a recurrence of "congestive fever"?) later that year. Silas Caldwell, who had bought the new plantation, quickly lost faith in the land he himself had selected: "Too much of our plantation," he now believed, was "too flat and wet. . . . I am afraid our slaves will be sickly owing to the local situation of our Farm."[25] Most of the land lay in flat tracts on both sides of the two branches of Perrys Creek, which joined each other on the plantation itself. (This was fertile soil, where cotton was still being grown 165 years later.) Only the plantation's northwest corner was a bit hilly, and the slaves' cabins were eventually moved there to distance them from the low-lying miasma. Contaminated drinking water may explain why dysentery struck Polk's bondspeople in the spring of 1838; Elizabeth and Nancy had still not recovered by June.[26] A year later seven or eight slaves were again "quite sick with . . . Billious Dysentery"; overseer George Bratton died of it, and Bratton's wife nearly perished, too. The demise of this white man was probably the decisive factor in persuading Polk's agents to shift the location of the slave settlement. "Your friends here speek of this being a sickly place," the new overseer soon reported, "and speek of its being proper to moove the cabins to some other point."[27]

Although the removal of the slaves' cabins to the opposite side of the hill may have improved matters, it could not solve various other problems. Overseer Garner implied that the shoes supplied to the slaves were of such low quality that they did not last through the winter. And even when the weather turned warm, slaves still had to work in mud; Garner notified Polk in May that the early corn looked bad, "on wet low land. I had to plow when the mules would mier [mire] to the [k]nees in places."[28]

A fundamental problem was that planters, in order to control their slaves, insisted on their living together in settlements where a white man could keep an eye on them—and where epidemics were certain to spread faster than they would have done if the blacks had scattered themselves across the countryside, as they did as soon as slavery ended. Although the Polk plantation seems never to have been hit by one of the truly horrendous epidemics that regularly carried off huge numbers of slaves on rice plantations, the frequent epidemics that did strike the Mississippi plantation were devastating enough. Twenty slaves (more than one-third of the population at that time) were stricken by a fever during a twelve-day period in 1849, from which one young child died. The worst epidemics were in 1852, when six slaves (11 percent of the population) seem to have perished within a few months of each other. First, a twelve-year-old boy died of pneumonia; then a whooping cough epidemic killed three infants; and finally, an epidemic of what the doctor called erysipelas of the internal organs made five adults very ill: the plantation's best worker, Henry Carter, succumbed to this disease, on top of pneumonia, and "old Cloe" (in her mid-sixties) apparently also died from the same illness. That autumn and winter so many hands were ill for so long that one-sixth of the cotton crop (perhaps thirty-five bales) wasted in the field; and the harvest of the remainder could not be completed until February 14.[29] The next year about five slaves had dysentery, and in 1854 a small typhoid fever epidemic killed the twenty-year-old Calvin.[30]

At Polk's plantation, as everywhere in the Deep South, chronic malaria doubtless plagued many slaves, reducing their resistance to other illnesses and causing the babies of infected mothers to be born underweight so that they succumbed to other maladies. This probably contributed substantially to the dreadful child mortality rate at Polk's plantation. The overseer's purchase for the slaves of quinine—a standard remedy to ease the symptoms of what was then known as "intermittent fever"—indicates his concern about malaria. When Polk bought slaves, he almost always did so in the upper or middle South; and slave traders understood that when bondspeople from these regions were deported to the Deep South, they were very likely to become ill with malaria.[31] President Polk's understanding was equally clear; thus, he instructed his agent, when he bought half a dozen slaves in 1846, that it might be cheaper to buy them in June but that they should be kept in Tennessee until the autumn, "as it would not be safe on account of sickness to send [the slaves] to my plantation until about the 1st of October." In 1856 both Caroline Johnson and Marina had malaria (which may explain why only two children of Marina appear to have survived until 1860). The mulatto Reuben was a privileged slave (one of the three whom Polk hoped never to sell out of the family) who had used his chronic malaria at the plantation as a means of persuading Polk to send him back to Tennessee in December 1836, where Reuben was allowed to rent out his own time in urban employment. But the fifteen-year-old Eliza was not so lucky: she perished in 1845 from what was probably an early bout of malaria before she had built up sufficient resistance to the disease.[32]

A different chronic health problem was that overseers—keen to produce the largest possible crops and fearing that slaves were malingering—tended to push slaves too hard, sometimes when they were in fact ill. John Mairs had the reputation of getting a lot of work out of the Polk slaves, and perhaps he had pushed Henry Carter too hard during the 1852 harvest. In any case, it was only a few weeks after Carter's death on October 21, 1852, that Mairs suddenly found it politic to assure Sarah Polk that although some of the slaves "are unwell with bad colds, I am not pushing, think it better to lose a little tim[e] than a negro."[33]

A further chronic problem was that pregnant mothers were expected to work in the fields until shortly before the baby was due and had to return to field labor a few weeks after a baby was born, subjecting the baby for most of the day to the (sometimes neglectful) care of young children or of women too old to be useful in the field.[34] The Polk records do not throw further light on these problems, but perhaps the excessive child mortality rate and the large number of deaths of women of childbearing age speak for themselves.

A final chronic problem was that a slave bought from a stranger might prove "unsound." Certainly the overseers would try, if possible, to blame the death of a young adult slave on a previous disability—implying that the agent who purchased the slave had been gulled and that the overseer himself bore no responsibility. Thus, in announcing to Sarah Polk the death of young Caroline Davis from pneumonia on February 21, 1850, John Mairs identified Caroline as "won that Mr. Samuel P Walker [James Walker's son] sent hear Las april frome Memphis. This negro was Diseased. She come her sick and has bin complayming of and on ever sens she has bin heare." Surely, Mairs implied, Mrs. Polk mustn't suppose that he himself could have caused Caroline's death by making an ill woman work out-of-doors in midwinter.[35]

If Mairs was engaged here in special pleading, the fact nevertheless stands forth that five out of seven of the young female adults (and two out of six of the young adult males) who perished at the Mississippi plantation had been bought by Polk from strangers.[36] One or two (like Matilda in 1839) may indeed have been afflicted when they were sold by a chronic illness that escaped the scrutiny of Polk's purchasing agents. And others may have been so disheartened by being torn away from family and friends that their resistance to disease was diminished. But Polk purchased from strangers almost half of the slaves he sent to Mississippi, and the death rate among these, although significantly higher than among his other slaves, was not immensely so.[37] Most Mississippi planters depended heavily on buying slaves from strangers, so this factor is unlikely to have been the principal cause for the unusually high death rate at Polk's plantation.

The melancholy fact is that most plantations had a very high child mortality rate, and Polk's plantation was (in this respect) unusual only in having a somewhat higher rate than was common among slaves everywhere in the South. The death rate among Polk's young adult slaves, however, appears to have been considerably higher than even the Southern norm (high as the latter was from poor nourishment, chronic malaria, the callousness of many masters, and epidemics resulting from the slaves being bunched together into settlements). Probably Caldwell was right in observing that too much of Polk's plantation was "too flat and wet." Polk's agents may have bought one or two unhealthy young slaves. But perhaps the main explanation for the unusually high mortality rate was that this was an absentee plantation, where for most of the year (and sometimes for several years on end) the master was seldom present to try to prevent the overseers from abusing their despotic power.[38]

8

┅━ ⊰◈⊱ ━┅

Family and Community

Two generations of scholars have richly demonstrated the strength of the slaves' family and community institutions. John Blassingame examined the slaves' ways of escaping their masters' surveillance by immersing themselves during the evenings and on Sundays in the community life of their own quarters. Eugene Genovese and Herbert Gutman challenged the older view that slavery had undermined family life among the bondspeople.[1] No historian today would picture the slaves as mere passive victims of oppression.

At first these studies may have implied that the slaves managed to avoid being damaged by their circumstances. But a balanced view is now emerging, which while indicating the vitality of the slaves' family and community institutions, calls renewed attention to the harm done to them.[2] The Polk records are imperfect for striking this balance, for they contain almost no direct evidence from the mouths of the slaves themselves. Indirectly, however, these records are of considerable value. Doubtless at the Polks' plantation, as elsewhere, family and community gave the slaves real protection from their masters' exactions. But the family life of the Polk slaves was less solidly based and their community less stable than might have been anticipated. A principal explanation lay in the institution of abroad marriages. Another problem arose from the slaves' seething discontent with bondage, which led many men (most of them married) to try at least temporarily to flee. And both family and community institutions were further weakened by the constant influx of newly purchased slaves, severed from all their previous community ties and also usually cut away from all of their previous family links. Community was also weakened by a high turnover among the slaves, as early death or other forces removed many of them from the plantation. Although the slave community at the Polk plantation was in one respect stronger than might have been expected, the plantation was in this regard atypical. At most frontier plantations, the community's solidity was probably weakened even more than at the Polk plantation.

Abroad marriages were common on small farms, where slaves were owned in such small parcels that they were obliged to seek partners away from home. The Polks' enterprise, however, was larger than the

100

Southern norm (comprising, as it did in 1849, fifty-six slaves), and abroad marriages might therefore have been relatively rare. Such was far from the truth. In fact, some of the women and more of the men had abroad marriages, even though the risks of entering such a marriage had been evident to the Polks' slaves ever since the founding of the Mississippi plantation. This was true despite the fact that Polk, unlike many masters, did sometimes attempt to prevent family disruptions.

In 1834, for example, Polk bought Mariah's husband, Henry Carter, from a mixture of motives (partly benevolent, partly self-interested).[3] At the same time, he broke up Caesar's marriage because he did not offer to sell Caesar to the owner of Caesar's wife. (Caesar's wife had concluded that she would have a better life on her own in Tennessee than by being subject to Polk's brutal overseer Ephraim Beanland.) Because Polk evidently did not try to buy Elizabeth's abroad husband, Elizabeth's marriage, too—like Caesar's—was shattered by the move to Mississippi.[4] This move seems also to have torn Eve away from the father of her first two children.

Eve subsequently married a slave on Polk's Mississippi plantation, and this was a long-enduring union. Eve's husband was Phil, who sometimes made shoes at night after working in the fields (or as a blacksmith) during the day. Eve and Phil's marriage lasted more than twenty years, their time together disrupted only by Phil's attempt at (permanent?) escape from the plantation in 1853.[5]

Another long-lasting home marriage was that between Maria Davis and Alphonso. Maria, raised in Virginia, had been separated from everyone she knew and had been sold at age fifteen to a slave trader who carried her to Tennessee and sold her to President Polk's agent in 1847. At age sixteen, Maria conceived by Alphonso the first of four children, of whom three quickly died. This union endured for at least a dozen years, broken only—as in Eve and Phil's case—by Alphonso's multiple attempts to flee. The marriage did come into dire straits when Alphonso's owner, Marshall Polk, Jr., threatened to remove him permanently from the plantation; but the young white man relented and apparently sold Alphonso to Sarah Polk, so the marriage was not, after all, destroyed.[6]

Yet another relatively long-enduring home marriage was that between Chunky Jack's son Manuel and a girl named Jane. Bought in 1846 by President Polk's agent when she was only twelve years old, separate from either parents or siblings, she was fifteen or sixteen when she started the first of six pregnancies by Manuel.[7] This resulted in a miscarriage. Two other children died young, but the marriage continued until 1860, when three of Jane and Manuel's young children were still alive. Manuel, however, had twice attempted to flee—once with Phil and once with Alphonso—and the first attempt was probably an effort at permanent flight.[8] Then in 1860 Sarah Polk appears to have destroyed the marriage by removing Manuel to Tennessee.[9]

Harbert and Mary, too, had a relatively long-enduring home marriage: they were probably married for fourteen years. But even more than Phil's,

Alphonso's, or Manuel's marriages, Harbert's was made unstable by his discontent with the plantation. Harbert fled some five times during the mid-1850s. He aimed at permanent escape, and almost certainly he was sold—never to see his wife again—in 1856.[10]

These four cases indicate that even when a slave couple had a home marriage, the husband's wish to flee was likely to threaten the solidity of the family. Moreover, several of the Polks' married men had abroad marriages, where the strains on family life were doubtless even greater. Among the men with abroad marriages were Addison—who fled at least four times—and Gilbert, the most indomitable of the Polk fugitives, who ran away no fewer than ten times.[11] Men with abroad marriages, like Addison and Gilbert, were even more likely than those with home marriages to be so discontented that they were willing to undertake the manifold dangers of flight.

In 1846, when President Polk sought to improve his long-term financial prospects by expanding his slave force, he made a brief effort to buy the spouses of slaves with abroad marriages. "Several of my men," the president informed his agent, "have *wives*, and several of my women have *husbands*, in the neighborhood. . . . If you find that any of their *wives* or *husbands* can be purchased at fair prices, and they are such as you think I ought to buy, you are authorized to purchase them." These suggestions did Polk's slaves no good. Polk could remember the names of only four of his slaves who had abroad marriages, though there seem to have been several others as well. Polk's agent did not think that two of the specified spouses were worth buying, and Polk's neighbor John Leigh declined to sell the husbands of Elizabeth and of Caroline Johnson, suggesting instead that Polk sell these two women to him. Polk rebuffed this offer: he needed more slaves on his plantation, not fewer, and he feared undermining discipline if he let slaves think they could eventually get away from his plantation by entering an abroad marriage. Even when Leigh formally proposed buying Caroline Johnson in order to unite her with her husband, the president refused.[12] After this brief flurry, Polk's slaves remained in exactly the same position they had been in when he raised the subject.

All of Polk's slaves were witnesses in 1852 to how insecure a slave's marriage could be when the husband and wife had two different masters. President Polk had bought Billy Nevels, age seventeen, in 1846. Nevels had married within a year or two a woman named Barbara, who was six years older than he, by whom he soon had two children. Although Billy and Barbara lived together on the plantation, they had two different masters, for Barbara was the property of Polk's nephew, the West Point cadet Marshall Polk, Jr. As soon as this young man was legally able to do so, he removed Barbara and her one surviving child to his own land in Tennessee, destroying forever her marriage. At the same time he also removed his slave Charles from the plantation, demolishing Charles's marriage to nineteen-year-old Rosetta (who three years earlier had been sold away from her parents). Thus the young white man, with this double blow, reminded every other Polk bondsperson of the fragility of the slaves' family institutions.[13]

The inventory of James Polk's slaves when he died in 1849 permits a systematic examination of these matters, and the instances of family disruption previously described may be collated with every other such case.[14] Twenty-six of Polk's bondspeople were married (or, in the case of Manuel and Jane, were on the verge of marriage) in 1849. It turns out that between 1834 and 1860 a *majority* of these people apparently suffered disruptions of their marriages by the actions of the Polks. Cloe lost her husband, Chunky Jack, when Polk sold Jack in 1834. Elizabeth's first abroad marriage was destroyed when Polk sent her from Tennessee to Mississippi in January 1835. Eve was separated from the father of her first two children when Polk sent her to Mississippi at the end of 1836.[15] Blacksmith Harry was separated from his second wife when, in 1848, President Polk forced Harry to leave Carroll County and reside on Polk's own plantation.[16] The marriages of Billy Nevels and Barbara and of Charles and Rosetta were smashed in 1852, when Marshall Polk forced Barbara and Charles to go to Tennessee. Harbert's marriage to Mary was terminated in about 1856, when Sarah Polk sold that persistent fugitive.[17] And in 1860 "the Slaves Giles [and] Manuel . . . [were] taken [by Sarah Polk] from said farm [the Polk plantation]," an action that apparently destroyed Giles's marriage to Daphney, as well as Manuel's to Jane. (These two women were left in Mississippi, whereas Giles and Manuel seem to have been taken to Tennessee, possibly at the request of Sarah's nephew William H. Polk.[18])

Thus fourteen of the twenty-six married (or soon to be married) slaves in the 1849 inventory experienced the forcible disruption of a marriage, and even the marriages of the other dozen slaves could not be solidly based. Half a dozen of the married slaves sought at least temporary escape from the plantation. Thus Gilbert fled from the plantation at least ten times, often toward Tennessee; Addison fled at least four times (twice to Tennessee); and Phil ran at least once, quite possibly in a vain effort to gain permanent freedom. Perry, too (who probably had an abroad marriage), fled once, although the buckshot that Leigh put into his thigh seems to have deterred him from further attempts at escape.[19] Even Henry Carter's marriage to Mariah was threatened when Henry's rage at overseer John Garner impelled this privileged slave to flee. Marina also left the plantation from time to time, overseer John Mairs regarding her as the most disruptive of the female slaves.[20] The marriage of Alphonso and Maria Davis was imperiled by Marshall Polk's original intention to remove Alphonso soon after he had claimed Barbara and Charles.[21] Caroline Johnson was never authorized to see her husband (the Leighs' driver) more than once a week because President Polk refused Leigh's offer to buy her.[22] Of these twenty-six married slaves, therefore, only the pygmy Garrison and his wife, Caroline

Harris, probably never felt the severe pressure on their marriages that arose from their enslaved condition.

If we turn to the twenty-four of James Polk's slaves who, in 1849, were still too young to be married, we find that many of them had already had traumatic experiences of family disruption. Nine of these twenty-four young slaves had already been permanently separated from both parents by sale. These were Caroline Childress (sold away from Tennessee at age fifteen by Sarah Polk's mother); Joe (sold away from Tennessee at age seventeen and one who ran away at least seven times); Jerry, Anderson, and Jason (whom Polk had just bought, each only ten or eleven years old and each separated from both parents); Sally, Agnes, and Calvin (whom President Polk had bought in 1846 at ages twelve or thirteen, each separated from both parents); and Caroline Davis (whom he had just bought at age nineteen).[23] Another of Polk's young slaves had been forcibly taken away from one parent: this was Turner, whose mother, Eve, had been separated from Turner's father when Polk deported Eve from Tennessee in 1836. Five of the other young slaves saw their father only once a week: these were the children of Elizabeth, whose husband, owned by John Leigh, was permitted to visit his family only from Saturday night until daybreak on Monday morning.[24] Consequently, just nine of Polk's young slaves had not thus far experienced some form of family disruption resulting from their enslaved condition; and three of these nine young children died soon after 1849.[25] It is not absolutely certain, of course, that every one of these family disruptions was permanent. It is possible, though improbable—given the absence of evidence to support such a speculation—that Sarah Polk sent Giles and Manuel back to Mississippi at some later time, after taking them away from the plantation in 1860. All in all, it is overwhelmingly clear that the Polks' bondspeople were injured by the enforced instability of family institutions on the plantation.

These slaves' community, too, was not so secure as they would have wished. When James Polk died in 1849, his Mississippi plantation had been established for nearly fifteen years: it then comprised fifty-six slaves,[26] and one might suppose that they would have lived together long enough to have formed a stable community. But in fact eighteen of the bondspeople had come to the plantation within the last four years (half a dozen of them only a couple of months before Polk's death). They brought no community with them, for blacksmith Harry had been torn from his children and his second wife in Carroll County, Mississippi; and although Harbert had been acquired with his wife and her child, each of the other fourteen recently purchased slaves had been bought singly, uprooted from every tie of kinship or familiar locale. They were obliged to start life anew among total strangers, in a totally unknown environment, and wholly without the consolation a free immigrant might have felt—of having chosen such a fate voluntarily.[27] In this respect, Polk's plantation was probably typical of many on the cotton frontier, where it was common for planters to expand their plantations by purchasing slaves from slave traders (who brought them from the upper and middle South). Frontier planters, it was said, raised cotton to buy more slaves and bought more slaves to raise more cotton. The South's booming market for labor facilitated this rapid expansion, with all of its disruptive effects on the slaves' family and community lives.

Perhaps almost equally typical, fewer than half of the slaves Polk sent to Mississippi in 1835 were still there twenty-five years later. Polk assigned twenty-one slaves to his plantation, mostly young and able-bodied;[28] but by 1852 eight of them had died (only two surviving into old age),[29] and four more had been removed from the plantation (two favored slaves by Polk himself, and two disfavored ones by his nephew Marshall Polk, Jr.).[30] Thus by 1860 only nine slaves from the original group were still on the plantation to carry on a sense of community.

In another respect Polk's plantation was not typical. What sense of community his slaves had developed in Mississippi by 1849 was partly produced from circumstances within the Polk family unlikely to have been closely replicated at most other new plantations. When Sam Polk—James Polk's father—died in 1827, he had owned about fifty-three slaves, whom he bequeathed in more or less equal shares to his wife, his six sons, and his one still unmarried daughter.[31] This democratic dispersal of "property" effectively destroyed the slaves' sense of community that had grown at Sam Polk's plantation, near Columbia, Tennessee, before 1827. The unusual thing about the Polk family, however, was that three of James Polk's younger brothers died as bachelors in the 1830s; five of their slaves, coming into James Polk's possession, survived long enough to work at his Mississippi plantation.[32] Another younger brother (who had married and fathered an infant son) also died young, leaving four of his slaves for the support of his mother until she died (when their possession would revert to the infant heir, Marshall Polk, Jr.), and old Mrs. Polk sent these four slaves to work on James Polk's plantation.[33] Furthermore, the financial incompetence of Polk's younger brother William led him to sell five inherited Polk slaves to James in 1838.[34] James Polk bought (or otherwise acquired the use of) four more slaves from his mother and his sister.[35] Consequently, about eighteen Polk family slaves eventually worked at James Polk's plantation, and the reestablishment of these old connections gave the slaves at his Mississippi plantation a greater sense of continuity and community than they could otherwise have felt. Thus when, in about 1842, the slave Joe—bequeathed by old Sam Polk to Sam's wife in Tennessee— was installed as the driver on James Polk's Mississippi plantation, a substantial number of the Mississippi slaves would have recognized him as a previous acquaintance. Similarly, when old Ben, Pompey, Alphonso, and blacksmith Harry arrived at the Mississippi plantation at various times between 1839 and 1848, these Polk family slaves would also have found

old acquaintances or relatives to introduce them to their new life.[36] Because of this reconcentration of family slaves, community ties on the Polk
plantation were probably a little stronger than on most frontier plantations.

Nevertheless, the Polk plantation deviated only to this limited extent
from the typical frontier pattern, where community was constantly eroded
by a planter's purchase of new, young slaves—usually bought separate from
parents or siblings—whenever he thought he could afford to do so, and
where death or removal caused a considerable turnover in the slave population. In their new environment the slaves valiantly built whatever community ties they could. But on the frontier, even more than elsewhere,
the South's booming market for labor power made its semicapitalist economic system much more dynamic—and the strength of the bondspeople's
community institutions much weaker—than in rural Russia, where the
sluggish, traditional economic system fostered the development among serfs
of powerful communal institutions.[37]

9

Privileges

Slave systems, as the historical sociologist Orlando Patterson has argued, frequently offered their bondspeople safety valves, which—by allowing steam to escape—made the system less likely to explode. In Cuba a safety valve was the institution of coartaçion, which permitted a substantial number of slaves to buy their own freedom, especially in cities.[1] In the United States the vast majority of slaves had no prospect of freeing themselves; but on James Polk's plantation there was a different safety valve, a privilege offered to few other American slaves: a system of overtime work (for pay), which Polk apparently copied from his neighbor John Leigh.

Polk's 920-acre plantation was larger than he needed. By 1842 his slaves had cleared two-fifths of this land—more than they could be expected to cultivate by working six days a week. And, as overseer John Mairs cleared some twenty-five acres during each of his first years at the plantation, Polk continued to suffer from a labor shortage even after he started buying large numbers of new slaves in 1846. Some cleared land might have to lie uncultivated unless the proprietor could find a way of inducing his slaves to work overtime.[2] Because Polk was not a sabbatarian, he had no religious scruples about Sunday work, but the custom of giving slaves one day off each week was so strong that he could not contemplate trying to *force* them to labor each Sunday.[3]

John Leigh had the brilliant idea at his plantation of turning over to his slaves some of the land—subdivided into small patches—where, if they wished, they could in their free time grow cotton for themselves.[4] As early as 1844 Polk instituted a similar scheme on his own plantation; from 1844 through 1846 his slaves raised four or five bales of cotton annually, for which he paid them in total an average of $126 per year. By the early 1850s, when the number of hands had grown, payments averaged about $200 a year. Thus the plantation's gross revenues (including the sale of the slaves' overtime crop) were 3 percent to 5 percent larger than they would otherwise have been; some or all of this surplus was paid back to the slaves through an incentive scheme that put cash into the pockets of every slave who worked overtime in this way. The slaves no doubt used their earnings to buy tobacco, sugar, and other supplementary household goods and apparel from traders or local merchants.

In 1846 the median annual sum paid to each overtime worker was $6.08. This was not a staggeringly large amount—for example, it was barely more than 1 percent of the $450 annual salary paid to the slaves' overseer, John Mairs, that year; and the sum was derisory compared to the $3732 cash profit, after payment of all expenses, that President Polk garnered from the plantation's operations.[5] Nevertheless, $6.08 might seem a good deal more than no cash at all, which was what most slaves could expect. The sum might be enlarged if a slave worked especially hard and skillfully on his or her patch of land.

By far the most successful worker in 1846—earning 70 percent more than any other slave—was Henry Carter, who was paid $16.20 for his crop. This was the man who, to forestall a whipping in 1840, had dared to fight overseer John Garner and had then fled 110 miles to seek Silas Caldwell's protection in Tennessee—an episode that had ended in Garner's dismissal. Henry Carter's wife, Mariah, was the infirm woman who had nevertheless increased her value to Mrs. Polk by learning to weave. Henry and Mariah's son, also named Henry, was the enslaved youth whom President Polk had brought to the White House.

Next after Henry Carter in annual earnings was Addison, with $9.50. Addison had previously fled the plantation at least three times. No doubt a major purpose of the incentive system was to stop slaves from running away by giving them a small "stake in society." In Addison's case the scheme failed, for he ran away again in 1848, getting all the way to Dr. Caldwell's plantation in West Tennessee, only to discover that his former protector had died.

Nineteen other slaves earned money in 1846 by raising cotton on their own patches. Of these, only Phil and his wife, Eve, labored as a pair. Five women worked on their own, two of whom had abroad marriages, and the other three women seem to have been unmarried. These women's annual earnings ranged from $4.20 to $7.50. Among the men, the superannuated Ben (a different Ben from the much younger one whom Polk had sold in Tennessee) earned just $2.80, the pygmy Garrison earned $3.60, and the earnings of the other able-bodied males ranged from $3.16 to $9.24.[6] Thus earnings varied greatly, depending on how much overtime labor a slave was willing to undertake. Not every slave felt that the pittances on offer were worth sacrificing much of the little spare time left after the week's six days of unpaid labor were ended.

Start-up problems accompanied the introduction of this scheme. There were two ways in which the slaves might have been paid: they could receive at Christmas a notional sum for each pound of the seed cotton they had picked (before it was ginned), in which case they might receive much less than the cotton actually sold for when it reached New Orleans; or they might defer payment until the ginned cotton was sold, in which case they would get the full price that their crop eventually fetched, but they might have to wait for months or even longer than a full year before Polk decided to sell the crop. There might also be a compromise, in which part payment was made in the year the cotton was picked and the remainder was paid when the last bales of cotton had finally been sold. This is what occurred with the 1844 crop, and it led to unrest among the slaves. At Christmas 1844 a mere $25 was distributed among all the slaves who had raised cotton, and nearly two years later they were still waiting for the rest of their money. "The Negroes are pressing me for their *pay*," the president's agent reported in November 1846, "for 5 bales cotton that they made and shipped with yours in 1844."[7] Payment for the 1845 crop was not quite so slow, two notional installments having been paid that autumn and the final installment paid in October 1846.[8] These delays caused the slaves to request all their money for the 1846 crop by Christmas 1846: "They want for their present crop the money for their cotton in the seed," Robert Campbell explained, "as they believe when it is baled and sent off they do not get justice." Campbell therefore paid for the slaves' whole 1846 crop that December, and—at Polk's instruction—he paid in metallic money (which the slaves liked) rather than in paper money. But in fact they lost out badly that year, for when the price of cotton rose, the president, not the slaves, pocketed the extra cash earned by the sale of their cotton. Although the slaves received almost as much cash from their 1846 crop as (eventually) they received from their 1844 crop, their share of the plantation's gross revenues had fallen nearly half, from 5 percent in 1844 to 2¾ percent in 1846.[9]

Probably the slaves' cognizance of this fact led, once again, to a deferred payment for their 1847 cotton, after the crop had actually been marketed. "As soon as the cotton is sold," the president assured his overseer in March 1848, "I will remit to you the [receipts for] the 4 bags [i.e., bales] belonging to the hands . . . that you may distribute it among them." Six months later prices were still low: Polk still had not sold the cotton, and the slaves were boiling with impatience to receive their cash. Perhaps it was no coincidence that at this moment Addison—the second highest earner in 1846—fled once again, even though this might have led to forfeiture of his share of the 1847 crop. Polk now offered the slaves another fork-tongued compromise: if they were unwilling to wait for him to sell the 1847 crop in New Orleans, he authorized his overseer to sell as many as eight bags of the 1848 crop at the (much lower) price he could get for them in northern Mississippi, so that Mairs could immediately pay the slaves a (much diminished) sum for both the 1847 and the 1848 crops.[10]

Here, as everywhere else in plantation life, there was constant struggle as masters and slaves both tried to improve their own position. In this instance, the masters kept the trump cards in their own hands. If payment was to be made before the crop was sold, the masters decided what price to offer for each pound of seed cotton; and they could use the offer of a good price for the *slaves'* own cotton as an incentive for the slaves to work hard during the week on the *masters'* crop. "For their good performance" in unpaid labor on the 1845 crop, Campbell notified the president, "I have paid them for their cotton in the seed at [the relatively high price of] $1.25 cents per hundred pounds." Similarly, the president sought to elicit good work by the promise of future largesse. "Tell them," he had instructed his overseer in September 1845, "that if I live to return, I will on my first visit to the plantation make them a handsome present."[11] Unfortunately for the slaves, Polk did not live to fulfill this promise.

From the masters' point of view, did the incentive system pay? To some degree the answer must be yes, for the scheme cost them nothing (paid for, as it was, by the slaves' extra, overtime production on land that might otherwise have lain uncultivated). And at first the number of fugitives seemed to decline. It is true that Gilbert, the most persistent of all the Polk dissidents, did flee late in 1844, undeterred by the fact that this might have cost him his share ($6.77, as it turned out[12]) of the proceeds of the slaves' 1844 crop. But during the next nearly four years apparently there was only one fugitive, the newly purchased seventeen-year-old Joe, brought unwillingly to the plantation in January 1847; wholly uninterested in incentive plans, he ran away four times during the next eighteen months. With this exception, Polk's slaves were relatively quiescent during this period, perhaps mainly because overseer John Mairs seemed at first less unpleasant than his predecessors and partly because the incentive system— despite uncertainties about when and how much the slaves would be paid— did indeed offer them a tiny stake in society.

But beginning with Addison's flight in autumn 1848, the number of fugitives returned to its normal high level.[13] Mairs had lost whatever novelty value he had had in 1845, and the incentive system could be seen to be what it was—a tiny mitigation that in no way changed the fundamental nature of the regime. The financial benefits of the incentive system must have seemed minuscule to the slaves when they contrasted their lives with that of the previously truly privileged slave, Long Harry, whom President Polk sent to the plantation in January 1848.

Harry had been the most favored of Polk's Mississippi slaves, and he was the most unusual.[14] For one thing, he communicated with Polk by post, and two of his letters (perhaps written by a white amanuensis) have been preserved and recently printed. By reading between the lines of Harry's transparent flattery, one can attempt to learn something of his mentality.[15] He was a skilled blacksmith, by far the most valuable of Polk's slaves, and for several years he was granted remarkable independence[16]— living thirty-five miles away from Polk's plantation and hired out to employers in Carroll County (at a rental ranging from $275 to $412 per year), who evidently allowed him to earn palpable sums for his own use.

Born in the late 1790s, Harry had never done field labor but had worked instead at the anvil from an early age. For some years his smithy was on a farm near Columbia, Tennessee, which was owned by old Sam Polk but run by James Polk's brother-in-law (and future partner) Dr. Silas Caldwell. Possibly Caldwell taught Harry to read and write. The blacksmith was a striking figure; a friend of James Polk later vividly recalled having seen Harry—"tall & muscular"—working at Caldwell's place in about 1822.[17] In the late 1830s Harry was rented to the overseer of Caldwell's West Tennessee plantation for $200 per year, and by 1841 James Polk was renting him to Carroll County (Mississippi) employers at an annual fee of $412. Even when the fee declined—to $325, then $300, then $275 (as Harry became older, and when low cotton prices before 1846 reduced what employers felt they could afford)—Harry was a much better source of income to James Polk than any of his other slaves.[18] The cash Polk received from renting out Harry was far more than the sum that Polk paid annually to all of his plantation slaves—about $126 per year during the mid-1840s—for the cotton they sold him through his incentive plan.

Harry's relatively independent life in Carroll County suited him, and when he sensed that Polk might curb his autonomy, Harry did everything possible to ingratiate himself with his master and to present reasons why he should be permitted to stay in Carroll County. Apparently Harry and his wife had been forcibly separated from each other for several years when he was working in West Tennessee and her master had deported her from central Tennessee to Mississippi; but now Harry was again near his wife and several of his children, and he wanted to stay with them. He seems to have gotten along with several of his employers in Carroll County and to have made a niche for himself in the local society (being on betting terms with some of the white men). Harry had grounds for supposing his independence would be reduced if he came under the direct control of his imperious master and of Polk's overseer in Yalobusha County.

For several years the interests of James Polk and his most valuable slave appeared to be congruent: Polk offered Harry the remarkably independent life of a highly skilled artisan working without close supervision, while Harry supplied Polk with a good source of income at a time when the need for a blacksmith at Polk's plantation was not yet large. But the arrangement was less satisfactory to Polk than he might have wished. Year after year there were problems in getting the employers who rented Harry to pay up. The greatest difficulty centered on collecting Harry's rental fees for the years 1836 and 1838, which came to a combined total of $400 and which, with accumulated unpaid interest, were valued by 1844 at $516. George Moore, Caldwell's overseer, had rented Harry for these two years, but Moore had never paid and he died insolvent. When bankruptcy proceedings finally ended in 1844, Polk could collect only 18 cents on each of the dollars owed him. Similar, if less drastic, problems arose in other years. Polk could at first collect only $50 of the $412 owed him for Harry's 1841 hire, and he was obliged to go to court to collect the rest. Only after another suit could President Polk's agent secure full payment of the 1846 rental, and this story was repeated a year later.[19]

Meanwhile, in 1846 the problem became acute because Polk was in Washington, unable to come to Mississippi to dun cash out of reluctant debtors; Polk's agent, Robert Campbell, balked at spending the time required to track down these debtors. In the correspondence between the president and his agent, Polk professed to wish to leave the decision about Harry's future to the blacksmith himself, but Polk soon decided to order Harry to leave his children permanently and go to the plantation. Harry, by now a widower, had recently remarried, and when Polk learned about this, it did not alter his determination that Harry must stay at the plantation. Harry was not permitted to rejoin his wife, nor did Polk try to buy her.[20] Campbell, meanwhile, accused Harry—as white men liked to accuse independent black men—of drinking more than was good for him.[21] Had James Polk's ears been so attuned, he might have found irony in a white man's charging a black man with intemperance: Polk's father had died of drink at the age of fifty-five, and James Polk's brother Frank had died of alcoholism at the age of twenty-eight.[22]

Blacksmith Harry bruited it about that his eyesight was failing—"he is so blind," Campbell reported in 1846, "that he cannot make a horse shoe nail." Doubtless Harry hoped to make Polk suppose that his services on the plantation would not be valuable.[23] But once the president made up his mind, he was inflexible: Harry must leave his children and move to the plantation by January 1848. This revocation of Harry's main privilege proved profitable to the Polks: besides doing the plantation work and training the young slave Alphonso in the blacksmith's trade, Harry earned money for the Polks by working for neighboring planters; he also made ironware, which the overseer sold in the local shops. By these means, Harry earned for Polk's widow in 1851—after deducting the cost of his materials and not including the value of his work for the Polk plantation itself—some $400. This was even more than he had normally earned for the Polks when he was rented out; for an "old" slave, already well into his fifties, these were remarkable earnings, putting a large query beside any notion that Harry had a serious drinking problem or that he was fast losing his sight.[24]

Harry was a proud man, and he sometimes addressed white people with a strong sense of his own worth. Soon after James Polk died, his executor Daniel Graham (who had held a high post in the U.S. Treasury during Polk's administration) visited the plantation on estate business and he asked Harry to repair a fine metal tongue on his elegant carriage. On Graham's return journey to Tennessee the tongue broke, and he threatened not to pay for Harry's work; but Harry resolutely requested that Graham pay, insisting that the "carage tongue was a fancy piece of work": even before it first broke, it had never been strong, and Harry could not be held responsible if Graham chose to drive a fancy carriage "on those bumpy rodes from here to Tennessee." Whether this reply secured payment from Graham is unknown, but it indicates Harry's reluctance to be pushed around by a white man. Harry's elder brother had been Jack Long, and perhaps some family disinclination to be submissive had led (in 1838) to Jack's being killed by James Walker's overseer.[25]

When Harry wrote to James Polk in the 1840s, however, his tone was different from that used to address Graham, for he enjoyed a privileged position he did not wish to jeopardize. Harry never, of course, uttered a word to Polk of his feelings when his brother Jack had been killed. Instead, he pulled out all the stops of apparently servile deference, especially when referring to Polk's mother. "Tell the old Lady Harry is hir se[r]vint untill d[e]ath," he addressed Polk in 1842, "& would be Gl[a]d to see Hir on[c]e mor[e]." Even though Harry's children were not owned by the Polks—and the blacksmith's virility, therefore, had not financially benefited them—Harry nevertheless spoke proudly of having sired eleven children, all of whom were still living and all of whom he named in this letter. He reminded Polk that "I have ben faithful over the anvill Block Ever [since] 1811." Cushioned among these personal appeals lay the real point of the letter: the blacksmith warned Polk that, at a time when cotton prices were low, his employer would not be able to afford quite so high a rental payment in 1843 as in 1842. Evidently Harry wanted to stay with his employer, and the letter was skillfully calculated to improve Harry's chances of doing so, even if a lower rent were offered.[26]

The most complex surviving communications from Harry were written two and a half years later, after news of Polk's victory in the 1844 presidential election had reached Mississippi. By now Harry had a different employer. As in the earlier missive, Harry sought to ensure that his next employer would be one who treated him well; but he did *not* wish to remain with his current employer, his (faint) praise of that man notwithstanding. To ensure that Polk did not misunderstand this letter (which was designed to avoid offense to Harry's present employer if it should fall into his hands), Harry soon, surreptitiously, got another white man to send Polk a candid communication in which Harry made utterly plain that "I do not want to live with Mr. Kimbrough any longer."[27]

In both of these 1844 letters the blacksmith aimed to insinuate himself with Polk so that Polk would let him continue to live near his family in his highly privileged position near Carrollton. In the longer of these letters Harry affected a suitably deferential manner, twice calling himself "an humble negro." Yet Harry adopted a remarkably familiar tone: twice he addressed the president-elect as "Master Jimmy." How many white men called Polk "Jimmy" to his face? Perhaps Harry still thought of Polk's mother as his mistress, and he therefore felt able to accost her son—elevated though Polk's position now was—in the same terms he would have used thirty years earlier.

At this time dozens of Democratic Party activists—hoping to secure jobs in the new Polk administration—were sending Polk ingratiating letters, assuring him of their joy at his election, boasting how much they had contributed to this happy result, and building their credit with him at the moment he began to distribute the spoils of office. Harry's strategy was identical (though the favor he sought was not an office in the new administration but security of tenure in his privileged Mississippi situation). Harry's employers seem to have allowed him enough free time so that by working at his trade he could earn a not inconsiderable income for himself. He had sufficient money to make big bets on the outcome of the presidential election, and naturally he backed Polk (it would scarcely have won his master's favor had he done otherwise). The scale of Harry's wealth may be judged by his winnings when Polk was the victor: $25 cash, eleven pairs of boots, one barrel of flour, lots of tobacco, and forty gallons of whiskey.

Perhaps much of the tobacco, and even several pairs of boots, were bet with other slaves; but surely Harry had made most of these wagers with white men. No doubt they had challenged him to give his reasons for thinking Polk deserved to win, and this had led Harry to make some "speaches" for his master. Possibly even more persuasive than speeches in winning votes for Polk was the distribution of whiskey; most of Harry's forty gallons of that liquid appear to have been dispersed *before* the election through white Democrats who offered Harry feudal protection. During the campaign Harry had run into difficulties with the local Whigs; and (he assured Polk that) he had "treated [the whiskey] all out in Electionaring for you through my [Democratic] friends who stood by me in Electionaring Troble. I tell you Master Jimmy that I made some big speaches for you and though an humble negro I made some votes for you." When the news of Polk's narrow electoral victory reached Carrollton, the disappointed Whigs sarcastically addressed Harry as though he himself were the victor. "I have been so over Joyed at the newse of your Elevation," Harry flattered his master,

> that I have hardly Known what I was and some of the whigs call me President to Plag[u]e me and to ridicule you. But this I know, that I have hardly Eate, drank, slep[t], or worked any since I heared the Glorious newse. You may be assured my dear Master Jimmy that I have done all in my Power for you. Though an humble negro I made some votes, for I have ben betting and lousing on you for the last siveral years [Polk having been defeated in both 1841 and 1843 when he had sought reelection as governor], but I have made it all up now.[28]

This grand display of fealty won Harry cash and, more important, it won him favor; for three more years Polk permitted him to remain in his privileged position in Carroll County. Privileges could always be revoked, however. Polk's agents eventually proved unwilling to continue chasing down Harry's employers to collect the annual fee for renting him. In January 1848 Polk finally tore Harry from his children and his second wife and forced him to live at the Yalobusha plantation, where his independence was curtailed.

Grants of privileges to slaves were common in the American South. Although those offered to Polk's bondspeople were somewhat different from the ones often granted elsewhere, the pattern was the same. A handful of slaves—like blacksmith Harry; Polk's personal servant, Elias, in Tennessee; or Henry Carter's young son, who served in the White House—might be afforded a remarkably privileged life, such as Harry enjoyed for several years in Carroll County, Mississippi. But a privilege of this kind might at any moment be withdrawn, as it was from Harry in January 1848. Alongside special privileges offered to individual slaves were general privileges—which might be extended to all the slaves on a plantation—such as the "privilege" of raising cotton in their own time for their own profit. Although such privileges did not alter the basic terms of servitude, masters liked to dwell on their own generosity in making these grants. But the more important realities at James Polk's plantation were registered not by these privileges but by the flood of male fugitives; by the balance sheet, which did indeed provide Polk's widow with the large (if not wholly regular) income at which her husband had aimed; by the master's avidity in entering the market for labor power—usually that of very young workers, separated from parents, siblings, or friends—in order to increase the revenues from his semicapitalist enterprise; by the dismal record of child mortality; by the frequency of early death among his young adult slaves (especially the young women); and by the relative fragility of the slaves' family and community institutions. Polk was able to overlook the inhumanity of the system and the evidence of his slaves' discontent because—having determined either to win or to lose more money by investing in a Mississippi cotton plantation—he had bet successfully, and by the late 1840s his cotton business was paying well.

Blacksmith Harry, too, had made a wager (on the outcome of the 1844 election) and this bet had, temporarily, served Harry's interests. Was the same thing true for the American people when, by their votes, they bet that year on a Polk presidency?

II

PRESIDENT

10

Polk's Early Response to
the Antislavery Movement

President James Polk was a product of the Jacksonian Democratic age. He represented the entrepreneurial and democratic spirit of the burgeoning southwestern planting frontier, not the relatively elitist spirit of the old Virginia Dynasty—of Presidents George Washington, Thomas Jefferson, James Madison, and James Monroe. But Polk did not possess the military reputation and commanding personality of his mentor, President Andrew Jackson, nor was Polk—as contrasted with Senators Henry Clay, Daniel Webster, and John C. Calhoun—a towering orator. Consequently some contemporaries made the mistake of writing him off as an insignificant figure: "Who is James K. Polk?" his Whig rivals taunted during the 1844 presidential campaign. Polk became known as America's first dark horse presidential candidate, nominated not because he was nationally famous and a proven political winner but, allegedly, because he could be foisted on an unsuspecting public by backstage managers who were devising secret schemes in smoke-filled rooms.

Although Polk's nomination was indeed the result of backstage maneuvers and although he had indeed been repudiated by the voters of Tennessee both in 1841 and in 1843, when he unsuccessfully ran for a second term as governor of that state, he was by no means insignificant. In a House of Representatives where congressmen—whose abilities generally were not transcendent—often served only a term or two, Polk's fourteen-year service and his methodical cast of mind set him apart. Understanding banking, he had led President Andrew Jackson's assault on the Bank of the United States. Polk was a workaholic who had labored hours and hours, intelligently, over the details of tariff legislation. His four years as speaker of the House of Representatives (1835 to 1839) had given him valuable experience in controlling that unruly body. By the time Polk was elected governor of Tennessee in 1839, he was already thinking he might one day become president of the United States, and his actions were those of an ambitious man.

The New York Democrat Martin Van Buren was then president, and he was sure to run for reelection in 1840. Polk's strategy was twofold: while he must assure Southern white people that he was sound on issues important to them, he must at the same time make himself attractive to enough Northern Democrats to secure nomination for a national office. At first the desired post was the vice-presidency, and when Van Buren was renominated for president in 1840, Polk hoped (in vain) for the vice-presidential slot. Even after Van Buren lost the 1840 presidential election, he remained the front-runner for the Democrats' presidential nomination once more in 1844, and Polk again sought the vice-presidential nomination on Van Buren's ticket.

But by 1844 circumstances differed substantially from those of 1840. A powerful Democratic faction, strongest in the South, had concluded that Van Buren was unelectable and should therefore be replaced as the party's nominee. When a strong movement had developed in 1843 to annex Texas, Southern Democrats sensed they had an issue that could enable them to defeat even the popular prospective Whig nominee, Henry Clay. To profit from this situation, Polk had to play his cards carefully. He had to robustly declare himself for the speedy annexation of Texas. But he also had to publicly support the nomination of Van Buren (whose stance on Texas long remained unknown) so that Van Buren's associates would back Polk for the vice-presidency. And if, by any chance, Van Buren should fail to secure the presidential nomination, Polk and some of his allies hoped Van Buren's lieutenants might turn to Polk for the presidency because Polk was one of the few leading Southerners who had seemed to remain steadfastly loyal to Van Buren during the runup to the Democrats' 1844 nominating convention.

For Polk to pursue this double strategy required him to avoid saying things about slavery that might alienate Northern Democrats. He might, of course, express himself in favor of annexing Texas, but he must not declare that slavery was a positive good, as Secretary of State John C. Calhoun notoriously did in an official letter of April 1844. Unlike Calhoun, Polk must present himself as a moderate Southern Democrat. The Northern public must not be encouraged to enquire into Polk's convictions about slavery. And because Polk's early career centered on economic issues such as the bank war, historians have also not enquired much about his early stance on slavery. His record turns out to have been somewhat less moderate than has been supposed.

During his first ten years in Washington (1825–35), Congressman Polk concentrated on such issues as the tariff and the Bank of the United States, and he seldom addressed the House of Representatives on the subject of slavery. In the few addresses he did make, he always supported what he supposed to be the interests of slaveholders. In 1826 he defended the U.S. Constitution's three-fifths clause, which granted the slave states extra political power (both in the House of Representatives and in the presidential electoral college) by counting three-fifths of the slaves as part of the total population that determined the number of a state's congressional seats. Polk implied that enslaved black people were an irksome presence in the United States, for which his contemporary generation of white people bore no responsibility: "This species of population was found amongst us [in 1776]. It had been entailed upon us by our ancestors, and was viewed as a common evil." Objectionable though this presence might be, there was nothing to be done about it; and the slaves (or at least, three-fifths of them) ought properly to be counted for representation because they would also be counted in allocating direct taxes among the states, should a war ever require the imposition of direct taxes. Unlike other sorts of property, this type might legitimately be counted in apportioning representation and direct taxes because slaves "were a species of property that differed from all other: they were rational; they were human beings." Polk's language was not clear. He spoke as though he felt that slavery itself were objectionable, for he remarked that "some of the States which then [in 1776] possessed it ["this species of population"] have since gotten clear of it." Yet the thrust of his argument was that no moral opprobrium should rest on the South for the existence of slavery. The South happened to have slaves, and it was perfectly fair that this form of property "should at least be in part represented" in apportioning congressional seats and electoral college votes.[1]

If in 1826 Polk seemed to feel that slavery's existence required some hint of apology or explanation, he never again displayed public embarrassment on the subject. In 1830 he told the House of Representatives (when it was debating a bill providing for the penitentiary punishment of criminals within the District of Columbia) that the penitentiary would be inappropriate for bondspeople because imprisonment "did not amount . . . to such an efficient restraint [upon slaves] as was necessary." Flogging was a superior restraint, both because "a slave dreads the punishment of stripes more than he does imprisonment" and because flogging a slave would have "a beneficial effect upon his fellow-slaves"—instilling into them the dread that was the best way of keeping them under control.[2] A year later Polk aligned himself with thirty-one other Representatives in opposing, unsuccessfully, a proposal from the Virginia Congressman Charles Mercer to urge the strengthening of America's feeble international commitment to enforcing the ban on the African slave trade.[3]

During the presidential election year of 1832, this courageous Virginian, Charles Mercer, was the object of Polk's open attack in an early exercise of the "politics of loyalty"—a competition among Southern politicians to outdo each other in professions of fidelity to the supposed interests of the slave states. "Colonizationists" like Mercer and, most notably, Henry Clay—the presidential candidate then opposing the bid of President Andrew Jackson for a second term—demonstrated their uneasiness about slavery. They wished to encourage slaveholders to free slaves voluntarily, on the condition that the freed people would be deported from the United States. To provide a financial incentive, colonizationists favored granting national or state funds to subsidize black people's deportation to Liberia, on the west coast of Africa. (Some colonizationists advocated deporting *free* blacks first, and not every colonizationist thought that free blacks should be allowed to decide for themselves whether or not to leave the United States.) Although Andrew Jackson, too, had favored colonization in 1817, when the Colonization Society's only declared aim was to remove free blacks from the United States, he (unlike Clay) had never wanted to use federal funds to encourage the manumission of slaves.[4] By 1832 Polk, having just established his new cotton plantation in West Tennessee, was looking forward to its first revenues, and he seems to have been eager to embarrass colonizationists. He probably had two reasons: he wanted no federal action of any sort in an antislavery direction, and he was glad to try to discredit a movement that, however cautiously, criticized slavery.

Forty English people, residents of the Cotswold town of Cirencester, presented Polk a splendid opportunity to prod a hornets' nest. These Britons petitioned Congress to aid the American Colonization Society, and in April 1832 Virginia Congressman Charles Mercer presented their petition to the House of Representatives, which at first referred it to its committee on colonization. To modern eyes the petition might seem outrageous, for it declared that "a mixed population of whites and blacks cannot . . . cordially unite," and it therefore advocated a permanent separation of the races through the "colonization" of the blacks. But to Polk the petition was outrageous for a different reason: it alleged (in Polk's paraphrase) that "human liberty could not long exist in a country where the mixed condition of freedom and slavery was found." For a bunch of foreigners to interfere "in the slightest degree [in this question] was uncalled for and impertinent."[5]

Polk called for reconsideration of the original vote on the Cirencester colonization petition. Like the proponents a few years later of the gag rule (which prescribed immediate rejection of antislavery petitions), Polk sought—instead of referring the petition to committee—some more summary way "to dispose of it so as to prevent similar annoyances in the future." He wanted to intimidate Mercer into withdrawing the petition, threatening that "if the debate [which Polk had instigated] was to go on, [Polk] warned gentlemen that a discussion would ensue, such as perhaps had never been witnessed in that Hall." As though in response to this cue, a South Carolina congressman soon rose to threaten war. Congressman James Blair declaimed that the Virginian Mercer, in giving countenance to the antislavery movement, was a "recreant to the cause" of the slave states. Furthermore, Blair argued that when the slave issue was seriously moved, "the South would meet it . . . in the open field, where powder and cannon would be their orators, and their arguments lead and steel." This debate occurred six months *before* the South Carolina election that placed a "nullificationist" majority in command of the state legislature; and the issue here was explicitly the central one, slavery, not the surrogate issue of the tariff. The provoker of this angry interchange was James Polk, who seemed to feel that slavemasters' best interests were served by isolating Virginia colonizationists and cutting them down to size, indirectly striking a blow at that arch-colonizationist, Henry Clay.[6]

The impulse that led Polk to provoke this debate in 1832—the wish to dispose of a petition from outsiders who criticized (however mildly) the institution of slavery, "so as to prevent similar annoyances in the future"— impelled the House of Representatives in May 1836 to try to dispose of *all* antislavery petitions by receiving but then immediately rejecting them. Many of these petitions prayed for Congress to abolish slavery in the federal District of Columbia—or at least to abolish the slave trade there—since lawmaking for the federal district was the responsibility of the national government. Polk was by now speaker of the House, and his procedural rulings enabled slave-state representatives, with the support of many Northern Democrats, to ram a gag rule through the House. Speaker Polk (in the historian Leonard Richards's words) had "stacked" the committee that drafted this new rule "with eight administration men and one border-state Whig." When the committee reported, Speaker Polk let advocates of a gag rule defend it at length; but when he saw former President John Quincy Adams rise to challenge the committee report, Polk gave the floor instead to a committee member, who called "the previous question," thus ensuring an immediate vote before an opponent of the measure had a chance to argue against it.[7] (These tactics were similar to those President Polk used to propel a declaration of war against Mexico through the House of Representatives a decade later.) The gag rule proved counterproductive for the proslavery cause because John Quincy Adams (and others) battled against it during the next eight years and—by defending white people's right to petition—gained the support of many thousands of Northerners who would never have supported the abolitionist movement itself.

As speaker, Polk had not needed to avow his own beliefs about the gag rule, except insofar as they might be inferred from his rulings on procedural matters. But when Polk became governor of Tennessee in 1839, he found an opportunity to publicize his views. Proponents of the gag rule in 1836 had been divided into two groups. On the one hand was John C. Calhoun's position, adopted by South Carolina's James Hammond, that Congress had no constitutional right to abolish slavery, even in the national capital of Washington, D.C., and that therefore Congress should refuse even to "receive" a petition praying for abolition in the district. On the other hand was the belief that Congress probably *did* have power over slavery in the district, though its proponents did not want Congress to exercise this power. South Carolina's Henry Pinckney (quietly backed by the 1836 Democratic presidential candidate, Martin Van Buren) therefore proposed that Congress should "receive" these petitions before immediately—without discussion—rejecting them. Neither Hammond's nor Pinckney's approach afforded antislavery petitioners the slightest hope of getting their ideas considered by Congress. Pinckney's resolution was adopted in 1836 because it promised to embarrass Van Buren less, with Northern voters, than would Calhoun's doctrine.[8] But when Polk finally expressed his own opinion in 1839, it turned out that by then he adhered to Calhoun's position. "To disturb [slavery] within the District of Columbia," Governor Polk averred, "would be a palpable violation . . . of the clear meaning and obvious intention of the framers of the Constitution. [The federal government has no power] to take cognizance of, or in any manner or to any extent to interfere with, or to act upon the subject of domestic slavery." Thus, in Polk's view, it would be unconstitutional for the federal government to take any antislavery action in the district or in the territories or to promote colonization.[9]

Privately, Polk may well have adhered to Calhoun's view long before he made his public avowal in October 1839. His own private circumstances seemed to be consistent with his new public stance. During the twelve months before October 1839, Polk had poured $14,000 into his Mississippi planting enterprise, doubling his capital investment there.[10] This was a huge sum for a man whose gubernatorial salary during the next two years would be fixed at a mere $2,000 per annum. Thus when he made his public avowal, Polk—who had already had a big financial interest in ensuring that the federal government should never "to any extent . . . act upon the subject of domestic slavery"—had just decided to greatly magnify that interest. His political conviction was congruent with what appeared to be his own financial interest.

Governor Polk's view of the limits on congressional power triumphed the next year when a renewed loyalty competition during the run-up to the 1840 presidential campaign led the House of Representatives to accept Calhoun's position. The House replaced the Pinckney gag rule with the even more Draconian rule that Congress would not even "receive" any petition bearing on slavery in the District of Columbia or anywhere else.

If Polk responded to the antislavery movement by attempting to throttle it with a gag rule (and by alleging that the Constitution banned the federal government from any type of antislavery action, anywhere), he also seized on abolitionism as a stick with which to beat his Whig opponents. As governor of Tennessee, he employed this strategy during the presidential election of 1840, when he worked with close political allies, such as Tennessee's U.S. Senator Felix Grundy, to cover the Whigs with abolitionist tar.

"Abolitionism," as used by Polk and his coadjutors, embraced any effort that might be construed as arising from a spirit hostile to slavery or sympathetic to free blacks. Were the Whig presidential candidate, William Henry Harrison, to be victorious, Harrison's administration was likely—Polk's Democratic allies claimed—to abolish slavery in the District of Columbia, to ban the interstate slave trade, to withdraw "in every possible way . . . the protection guaranteed by the Constitution to slave property," and to encourage "those who [by aiding fugitive slaves] steal it." Polk's allies blasted Southern Whigs who refused to support the most drastic version of the congressional ban on the consideration of antislavery petitions. A Whig committee in the House of Representatives came under fire for iniquitously blocking a proposed ban on free blacks' testimony "in courts martial held in the Slaveholding States or Territories." Whigs in Pennsylvania were lambasted for opposing the state's new ban on blacks' voting. These examples were all said to illustrate the insidious influence of abolitionists on the Whig Party.[11]

The Southern Democrats' principle was guilt by association. In a public letter to Senator Grundy, Governor Polk charged, "The Federalists [i.e., the Whigs, whom Polk always called Federalists] and their allies the abolitionists [are acting] against the cherished principles of our Republican institutions."[12] Southern voters, Grundy and his associates urged, should "reject and repudiate all connection, direct, or indirect, with Abolition and its allies." The securing of slave property, they declared, was by far the most important issue presented to Southern voters, in comparison to which all other political disputes sank into insignificance. "Of what importance," these Democratic leaders cried,

> is it to [the Southern people] whether we have a national Bank or not; a protective tariff or not; internal improvements or not; if a faction shall obtain a controlling power in the Government, which shall rob them of their property, desolate their fields, destroy their dwellings, and massacre their families? This subject transcends and supercedes all others.[13]

"Property" here means slaves.

Polk and his allies threatened during the 1840 campaign that if abolitionist propaganda were not suppressed and if abolitionists gained power in Washington through a Whig victory, disunion was likely to follow. Thus Governor Polk wrote publicly on October 2, 1840, that circulation of abolitionist documents (such as the proceedings of the World Anti-Slavery Convention in London) might provoke slave insurrection and "may endanger [the Union's] existence if the wicked agitation . . . is persisted in."[14] The previous day the Tennessee Democratic Central Committee (which Polk had called into existence, and whose actions he seems to have orchestrated) had published an address that quoted the national Democratic Party's resolution that

> all efforts . . . made to induce Congress to interfere with questions of slavery [e.g., in the District of Columbia or in the territories], or to take incipient steps in relation thereto [e.g., by receiving antislavery petitions], are calculated to lead to the most alarming and dangerous consequences, and . . . all such efforts have an inevitable tendency to . . . endanger the stability and permanency of the Union, and ought not to be countenanced.[15]

This pronouncement of the national Democratic Party did not, however, go far enough toward condoning disunionism to satisfy Polk and his associates. The Tennessee party's address noted, with ill-concealed gusto, that the manifesto issued by Southern Democratic leaders in July (quoted in preceding paragraphs here) "has given great offense to the Abolition party in the North," and the abolitionist leaders there had urged abolitionists to vote for Harrison. Polk's colleagues advised that on election day Southerners should remember the abolitionists' support of the Whigs: the Southern people should "not allow their dearest interests to be trifled with by politicians, aiming to acquire power by means which set at defiance the compromises of the Constitution, and must if not resisted terminate in the loss of our glorious Union."[16] Evidence of this sort indicates the centrality of the slavery issue to Southern Democratic politicians and their eagerness to condone disunionism as a justifiable response to the antislavery movement.

Revisionist historians have in recent years doubted that slavery was the principal issue. What most affronted these Southern leaders and their constituents, it has been asserted, was the threat to their republican equality (and thus the challenge to their honor) implicit in the antislavery campaign.[17] But the evidence just examined does not support this interpretation. True, the July manifesto signed by Southern Democratic congressmen *did* claim that a Whig victory would "make the Southern States and Southern Statesmen, not the equals, as the Constitution makes them, but the provinces, inferiors and vassals of the Northern States and Northern men." However, this brief reference to degradation of the South was relegated to the peroration of thirteen closely packed pages devoted otherwise solely to the slavery question. These Southern congressmen seemed as sophisticated as any modern historian in analyzing the roll-call votes on the Pinckney gag rule in order to detect the perfidy of Northern, and even some Southern, Whigs on this issue. Only after blasting, page after page, "Abolition and its [Whig] allies" for undermining slavery, do the authors add to the substance of their real charges against the antislavery movement an appeal to honor and to Southern equality.[18]

Polk and his Tennessee allies had *not* made slavery their central issue at the beginning of the presidential campaign. The first Tennessee Democratic address (published on July 4, 1840, a fortnight before the Southern Democratic congressmen in Washington composed their onslaught on abolitionism) had downplayed slavery. Although that early address briefly accused Harrison of alliance with abolitionists and claimed that many delegates to the Whig national convention were abolitionists, these were the only references to the slavery question.[19] Probably Tennessee Democrats feared that if they stressed the slavery question, their incumbent presidential candidate—the New Yorker, President Martin Van Buren—might not seem so attractive to Tennessee voters as the Virginia-born Harrison; and therefore they sought at first to skirt that issue. Apparently it was only toward the end of the campaign, when their focus on economic issues proved not to galvanize enough Democratic support in Tennessee, that the state's Democratic leaders—almost in desperation—gave greater emphasis to the slavery question and to the alleged alliance of Whigs with abolitionists.[20] This strategy failed: Harrison not only won the national election but even decisively defeated Van Buren in Tennessee (where Polk had won the governorship by a narrow margin in 1839).[21] What Southern Democrats needed for the next presidential election, in 1844, was a slavery-related issue with which to assault the Whigs more effectively than by accusing them of being soft on the (rather feeble) abolitionist movement. During 1843 and 1844, John Tyler—the Virginian who succeeded to the presidency after Harrison's death in 1841—and his Secretary of State Abel Upshur (and after Upshur's death, Secretary of State John C. Calhoun) furnished the Southern Democrats with exactly the issue they needed: Texas.

Polk, whether defending the three-fifths clause or opposing greater international cooperation in enforcing the ban on the African slave trade, never wavered in defending what he supposed to be the interests of the slave states. He claimed that the federal government had no power to touch slavery, not even in the District of Columbia or in the territories. He aimed to prohibit all expression of antislavery sentiment in Washington and to destroy the Whig Party by taunting it for its supposed alliance with abolitionism. Polk's policy typified that of almost the whole Southern Democratic Party.

This policy, it may appear, was unlikely to serve the long-term interests of slavemasters, for the strength of Northern antislavery sentiment was certain to grow and eventually to express itself in those areas subject to federal jurisdiction—that is, the federal capital in Washington, D.C., and the federal territories. Slavemasters might better have confined their defense of slavery to the states where it already existed. The Tenth Amendment was understood by almost everyone, both in the North and in the South, to ban federal action against slavery within the Southern states: "the powers not delegated to the United States by the Constitution, nor prohibited by it to the States, are reserved to the States respectively, or to the people." This constitutional guarantee offered slavemasters all the security they needed for years and years to come.

The long-term interest of slavemasters evidently required that they distinguish between the various strands of antislavery opinion. Genuine abolitionists remained a small minority in the North until well into 1862, when shattering military defeats finally convinced many reluctant Northerners that emancipation might after all be their best route to winning the Civil War and securing their other goals. Before then, the great majority of Northerners sought at most a limited antislavery policy, falling far short of what abolitionists desired. Of course, Northerners could not be expected to accept indefinitely the ban in Washington of every antislavery utterance nor the falsehood that everyone who felt uneasy about slavery was in the pocket of "abolitionists" nor—above all else—disunion as a legitimate means of resisting the antislavery movement. But nearly all Northerners accepted the Tenth Amendment's ban on federal antislavery action within the Southern states. It might seem that it was in the long-term interest of slaveholders to conciliate moderate antislavery opinion in the North instead of seeking only those "doughface" Northern allies who could be expected to accede to most proslavery demands.

Why did not James Polk pursue some such conciliatory policy, which would so clearly (with hindsight) have served the long-term interests of the slaveholders? One answer is that he was himself a slavemaster, expanding his enslaved labor force as rapidly as he felt he could afford to do, caught up in his own short-term financial aims, and oblivious to the long-term interests of other slavemasters.

A second answer is that it suited Polk's short-term political interests to picture the antislavery movement as an undifferentiated mass of abolitionists (rather than to distinguish between the various elements within this complex movement): then he could charge the whole Whig Party with being soft on abolitionism.

A third answer lies, perhaps, in Polk's lack of faith in paper constitutions, specifically, in his lack of faith in the binding power of the U.S. Constitution. Ever since the French Revolution, the world has seen that an apparently well-constructed paper constitution can prove an inadequate guarantee that rulers will actually be bound by the constraints theoretically imposed on them. Today we understand that a constitution needs to be supported by a political culture that constrains the rulers to accept the limits theoretically imposed on them, and we observe that it sometimes takes fifty years or more for such a culture to grow and to solidify itself so that the rulers do in fact feel constrained to remain within the limits set out in the constitution.[22] Some such apprehension may have guided Polk. When he was born in 1795, it was only twenty years since a centralizing power (the British government) had attempted to fasten unrepresentative, outside rule on the colonies of North America; and when Polk was already nineteen years old (in 1815), a British army appeared at New Orleans to attempt again to dictate terms to the Americans. Sensing a parallel between British dominion and Federalist rule, Polk feared that the paper U.S. Constitution—which had only gone into operation six years before Polk was born—might alone prove an inadequate constraint on the Federalists and their Whig successors. A political culture must be grown that would really confine the "Federalists" within the limits theoretically imposed on them by the Tenth Amendment. It was not enough to wait passively for the paper constraints theoretically imposed to enforce themselves. Rather, defenders of slavery must actively ensure that a safe political culture be established: Northern politicians must understand that they *must* be bound by the Tenth Amendment. The way to develop this culture, Polk thought, was to establish the principle that Congress must never interfere *anywhere* with slavery—not in the states, not in the District of Columbia, not in the territories. Only by establishing some such principle could the South be assured that Northern politicians would in fact be bound by the Tenth Amendment and would keep their hands off slavery in the Southern states.

These three reasons go far to explain Polk's shortsightedness, and the same reasons apply to Democratic leaders in other parts of the South. But they do not tell the whole story. Polk's stance on Texas annexation and the issues arising therefrom may throw light on these matters.

II

Texas and the Mexican War

James Polk was nominated for president in 1844 mainly because Southern Democratic leaders wanted to increase the prosperity and political
power of slavemasters (as well as would-be slavemasters and prospective
emigrants from the non-slaveholding class) by annexing the huge slaveholding republic of Texas—which had declared independence from
Mexico eight years earlier. Polk won the presidential election by a narrow
margin, and within a few months Texas was acquired. A war with Mexico
soon followed, in which the Americans' breathtaking military victories
against that relatively weak nation perhaps fed the recklessness with which
Deep South politicians later embarked on secession, imagining that, if this
led to war, Southern soldiers might reenact against the North the glorious
triumphs with which they had routed the Mexicans.

The Civil War arose from a long-festering dispute about whether slavery was to be legalized in the Western territories. After 1854 that dispute
focused on Southern efforts to legalize slavery in Kansas; but by 1850 civil
war already threatened over the status of slavery in the Mexican Cession.
This was the huge area (including modern California, New Mexico, Arizona, Nevada, Utah, much of Colorado, and a bit of Wyoming) seized from
Mexico in the Mexican War of 1846–48. That war had been precipitated
by a border dispute between the Republic of Mexico and the independent Republic of Texas. When the United States annexed Texas in 1845,
President Polk had adopted the Texans' border claims, and the Mexican
War had quickly ensued. To understand the origins of the Civil War, therefore, it is necessary to consider the annexation of Texas.

So securely is Texas now embedded in the American political and
economic fabric that the events of 1844–45 have an air of inevitability or
even the aura of a great national triumph. Yet Polk was elected by a hairs-
breadth in 1844: he would have been defeated in the presidential election
if just a few thousand Whiggish voters in New York State had cast their
ballots for the Whig candidate—the Kentucky slavemaster Henry Clay—
instead of throwing them away on the candidacy of the Liberty Party's
James Birney.[1] If Polk had lost the election, there is good reason to suppose that reasonable American territorial aspirations, extending to the
Pacific Ocean, could have been satisfied without the war against Mexico,

and the subsequent political battle over slavery in the Mexican Cession would have lost some of its fierceness.

American settlers in the Mexican province of Texas, seeking independence, had defeated a Mexican army in 1836. Several years earlier Mexico had decreed that no new slaves were to be introduced into Texas, and in 1830 certain steps had been taken toward enforcing this ban. Securing their slave property had been one of the Texans' principal aims in their drive for autonomy and eventually independence. As of 1836 there were only about 5,000 slaves in Texas, whereas the Anglo population was some 30,000. The American settlers hoped in 1836 for speedy annexation to the United States, but—because President Andrew Jackson did not wish to jeopardize the chance that his chosen successor (the New Yorker Martin Van Buren) would win the presidential election of 1836—Jackson did not act.[2]

To vastly extend the domain of slavery—as annexing Texas would do—was not then electorally popular in the North, and during Van Buren's presidency he, too, failed to act. But when the Virginia states' rights enthusiast John Tyler succeeded to the presidency in 1841 (and alienated his Whig supporters by vetoing their economic legislation), Tyler and his Virginia ally, Secretary of State Abel Upshur, turned to the Texas issue in order to strengthen Southern slavery—and perhaps to win the presidency for Tyler in the 1844 election. Tyler indicated the depth of his commitment to slavery by appointing John C. Calhoun secretary of state in 1844 (when Upshur was killed in an accident); Calhoun's much-publicized letter to the British minister Richard Pakenham argued that the United States must annex Texas because slavery was a positive good, which needed to be defended against Britain's dangerous abolitionist policy.[3] The number of slaves in Texas had shot up to 27,000, and they already made up nearly 27 percent of the population.[4] This was the situation by April 1844, as James Polk angled for the presidential nomination.

Polk and his allies pursued their goals efficiently. Although a rule requiring a two-thirds' majority to nominate a candidate had first been implemented at the Democratic Party's convention in 1832, the custom was not yet firmly established. When the party convention opened in 1844, the matter remained undetermined. Everyone knew that fixing a two-thirds rule would probably enable the Southern states to block the candidacy of Van Buren. Polk did not attend the convention, but his Tennessee backers were in a state delegation that voted (along with Van Buren's other opponents) for the two-thirds rule. This rule having been adopted, Van Buren gained a majority for the nomination but could not garner the required two-thirds of the votes; eventually the nomination went to Polk, who had persuaded Van Buren's supporters that he had remained loyal to their candidate.[5]

Inconsistently, the backers of Texas annexation adopted precisely the opposite procedural rule in the U.S. Senate. The U.S. Constitution required a two-thirds' majority for ratification of a treaty, and in June 1844 the Senate rejected Texas annexation. Although defenders of slavery relied on strict construction of the Constitution in order to make the institution secure in the Southern states, the annexationists now bent the Constitution by evading its treaty clause. They sought instead to annex territory by an unprecedented route—a joint resolution of Congress, which would require only a majority, not two-thirds of the vote. Yet even after Polk had won the 1844 election on a platform of Texas annexation, it proved almost impossible to secure even a simple majority in the Senate. President-elect Polk finally achieved this end in February 1845 when he deceived several senators, in private consultations, about how he would implement an annexation resolution if they voted for it. (He led these senators to believe that when he became president, instead of proceeding immediately with annexation on the terms previously agreed on between Texas and President John Tyler's administration, he would appoint commissioners to renegotiate the matter to make war with Mexico less likely.) The Texas annexationists—and Polk most of all—were determined to reach their objective by whatever means lay to hand. The situation was somewhat obscured because the Democrats linked annexation to a demand that American claims to the Oregon territory be extended far north of the Columbia River. Thus a contingent of Northern Democrats (especially from Ohio, Indiana, Illinois, and Michigan) vigorously supported a joint program of expansion in the Northwest along with annexation of Texas.[7] The drive for Texas was propelled above all else, however, by the desire of many slavemasters and would-be slavemasters to extend the realm of slavery.[8]

Polk's advocacy of slavery's expansion arose partly from his family's experience. His grandfather Ezekiel Polk (who at his death in 1824 owned twenty-four slaves) had been lured repeatedly to the West by the prospect of improving his fortunes. Briefly sheriff of a North Carolina county in 1782, Ezekiel was then appointed a surveyor for Carolina speculators in Tennessee lands; he permanently abandoned Carolina in 1803 (at age fifty-five) to develop a plantation in middle Tennessee. Dissatisfied, he soon moved south to Maury County, Tennessee, where he had previously acquired several thousand acres of valuable land; then in 1821 the seventy-three-year-old slavemaster-pioneer relocated his slaves once again to clear a tract of land, this time in the fertile "Western District" of Tennessee, where he soon planned the "great eight-room house" that would properly proclaim his social status. Polk's father, too, had moved from North Carolina, in 1806, to found a plantation in central Tennessee.[9] Polk himself had established his own plantation in West Tennessee in 1831; he had moved his field of operations to virgin land in Mississippi at the end of 1834, and he was actively exploring the chances of shifting his slaves to Arkansas later during the 1830s and 1840s. He knew from his own experience how opening western lands to the spread of slavery could improve a person's economic prospects. Furthermore, one of his great uncles had emigrated to Texas and reported to him in 1836 the famous events at the Alamo. That year, two of Polk's cousins participated in the military side of the Texas revolution. And in 1845, when President Polk wanted a confidential agent to assure Texans that he would back their flimsy claim to the Rio Grande boundary, he turned to his old friend Arkansas Governor Archibald Yell, who previously had acted as Polk's agent in buying and selling Arkansas land with the thought that Polk might shift his plantation operations from Mississippi to that western state. The westward expansion of plantation slavery held deep personal meaning to the president.[10]

The annexation of Texas, the Mexican War, and the subsequent political battle over slavery in the conquered territory are often examined separately. This is certainly how Polk sought to present these events. Yet, because the three issues were intimately interwoven, they cannot be properly viewed unless the interrelations among them are constantly held in mind.

When Polk annexed Texas, he adopted the Texans' claims to the Rio Grande as their boundary, not only for their southern boundary but for their western border too. Texas had a sound claim to the Nueces River as its southern boundary, some 150 arid miles short of the Rio Grande, and it might perhaps have plausibly claimed even the watershed between the Nueces and the Rio Grande. Also, Texas might have reasonably claimed as its western border a line running from the headwaters of the Nueces River north and northwestward, or even a line from the watershed between the Nueces and the Rio Grande to the southeast corner of present-day New Mexico and thence straight north. This last line would have run some 200 miles east of the Rio Grande, as that river flows from the Rocky Mountains of Colorado almost due south through New Mexico to El Paso (see map 11.1). The Texans, by extending their appetite westward to the Rio Grande, thus sought to devour more than half of the present state of New Mexico, including Santa Fe, Albuquerque, and Taos, to which they had no remotely legitimate claim. And on their southern border, the Texans' demand for the Rio Grande encompassed Mexican posts at Santiago and Laredo and settlements north of Matamoros, to which again Texas had no legitimate claim. Even the historian Justin Smith—a vigorous defender of the Mexican War—acknowledged (in a footnote) that he regarded the Texans' boundary "claim and all conclusions based upon it as unsound." And Polk's secretary of state, James Buchanan, had declared in 1844 that Texas's claim "to that portion of New Mexico which lies east of [the Rio Grande], and north of [El Paso], is certainly of a very doubtful character; and it is one upon which we ought not to insist."[11] Polk did insist. He need not have adopted the Texans' grandiose border claims, but he did so. These claims—increasing the assurance that Mexico would

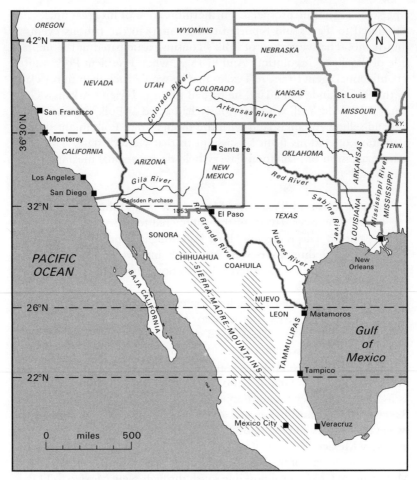

Map 11.1   Texas, Mexico, and the Mexican Cession

strenuously resent the annexation of Texas by the United States—furnished Polk the provocation that led in 1846 to war with Mexico, and the war enabled the United States to conquer a vast western domain, including California.

Even if Texas had been annexed with reasonable boundaries, war with Mexico might possibly have ensued, for the Mexican government had never offered to recognize Texan independence until May 1845, after the United States had proposed to annex Texas; and Mexico was even less happy at the idea of Texas's joining the United States.[12] But Mexico would probably have swallowed its unhappiness—and avoided war—if the United States had not demanded the Rio Grande boundary.[13] To Mexico, Polk's demand for the Rio Grande boundary was (1) a claim to take over long-established Mexican communities at and near Santa Fe; (2) a humiliating grab for the large, though unfertile, portion of the province of Coahuila, lying between the Rio Grande and the Nueces River, even though the Nueces had always (before the Texan claim of 1836) been accepted as the border between Texas and Coahuila; and (3) an American assertion of the right to aim artillery at what was by far the largest town in the whole region, Matamoros, situated on the south bank of the Rio Grande. Many Mexican military and civilian leaders were very reluctant to enter into a war with the United States, which they feared Mexico could not win.[14] Because of this reluctance, Texas could probably have been annexed without war if the United States had not insisted on the Rio Grande as the boundary. A principal difference between Polk and the Whig Henry Clay— Polk's opponent in the presidential election of 1844—had been that Clay favored annexing Texas in some cautious way that would not precipitate military conflict.[15] If Clay had won the election he certainly would not have demanded the Rio Grande as Texas's border.

President Polk insisted on the Rio Grande. He then ordered General Zachary Taylor to encamp his army "on or near the Rio Grande" in order to establish the claim. Taylor planted his troops in disputed territory just south of the Nueces River, although he cautiously held them back 150 miles from the Rio Grande, and Mexican authorities were reluctant to respond to this limited provocation. Polk repeatedly—on October 16, 1845, and January 13, 1846—urged Taylor to place his army "as near [the Rio Grande] as circumstances will permit," but Taylor delayed moving until early March, and his troops did not reach the Rio Grande until March 28, 1846. No Mexican attack being immediately forthcoming, the impatient Polk, with the acquiescence of his cabinet, decided to ask Congress to declare war on Mexico. But before he actually sent his war message to Congress, Polk learned—fortunately, from his point of view—that a Mexican force had finally crossed the Rio Grande to ambush some of the recently arrived American soldiers.[16] Polk was therefore able to redesign his war proposal: he alleged that war already existed "by the act of Mexico herself." Congress need not declare war at all but merely "recognize the existence of the war" already started by the enemy.[17]

Anxious lest his conduct of affairs meet strong Whig opposition in Congress, Polk prepared to tack a preamble, acknowledging a state of war, onto an appropriation bill that provided financial support for General Taylor's army. Polk's Democratic lieutenants in Congress refused to let the two matters be voted on separately, and thus no congressman could vote against war without also voting against supplies for the American soldiers. Only a handful of brave congressmen (fourteen of them) were willing to vote against this unjust war and thereby (because of the Democrats' stratagem) to court the opprobrium likely to be directed against anyone daring not to support American soldiers, exposed as they might be to assault from a more numerous Mexican army.

This parliamentary trick, however, was not sufficient for Polk. His lieutenants also arranged that consideration of the House appropriation bill, to support General Taylor's army, was to be terminated within two hours; and they then filled three-quarters of this time with a reading of the president's message and the supporting documents. At the last moment they sprang, as an amendment to the appropriations bill, a preamble declaring that a state of war already existed: thus actual debate on the declaration of war was effectively precluded in the House of Representatives (where Polk faced the strongest Northern and Whig opposition).[18]

It was a disgraceful episode. Rational consideration of whether or not to go to war for an "indefensible"[19] border claim was swept aside. A president whose political career was founded on strict observance of the Constitution played fast and loose with proper parliamentary procedure. He seemed to appeal to constitutional restraint only when it suited him to do so. And by whipping the war resolution through the House against the wishes of 35 percent of its members,[20] the president planted the seeds of a towering political conflict over war aims: was slavery to be legalized in the territory Polk wished to seize from Mexico?

Polk's subsequent policy toward Mexico was consistent with his opening salvo. The war was scarcely launched before the president told the cabinet he hoped to acquire all of Mexico north of the twenty-sixth parallel—not only New Mexico and California (which then contained present-day Arizona, Nevada, Utah, and parts of Colorado and Wyoming) but also another 300,000 square miles of Mexican territory, including most of the present-day Mexican states of Nuevo Leon, Coahuila, Chihuahua, Sonora, and Baja California.[21] Once General Taylor had won a few battles in northern Mexico, Polk began to think that his grandiose territorial aspirations might be realized. "You need not be surprised," the president wrote his brother in October 1846, "if other Provinces [besides California and New Mexico] also are secured. . . . The longer the war . . . the greater will be . . . the indemnity required."[22] (A few months later, Mexican authorities somehow got wind of Polk's appetite for the twenty-sixth parallel. Mexican nationalists then used allegations of Yankee land hunger to repel an unofficial American peace overture tendered early in 1847.[23])

Normally, Polk's military and diplomatic tactics were incremental. He applied military pressure first, thereafter making a demand on Mexico that no Mexican government would be likely to accept. Then, when his demand was not met, he applied additional military force and committed his negotiators to a new, more ambitious goal, which again the Mexican government—sometimes to Polk's surprise—would also be unwilling to accept; and the process was repeated. Thus Polk began by ordering General Taylor's army to the Rio Grande. While Taylor was still encamped at Corpus Christi (just south of the Nueces River), Mexico indicated willingness to talk to a special American commissioner, presumably about whether they might accept their loss of Texas to the United States in return for an American payment (such as had previously been paid to France for the Louisiana Purchase). Polk—regarding the annexation of Texas, without any cash payment to Mexico, as a nonnegotiable fait accompli—declined to discuss this issue, as the Mexicans seemed to have offered to do.[24] Instead he appointed a "minister plenipotentiary"—not the ad hoc commissioner whom the Mexicans had requested—and instructed him to offer $5 million for the remainder of New Mexico *west* of the Rio Grande; the agent was to offer up to $20 million more for parts of California.[25]

When Mexico, predictably, declined to negotiate on these terms. Polk threatened war; he also posted the American navy to the Mexican port of Veracruz (ready to cut off the tariff revenues on which the Mexican government relied to pay its soldiers); and he sent General Taylor specific authorization to occupy the north bank of the Rio Grande, directly opposite the Mexican town of Matamoros. At that time Matamoros was much the largest town in the whole region. Its population of 15,000 was triple that of either Houston or Galveston (the largest towns in Texas).[26] Taylor's encampment within artillery range of this important urban center led, predictably, to the Mexican ambush, which then covered Polk's (previously determined) decision to go to war.

Taylor's subsequent victories in northern Mexico during the next few months failed to produce the expected Mexican submission, whereupon Polk resolved to carry the war to central Mexico. His cabinet, however, was reluctant to extend military operations toward Mexico City. Once again, therefore, Polk employed incremental tactics: in November 1846 he got the cabinet to agree at least to a landing at Veracruz. In practice, this was sure to result in the desired military campaign toward Mexico City (for no invading American army was likely to sit passively on the pestilential coast near Veracruz during the long summer of 1847, watching its soldiers die of malaria and yellow fever, when a campaign into the mountains would offer respite from these scourges). Thus, by proceeding one step at a time, Polk eventually secured his cabinet's assent to the campaign toward Mexico City.[27]

Once General Winfield Scott's army had captured Veracruz—and with the prospect of Scott's march inland—Polk formulated instructions for a new diplomatic agent, Nicholas Trist. Before launching the war, Polk had set his minimum demand as, in effect, Mexican submission to the virtually uncompensated loss of Texas, but now the president's minimum demand was far more ambitious. He presented Mexico with the ultimatum to cede California and New Mexico, for which the United States would pay up to $20 million (and would waive various financial claims against Mexico), or the war would continue. Trist should also attempt to purchase Baja California (the long peninsula stretching 800 miles southward from San Diego) and to secure American transit rights from the Gulf of Mexico across the Isthmus of Tehuantepec (350 miles southeast of Mexico City) to the Pacific Ocean.[28]

Five months later the Mexican government still refused to submit to the ultimatum, even though Scott's army had smashed the defenses of Mexico City and was poised to occupy the city itself. When news of this refusal reached Washington, Polk ordered Trist to break off contact with the Mexicans and return home, and the president once again put incremental tactics into service. A movement had developed in the United States to keep permanent possession of substantial portions of present-day Mexico. The two most important members of Polk's cabinet favored this policy. Secretary of State James Buchanan—a Pennsylvanian seeking the support of expansionists for the Democratic presidential nomination in 1848— wanted to keep the northeastern part of present-day Mexico, between the Gulf of Mexico and the Sierra Madre. Secretary of the Treasury Robert Walker (a Mississippian) hoped, like some other Democrats, to annex *all* of Mexico.[29] Polk himself had envisaged, almost from the beginning of the war, seizing (besides California and New Mexico) most of the five other northern states of Mexico. Thus when the president told his cabinet in October 1847 that he favored further military operations and "establishing more stable Governments than those [previously] established," it seems certain that he contemplated further territorial aggrandizement. In his annual message to Congress (December 1847), Polk called for annexation of New Mexico and the Californias (in the plural, thus including Baja California), and he threatened to up the ante because of "the obstinate perseverance of Mexico in protracting the war." If Mexico would not submit, Polk warned, the United States must "tak[e] the full measure of indemnity into our own hands"—that is, the United States must permanently seize even more territory. But guerrilla warfare against the American armies apparently had turned Polk against his original idea of seizing all of Mexico north of the twenty-sixth parallel: he seems now to have hoped instead to grab the Mexican port of Tampico (at the twenty-second parallel); to secure an American right of passage across the isthmus of Tehuantepec, from the Gulf of Mexico to the Pacific Ocean; and "perhaps to make the Sierra Madra [*sic*] the line," thus seizing the province of Tamaulipas and all the rest of Mexico between these mountains and the Gulf of Mexico.[30]

The Mexicans had surprised Polk by their stubborn resistance to his idea that they should acknowledge defeat and sign a peace treaty. Consequently, the war had dragged on much longer than the president had anticipated. During this time a series of military triumphs fed American patriotic fervor, especially in the South and Southwest, from which a disproportionate number of the American soldiers had been recruited. (Yet when the final toll was counted, it turned out that 14 percent of the American soldiers had died.[31]) The Whigs had been making big gains in the midterm congressional elections,[32] and the next presidential election was on the horizon. Public opinion was divided: some Whigs wanted no territorial conquests at all; apparently most Americans would have been satisfied to settle for New Mexico and California, and they wanted an end to the war; but vociferous groups within the Democratic Party sought even more territory from Mexico.

Favoring this last course, Polk aimed to increase the pressure on Mexico by recalling his envoy, Nicholas Trist, rather than amending Trist's original instructions. Thus when Trist—violating repeated orders to return home—remained in Mexico City and finally secured a treaty consonant with those original instructions, Polk had no firm ground on which to reject the work of his insubordinate emissary. Trist had even acquired California and New Mexico for only $15 million, although authorized to pay $20 million. Yet astonishingly, because on November 16, 1847, Trist had received the orders to leave Mexico, the angry president refused to pay Trist's salary for the period—November 16, 1847, through February 2, 1848—during which he had skillfully negotiated the treaty that secured everything he had previously been instructed to get.[33] Nevertheless, and inconsistently, Polk probably breathed a sigh of relief that Trist had enabled the United States to terminate without loss of face a war in which American losses had been considerable. The president, however, would assume no responsibility himself for ending hostilities, leaving it instead to the senators—eleven of whose appetites for Mexican soil remained unsatiated—to decide for themselves whether or not to halt the war with territorial acquisitions smaller than Polk had originally desired.[34] Trist's treaty added a mere 650,000 square miles to U.S. territory, whereas Polk had once hoped for about 950,000 square miles.[35] Happily, the war was by now sufficiently unpopular in the United States that the Senate eventually voted by thirty-eight to fourteen (with four dissatisfied senators abstaining) to accept Trist's treaty. Part of the opposition or abstention came from senators—like slave-state Senators James Westcott, Dixon Lewis, Sam Houston, and David Atchison and the Illinois Senator Stephen Douglas (whose wife stood to inherit over 100 slaves and a great Mississippi plantation from her rich father)—who would have liked hundreds of thousands of square miles more of Mexican territory.[36]

Polk's unsettling experiences in governing his slaves may illuminate how he conducted diplomacy and the war. Having been subjected when he was sixteen to an excruciating (unanesthetized), pioneering operation to remove a urinary stone, and having grown up a frail and relatively bookish youth (whose later marriage remained childless), Polk always felt a need to prove himself.[37] When he compromised with his fugitive slaves (having them whipped but then sometimes selling a favored bondsman into the slave's familiar central Tennessee homeland or requiring that Dismukes's whipping of Gilbert and Addison be witnessed by Polk's agent Bobbitt), these halfway measures were ineffectual in curbing flight. Unsatisfying experiences of this sort may have reinforced Polk's feeling that he must act in an authoritative, decisive way if his presidency was to be a success. Once president, he immediately effected Texas annexation in the speediest possible manner, disregarding the outcry this aroused; he took an aggressive stance toward Britain, depending on the Senate to assume responsibility for retreating from his untenable territorial claims against Canada; he forced through Congress a hasty declaration of war on Mexico; and he pursued against Mexico territorial ambitions predictably unacceptable to any government of that nation, once again depending on the Senate to take responsibility for backing down from his most far-reaching goals. These seem to be the actions of a man who felt he must prove himself, not only by being a workaholic,[38] but also by repeatedly flexing his muscle in order to achieve his foreign policy goals.[39] May not the humiliations Polk had experienced in governing his slaves have contributed to his determination to show the Mexicans, and even the powerful British, who was boss?

American expansion to the Pacific has often seemed predetermined, as Manifest Destiny, but it need not have been precisely so. Had Henry Clay been elected in 1844, he would not have demanded the Rio Grande as Texas's border, and this rich source for dispute with Mexico would not have existed. Mexico, then, might well have accepted—at least informally, if not soon by formal agreement—the annexation of Texas to the United States, especially if financial compensation had been tendered. American settlers (mostly from the North) would then have infiltrated California, as Americans (mostly from the South) had previously done in Texas; and quickly a movement for Californian autonomy, followed by independence from Mexico, would have ensued, similar to the one that had already succeeded in Texas. California no doubt would then have been annexed to the United States. This whole process would have been accelerated by the Gold Rush (which of course no one could foresee). Mexico probably would have tried to put a military halt to the process, but its efforts would probably have been even less effectual than they had been against Texas. No protracted war—perhaps no war at all—had to have occurred. The boundary between the United States and Mexico would *not* be identical to the present boundary: Texas would not extend southward quite as far as the Rio Grande, and the Mexican border might extend many miles into present-day New Mexico. Would this diminution of U.S. territory have been worthwhile for the sake of avoiding an aggressive and unjust war against Mexico? In particular, would it have been worthwhile if—by renouncing an extended war against Mexico—the Americans had been able to avoid the bloodbath that followed so soon thereafter, the American Civil War?

12

Slavery and Union

Historians rightly see the dispute over the booty from Mexico as the first scene of a tragedy that led, almost inexorably, from the political battles of 1846–50 between Northerners and Southerners to the military battles of 1861–65. Yet Polk professed surprise that anyone should suppose a connection between his war against Mexico and the slavery question. That Polk was a "Continentalist," not a slavery expansionist, has become the standard view of his presidency. Polk was a nationalist, it is said, not a sectionalist: his purposes were to serve the interests of the whole nation, not to advance those of his native South. Sectional controversies did, of course, arise from the Mexican War, but these—it would seem— were the unintended and unforeseen consequences of a war whose purposes were truly national.[1]

Several replies may be suggested to this view of Polk's war. For one thing, sectional controversy was *not* unforeseen. Southern Whigs predicted that conquering territory from Mexico would provoke political conflict about slavery in the new territory, a conflict likely to ruin the Whig Party. Hence Southern Whigs rallied during the Mexican War behind the phrase "No Territory"; this neutral slogan might enable them to continue their alliance with Northern Whigs without requiring them to subscribe to any electorally unpopular antislavery declaration.[2] Northern Whigs, too, foresaw that grabbing land from Mexico would entail a fight about slavery. Their reluctance to increase the number of slave states (and the reluctance of Northern Democrats to lose support from the Northern electorate on this issue) had already delayed the annexation of Texas for eight years, and Northern Whigs were sure to look at the acquisition of any further Mexican territory—especially that south of 36°30'—with skepticism.[3] Similarly, the Northern Van Burenites (who felt that slave-state Democrats had robbed their candidate of the Democratic presidential nomination in 1844 because he was cautious about acquiring new slave territory) would surely look askance at acquiring even more territory from Mexico, which might further increase the slave states' political power.[4]

Even James Buchanan, Polk's secretary of state, could see from the outset that the slavery question was sure to arise once territory was seized from Mexico. At a cabinet meeting on June 30, 1846—seven weeks after the declaration of war—Buchanan opposed permanent seizure of provinces south of New Mexico because of

> the unwillingness of the North to acquire so large a Country that would probably become a slave-holding country if attached to the U. S. . . . If we attempted to acquire all this territory [north of 26°], the opinion of the world would be against [us], and especially as it would become a slave-holding country, whereas while it was in possession of Mexico slavery did not exist in it.[5]

Buchanan apparently assumed that slavery would be legalized in any U.S. territory south of the Missouri Compromise line (36°30'), and this evidently was Polk's presumption as well. Historians have often quoted Polk's indignant outburst on August 10, 1846, just after the Wilmot Proviso had been introduced, "What connection slavery had with making peace with Mexico it is difficult to conceive."[7] But this diary entry was disingenuous, for Polk knew perfectly well (from Buchanan's interventions in cabinet discussions on June 30 and July 7, 1846, if from nowhere else) that conquering territory in the Southwest was bound to stir Northern anxiety about slavery, just as annexing Texas had aroused anxiety. Controversy over slavery was as certain to follow a war of conquest as the month of August follows, in due course, March.

Indeed, Polk surely had sensed this in March 1846 when—as he impatiently awaited news that General Zachary Taylor had moved his troops to the Rio Grande—he discussed with his brother-in-law John Childress buying more slaves for the Mississippi plantation, but doing so secretly. Polk's consciousness of the connection between slavery and a war of conquest reappeared on June 2, 1846 (three weeks after the declaration of war), in the president's words that finally authorized Childress to buy these slaves: "I need not repeat the reason which I assigned to you [in March] why it should not be made public that you are making purchases for me." Thus on August 13, 1846—five days after the House of Representatives adopted the Wilmot Proviso—Polk's order to his cousin Robert Campbell that Campbell must keep these purchases secret was a mere reaffirmation of a plan conceived months before antislavery congressmen introduced the proviso. Polk's anxiety that the public might learn of his slave purchases indicates his awareness that war with Mexico was likely to provoke controversy about slavery.[8]

Did Polk attack Mexico without the intention of thereby increasing the number of slave states? Possibly the president did not consciously seek that goal, but only because his convictions about slavery were so deeply imbedded that they might not have been at the front of his mind in 1845 and 1846, when he decided on the policies that led to war. The question of slavery in what became known as the Mexican Cession was for Polk a matter of rights, not only of negotiable interests. Polk felt that, as a matter of abstract principle, slavemasters had a *right* to take their slaves anywhere in American territory, even north of 36°30', whether or not it should actually prove practicable to establish slavery there.[9] Polk acted on this conviction in California and New Mexico. He secretly negotiated with John C. Calhoun in July 1848, promising implicitly that—if Calhoun could get Congress to agree that federal judges (not Congress nor the territorial legislatures) were to decide the future of slavery in these territories—he would appoint judges there who shared Calhoun's belief that slavemasters had a right to take their slaves anywhere in the territories.[10] Because the House of Representatives never acceded to this plan, the president never had an opportunity to fulfill his implicit promise.

Even before this conversation with Calhoun, however, Polk had concluded that the South would probably have to abandon his abstract principle. He decided that "Southern rights" might reasonably be compromised to the extent that they had been sacrificed in the Missouri Compromise of 1820—that is, that Congress might ban slavery north of 36°30' on condition that it would be legalized south of that line.[11] Thus, if Polk had had his way, slavery, though banned north of Monterey, California (which lies about 100 miles south of San Francisco), would have been legalized in the huge Californian expanse lying south of that line.

But the House of Representatives would not agree to extend the Missouri Compromise line, and President Polk eventually accepted the idea that all of California might become free, if it skipped the territorial stage. (The ban on slavery would be imposed by the convention that wrote the constitution for the new state.[12]) Polk—unlike Calhoun, who by 1849 had progressed to a more advanced position—was willing to accept this idea because it did not violate the principle of *congressional* noninterference with slavery. Polk had always believed that a state government had the power to legalize or to ban slavery; his principle was that Congress had no power to do so (or, at least, not south of 36°30').

Thus, long before the end of his four-year term, the president had determined a position from which he was wholly unwilling to budge. In August 1846 the House of Representatives had passed the Wilmot Proviso, which—if the Senate had concurred—would have banned slavery from every part of any territory conquered from Mexico. Although the Senate did not concur, Polk was angered by the flaring up of this issue; when the House twice again passed the Proviso (in February 1847 and December 1848), he determined to veto it if the Senate, too, should ever try, by enacting the proviso, to deny the South its rights in the territories. Polk's hostility was directed against the nascent free-soil movement, whose participants nearly all believed that Congress had no power over slavery in the *states* but who sought a congressional ban of slavery in the federal *territories*.

During the months between the House's first and second adoption of the Wilmot Proviso, the president was occasionally reminded of his own connection with the slave system. In October 1846 Polk rebuffed his neighbor John Leigh's offer to buy Caroline Johnson so that her husband (Leigh's driver) would be with her every night. In December, the president—anticipating that his revenues from the 1846 cotton crop would be by far the highest they had ever been—urged his agent to buy several more slaves (in addition to the half dozen just acquired) and to do so speedily, "as I think it possible that such property will continue to rise in price for several months to come." The next month Polk learned that an angry buyer in New Orleans had rescinded a large purchase of the president's cotton because ten or fifteen bales of it were faulty goods, deceptively packed by Polk's overseer. At this time Polk reiterated to his slave-purchasing agent "my former request, that as my *private business* does not concern the public, you will keep it to yourself." The president's strong sense that his involvement with slavery was his own private business surely intensified his hostility to the Wilmot Proviso, with its implication that slavery was *not* entirely a private matter.[13]

Any enactment like the Wilmot Proviso would be unconstitutional, Polk averred in the draft he finally prepared (early in 1849) to use as a veto message: it would deprive the Southern states and their citizens of that equality with the nonslave states and their citizens that was the fundamental principle of the Constitution. "The territorial possessions acquired [from Mexico] were purchased by the common blood and the common treasure of citizens of all the States, Slaveholding and non-Slaveholding," the president declaimed in his draft (clearly illustrating how the Mexican War exacerbated the slavery issue). "It [*sic*] belongs equally and alike to all the States." Implying that slave states might, understandably, break up the Union if the proviso were enacted, Polk placed responsibility for any such denouement on the free-soilers: "Surely there can be no adequate motive for any lover of our glorious Union, to press this delicate question [of slavery in the territories] to an extreme point, by which the blessings of liberty, may be put in jeopardy or lost forever."[14]

Polk's attitude to the proviso was shared by virtually every Southern Democratic Senator (except Missouri's Senator Thomas Benton[15]), and by most Southern Whigs as well. This was the issue that already threatened in 1850 to lead to secession before the "Armistice of 1850"[16] was arranged, and (in modified form) it was the issue that did in fact lead to secession in 1860–61. "The idea of secession as a possible recourse," according to the historian David Potter, "first won widespread acceptance in the South during the prolonged deadlock of 1846–1850." So strongly was the matter felt in South Carolina and Georgia that by 1851 these two states were already virtually committed to secession if the national government banned slavery everywhere in the territories.[17] With hindsight, one can see that someday the North was likely to insist that the national government would make it illegal for slavery to expand. Thus the secession movement that swept the Deep South in 1860–61 had become very probable in 1851, and indeed was on the cards in 1846–47, from the moment the depth of Southern hostility to the Wilmot Proviso manifested itself.[18]

The crucial question is not "Why did South Carolina lead the secession movement?" but "Why did the Democratic Party of both the Deep South and the middle South share South Carolina's stance toward the territorial question?" President Polk was by far the most powerful leader of the Southern Democrats during the late 1840s, and his view of the Wilmot Proviso typified that of Southern Democrats. It is Polk's stance—more than that of John C. Calhoun and Calhoun's South Carolina associates—that must be fathomed if one is to understand the secession of the other Deep South states, and eventually of those in the middle South.[19]

The hope of extending slave-based plantation agriculture into the Mexican Cession was not the heart of the matter. It is true that Polk favored opening new lands for settlement by American slavemasters; this was obviously his aim in rushing through the annexation of Texas. It also lay behind his (abortive) efforts in 1848 to purchase Cuba,[20] where slave-based sugar plantations were booming and where there would have been splendid opportunities for the investment of American capital into the further development of the sugar industry. Similarly, it could have proved feasible to raise cotton in California with gangs of slaves. Southern Democrats were disappointed when the unexpected rush of free-state gold-seekers in California led promptly to the adoption of a free-state constitution, which excluded slavemasters from enjoying the fruits of conquest.[21] And no doubt Southern leaders cherished a vague hope that, one way or another, slaves could be profitably employed elsewhere in the little-known southern reaches of the Mexican Cession—surely as domestic servants, perhaps as laborers in mining ventures, or possibly in some undetermined sphere of agricultural production.

However, enough was known in 1846 of the arid, mountainous character of the Mexican lands east of present-day California that lust for plantation profits can scarcely have been the driving force behind most Southern Democrats' hunger for Mexican territory. More significant was their desire to enhance the South's political power, especially in the U.S. Senate. Even under the distorting influence of the three-fifths clause, the U.S. House of Representatives already had a substantial Northern majority by 1846, and it was to the Senate that Southern white people increasingly looked as their bulwark against Northern antislavery assault. By 1848—after the admission of Texas, Florida, Iowa, and Wisconsin to the Union—there were still as many slave states as free states (and thus as many slave-state as free-state senators), but this balance was sure to end when more free states were created from the Louisiana Purchase territories north and west of Missouri.

Polk's first act as president had been to accept the proposal that Texas might one day divide itself into five slave states, which would enhance

Southern power in the Senate;[22] and no doubt he anticipated that the territory seized from Mexico—at least south of 36°30'—might one day be created into slavery-friendly states, which when represented in the Senate, would vote with the South on slavery-related issues. This would not require the establishment of great slave plantations in these newly conquered areas. All that would be needed was the presence of some domestic slaves and a few employed in small-scale agriculture or perhaps in mining, as well as a state legislature that chose to protect the economic interests of the local slavemasters. After all, every American state south of 36°30' (and several north of that line, such as Maryland, Virginia, Kentucky, and Missouri) sent strong defenders of slavery to the U.S. Senate, and it was an easy inference that senators from any states carved from conquered territory south of 36°30' would also be allies of the older slave states. Polk may not consciously have thought in this way, and he certainly made no such explanation of his motives to the public. But evidently he felt that territory south of 36°30' was likely in due course to produce slavery-friendly senators and representatives, even if slaves should prove to be sprinkled only lightly across the region. Polk's additional hope—that his defeat of the Mexican army would enable him to add Nuevo Leon, Coahuila, Chihuahua, Sonora, Baja California, or perhaps Tamaulipas to the war's booty—was undergirded by the presumption that these areas, too, would in due course produce senators and representatives friendly to the "Southern institutions" of the older slave states.

Yet the most important of all Polk's motives, largely explaining his profound hostility to the Wilmot Proviso, was his determination that Southern "rights" must be asserted.[23] These were of two sorts—the rights of *individual* Southern white people to take slaves wherever they wished in the national territory, and the rights of Southern *states* to limit national authority over slavery. Polk's instinct was Calhounite: that individual slavemasters had the abstract right to take their slaves anywhere, even north of the 36°30' line. On this right, however, President Polk, unlike Calhoun after February 1847,[24] was willing to compromise. To Polk the nonnegotiable right was that of Southern states to avoid any congressional ban on territorial slavery south of 36°30'. This meant, preferably, that the Missouri Compromise line would be extended to the Pacific Ocean; alternatively, however, it might mean—as in the case of California—that Congress would skip entirely the formal organization of a territorial government and immediately admit the area to the Union as a state (with the right, when it wrote its state constitution, to decide for itself the future status of slavery). Polk remained inflexibly opposed to a *congressional* ban on slavery in California or anywhere else south of 36°30'. This, he averred, would violate the rights of both individual Southern people and the Southern states, and he would brook no substantial sacrifice of Southern rights.[25] For Congress to pass the Wilmot Proviso, he said, would threaten disunion; and the tone of his prospec-

tive veto message was that, under such provocation, secession would be
perfectly understandable.[26]

So strongly did Polk believe in Southern rights that he underscored
them even in the 1848 presidential message in which he reluctantly accepted a congressional ban on slavery in the newly settled territory of
Oregon. This region lay entirely north of 36°30'—indeed, the border between California and Oregon was at the forty-second parallel, 380 miles
north of 36°30', and everyone could see that slavery could never be legalized there. Nevertheless, it was important to Polk to establish a claim that
slavery was being banned there only because Oregon lay entirely north of
36°30', not because Congress possessed any general power to ban slavery
from a territory. The principle of federal noninterference with slavery must
be asserted, and this principle must be compromised no further than the
South had previously accepted in the Missouri Compromise of 1820, with
its division of Louisiana Purchase territory at 36°30'. The real issue was
the security of slavery within the slave states themselves, and that security
could be achieved only by a determined defense of the general principle
of federal noninterference. In one of the strongest proslavery declarations
of his career, the president asserted that the slavery question "does not
embrace merely the rights of property, however valuable, but it ascends far
higher, and involves the domestic peace and security of every [white] family." Polk, having two months earlier authorized the sale of the persistent
fugitive Joe—who had already fled the Mississippi plantation four times since
his purchase in 1847—perhaps felt especially conscious at this moment of
the desirability of protecting the security of slavemasters' families.[27]

In examining Polk's motives for embarking on the Mexican War and
for intransigent opposition to the Wilmot Proviso, one does not deny that
Polk was a continentalist. He and the Southern Democratic Party shared
with many Northerners—especially but not exclusively Democrats—a
desire to see the American flag carried to the Pacific Ocean. Northwestern farmers in the early 1840s were already settling in the Oregon territory
(whose border with Canada had not yet been fixed); northeastern merchants were keen to possess the harbor of San Francisco as a base from
which to increase American commerce with the Far East; and northeastern zealots, like the New Yorker John L. O'Sullivan, filled the air with
rhetoric about carrying the blessings of republican institutions to the Pacific and driving back the perfidious British.[28] There can be no doubt that
Polk, whose republican convictions and anti-British sentiments were as
profound as O'Sullivan's, shared this nationalist fervor. Several generations
of historians have demonstrated that Polk was no mere Southern sectionalist;
he was indeed a continentalist.[29]

But his Southern Democratic version of continentalism contained
several unexpungeable adjuncts. No doubt Polk, and the Democratic Party
platform on which he stood in 1844, advocated extending Oregon's border much farther north than the British preferred; and President Polk reck-

lessly pushed this claim, threatening Britain with war and foisting on the Senate the responsibility for retreating from his extravagant claims[30] (just as in 1848 he forced the Senate to assume the responsibility for retreating from his war against Mexico). Polk, however, had gained the Democratic nomination because he demanded Texas, not Oregon (which he added to win support from Northern Democrats). The annexation of Texas—for the benefit of Southern white people—was Polk's primary purpose in 1844–45.[31] And when by 1846 he began to reveal his further aim of expansion to California, he sought not only national extension but also the possibility that slavery would spread to parts of the Mexican Cession, that new territory south of 36°30' would in due course enhance the political power of the slave states, and that Southern rights would be tenaciously defended within the conquered realm. This was continentalism, to be sure, but with a strong Southern flavor.

There was a deep contradiction between Polk's hostility to the Wilmot Proviso and his attachment to the Union. He threatened, and his Southern Democratic associates constantly reiterated, that congressional adoption of a ban on territorial slavery south of 36°30' would provoke disunion; they seemed to imply that disunion under such provocation would be understandable and perhaps condoned. Polk's references to disunion were always coded and always implied that the burden of responsibility would fall on the North. In the draft message prepared for his veto of the Wilmot Proviso, the president wrote (as previously quoted) that if the free-soil principle were enacted "the blessings of liberty, may be put in jeopardy or lost forever." In the Oregon message, Polk, thinking of the free-soilers, posed the rhetorical question, "Ought we at this late date, in attempting to annul [the Missouri Compromise] . . . to endanger the existence of the Union itself?" During the 1840 presidential campaign, the Tennessee Democratic Address #2 (quite surely drafted by Governor Polk) had declared that Northern efforts to defy the compromises of the Constitution "must if not resisted terminate in the loss of our glorious Union."[32]

This was all very well as rhetoric, designed to win votes at home and to scare Northern Democrats into voting against anything resembling the Wilmot Proviso. But what would Deep South and middle South Democrats do if Congress ever seemed on the verge of enacting a ban on territorial slavery? Would they in fact secede, a course of action that their rhetoric seemed to condone?

It is customary to sharply distinguish "extreme" Calhounites from the "moderate" Southern Democrats like Polk. One may observe, however, that by 1839 Governor Polk had adopted Calhoun's stance that Congress had no power over slavery anywhere, for example, not in the District of Columbia nor in the territories. For this reason and others, Calhoun was delighted when Polk won the Democratic presidential nomination in 1844. "The prospect is now fairer to return to the good old Republican doctrines of '98 . . ." Calhoun wrote enthusiastically during the 1844 canvass, "than it has been since 1828. . . . [The South] look[s] forward to Mr. Polk's administration. . . . If he should realize their expectation, of which I have much confidence, his administration will mark a great & salutary era in our political history." Calhoun's associate Francis Pickens (Carolina's governor during the secession crisis of 1860) had jubilantly reported in May 1844 that "Polk is nearer to *us* than any public man who was named [at the Democratic convention]. He is a large Slave holder & plants cotton—*free trade*—Texas—States rights *out & out*."[33] There were, to be sure, real differences between Polk and Calhoun. Early in 1847, for example, the president considered Calhoun "the most mischievous man in the Senate to my administration." Polk attributed Calhoun's disobliging conduct to his presidential ambitions: "I now entertain a worse opinion of Mr. Calhoun than I have ever done before." Two years later Polk pointedly asserted to Calhoun "that I gave no countenance to any movement which tended to . . . the disunion of the States." Yet the next day the president, while denying that secession was yet appropriate, indicated to a Tennessee congressman that it might one day become so:

> It was time enough to think of extreme measures when they became inevitable, and that period had not come. . . . [I was] as much attached to Southern rights as any man in Congress, but I was in favour of vindicating and maintaining these rights by constitutional means; and . . . no such an extreme case had arisen as would justify a resort to any other means; . . . when such a case should arise (if ever) it would be time enough to consider what should be done.[34]

By 1861 most Southern Democrats believed that "an extreme case" had arisen, and nearly all of them then followed South Carolina's lead into secession. Perhaps they were cleverly maneuvered by fire-eaters into pursuing a secessionist course that did not come naturally to them. But it is more plausible, I believe, to conclude that after 1846 most Southern Democrats had staked out a position that was very likely to lead them into secession if a political party committed to a congressional ban on all territorial slavery should ever gain power in Washington. The real responsibility for widespread secession, in other words, lay at the feet of "moderate" Southern Democrats like Polk and cannot be assigned principally to South Carolina secessionists, who could never have achieved their aims if they had not been able to depend, with reasonable confidence, on the support of Southern Democrats throughout the Deep and middle South.

James Polk himself, however, may not perfectly illustrate this argument. He did indeed commit himself, from 1846 until his death in 1849, to inveterate hostility to a congressional ban on territorial slavery. But if he had lived until 1861 he might *possibly* have favored a Unionist course in

Tennessee, even until the time of the state's referendum on secession in June 1861. This surmise is suggested by the careers of two of Polk's close Tennessee associates.

Unionism was always strong in relatively slaveless East Tennessee, which even in June 1861 voted 34,023 to 14,872 against secession.[35] But where slavery was strongly entrenched—in Polk's middle Tennessee and in West Tennessee—secessionists were sweepingly successful once Lincoln's call for soldiers in April 1861 had obliged Tennessee to take sides between the Union and the Confederacy. East Tennessee's U.S. Senator Andrew Johnson (who in the 1860 presidential campaign had supported the Southern Democratic candidate, John Breckinridge) was the only senator from a Confederate state to remain loyal to the Union. In middle Tennessee, however, Unionism was concentrated in the Constitutional Union Party (the successor to the old Whig Party). By May 1861 middle Tennessee's Democrats overwhelmingly backed secession, only two of the region's prominent Democrats still remaining Unionists.[36] Both of these men— William Polk and Judge John Catron—had been close associates of James Polk.

Polk's much younger brother William Polk—a Democratic U.S. congressman from 1851 to 1853—supported Stephen Douglas in the 1860 presidential election instead of John Breckinridge (whose platform of a federal slave code to protect slavery everywhere in the territories was much more popular among Tennessee Democrats than Douglas's "popular sovereignty" position). In May 1861 William Polk chaired the Tennessee Unionist convention (combining Unionist Democrats with Constitutional Unionists), which nominated a gubernatorial candidate for the August election. When that candidate declined the proffered nomination, William Polk himself became the Unionists' (unsuccessful) candidate. It is said that the Lincoln administration, as a reward for William Polk's Unionism, offered him early in 1862 the post of loyalist governor of Tennessee, which William (shying away from a position of such decided danger and unpopularity in middle Tennessee?) declined.[37] Only after William Polk turned down this offer, apparently, did the post go to Senator Andrew Johnson (from Unionist East Tennessee), who then became Lincoln's running mate in the 1864 presidential election.

The second of James Polk's Democratic Unionist associates was U.S. Supreme Court Justice John Catron, a long-time colleague whom James Polk named in 1849 as an executor of his will. In the Dred Scott case, Catron concurred with Chief Justice Roger Taney's Calhounite conclusion that Congress had no constitutional authority to ban slavery in the Louisiana Purchase territory and that, therefore, the Missouri Compromise's ban on slavery north of 36°30' had been unconstitutional.[38] Yet early in 1861 Catron (acting in his role as a circuit court judge in Missouri) issued an uncompromisingly Unionist judicial ruling. Catron became so unpopular with Tennessee secessionists that he was driven from his Nashville residence and had to live in Washington until Nashville was captured by the Union army. Catron's stance showed that inveterate hostility to a congressional ban on territorial slavery need not preclude vigorous Unionism. But Catron's position was exceptional in that the strength of his Unionist convictions was supported by the salary and status of his being a lifetime appointee to the Supreme Court.[39]

The Unionism in 1861 of Judge Catron and William Polk suggests that James Polk himself might *possibly* have assumed a Unionist stance had he not died young. It seems much more likely, however, that he would have taken the road followed by the former Tennessee congressman Cave Johnson (postmaster general in Polk's cabinet), who in early years had been the closest of Polk's political allies. Cave Johnson opposed Tennessee's secession until April 18, 1861, but backed the Confederacy once Lincoln's call to arms had obliged Tennessee to take sides in the war.[40] Middle Tennessee Democrats overwhelmingly supported secession after mid-April 1861 (indeed, many of them did so much sooner), and there is no convincing reason to suppose that Polk would have resisted the torrent of Democratic opinion when even his archrival John Bell, the Constitutional Unionist presidential candidate in 1860, was swept along with the current. Polk's economic interest—unlike that of Catron and William Polk—would also have impelled him in the Confederate direction. He would have depended on revenues from his Mississippi plantation to sustain himself and his wife during his retirement. Had Tennessee remained with the Union after April 1861, Polk's position would have resembled that of the Illinois Senator Stephen Douglas (who from 1848 to 1861 greatly profited from the Mississippi cotton plantation and its 142 slaves owned, first, by Douglas's wife and then by their two minor sons). Senator Douglas learned in 1861, a few weeks after the firing on Fort Sumter, that every New Orleans factor would stop payment to him in Illinois of the revenues from his Mississippi plantation.[41] Could Polk have felt financially secure in a Unionist Tennessee after April 1861, when the Union was at war with Confederate Mississippi?

Whatever way Polk might have answered that question, the fact remained that the profound hostility he and other Southern Democrats harbored against a congressional ban on territorial slavery was diametrically opposed to the Unionism that most of these Democrats also professed, but which the great majority of them abandoned when they had to choose. Only a handful of exceptionally placed Southern Democrats—like Justice Catron, Senator Andrew Johnson (whose East Tennessee constituents remained Unionist), or the Douglas Democrat William Polk—proved steadfast to the Union. The logic of the Southern Democratic leaders' earlier position (that disunion was probable and might be condonable if Congress banned territorial slavery) impelled most of them toward secession. Their constituents, who had been told repeatedly that there was no difference between free-soilers and abolitionists—both groups equally intolerable as wielders of power in Washington—naturally cheered Southern Democratic leaders when they adopted a secessionist course. The explanation for the widespread success of secessionism lay primarily in the doctrines preached for years by Southern Democratic leaders, like James Polk, everywhere in the Deep and middle South. The South Carolina secessionists merely lit the inflammable tinder that others had scattered so assiduously throughout the region.

Thus the annexation of Texas, the Mexican War, and the territorial slavery issue made up the interconnected elements of a single story. In annexing Texas, Polk was impelled by the wish to expand slavery, but this was not his principal motive later, when he launched the Mexican War. Here he was a continentalist, pursuing nationalist aims, to which any hopes he may have had of expanding the area of plantation slavery or even of increasing the political power of the slave states were subordinate. His war with Mexico was nevertheless as dangerous to the Union as though slavery expansion had been his primary aim because he assumed that Southern rights must be respected in the new territories, even if their acknowledgment should not lead to an expansion of plantation slavery. He had convinced himself, unnecessarily, that the defense of slavery in the states where it already existed required the assertion of Southern rights in the territories as well. The Mexican War need not in itself have threatened the Union, but in combination with the tacit assumption—soon made explicit—that Southern rights must not be substantially infringed in the Mexican Cession, it was sure to do so.

13

Alternatives

Since the territorial policies pursued by James Polk and lesser Southern Democrats proved disastrous to Southern whites, one wonders whether some alternative policy could have averted the cataclysm. If so, why was it not adopted?

To some modern Americans, the program advocated by the former president John Quincy Adams might seem to have offered a preferable alternative. Adams, like Polk, was a continentalist. Adams always favored an expansionist policy in the Northwest, and in 1845–46 he heartily sympathized with President Polk's aggressive stance toward Britain over Oregon. Adams's continentalism also embraced the Southeast. As secretary of state, Adams had in 1819 negotiated the acquisition from Spain of Florida, to most of which the United States had no shred of a legal claim; publicly he always supported the entry of Florida into the Union as a slave state, when its free population so warranted. In that same negotiation with Spain in 1819, Adams had been the last member of President James Monroe's cabinet to acquiesce in abandoning any claim to Texas. (American claims to any part of Texas were, in any case, as fragile as were Spain's claims to the region between California and the Columbia River; and Spain renounced those claims at the same moment that the United States renounced its claim to Texas.) Monroe's cabinet felt, and Adams agreed, that renouncing a weak claim to Texas was justified in order to get Spain to peacefully cede Florida to the United States. The Senate agreed, too, accepting without one dissenting vote the treaty that swapped any claim to Texas in return for the actual possession of Florida. And at that time General Andrew Jackson concurred.[1]

Jackson later changed his mind, and he then accused Adams of having betrayed the South by abandoning a viable American claim to Texas. After Texas declared its independence from Mexico in 1836, Congressman Adams found enough Northerners opposed to adding more slave territory to the Union so that he and a few colleagues were able to block the annexation of Texas for eight years. It may tempt modern Americans to suppose that Adams's policy—of acquiring no new slave territory—would have best promoted the national interest since by settling the territorial slavery issue at an early stage, it could have eliminated the later dispute that led to the Civil War.

But Adams's program had no chance of permanent success. The anti-slavery movement was still too weak in the North to have blocked Texas annexation indefinitely. And when the South's lust for Texas grew, while a Northern movement burgeoned to drive Oregon's borders farther north than the Columbia River, some version of Texas annexation became irresistible. As Henry Clay (declaring that the institution of slavery was "destined to become extinct, at some distant day") argued in a presidential campaign letter of 1844, "It would be unwise to refuse a permanent acquisition [Texas] . . . on account of a temporary institution." Clay's argument suggests that the annexation of the slave-based Texas Republic could not have been prevented. But almost surely Texas could have been annexed in a different way from Polk's, with different borders; and this probably could have occurred without more serious consequences than sporadic border warfare with Mexico. Had the United States paid for Texas, there might have been no war at all. Indeed, a policy different from Polk's—more diplomatic, less aggressive, and less provocative—probably could have secured without a war not only Texas but also California and New Mexico. According to David Pletcher, the premier historian of *The Diplomacy of Annexation*, "the Mexican War was . . . an unnecessary gamble":

> Polk's alarums and excursions present an astonishing spectacle. Impelled by his conviction that successful diplomacy could rest only on a threat of force, he made his way, step by step, down the path to war. . . . Polk's background and character militated against . . . reliance on conventional diplomacy. Instead of carefully exploring issues and interests, he chose a policy based on bluff and a show of force. . . . He served his country ill by paying an unnecessarily high price in money, in lives, and in national disunity.[3]

If war with Mexico—or at least a big war—could have been avoided, much of the steam would have been taken out of the early stages of the territorial slavery dispute. Southern leaders might have perceived that Texas was the last place in North America to which they could really aspire to spread plantation slavery. Once the South had acquired the votes of Texas's two senators, Southern Democratic leaders might better have abandoned their efforts to add further slavery-friendly votes to the Senate, and they might better have given up their escalating demands for "Southern rights" in the territories. Had the United States pursued a less unjust policy toward Mexico and had there been no big war between the two nations, it would have been much less difficult for Southern leaders to advocate a rational policy toward territorial slavery. But once the United States had been dragged by the Polk administration into an unnecessary war with Mexico; once thousands of Southern soldiers had trooped off to Mexico, many dying there; once the United States had expended substantial sums to support its armies; and once Southern voters (and many Northern ones too) had thrilled to the stories of General Taylor's triumphs in northern

Mexico and General Winfield Scott's amazing campaign through central Mexico to Mexico City itself, naturally, then, Southern voters demanded that the South have its equal share of the booty. The cry that Southern rights had to be vindicated became much more powerful than it need have been.

Yet the Mexican War merely exacerbated—however greatly—the fundamental question, which was how the South might best respond to the unavoidable growth of antislavery sentiment in the North. Southern whites were ill served by the stress that Southern Democratic leaders laid on states' rights. It is a striking fact that the United States has been the only country where slaveholders have fought a war aimed at preventing the central government from acting against slavery. Everywhere else slavemasters accepted the power of the central government to act as it determined, whatever slavemasters might think. British West Indian slavemasters submitted peacefully to the British Parliament's Emancipation Act of 1833, French slaveholders in the Caribbean submitted to the French government's abolition decree of 1848, Cuban masters accepted the decisions of the Spanish government from 1870 to 1886, and Brazilian masters submitted to their government's acts from 1871 to 1888.[4] Only Southern slavemasters fought a war in a vain attempt to stave off the inevitable. They did so, in large measure, because they believed in states' rights.

But so, to a substantial degree, did most Northerners. When Lincoln was elected president he was pledged to and believed in the doctrine that slavery was untouchable in each state, not to be disturbed by the national government.[5] Southern Democratic leaders like Polk, however, deliberately confused the important distinction between moderate antislavery Northerners (like most backers of the Wilmot Proviso) and abolitionists. The former believed that the national government had authority over territorial slavery (because the national government owned and governed the territories), but they thought it had no power over slavery within the states (because the Tenth Amendment protected the states from unauthorized intrusions of national power). The abolitionists, by contrast, hoped in one way or another to achieve the speedy emancipation of slaves in the states themselves. The states' rights doctrine did not, then, divide Southerners from free-soilers in regard to slavery within the slave states, but it did encourage Southern Democrats to demand the South's "equal rights" in the territories as well. Southern Whigs were less enamored of states' rights than were Southern Democrats, and this encouraged Southern Whigs, as a rule, to take a more rational view of the territorial slavery question (and of other slavery-related issues).

Insisting on "equal rights" in the territories, most Southern Democrats soon denied that either Congress or a territorial legislature (prior to the territory's applying for statehood) had the authority to ban slavery in any territory. Calhoun enunciated this position in 1847, and in ambiguous form it seemed soon to have been accepted even by the Northerner Lewis

Cass so that he could garner the Southern support necessary for his two-thirds' majority as the Democratic presidential nominee in 1848.[6] This reasoning lay behind Southern insistence on repealing the Missouri Compromise in 1854 and behind the Supreme Court's ruling in 1857, in the *Dred Scott* case, that the Missouri Compromise's ban on territorial slavery north of 36°30' had been unconstitutional. By 1860 Southern Democrats demanded enactment of a congressional slave code in order to enforce the right of slaveholders to take slaves anywhere in the territories; this demand provoked them to split the national Democratic Party into a Northern and a Southern wing, increasing the likelihood of a Republican being elected to the presidency that year.[7] This whole disastrous policy arose from the demand of Southern Democrats for Southern rights in the territories.

Had James Polk lived until 1860, perhaps he would not have supported the demand for a congressional slave code, but every other part of this policy was consistent with Polk's own desire for the utmost feasible assertion of Southern rights in the territories. Polk's friend Justice John Catron was a prime actor in securing the U.S. Supreme Court's *Dred Scott* ruling against the Missouri Compromise and in the negotiations through which President-elect James Buchanan (having learned that this decision was forthcoming) pretended in his inaugural address that he did not already know the Court's intention.[8] The absolute insistence on maintaining Southern rights in the territories—in pursuit of which Polk was a principal leader—was almost certain to lead Southern whites into secession and disaster. Tennessee "should not have seceded," the East Tennessee Unionist Whig leader, Judge Oliver Temple, wrote many years after the Civil War:

> It was a stupendous folly. . . . By it every material interest of the State was laid low in ruin. Slavery, which seemed to have been the first consideration in the minds of the Southern people, was forever destroyed. . . . The Abolition party proper constituted but an insignificant part of the Northern people. Slavery was really in no danger, and would exist to-day [1901], but for the transcendent madness and folly of its friends.[9]

Were foresight a predominant human trait, a majority of Southern white voters would have recognized that sooner or later the Northern majority would insist that the national government act to confine slavery within the states where it already existed. This impulse was not yet vigorous enough in the North by 1844 to prevent the annexation of Texas as a slave state, but the strength of the movement was already evident in 1846, when a majority in the House of Representatives voted for the Wilmot Proviso, only to be stopped by the opposition of Southerners and of a few Northern Democrats in the Senate.[10] Although the vast majority of Northerners were willing to abide within the limits imposed by the Tenth Amendment, many of them criticized slavery, and a good many began to wish to establish conditions under which slavery might eventually die out. This was a fundamental impulse behind the free soil movement; and from the moment in 1846 when the Wilmot Proviso passed the House of Representatives, a prescient Southern white might have sensed that the battle for Southern rights in the territories was, in the long run, hopeless and should be given up.

Abandoning this battle, however, would have had serious implications, which few Southern leaders were prepared to face. If the South gave up its struggle for Southern rights in the territories, Southern whites would be acknowledging that they would one day be substantially outnumbered in the Senate, as well as in the House of Representatives. And if Delaware and Maryland, or perhaps even Kentucky, should ever emancipate their slaves, the day might not be distant when the free states could muster a three-quarters' majority to amend the U.S. Constitution in some antislavery direction. Meanwhile, a Northern majority in both Senate and House might feel free to harass the slave states, perhaps by abolishing slavery in the federal District of Columbia or by trying to restrict the interstate sale of slaves.[11] Southern leaders, vociferously pursuing their futile goal of asserting Southern rights in the territories, preserved for themselves and their constituents the illusion that slavery could be insulated forever against any intrusion by the national government. We can see that this was indeed an illusion; that the national government was certain one day to make its influence felt, however mildly at first; and that, of course, in the long run slavery was doomed. It would have been reasonable for Southern leaders, therefore—even when thinking only of the interests of Southern whites— to consider how Southern states could best adapt themselves to a world where the antislavery movement was gaining force while protecting the whites' interests as far as feasible.

James Polk could not have been expected to acknowledge in the 1840s what we can see now—that *eventually* the Southern states would have had to adopt some scheme of so-called *post-nati* emancipation. This method (which had been adopted in Pennsylvania, New York, and New Jersey and thoroughly canvassed in Virginia at its 1831–32 convention) would free at the age of twenty-eight, twenty-five, or possibly twenty-one all slaves born after a specified date.[12] Slavery would gradually die out during a long period, when slaves born before the specified date died one by one and when those born after that date reached their twenties and became free. The scheme would be relatively painless to slavemasters because for many years they would continue to profit from the labor of all their slaves born before the specified date, as well as from the work of newly born slaves until they reached their twenties. The cost to taxpayers would be limited because the whole, or the principal, financial compensation to slavemasters for losing their property would be paid by the labor of the slaves themselves during the next generation or more. The scheme would have been heartless to the slaves themselves—to every slave already alive and also to the newly born until they reached their twenties—and it would not have been acceptable to immediate emancipationists in the North. But it could have been accepted by the great majority of Northern Democrats and by most Northern Whigs, including Abraham Lincoln.[13] In any case, if such a plan had been adopted by Southern states, they would have been perfectly free to do as they chose, unhindered by the objections of Garrisonian abolitionists that post-nati emancipation was slow and immoral.

Post-nati schemes of emancipation were seriously considered by some Southern leaders between 1783 and 1832 and even by a few of them (nearly always Whigs) thereafter. But the water was normally muddied by the intrusion of the colonization issue.[14] Often the term "colonization" was a euphemism for the idea of forcibly deporting from the United States—to "colonize," say, Liberia in West Africa—any blacks who might be emancipated from slavery. Post-nati emancipation in Northern states had not been tied to colonization,[15] but when such schemes were discussed in the South, it was nearly always within the context of deporting the freed people. This doomed these emancipation schemes, for almost everywhere in the Southern low country and Piedmont (except in Delaware and parts of Maryland), the value of land depended on the availability of a large supply of cheap labor to till it. If the slaves had all been deported, land values everywhere in the plantation South would have plummeted. There was no chance that any substantial number of Mississippi landowners, who had children to whom they could bequeath their land, would back a scheme sure to wreck their children's economic prospects. In the absence of enough landless white people willing to work as laborers, plantation owners believed that they required cheap black labor—preferably (most planters thought) slaves who did not need to be paid wages but, in any event, workers who could be made to work for small compensation. It is inconceivable that the Deep South would ever—before the mechanization of its agriculture in the mid-twentieth century—have deported its black laborers, and the same was true for most areas of the middle South as well. As a practicable policy, colonization was in most parts of the South an illusory scheme, permitting some slavemasters to soothe their consciences about their own conduct by persuading themselves that they really favored freeing their slaves. But it was more than that. It also served the valuable function of keeping alive, even in parts of the South, the sentiment that the institution of slavery must some day come to an end.

Although talk of colonization was therefore useful as a means of keeping post-nati emancipation on the agenda of some Southern and Northern whites, the idea of deporting freed people would eventually have had to be abandoned (for the reasons just stated) once post-nati emancipation was to be converted into a practical program. But this would have run into the powerful belief of many Southern whites that any blacks continuing to reside in the South must be controlled if white people's lives and property were to be secure, and slavery was alleged to be the only efficacious means of exerting this control. A large (but indeterminately large) fraction of this sentiment was rationalization by proslavery propagandists like J. D. B. DeBow, who wished to preserve slavery for economic reasons but who fostered anxiety about racial control to whip up support for slavery among Southern whites who had no economic stake in the system. Genuine anxiety that blacks would run out of control if not enslaved was widespread among non-slaveholders, and fears of a potential "war of the races" could always be stirred by demagogues whose allegiance to slavery arose primarily from their economic stake in the system.[16]

So great and so widely distributed were the economic advantages of slavery to white people, and so common were the racial fears that impelled many non-slaveholders to support or at least to tolerate the slave system, that few Southern leaders after 1832 had the courage to broach discussion of post-nati emancipation. Those few were mainly concentrated in the border South or in the parts of western Virginia that, in 1863, having seceded from Virginia, formed the Unionist state of West Virginia. A scheme of post-nati emancipation, seriously discussed in Kentucky in 1851, was overwhelmingly rejected. Some discouraged emancipationists there decided then that no such scheme was likely to succeed unless they could enlist the aid of antislavery Northerners. An alliance between Southern emancipationists and moderate Northern free-soilers seemed their only route to success.[17]

A principal cause for the failure of the Southern emancipation movement (such as it was) was the venomous hostility directed against any such scheme by the Southern Democratic Party. Emancipation would lead to a war of the races! It would undermine the property rights of Southerners! It was a scheme promoted by abolitionist fanatics and traitors to the South! These withering objections were directed by Southern Democrats against the mildest of antislavery proposals.

Freedom of expression about slavery was substantially curtailed in the South after about 1832. That this occurred was not inevitable. It resulted from conscious decisions by politicians like James Polk, for example, who in 1832 isolated and cut down to size the Virginia colonizationist Congressman Charles Mercer. It was the consequence of decisions, such as Speaker Polk's in May 1836, to prevent opposition leaders from arguing against a congressional gag rule on discussions of slavery. It was produced by those assaults (e.g., Governor Polk's Tennessee Democratic Address of 1840) on Southern Whigs that labeled Whigs traitors to the vital interests of the South because of their putative association with abolitionists. By hindsight, it may appear that Democratic efforts of this sort to stifle discussion of the slavery issue ran contrary to the long-term interests of Southern whites.

Influential Southern Democrats like President James Polk might better have told their people the following:

1. Once Texas had been annexed, there were no further great profits to be made from trying to establish slavery in Mexican territory (except in California, which was too far from Texas for slavemasters ever to feel secure there).

2. There was no point in trying to establish Southern rights in Mexican territory because the political leaders of new states formed from that region might never prove reliable allies of slave-state senators and congressmen.

3. In due course the national government, under Northern influence, was certain to put pressure on the slave system by banning slavery in the territories or by abolishing slavery in the District of Columbia. This presented no great threat to slavemasters because there was an important difference between the numerous Northern free-soilers and the relatively few but more determined abolitionists.

4. Protected by the Tenth Amendment and by the willingness of an overwhelming majority of Northerners to abide by the limitations on national power that the amendment imposed, Southern whites would be able to continue profiting from slavery long into the future.

5. Southern white people should therefore repudiate in the strongest terms any claim that secession would be an understandable, perhaps condonable, response to antislavery action in the federal territories or in the federal District of Columbia.

6. It befitted Southern whites, as a liberty-loving people, to cherish the free expression of opinion. This implied that critics of slavery and advocates of gradual emancipation should be allowed their say in Washington and in the South. Free discussion was likely to lead to the most rational decisions about how to secure the long-term interests of Southern whites.

A program of this sort would have appealed entirely to the self-interest of Southern whites without invoking the slightest reference to the welfare of African Americans; and it might therefore be supposed to have stood some chance of being successfully presented to the Southern white electorate. Had policies of this sort triumphed in the South, slavemasters could have continued to reap the profits of slavery for many years after 1860. But when the cotton boom of the 1850s finally came to an end, the speculative boom in slave prices would have terminated, and slavemasters would have felt less prosperous than they had done. With the building of more railways, the growth of Southern cities, and the spread of industrialization, increasing numbers of Southern entrepreneurs would have perceived better ways of investing their capital than in buying slaves, and the price of slaves would have declined. Southern humanitarian impulses, previously diverted into the paternalist cul-de-sac, would once again, with growing force, have impelled examination of schemes of gradual emancipation.

One by one Southern legislatures could have adopted some such scheme. This would have been relatively painless for the planters because the costs of emancipation would no doubt have been placed largely on the shoulders of the slaves themselves (as had previously occurred when northern states had enacted post-nati legislation). When gradual emancipation laws were finally passed in the South, they would presumably have been detached from the colonization idea since Southern landlords would scarcely have tolerated the deportation overseas of many of their black laborers (nor would many taxpayers have been willing to pay the costs of transporting these laborers out of the country). Emancipation could eventually have arrived without the deaths of 250,000 Southern white males, without revolutionary turmoil, and without the devastation of the South.[18]

Yet Southern Democrats in the 1840s and 1850s need not have advocated or even foreseen gradual emancipation. All they needed to do was to forcibly discountenance secession; avoid stirring up unnecessary anxieties; and counsel free, calm discussion of Southern whites' best options. Why did it not occur to Polk and his Southern Democratic colleagues that a program of this sort was best adapted to serve the interests of Southern white people?

Policies that might eventually have led in this direction were indeed proposed by certain Southern leaders. Among Polk's contemporaries, the three most prominent were Polk's opponent in the presidential election of 1844, the Kentucky Whig Henry Clay; the Missouri Democratic Senator Thomas Hart Benton; and the Tennessee Whig John Bell, Polk's rival for the speakership of the U.S. House of Representatives (Bell won in 1834, Polk in 1835). Bell was the Constitutional Unionist candidate for the presidency in 1860, when he won the states of Tennessee, Kentucky, and Virginia. These three Southerners all advocated policies that might have better served the long-term interests of Southern white people than did Polk's.

Senator Benton, for example, opposing the immediate annexation of Texas in 1844, tried to divide Texas so that a substantial part of the region could enter the Union as a free state.[19] Later, just after the end of the Mexican War, he played a central role in blocking the efforts of Polk and others to legalize slavery everywhere in the Mexican Cession south of 36°30'.[20] And in 1849 Benton courageously devoted half the year to making anti-Calhounite speeches across the length and breadth of Missouri. He opposed extending slavery into any area where it had not previously existed. Unlike the Calhounites, Benton believed that Congress *did* have the power to exclude slavery in the territories, although it did not have to exercise that power since slavery had already been banned in the Mexican Cession by Mexican law.[21]

Like Benton, Henry Clay sought to avoid war over Texas, and he hoped for some method of annexation that might prove acceptable to most Northern Whigs. Clay had long supported a colonizationist scheme of gradual emancipation, subsidized by federal funds; as late as 1849 he publicly declared himself in favor of a post-nati scheme of emancipation in Kentucky.[22] John Bell's was another powerful Southern Whig voice against what he regarded as the reckless expansionist policies pursued by Southern Democrats like Polk. Bell opposed Tennessee's secession until after the firing at Fort Sumter, when he, unlike Judge Catron, finally succumbed reluctantly to popular secessionist pressure in Nashville.[23]

To be sure, two of these three Southern leaders were from border states—Missouri and Kentucky—whereas Polk was from the middle South state of Tennessee. Also, the two most prominent of these leaders—Clay and Bell—were Whigs, whereas Polk was a Democrat. This gets close to the heart of the matter, for the Whig Party produced—with the important exceptions of certain dyed-in-the-wool conservatives like the Virginians John Tyler and Abel Upshur[24]—most of those Southern leaders who adopted a relatively moderate stance on the slavery question. For example, the Virginia emancipationist Congressman Charles Fenton Mercer (whose colonization petition James Polk skewered in 1832) became a Whig, and John Berrien, a Whig senator from the Deep South state of Georgia, made able speeches to halt the suicidal course pursued by his Democratic rivals.[25]

Whigs differed from Democrats on economic policy, states' rights, and popular (white males') rights, and their stance on all these matters tended to make them more moderate on slavery than were the Democrats. The rhetoric of electoral competition between Democrats and Whigs seemed to suggest that Whigs favored rapid strides toward a modern commercial economy, whereas Democrats held to old-fashioned noncommercial ideals. But in middle Tennessee—and perhaps in many other parts of the South— entrepreneurial groups in both parties favored commercial development,[26] and the real choice lay between two different routes to achieve that goal. Whigs wanted the national government to foster development by rechartering the Bank of the United States in order to supply and regulate the credit system, by enacting a protective tariff to foster the growth of American industry (including the slave-based sugar industry of Louisiana), by subsidizing transportation projects ("internal improvements"), and by selling government-owned land to farmers at prices high enough to generate the funding for internal improvements (and possibly also the funding for a colonization scheme). Democrats mistrusted all of these federal initiatives. Their policies promoted during the mid-1830s the unconstrained expansion of credit by state banks and the subsidization of internal improvements by state governments, not by the federal government. Their policies of reducing federal land prices and of enacting a revenue tariff favored agricultural entrepreneurs rather than manufacturers. The agrarian language within which the Democrats' economic policies were clothed lent a decep-tively old-fashioned air to their whole program, helping to enlist behind the Democratic Party subsistence farmers, as well as many agricultural and commercial entrepreneurs who were as keen to enter the modern com-mercial world as the most up-to-date New York merchant. When James Polk sought votes from small farmers, he acknowledged that even they were implicated in a market economy. Thus he was much applauded for a free-trade toast (at an 1830 political dinner in his congressional district): "Sell what we have to spare in the market where we can sell for the best price; buy what we need in the market where we can buy cheapest."[27]

Because Whigs turned to the national government to further their economic program, they were accused by their Democratic opponents (like James Polk) of favoring "consolidation"—that is, the enhancement of centralized governmental power. Democrats, who favored states' rights, alleged that Whig centralization violated the U.S. Constitution: the Bank of the United States was unconstitutional, federal promotion of internal improvements was unconstitutional, and a protective tariff was unconsti-tutional.[28] Against these Whig proposals, Democrats such as Polk asserted the rights of state governments to resist encroachment by the national government.[29] The Democrats' states' rights stance made it easy and logi-cally consistent for them to decry any move by the national government to restrict the rights of slavemasters, for example, by imposing a congres-sional ban on territorial slavery.

Yet logical consistency with a states' rights economic program can go only so far in accounting for the Democrats' position on slavery. After all, James Polk proved the most vigorous of all American presidents in wield-ing the power of the national government when he felt it served the in-terests of slavemasters, as he did in his aggressive policy of Texas annexation and in espousing the claims of Texans to boundaries as wide as they chose to assert. By 1860 most Southern Democrats favored wielding the power of the national government in the territories to enact a territorial slave code, which would protect the rights of slavemasters to take slaves anywhere in that area. Something more powerful than logical consistency drove the Southern Democrats into their determined hostility to any encroachment on Southern rights.

Perhaps more significant in this regard than their disputes about eco-nomic policy and states' rights were the disagreements between Whigs and Democrats about popular rights. In the surge toward Jacksonian Democ-racy, Democrats applauded the extension of numerous rights to ordinary white males—the right to vote, the right to hold governmental office, the right to have personal contact with political representatives (who prefer-ably should be limited to brief terms of office), the right to pursue one's individual economic interest unconstrained by governmental restriction, and the right of a majority to impose its will on a minority (requiring members of the minority to conform to majority opinion or to leave the community). Whigs were more cautious about all of these matters. If Whigs remained skeptical about universal (white male) suffrage, they quickly learned to keep their opinions private, and by 1840 Whig politicians had proved as adept as Democrats in courting the favor of ordinary voters.[30] (For example, James Polk was defeated in his bids for reelection as Tennessee's governor, both in 1841 and 1843, by the Whig "Lean Jimmy" Jones, a better-tempered and even more skilled stump speaker and master of the art of ridiculing one's opponent than was Polk himself.)[31] Yet Whigs retained, unlike Democrats, a considerable sense that minority rights sometimes needed to be protected against the will of a popular majority. Southern Whigs like Henry Clay and John Bell were accustomed to rubbing shoulders, fairly comfortably, with Northern Whigs of evangelical background, who felt moral repugnance for slavery. A few Southern Whigs—because of similar personal contacts and because of their mistrust of untrammeled majority rule—even opposed the efforts of a congressional majority to stifle with the gag rule any expression of dissent by the unpopular abolitionist minority. Whigs also tended to retain a sense that it was legitimate for government to impose restrictions on people's pursuit of their own economic self-interest. Whigs, for example, sometimes favored enactment of Sabbatarian legislation, curtailing the right of an individual to conduct business on a Sunday.[32] For these reasons, Whigs were likely to be more tolerant than Democrats toward proposals for governmental restriction of an individual slavemaster's right to take slaves everywhere in the territories.

This sketch of the opposing views of Whigs and Democrats—especially the Democrats' endorsement of unconstrained economic individualism—may help explain James Polk's shortsightedness about the slavery issue. The problem was not simply that Polk owned slaves, for Henry Clay and John Bell each owned as many slaves as (or more than) Polk, yet they favored more cautious policies respecting slavery. In any case, politicians tend to promote policies that they think will be popular with their constituents rather than those that arise solely from their own economic interest. (Alison Freehling has demonstrated that delegates' votes on antislavery proposals at Virginia's 1832 convention depended mainly on which region of Virginia the delegates represented—heavily or only thinly populated with slaves—not primarily on how many slaves the individual delegate owned.[33]) A middle Tennessee Democratic politician who owned thirty-eight slaves—as did James Polk when he was elected president—might advocate a more aggressive assertion of Southern rights than a Kentucky Whig like Clay, the master of about fifty slaves.[34]

When Southern Democrats inveighed against emancipationist proposals such as those of Clay, they invoked the horrors of murder and rape, which they claimed would ensue if blacks were freed. The value of slavery as a form of racial control was constantly asserted to enlist the support of non-slaveholders for the slave system and to allay genuine fears by slavemasters that (because even slaves were often unruly) freed blacks might prove wholly ungovernable. Yet if slavery had been an unprofitable system, Southern leaders surely would have quickly abandoned such a system, and little would have been heard about slavery's utility as a means of racial control. Instead, Southern white leaders would have set about devising new forms of racial control, as most of them promptly did in the years after 1865. In the antebellum South, then, racial control provided a powerful argument in support of the status quo but was not the principal reason that James Polk promoted Southern rights as vigorously as he did.

Polk's circumstances were different from those of the three other upper South leaders who have been mentioned. Senator Benton's Missouri, except for a thin sliver of land, lay entirely north of the 36°30' line; and although Benton owned a few slaves on a Kentucky farm, his Missouri residence was in the booming city of St. Louis, with its commercial ties to the East, West, and North, as well as to the South. Slaves made up in 1840 only 15 percent of Missouri's population (a smaller proportion than in 1830), and Benton courted the votes of small, non-slaveholding farmers. He also gained support from antislavery German immigrants in St. Louis, and he might well feel that, except for a relatively small number of slavemasters, his state's future lay more with the North than with the cotton kingdom.[35] Henry Clay, too, was from a border state, a relatively northern part, and although Clay owned about 50 slaves, they raised hemp, grain, livestock, and tobacco—not, during antebellum years, hugely profitable crops.[36] Clay (and his Kentucky constituents) were not caught up in the frenetic cotton boom that had raged through the Deep South in the 1830s. John Bell, who with his wife apparently owned about 160 slaves in 1856, used them to manufacture iron near the Cumberland River (on Tennessee's northern border) and also perhaps to mine the coal in Kentucky that supplied these Tennessee iron mills. Thus the slavemaster Bell had a common interest with Pennsylvanians in a tariff on iron. Although Bell shared the caution of many other well-established Whig slavemasters about rocking the federal ark too hard, his economic interest pushed him even further in the direction of conciliating Northern Whigs.[37]

Polk, by contrast, was oriented toward cotton and toward Mississippi. He himself had been an enthusiastic participant in Mississippi's cotton boom of the mid-1830s, and he looked for a renewal of that boom to secure his own financial position. He and his Southern Democratic colleagues represented smaller slavemasters or would-be masters—allied with non-slaveholding, subsistence farmers—rather than the better-established planters (and the residents of areas deeply implicated in the market economy), who tended to support Henry Clay's and John Bell's Whig Party.[38] These smaller men-on-the-make thought often of their own short-term economic and social prospects, seldom of the long-term welfare of Southern whites, and Polk offered them no guidance toward understanding the latter. The mastery of slaves perhaps bred into Polk and his peers an even stronger tendency to be domineering than is common among human beings; but he was domineering over recalcitrant Whig congressmen or over Mexicans, not over the passions of his own Southern white constituents. No doubt Polk's was a continentalist vision, but his prospect was of territorial aggrandizement (and national grandeur) linked by an unbreakable chain to a price tag, on which were engraved the words, "Southern rights."

The Southern Democrats' ideologies of states' rights and unconstrained economic individualism meshed with the exigent short-term interest of cotton-planting entrepreneurs (or would-be entrepreneurs), forming a lethal aggregate. This combination of ideology and short-run advantage blinded a majority of Southern whites to their own long-term interests. President Polk might have wielded the extensive powers of his office to help his Southern constituents understand those interests. His failure to do so did not arise solely from his own immersion in establishing a cotton plantation on the Mississippi frontier. That experience did, however, make it easy for Polk to become a true representative of those other slavemaster-entrepreneurs—medium-sized planters, small entrepreneurs with ambition, and would-be entrepreneurs—who avidly sought their own short-term economic advantage, giving scarcely a thought to the long-term interests of Southern white people. The contrast between what Polk might have done as an intelligent, farsighted promoter of his own people's welfare and what he actually did as president was striking indeed.

EPILOGUE

Slavery and the Civil War

Americans of all backgrounds share an interest in trying to understand the origins of the nation's greatest catastrophe. Several influential modern historians have seemed to place ultimate responsibility for the Civil War on Northern Whig and Republican leaders. These writers suggest that if the North had been willing to follow the lead of Northern Democrats, perhaps calamity might have been averted because these Democrats (unlike most other Northerners) were willing to make the compromises that might have kept the Deep South and the middle South in the Union. In this view, most Northerners, except for the Democrats, failed to understand the political constraints within which Southern leaders were obliged to operate. Only the Northern Democrats—and not even all of them—understood that national interference with slavery could not be accepted by any Southern leader who required popular support and that any challenge to slavery would be considered an affront to Southern honor, to be resented and ultimately to be repelled.[1]

Two problems with this interpretation spring to mind. The Northern Democratic Party—as represented, for example, by Senator Stephen Douglas in the Lincoln-Douglas debates of 1858—sought to extract every possible vote by pandering to and inflaming the racial prejudices of the Northern electorate.[2] On the face of it, it seems unlikely that a modern reader would feel great respect for the judgment of this party's leaders.

The other problem lies in the policies actually pursued by the national Democratic Party during the antebellum period. Except for a few months in 1841 and a brief interlude between 1849 and 1853, the party (along with John C. Calhoun's "Whig" allies, President John Tyler and Secretary of State Abel Upshur) dominated the American political scene from 1828 through 1860. During this period Democratic leaders attempted to suppress all congressional discussion of slavery; they insisted on adding the huge slave republic of Texas to the Union and used dubious means to secure this end; they—in the opinion of Whigs like the Tennessee leader John Bell—were reckless and aggressive in pursuing their expansionist policy against Britain and Mexico; some of them did their best to grab additional slave territory in Cuba and in Central America; they repealed the Missouri Compromise; and Democratic administrations attempted to protect slavery in Kansas against the wishes of most settlers there. Thus the Democrats planted the seeds of the Civil War: first, by encouraging the slave states to suppose that Northern antislavery sentiment could be indefinitely ignored, then by conjuring up in the North exactly that determination—whose harbingers the Democrats had deplored—to constrain proslavery influence in the national government.

A different line of enquiry, in trying to comprehend why a different policy did not carry the day, might look to the South. Perhaps too much attention has focused on the state of South Carolina, whose leader John C. Calhoun has sometimes been perceived as the central figure in the Southern drama. No doubt South Carolina led the way, both during the nullification crisis of 1832–33 and when it seceded in December 1860; and the state's leadership has deserved full scrutiny. But the Civil War could never have assumed its actual form without the backing given to South Carolina by Mississippi and the rest of the Deep South and ultimately by Tennessee, Virginia, North Carolina, and Arkansas. The key question is, Why did the Deep South and eventually the middle South, too, follow South Carolina into secession? Here the role of the Democratic Party is all-important, and insofar as President James Polk was a powerful leader of that party, his career as slavemaster and as president may offer insight into the fundamental origins of the Civil War.

I certainly do not argue that Polk's policies arose from a mere defense of his economic interest in his Mississippi plantation. Nor, clearly, am I alleging that the shortsightedness of a Southern politician's perceptions increased in proportion to the number of slaves that politician owned. Owning slaves did nevertheless help to shape Polk's political vision, and what was true for Polk was probably true for most other Southern Democratic slavemasters and, to a lesser degree, of most Southern Whig slavemasters as well.

Polk felt that running his slave plantation was his own private business, not a matter of legitimate public concern. "There is nothing wrong [in] it," he wrote in 1846 to his cousin, then engaged in secretly buying for the president half a dozen slaves, aged twelve to seventeen, "but still the public have no interest in knowing it."[3] This was the expression of a defensive mentality, which boiled with resentment when outsiders suggested that the federal government had any right to interfere with the private business of a slavemaster. This mentality would ultimately lead to secession as a legitimate response by the slavemasters to the prospect of what seemed to be substantial federal interference with their rights.

Polk's slaves reminded him, by the persistence of their efforts to flee his plantation, of their dissatisfaction with their lives. Nor can Polk have failed to notice the large number of slave children who died at his plantation, and the considerable number of young adults who perished there as well. He probably was conscious that, although he had sometimes bought or sold a slave to prevent the disruption of a marriage, his buying, selling, or moving other slaves from one place to another had disrupted several other families. Perhaps he felt that running a slave plantation was not a very salubrious business, and this feeling may have contributed to his intention, written in his will, to emancipate his slaves after his own death if his wife should predecease him.

But he considered the connection between himself and his slaves to be a private matter because his slaves were property, private property, and the public had no legitimate interest in how he handled his property. Slaves were an investment, and Polk invested thousands of dollars in buying more of them to increase the income he derived from his Mississippi plantation. He thought that investing in slaves on a cotton plantation was the best way to secure a reasonable income to supplement his congressional or gubernatorial salary and to ensure a good retirement income. Perhaps Polk's decisions as a private slavemaster were no more objectionable than those of most others of his kind. But statesmen have some responsibility to rise above short-term calculation and to think of the long-term interests of their own people—or even of their own nation. Instead of rising to the occasion, Congressman Polk (and later President Polk) brought to the national stage the constricted views of a Tennessee slavemaster. It would be intolerable, he felt, for outsiders to seize through the federal government power to interfere with a gentleman's pursuit of his own private business. The Union was indeed a blessing, but if Northerners ever brought things to an "extreme case," Southerners might be obliged to secede in order to preserve their society from the incursions of those who failed to acknowledge the right of private property in slaves.

For Southern white people what seemed to be at stake above all else was a social system permitting slavemasters to enrich themselves—and would-be slavemasters to hope to enrich themselves—in ways unparalleled in contemporary Southern circumstances. If a poor man would "just move into a rich neighborhood and jest be a little sassy [i.e., stop letting poor neighbors sponge off him], he'd get rich," a cotton planter's son exclaimed in 1853. "Never knew a man that was industrious and sassy in this country [northern Mississippi] that did n't get rich, quick, and get niggers to do his work for him. Anybody ken that's smart."[4] The South was bursting with slaveholding entrepreneurs (and would-be entrepreneurs like this one), and they dominated society. They found in James Polk a true representative of their wishes—one who, because he was less blatantly proslavery than John C. Calhoun, was able to garner enough political support in the North to make his way to the presidency; and one who so combined the roles of masterful deceiver, imperious organizer, jingoist bully, and lucky gambler that he could effect imperial conquests such as no other American president has aspired to. The expansion of slavery into the West—into Texas and perhaps beyond—for the benefit of Southern slaveholding entrepreneurs and would-be entrepreneurs was only part of Polk's aim; yet to all of his expansionist program was attached from the outset an important proviso (which might be called the Southern Democratic Proviso), stating that "Southern rights must, at all costs, be maintained in the new territory."

These rights had to be maintained because the security of the whole social system appeared to be at stake—the social system that enabled slavemaster-entrepreneurs to make their way in the world. To Southern Democratic leaders like Polk, it seemed essential to kill, as though it were a vicious snake, any assertion (such as that of the Wilmot Proviso) that the national government possessed any power to interfere with slavery. This principle might perhaps be compromised to the extent that an earlier generation of Southern statesmen had been willing, in 1820, to sacrifice it—that is, as far as 36°30'. But beyond that line there could be no real compromise, for otherwise the rights of the Southern states and their citizens would be imperiled. The monstrous phantasm of federal power would rear its venomous head, threatening to strike at that social system in which slavemaster-entrepreneurs found their profit, their power, and their status.

Not every slavemaster, of course, was an expanding entrepreneur like James Polk. Rich Southern businessmen such as the greatest of South Carolina rice planters, Nathaniel Heyward, often had children who became indolent inheritors of wealth (just as vigorous entrepreneurs in the North often produced children who lived lazily from the proceeds of inherited stocks and bonds). But the dominant ethos of the burgeoning Southwest—Tennessee, Mississippi, Louisiana, Arkansas, and Texas—and of the whole cotton belt, and of much of the rest of the South as well, was the spirit of slave-based enterprise, as typified by James Polk and his entrepreneurial brother-in-law James Walker. The perceived short-term interests of slavemaster-entrepreneurs and would-be entrepreneurs throughout the Deep South and the middle South dominated Southern political life.

Slavery also offered Southern whites a mode of racial control. Politicians like James Polk stressed this function of the system when they sought maximum emotional response to their appeals to kill the prospect of federal interference. According to slavery apologists like Polk, the lives of Southern white people, especially the sexual purity of Southern white women, were at risk whenever Southern rights were threatened. The preservation of slavery, President Polk instructed the House of Representatives in 1848, "involves the domestic peace and security of every [white] family."[5] This cry resonated with a Southern electorate genuinely alarmed that unenslaved blacks would run wild in the South. Yet it is evident, with hindsight, that if slavery had not been profitable, the system would quickly have died and Southern whites would have devised a different way of keeping African Americans under their thumbs. The cries for slavery as a system of racial control were, although responding to genuine fears, essentially rationalizations for securing a system that enriched Southern entrepreneurs and appealed to the hungers of would-be entrepreneurs.

Some historians have suggested that proposals to curb territorial slavery were resented in substantial measure because of their perceived insult to Southern honor. And indeed there can be no doubt that an honor ethos (demanding that affronts to the male ego be strenuously resented) pervaded Southern society. The affray in which James Polk's younger brother William insulted a fellow townsman (by horsewhipping him) and then killed him a few days later in broad daylight before 100 witnesses (when the insulted gentleman predictably sought to vindicate his honor with a gun) merely illustrates the wide reach of an honor ethic.[6] But the need to uphold Southern honor (like the need to maintain racial control) served as an argument that politicians pulled out of the bag to add emotional fervor to a defense of slavery primarily motivated by other forces. In their Address of 1840, Southern Democratic leaders focused their antiabolitionist arguments on the real issue—the security of the slave system—and appealed to Southern honor only in the brief peroration. Soon Southern leaders began waving the flag of honor at earlier points of the disputation; and in President Polk's draft veto of the Wilmot Proviso, he did indeed plan to declare, if Congress passed the proviso, that "for the first time in the history of the Government . . . the [Southern] States and the citizens of the [Southern] States . . . are sought to be reduced to a humiliating condition of inequality (with) and inferiority to their confederate States and their citizens."[7]

But why did the defense of slavery call forth appeals to Southern honor when they had been little heard in protests against a high tariff, against the Bank of the United States, or against federal improvements? Evidently the defense of slavery touched the most sensitive area of Southern life. At stake was not just the price of imported ironware, the vesting of control over the national credit system in the hands of the private banker Nicholas Biddle; or the financing of a road across the Allegheny Mountains. The issue instead seemed to be the security of the whole Southern social system: was the South to remain a slave society, whose slavemaster-entrepreneurs could freely enrich themselves by using enslaved labor (and whose families would feel themselves protected from blacks' putative violence by a Draconian system of racial control)? Or was the federal reptile to be permitted to threaten the life of this peculiar social system? Well might a politician cry that honor was at stake when the stakes seemed so large.[8]

The social history of James Polk's plantation may also remind us that many slavemasters preferred to envelop their plantation operations within a sweet-smelling haze of paternalist rhetoric. If the president of the United States was spending every spare penny of his plantation profits in buying children as young as ten years old—separated from mother, father, siblings, and friends—so that he could amass a substantial force of enslaved laborers to support himself in gentlemanly style during his retirement, this fact must be hidden from the public. The voters must believe instead that Polk seldom entered the market for enslaved labor—and then only in order to bring black families together. Although the Polk slaves did indeed experience certain instances of genuine benevolence, events at the plantation seldom matched the paternalist talk. Thus Caroline Johnson was never permitted to live with her husband at John Leigh's plantation, and the marriages of Barbara to Billy Nevels and of Barbara's brother Charles to Rosetta were permanently shattered when Polk's nephew decided to carry off his "property" to Tennessee. In 1834 James Polk reappointed the brutal overseer Ephraim Beanland, even after Beanland had driven the majority of Polk's Tennessee male hands into temporary flight and had stabbed Caroline Johnson's father, Chunky Jack. The numerous flights of Polk's slaves—even of his most valued plantation hand, Henry Carter—indicated how discontented they were with their lot. Moreover, the flights were often repeated, with Gilbert running away at least ten times and Joe fleeing at least seven times before he was sold by Sarah Polk at James Polk's wish. Child mortality at Polk's plantation was about double the contemporary rate for free children. This inhumane system survived in the South, and was vigorously protected by the region's leaders, because it paid well. Polk's plantation, for example, earned virtually an 11 percent profit on its capital investment over the thirteen-year span from 1845 through 1857, even taking into account the loss of more than half of the crops in two of those years; and the capital gains were even greater in 1858 and 1859, when the market value of slaves skyrocketed.

Thus the resulting suicide of the slave system from 1860 to 1865 cannot be attributed primarily to an eccentric group of South Carolina extremists, even though that state took the lead in resisting federal interference with slavery.[9] The real responsibility for secession was widely spread throughout the Deep South and the middle South, and it fell most heavily on Democratic Party leaders such as James Polk and his successors.[10] They constantly gave the wrong signals to the Southern electorate. Their ideology—states' rights plus unconstrained economic individualism—meshed perfectly with the perceived short-term interests of slavemasters (and would-be slavemasters). The prolonged cotton boom of the mid-nineteenth century might sometimes be temporarily checked, as it was between 1837 and about 1843, but usually slave-based cotton entrepreneurs were on to a very good thing, and they knew it.

The understanding of the Civil War's origins has recently been enhanced by the publication of Leonard Richards's *The Slave Power*. Richards depicts the role of Northern Democrats (especially of the so-called "doughfaces" among them) in upholding during the antebellum years Southern domination of the federal government.[11] A similar reappraisal is needed of the role of Southern Democrats in upholding that domination and in shaping its character.[12] The present sketch of President Polk's career may suggest one direction in which such an analysis of Southern Democratic policies could lead.

With respect to slavery, Polk and his Southern Democratic colleagues (aided by many of their Northern Democratic allies) did nothing at all to open the eyes of the electorate to the long-term interests of Southern whites. Instead of distinguishing, as they might have done, between Northern free-soilers and abolitionists, Southern Democrats lumped the two groups together as dangerous abolitionist fanatics. Instead of fostering free discussion of slavery's future and tolerating rational consideration of schemes of post-nati gradual emancipation, Southern Democrats eschewed any suggestion that slavery might one day come to an end. These leaders did not need to declare (as John Calhoun declared) that slavery was a blessing, which should be continued in perpetuity. All they had to do to ruin the South was to declare (as James Polk did) that they believed in unconstrained economic individualism and in an expanded version of states' rights; this ideology was as sufficient to blind its adherents to the future as was the "perpetualist" language of Calhoun.[13]

If the indefinite continuation of slavery were indeed a vital interest of Southern white people (as the dominant entrepreneurs and would-be entrepreneurs so deeply felt) and if the federal government had no right to interfere with slave-based entrepreneurs in the Southern states, it seemed logical to Polk and many other Southern Democratic leaders to demand Southern rights in *every* slavery-related field touched by the possibility of federal interference. Because Polk had rammed the annexation of the huge slave republic of Texas through a doubtful Congress and because he launched an unnecessary war against Mexico, both North and South felt considerable passion about the issue of Southern rights in the newly conquered territories. Although President Polk cooperated with Calhoun's attempt to engineer the legalization of slavery everywhere in the Mexican Cession (by judicial fiat), Polk and some of his Southern Democratic colleagues were willing (during the 1840s) to compromise the territorial issue up to a certain point—preferably to the 36°30' line. But Southern rights must be vindicated in some substantial form. The Tenth Amendment was not enough. Unnecessarily, Polk and most Southern Democrats went beyond states' rights to the principle that Congress must never infringe slavemasters' rights *anywhere* (except perhaps north of 36°30'). They demanded further guarantees, beyond the Tenth Amendment, that Northerners would never use federal power to undermine slavery in the states. The Wilmot Proviso was intolerable, and if the North insisted on banning slavery everywhere in the territories, Southern Democrats threatened—not merely warned, but also threatened—that the Union was in jeopardy. Secession, in other words, was on the cards from the moment Polk launched his war against Mexico in May 1846; and although the president sometimes distanced himself from Calhoun, the language of Polk's address to the House of Representatives in August 1848 and of his draft veto of the Wilmot Proviso suggested that, when the crunch finally came, nearly the whole Southern Democratic Party would follow South Carolina into secession.

That combination of ideology and short-term socioeconomic interest, which was so potent in the 1840s and 1850s, has not been wholly absent from more recent American history. A philosophy of unconstrained economic individualism and states' rights, combined with the perceived short-term economic interests of Southern landlords, led to perpetuation in the South, after the Civil War, of a caste system which corrupted human relations well into the twentieth century. In addition, an ideology of unconstrained economic individualism and of states' rights, joined to the short-term economic interests of a different group of entrepreneurs, led to the catastrophe of the Great Depression and to the sharp social conflicts in the United States during the 1930s. James Polk and his Southern Democratic colleagues had preached a similar ideology, which seemed exactly suited to the short-term interests of the entrepreneurs of his own semicapitalist slave society.

We modern Americans like to distance ourselves from James Polk's world by (correctly) naming it a slave society and ours a free society. We repudiate the slave system that was so important to our ancestors, but we are slower to repudiate the politics that walked arm in arm with that social system. Nostalgia for the Civil War era still pervades our culture as we relive vicariously, again and again, the glorious battles that some of our forebears fought to preserve their imperiled way of life. We no longer view plantation slavery through rose-tinted glasses, yet we remain reluctant to acknowledge that our political leaders betrayed us and that our ancestors often followed them uncritically. Our leaders' pursuit of short-term interests resulted in a horrendous national tragedy and in the South's desolation. Only when we reexamine our leaders' false turnings are we likely, finally, to forsake our strange esteem for the men who led us into disaster.

Appendix A

Polk Plantation Demography, 1835–59

Note: Abbreviations are listed and explained at the beginning of the notes section.

This appendix—after specifying the sources for statements in chapter 7 about demography—supplies five tables: (1) a chronological list of births at the plantation, (2) a chronological list of deaths, (3) calculations of the plantation's natural population growth, (4) a chronological list of slaves imported into and exported from the plantation, and (5) (based on the four previous lists) an annual tally of the plantation's population. From these lists, historians will be able to check the assertions in the text about child mortality, family size, and population growth.

The most important source is the 1849 inventory of Polk's Mississippi slaves, listed in family groups with valuations, at the Yalobusha County court house [JP estate inventory, Dec. 5, 1849, Yalobusha County Inventory book E, pp. 31–35, Coffeeville, Mississippi (hereafter JP, 1849 inventory)]. Nearly as helpful is the listing of his widow's slaves in 1860 [Sarah Polk, sale agreement, Jan. 25, 1860, James Polk MS, Tennessee State Archives, Nashville (hereafter SP, 1860 agreement)], a nearly correct version of which is easily accessible (Bassett, p. 275). The main James Polk Papers, at the Library of Congress, contain lists of his slaves assigned to the plantation late in 1834, with their ages and valuations (Sept. 5, 26, 1834), and lists of his field workers in 1844 and 1846 (RC to JP, Jan. 9, 1847). These papers also contain bills of sale (or other records), supplying the ages and prices of almost every slave bought by James Polk. Polk's 1831 will and records of the litigation surrounding his father-in-law's estate give further names and prices of slaves. The 1826 will of Polk's father contains the names of several slaves who, although originally willed to Polk's brothers, eventually came into his possession after the deaths (during the 1830s) of four of the brothers. Polk's notes on the back of an old envelope (the envelope is dated May 3, 1842) identify some of his field workers that autumn.

Overseers' letters give the birthdates of many babies and often name their mothers; the letters also record the deaths of slaves, along with the causes. But as many overseers' letters are no longer extant (and virtually none have survived for the years 1843–44 and 1857–59), much inference is required. The list of slaves in 1860, however, provides a good basis for many of these inferences, especially because young boys and girls are listed separately from adults; also the names of both the older slaves and of the young children are evidently written more or less in order of their descending ages. From these sources one can identify with reasonable assurance forty-eight children born at the plantation from 1835 to 1859, of whom twenty-one had died by January 1860 (see table A1).

The greatest uncertainty pertains to the number of children who were born and died at the plantation without either event's being mentioned in an extant letter. I estimate that there were at least seven such babies—one born in 1843, one in 1844, two in 1857, two in 1858, and one in 1859 (all of these being years from which almost no overseers' letters have survived). Although this estimate is almost certainly too small, I have preferred to avoid any appearance of exaggerating the child mortality rate. Even this minimum estimate of seven unrecorded babies who died before 1860—raising the total number of babies born at the plantation to fifty-five, of whom twenty-eight died by 1860—indicates a child mortality rate of 51 percent, and the reality was almost certainly even grimmer (see chapter 7, note 24). The estimated numbers of births and deaths in each of the two periods, 1835–49 and 1850–59, is shown in table 7.1.

Discussion of child mortality rates at the plantation appears in chapter 7, notes 4 and 21 and especially in note 24; details are supplied in table 7.2 and in table A1.

The manuscript U.S. censuses of 1840 and 1850 are of a certain but only limited value for the Polks' plantation. Neither census names individual slaves (thus white people trained themselves to regard these black human beings as nameless chattel), and the 1840 census (Yalobusha County, p. 284) did not even assign exact ages. Instead it grouped Polk's twenty male slaves into five categories (ages zero–nine, ten–twenty-three, twenty-four–thirty-five, thirty-six–fifty-four, and fifty-five plus) and divided his sixteen female slaves into the same groupings. Evidently overseer John Garner supplied rough and ready guesses of the slaves' ages (e.g., he seems to have reported forty-one-year-old Allen as fifty-five plus). And although the 1850 census (Yalobusha County, Schedule 2, pp. 33–34) purports to give the exact age of each slave, it contains palpable errors. Thus Maria Davis's one-year-old son, John, is apparently listed as seven years old, and the age of Daphney's four-month-old infant, Silas, is similarly misreported. Furthermore, overseer John Mairs seems to have alleged many male slaves to be younger than they actually were. The 1860 census (Yalobusha County, Schedule 2, pp. 69–70) also contains obvious errors: thus it claims—incredibly and contrary to SP, 1860 agreement—that all twelve children under the age of ten were males. In any case, the 1860 census is unhelpful because by August of that year (when the census was taken) Sarah Polk had removed six of her slaves from the plantation, and her new business partner evidently had sent ten of his own (of unknown ages and sexes) to augment the plantation's work force. The 1840 and 1850 censuses are nevertheless of some value—for example, in suggesting that neither Dicey nor Caesar had died until after 1840 and that "Joe 1" must have been at the plantation in 1850, even though his name does not appear in JP, 1849 inventory.

The other records, previously described, offer a surprisingly clear picture of plantation demography. The details are contained in the following five tables (A1–A5).

Table A1
Births of Polk Plantation Slaves (chronological), 1835–59

Children	Mothers	(a) Births (year)	(b) Deaths (year)	(c) Children Alive in 1860	(d) Sources*
Malinda	Elizabeth	1836?	—	Malinda	J, S
Anon 6	Eve?	1836?	1841?	—	WHP to JP, 12/17/36; C (1840)
Jim	Elizabeth	1838?	—	Jim	J, S
Anon 2	Elizabeth	1839?	1840	—	A, 10/4/40
Angeline	Eve	1840?	—	Angeline	J, S, A, 8/1/40
Anon 5	Matilda	1840	1840	—	A, 5/3/40
Andy	Elizabeth	1841?	—	Andy	J, S
Charity	Daphney	1844?	1849	—	A, 1/22/45 (12/28/44), 4/19/49
Julius	Eve	1845	—	Julius	J, S, A, 9/24/45
Davy	Elizabeth	1845	—	Davy	J, S, A, 10/28/45
Anon 7	Marina?	1846	1846?	—	A, 7/22/46 (4/26/46)
Frank	Daphney	1846	1854?	—	J, A, 7/8/46; C (1850)
Fanny 1	Elizabeth	1847	1850	—	J, A, 11/5/47, 10/8/50
Luchas	Eve	1847	1849	—	A, 10/1/47, 2/8/49
Lily	Daphney	1848	—	Lily	J, S, A, 7/6/48
Eliza 2	Barbara	1849	1851	—	J, A, 2/8/49, 7/8/51
John	Maria Davis	1849	—	John	J, S, A, 4/19/49
Silas	Daphney	1850	1851	—	A, 6/7/59, 5/18/51
Irvin	Eve	1850	1850	—	A, 8/10/50, 11/6/50
Mary An 1	Eve	1850	1850	—	A, 8/10/50, 11/6/50
Clay	Marina?	1850?	—	Clay	S
Burrel	Sally	1851	1851?	—	A, 3/5/51
Marthy	Barbara	1851	—	Marthy?	A, 4/16/51
Judy	Maria Davis	1851	1852	—	A, 9/10/51, 8/18/52
Anon 4	Eve	1851?	1852?	—	A, 9/20/52
George	Agnes?	1851?	—	George	S, A, 3/3/53
Willis	Jane?	1851?	—	Willis	S
Mary An 2	Daphney	1852?	1852?	—	A, 8/18/52
An Marie	Eve	1852	—	Any	S, A, 11/1/52
Violet	Jane	1852	—	Violet	S, A, 11/12/52
Carter	Caroline Childress?	1852?	—	Carter	S
Fanny 2	Maria Davis	1853	1854?	—	A, 7/9/53
Edward	Marina	1853	—	Edward	S, A, 8/16/53
Paul	Daphney	1853	—	Paul	S, A, 8/22/53
Ananias 1	Eve	1853	1854	—	A, 8/22/53, 7/6/54
Patson	Jane	1854	1855	—	A, 4/9/54, 8/1/55
Louisa	Sally	1854	—	Louisa	S, A, 10/11/54
Anon 9	Jane	1855	1855	—	A, 6/17/55
Henry Polk	Eve	1855	—	Henry	S, A, 8/29/55
Zach	Daphney	1855	—	Zach	S, A, "9/8/55"
Osburn	Caroline Harris	1855	—	Osburn	S, A, "9/8/55"
Ted	Caroline Childress	1856?	—	Ted	S

Children	Mothers	(a) Births (year)	(b) Deaths (year)	(c) Children Alive in 1860	(d) Sources*
Daniel	Maria Davis	1856	—	Daniel	S, A, 8/2/56
Manuel	Jane	1856	—	Manuel	S, A, 9/13/56
Susan	Malinda	1856	—	Susan	S, A, 12/3/56
Anon 14	Sally	1857	1857	—	A, 2/12/57
Ananias 2	Eve?	1858?	—	Ananias	S
Eliza 3	Malinda?	1859?	—	Eliza	S

		Births	Deaths	Children Alive in 1860	
Subtotal		48	21	27	
Unrecorded births at plantation of children who died unrecorded (est.)		7	7	0	
Total		55	28	27	

Child mortality rate (est.): (b)/(a) = 28/55 = 51%.

*Sources: A = agent's (e.g., overseer's) letter.
C = census (U.S. Census Bureau, manuscript).
J = JP, 1849 inventory.
S = SP, 1860 agreement.

Surmises: The list of young slave children living at the plantation in 1860 includes seven whose mother's names are uncertain:

Ananias 2	b. 1858?
Eliza 3	b. 1859?
George	b. 1851?
Willis	b. 1851?
Clay	b. 1850?
Carter	b. 1852?
Ted	b. 1856?

All seven children were born after 1849 (their names not being in JP, 1849 Inventory). I infer the approximate years of their births from their places on SP, 1860 Agreement, which lists young children more or less in order of decreasing age and monetary value. I surmise that Ananias 2 was a child of Eve, because Eve had lost another child of that name in 1854. I guess that Eliza 3 was a child of Malinda, named after Malinda's mother, Elizabeth. When Agnes died in 1853 she apparently left a surviving child (JM to SP, 3/3/53); I surmise that this was George. Willis, probably born about June 1851, is likely to have been Jane's child (Jane, after miscarrying on about May 1, 1850, bore other living children in November 1852, March 1854, June 1855, and August 1856). Clay may have been a child of Marina, named after Claiborne (a brother of Marina?), who had been owned by Silas Caldwell when Marina also belonged to Caldwell. Carter (a girl probably born just after Henry Carter's death in 1852, and presumably named in his memory) is likely to have been a child of Henry Carter's son Wilson. I guess that Wilson (the brother of President Polk's White House servant Henry) married Caroline Childress (raised as a house servant by Sarah Childress Polk's mother) and that Caroline Childress, in addition to being Carter's mother, may also have been the mother of Ted.

Name	Birth (year)	Death (year)	Sources on Death★
Hardy	1808	1835	Caldwell to JP, 2/11/35
Abe	1812	1836	Caldwell to JP, 1/16/36
Lucy	1792?	1838	A, 11/24/38
Anon 5	1840	1840	A, 5/3/40
Anon 2	1839?	1840	A, 10/4/40
Anon 6	1836	1841?	WHP to JP, 12/17/36; C (1840); I
Caesar	1806	1841?	I
Dicey	1817	1841?	WHP to JP, 12/2/37; I
Fan	1828	1843?	I
Matilda	1814	1843?	A, 7/5/40, 10/4/40; I
Old Charles	1785?	1844?	A, 10/14/34; I
Eliza 1	1830	1845	A, 9/24/45
Anon 7	1846	1846?	I
Caroline Henly	1830	1848	A, 7/20/48
Luchas	1847	1849	A, 2/8/49
Charity	1844?	1849	A, 4/19/49
Caroline Davis	1829	1850	A, 3/15/50
Fanny 1	1847	1850	A, 10/8/50
Irvin	1850	1850	A, 11/6/50
Mary An 1	1850	1850	A, 11/6/50
Eliza 2	1849	1851	A, 7/8/51
Silas	1850	1851	A, 5/18/51
Burrel	1851	1851?	I
Mariah Carter	1814	1851?	J, I
William	1839	1852	A, 8/3/52
Mary An 2	1852?	1852	A, 8/18/52
Judy	1851	1852	A, 8/18/52
Anon 4	1851	1852	A, 9/20/52
Henry Carter	1812	1852	A, 10/21/52
Old Cloe	1788	1852	A, 9/20/52; I
Old Sarah	1774	1852	A, 12/21/52
Agnes	1833	1853	A, 3/3/53
Old Ben	1784?	1853?	C (1840); J; I
Calvin	1833	1854	A, 2/25/54
Ananias 1	1853	1854	A, 7/6/54
Frank	1846	1854?	J, I
Fanny 2	1853	1854?	I
Anon 9	1855	1855	A 6/17/55
Patson	1854	1855	A, 8/1/55

continued

Name	Birth (year)	Death (year)	Sources on Death★
Anon 14	1857	1857	A, 2/12/57
Caroline Johnson	1818	1857?	A, 9/13/56; I

		Deaths	Unreported Deaths of Unreported Births (est.)	Total Deaths
Subtotals:				
1835–49		16	2	18
1850–59		25	5	30
Total: 1835–59		41	7	48

★*Sources*:

A = agent's (e.g., overseer's) letter.

C = census (U.S. Census Bureau, manuscript).

I = inference:

Before 1849: from absence of name on JP, 1849 Inventory and absence from lists of earners in 1844 and 1846 (RC to JP, 1/9/47).

After 1849: from absence of name on SP, 1860 Agreement.

J = JP, 1849 inventory.

S = SP, 1860 agreement.

Table A3
Natural Population Growth at Polk Plantation, 1835–59

	(a) Births	(b) Births	(c) Births	(d) Deaths	(e) Deaths	(f) Deaths	(g)
	Listed in Table A1	Unreported, of Children Whose Deaths Were Unreported (est.)	Total (est.) $[(a) + (b)]$	Listed in Table A2	Unreported, of Children Whose Births Were Unreported (est.)	Total (est.) $[(d) + (e)]$	Natural Population Growth $[(c) - (f)]$
1835–49	17	2	19	16	2	18	1
1850–59	31	5	36	25	5	30	6
Total	48	7	55	41	7	48	7

	Imports		Exports	Net Imports
1835	Original group (21)*: Abe, Addison, Barbara, Caesar, Charles 1, old Charles, Dicey, Elizabeth, Eve, Garrison, Giles, Hardy, Henry Carter, Henry (Mariah's), Jim Turner (Eve's), Lucy, Mariah, Phil, Reuben, old Sarah, Wilson (Mariah's).			
1836			Reuben	
1837	Imported: Nancy			
1838	Purchased (9): Caroline Johnson, Charles 2, Cloe, Eliza 1, Fan, Gilbert, Manuel, Marina, Perry		Nancy	
1839	Purchased (4): Allen, Daphney, Matilda, William. Imported: old Ben			
1840			Sold: Charles 2.	
1841			Henry (Mariah's)	
1842	Imported (4): Alphonso, Bob, Joe 1,† Pompey			
1845	Purchased: Caroline Childress			
1846	Purchased (9): Agnes, Billy Nevels, Calvin, Caroline Henly, Harbert, Jane, Lewis, Mary, Sally			
1847	Purchased (2): Joe 2, Maria Davis			
1848	Imported: Harry (blacksmith)			
1849	Purchased (6): Anderson, Caroline Davis, Caroline Harris, Jason, Jerry, Rosetta			
1851			Bob†	
1852			Barbara,† Charles 1,† Marthy	
1853			Sold: Joe 2	
1856			Sold: Harbert	
Subtotals: 1835–49:	59		4	55
1850–59	0		6	−6
Total: 1835–59	59		10	49

*As explained in chapter 4, during Polk's partnership with Silas Caldwell (1835–36), only nine of Polk's slaves worked at the new Mississippi plantation, joined by nine of Caldwell's. The rest of Polk's slaves worked at Caldwell's West Tennessee plantation, apparently not moving to Mississippi until the partnership was dissolved at the end of 1836. By this time Hardy, a 26-year-old slave of Polk, had died, before he could be sent on from Tennessee.

†Joe 1, Bob, Barbara, Charles 1: JP, 1849 Inventory, lists only one Joe, although two slaves of that name worked at the plantation. One of them (Joe 2) was a frequent fugitive, purchased in 1847; I believe he was sold in 1853, after he had fled at least seven times. The other Joe (Joe 1) was a privileged slave owned by Polk's mother and lent by her in about 1842 to work for James Polk in Mississippi. This Joe seems to have acted as a driver on Polk's plantation. James Polk's executor Daniel Graham doubtless knew that Joe 1 was owned by Polk's mother, and Graham therefore omitted this Joe from the 1849 list of slaves owned by Polk. In 1850 Graham seems to have learned that Bob was in fact owned by Marshall Polk, Jr., not by James Polk; Graham therefore omitted Bob's name from an 1850 copy of the 1849 list (Yalobusha County Inventory Book E, p. 33: Bob's name was listed in the original 1849 Inventory, p. 32). But in 1850 apparently Graham still didn't know that young Marshall Polk also owned Barbara and Charles, and the names of these two slaves (and of Barbara's child) therefore appeared in both the 1849 Inventory and its 1850 copy.

In 1852 Polk's mother died, and she appears to have bequeathed Joe 1 to Polk's widow. Thus the 1860 list of Sarah Polk's Mississippi slaves includes Joe 1. Joe 2, however, is missing from that list; I infer that he had been sold.

Table A5
Population of Polk Plantation, 1835–59 (annual)

	(a)	(b)	(c)	(d) Births — Unrecorded, Of children Who died Unrecorded Before 1860 (est.)	(e) Total [(c) + (d)]	(f)	(g) Deaths — Unrecorded of children born Unrecorded (est.)	(h) Total [(f) + (g)]	(i) Total — Population at end of year [previous (i) + (a) − (b) + (e) − (h)]
	Imports	Exports	Known			Known			
1835	21	—	—	—	—	1	—	1	20
1836	—	1	2	—	2	1	—	1	20
1837	1	—	1	—	—	1	—	—	21
1838	9	1	1	—	1	1	—	1	29
1839	5	—	1	—	1	—	—	—	35
1840	—	1	2	—	2	2	—	2	34*
1841	4	1	1	—	1	2	—	2	32
1842	—	—	—	—	—	—	—	—	36
1843	1	—	1	1	1	3	1	4	33
1844	—	—	1	1	2	1	1	2	33
1845	1	—	2	—	2	1	—	1	35
1846	9	—	2	—	2	1	—	1	45
1847	2	—	2	—	2	1	—	—	49
1848	1	—	1	—	1	1	—	1	50
1849	6	—	2	—	2	2	—	2	56
1850	—	—	4	—	4	4	—	4	56
1851	—	1	6	—	6	4	—	4	57
1852	—	3	4	—	4	7	—	7	51

1853	—	1	4	—	4	2	2	52
1854	—	—	2	—	2	4	4	50
1855	—	1	4	—	4	2	2	52
1856	—	—	1	—	4	—	—	55
1857	—	—	1	2	3	2	4	54
1858	—	—	1	2	3	—	2	55
1859	—	—	1	1	2	—	1	56
Subtotals:								
1835–49	59	4	17	2	19	16	18	56
1850–59	0	6	31	5	36	25	30	56
Total	59	10	48	7	55	41	48	56

★This figure of thirty-four slaves at the *end* of 1840 is consistent with the 1840 census, which recorded the presence of thirty-six slaves in the *summer* of 1840. No doubt the census taker included Charles (who was sold later in 1840) and Elizabeth's youngest child (who died about Oct. 1, 1840).

Sources: columns (a) and (b): table A4; column (c): table A1; columns (d) and (g): my estimate that at least seven children were born unrecorded, who died unrecorded before 1860, is discussed in the fourth paragraph of this appendix. In the absence of information about when the seven children died, I have somewhat arbitrarily assigned each death to the same year as that child's birth: this procedure is more or less consonant with the fact that a majority of all those slave children who died before age fifteen perished before their first birthday (my *Them Dark Days*, p. 537). *Column (f):* table A2.

Appendix B

Capital Investment in
the Polk Plantation, 1835–60

This appendix explains the basis for table 5.1. Two major sources confirm that the totals are approximately correct. (1) The assessors of Polk's estate in December 1849 (JP, 1849 inventory) valued the plantation's animals and equipment at $3,830 [the figure that appears in the 1849 subtotal of table 5.1, column (b)], and Daniel Graham's slight correction in 1850 (Inventory Book E, p. 33) of the original inventory set the value of the slaves at $27,100. My subtotal of columns (d), (f), and (g) agrees with Graham's figure. (2) When Sarah Polk sold a half-share of the plantation and its fifty-six slaves in January 1860 (SP, 1860 agreement), the planta- tion was valued at $60,000; this is the total that appears at the bottom of my column (h). Furthermore, the principal figures in columns (b), (c), and (d) are exact. The figures in columns (e), (f), and (g), however, are estimates. The sources for the figures and estimates in each column of table 5.1 are specified below.

Column (b): Animals and Equipment

1834: Silas Caldwell to JP, Feb. 11, 1835, *Corr.*, III, 94.

1838: Caldwell's 1834 investment in animals and equipment was about $1500 (ibid.). I surmise that this figure was the same when Caldwell sold out to WHP at the end of 1836 and when WHP sold out to JP at the end of 1838.

1845–49: In December 1849 the animals and equipment were valued at $3830 (JP, 1849 inventory). As John Mairs—soon after he had become overseer in 1845—had made the plantation self-sufficient in food (even pro- ducing a surplus), I infer that he was also efficient in building up the number of animals on the plantation. For example, the number of stock hogs, pork hogs, and sheep nearly doubled between January 1846 and December 1849 (RC to JP, Jan. 17, 1846; JP, 1849 inventory). Therefore I attribute the $1000 increase since 1838 to Mairs's administration, and I distribute this increase equally over the first five years after Mairs became overseer.

1850–60: The overseer in 1860 (G. W. Peale) told the census taker that the plantation's animals and farming equipment were worth $3050 on June 1, 1860. I surmise that this figure would have been about $280 higher in January 1860, before the completion of the winter slaughter of hogs; this would bring the total in January 1860 to $3330. I distribute the $500 decline since December 1849 equally over the ten years, 1850–59 inclusive. (U.S. manuscript Census of Agriculture, 1860, Yalobusha County, Southwest Beat, pp. 26–27, line 38.)

Column (c): Land

1834: Polk's half-share of the 920-acre plantation cost $10 per acre (Silas Caldwell to his wife, Dec. 26, 1834, Polk MS).

1838: Indenture, Nov. 3, 1838, between WHP and JP, Polk MS.

1844: JP, memo, Dec. 16, 1844, Polk MS. In 1836 WHP paid Silas Caldwell $7000 for Caldwell's half of the 920-acre plantation (indenture, Sept. 4, 1836, Polk MS). Thus WHP lost $950 when he sold out to JP in 1838 and 1844.

1847: Forty acres of the 960-acre tract had been owned solely by Silas Caldwell (the other 920 acres being jointly owned), and they remained in Caldwell's possession until his death in 1846. They then came into James Polk's possession, perhaps through a legacy. Polk had to pay $175 in legal fees and back taxes to secure possession. I estimate the value of this land at $8.75 per acre (RC to JP, Jan. 9, 1847; JM to JP, Feb. 6, 1847; JP to James Brown, May 18, 1847; to J. T. Leigh, Nov. 24, 1847, May 1, 1848; to RC, May 1, 1848, letterbook, Polk MS).

1854: Sarah Polk bought a 155-acre tract from her overseer in 1854 (SP, 1860 agreement). This almost certainly was woodland unsuited to cotton planting, and I estimate the total purchase price at $200.

Column (d): Slaves

1834: JP, schedule of slaves, (Sept. 5, 1834), Polk MS. This list of seventeen slaves belonging to James Polk omits Garrison (who was owned by Jane Polk until 1847) and three superannuated slaves (old Charles, Lucy, and old Sarah). I have corrected the mistaken addition on this document. An accurate transcription of each slave's valuation (except for Young Charles's, which was $325) is easily accessible in Bassett, p. 47.

1838–49: The valuations of all slaves bought by James Polk are on bills of sale, or in letters from Polk's agents in the Polk MS. References for each purchase are in the endnotes to chapter 1.

Valuation of Slaves Imported, 1838–48

1837: *Nancy.* I do not count this house servant, who was at the plantation in 1837 but appears to have been sent back to Tennessee within a few months.

1839: *Old Ben.* I do not count him as capital investment, as he probably had no monetary value by 1839.

1842: I estimate the 1842 values of these slaves as follows: (1) *Pompey*, $500; (2) *Alphonso*, $700; (3) *Joe 1*, $750. Daniel Graham's correction (Inventory Book E, p. 33) of JP, 1849 inventory, values Pompey then at $500; Alphonso plus his young wife and infant were then valued at $1500. On Joe 1, see table A4, note †. (4) *Bob*: I never count him as capital investment because the Polks rented him (from Marshall Polk, Jr.) from 1842 to 1851; Daniel Graham's amendment (Inventory Book E, p. 33) of JP, 1849 inventory, correctly deletes Bob's name from among those who had been owned by James Polk.

1848: *Blacksmith Harry.* I do not count him as part of the plantation's capital investment because figures on the income from his blacksmith's business are extant for only one year (and I have not counted them as part of the plantation's income for that year). By 1860 Harry was about sixty-three years old, and he probably no longer had any monetary value. On Harry, see chapter 9.

Column (e): Value Added or Lost to Land by Clearing or by Price Inflation or Deflation

1849: Five hundred and eight acres of the 960-acre plantation had been cleared by 1849 (JM to JP, Apr. 19, 1849, Polk MS), and this substantially increased the real worth of the land. But the collapse of land prices (after the end of the 1830s boom) canceled this increase. Indeed, although Polk had by 1849 spent $11,000 on the plantation land, overseer John Mairs told the 1850 census taker that it was worth only $7,330. I suppose that Mairs—anxious to keep down property taxes—undervalued the land by perhaps one-third and that it was really worth about $11,000 in 1850. That is, I suppose that the collapse of land prices after the 1830s boom exactly offset all the increases in the land's value that would otherwise have accrued from being cleared [1850 U.S. manuscript Census of Agriculture, Yalobusha County, pp. 19–20 (i.e., pp. "933–34"), line 34]. Mairs told the census taker that 700 acres were "improved," contrary to his more accurate reports to his employers, which show that only about 537 acres could have been cleared by June 1, 1850. I infer that Mairs told the census taker the total number of acres that he believed were suited, eventually, to raising cotton, the rest of the plantation being hilly woodland unsuited to improvement.

1860: Although the overseer in 1860 told the census taker that the land was only worth $10,000, I surmise that again its value was understated by about one-third and that its real value was about $15,000. Of its $4,000 increase in value since 1849, I attribute $200 to Sarah Polk's purchase of land from John Mairs in 1854, $1,900 to the clearing of another 190 acres during the 1850s (at $10 per acre), and the last $1,900 to appreciation of land prices during the boom of the 1850s. I have spread this appreciation equally over the years 1852–59 except for surges of inflation in 1853 and

1859. By 1851, 566 acres had been cleared (JM to SP, May 18, 1851, Polk MS), and I surmise that from 1852 through 1859 Mairs continued clearing an average of 16½ acres per year. Thus by 1860, 698 acres would have been cleared; the new overseer reported that year that the plantation contained 700 improved acres (1860 U.S. manuscript Census of Agriculture, Yalobusha County, Southwest Beat, pp. 26–27, line 38).

My estimate that the overseers understated the cash value of the plantation land by one-third, to both the 1850 and the 1860 census takers, is congruent with the 1849 valuation of Polk's estate and with Sarah Polk's sale agreement in 1860. In 1849 the assesssors of Polk's estate set the value of his Mississippi slaves at $27,100; and it is unlikely that the value of the 508 acres of cleared land, which these slaves worked, was anywhere as small as the $7,330 that Mairs reported. A figure of $11,000 for the land's value would lessen the disproportion between Polk's investment in land and his investment in slaves. Similarly, when James Avent contracted early in 1860 to buy a half-share of Sarah Polk's Mississippi estate (whose total valuation was $60,000), it is improbable that the land was worth only $10,000 of this total, for this would imply that the slaves were valued at about $46,700 (the remainder being the value of livestock and farm equipment). It is much more likely that the land was worth about $15,000, and the slaves about $41,700. This valuation of the slaves is congruent with the inflation of the New Orleans slave price index during the 1850s, but a valuation of $46,700 would not be. See column (f) below.

Column (f): Value Added or Lost to Slaves by Price Inflation or Deflation

As slave prices were higher in Mississippi than even in the cotton counties of southwestern Tennessee, I have assigned a modest increase in their value ($500, i.e., about 6 percent) when Polk deported his slaves from Tennessee to his new Mississippi plantation at the beginning of 1835.

1835–48: Slave prices rocketed in 1836–37 but collapsed in 1838, falling back by 1840 to the level of the early 1830s. In 1841–42 they collapsed even further, dropping by nearly one-third. Only when the annexation of Texas became certain, early in 1845, did prices gradually rise again, and they reached the 1840 level by 1848. The figures in column (f) reflect these fluctuations (as indicated by the New Orleans slave price index, which is cited below), but in a much less pronounced form: my estimates allow for a one-sixth increase, by 1837, in the value of Polk's original stock of slaves (canceled by 1840) and for a 10 percent decrease in their value between 1840 and 1842 (regained gradually by 1848).

1849–59: After 1851 a sustained boom for slave prices set in. I have estimated—for the years indicated by the New Orleans slave price index (but at a slightly lower rate of increase)—that the value of Sarah Polk's slaves (the ones left after she lost Charles, Barbara, and Marthy and after she had sold Joe 2 and Harbert) increased by about 9 percent from their 1849 valuation in 1852, about 12½ percent in 1853 and again in 1854, and by 9 percent from their 1849 valuation in 1858 and about 25 percent in 1859. Although these increases are a little smaller than would be suggested by the New Orleans price index, they are congruent with the $60,000 value set on the whole estate in January 1860. Evidently Sarah Polk's new business partner got what seemed to be a good bargain when he paid just $30,000 for his half-share of the enterprise.

I seek in these estimates to apply the principle enunciated in the famous article by Alfred Conrad and John Meyer ("Economics of Slavery in the Antebellum South," esp. pp. 106–10), that is, that calculations of planters' profits should take account of the increased value of their slaves as that population grew. And, like Randolph Campbell (*Empire for Slavery*, pp. 69–73), I seek to extend that principle to the calculation of capital losses, as well as to capital gains, in the values of slaves. I suppose that this practice may bring us closer to understanding how planters perceived the fluctuations in the values of their slaves.

The New Orleans slave price index is in Laurence J. Kotlikoff, "Quantitative Description of the New Orleans Slave Market," p. 35. I am greatly indebted to Stanley Engerman for this reference.

Column (g): Value Added to Slaves by Population Growth

As shown in table 7.1, the natural population growth at the Polk plantation was only one slave (from 1835 to 1849) and six slaves (from 1850 to 1859). Table A5 shows that this growth occurred only in 1847 and again from 1855 to 1859; thus, the child born in 1847 was still very young in 1849, and the children born from 1855 to 1859 were still young in January 1860. I have therefore set low figures for the estimated "Value Added to Slaves by Population Growth" in each of those years. The causes for the low population growth are discussed in chapter 7.

Appendix C

———— ≓◆≓ ————

Profits from the Polk Plantation, 1835–57

This appendix presents the figures on revenues, expenses, and capital gains, on which the profit rates in table 4.1 (in chapter 4) are based. The appendix also identifies the sources from which table C1 is constructed.

Table C1

Profits from the Polks' Share of the Mississippi Plantation, 1835–57 (dollars, est.)

Year of Crop	(a) Risk Capital at Beginning of Year	(b) Gross Revenues on That Crop	(c) Recurrent Expenses	(d) Cash Profit [(b) – (c)]	(e) To Land by Clearing or Price Inflation	(f) by Price Inflation/ Deflation	(g) by Natural Growth of Population	(h) Total Profit [(d) – (g)]	(j) Rate of Cash Profit [(d)/(a)] (percent)	(k) Rate of Total Profit [(h)/(a)] (percent)
1835	14,150	1850	1100	750		650		1400	5.3	9.9
1836	14,800	2221	725	1496		600		2096	10.1	14.2
1837	14,800	1800	888	912		600		1512	6.2	10.2
1838	15,400	1780	717	1063		–1200		–137	6.9	–0.9
1839	26,100	3128	1444	1684		–150		1534	6.5	5.9
1840	28,060	[2480]*	1424	1056				1056	3.8	3.8
1841	27,310	[2750]	1254	1496		–150		1346	5.5	4.9
1842	26,710	3840	1269	2571		–650		1921	9.6	7.2
1843	28,010	?	1179	?		?		?	?	?
1844	28,010	2725	1332	1393				1393	5.0	5.0
1845	30,010	3869	1367	2502		150		2652	8.3	8.8
1846	30,810	5188	1456	3732		350		4082	12.1	13.2
1847	35,630	3807	1477	2330		–150	100	2280	6.5	6.4
1848	37,810	3624	1392	2232		450		2682	5.9	7.1
1849	38,460	6561	1425	5136				5136	13.4	13.4
1850	41,930	6096	1441	4655	250			4905	11.1	11.7

Undistributed Capital Gains: Polks' Share of Value Added/Lost — To Slaves [columns (f) and (g)]

1851	42,130	5437	3897	300			4197	9.2	10.0
1852	42,380	6909	5357	400	2100		7857	12.6	18.5
1853	43,330	2755	1339	500	3000		4839	3.1	11.2
1854	46,080	2537	947	400	3000		4347	2.1	9.4
1855	49,630	5972	4233	350		200	4783	8.5	9.6
1856	50,130	7359	5571	350		400	6321	11.1	12.6
1857	50,230	6266	4643	350		200	5193	9.2	10.3

Average Annual Rate of Profit, 1835–44 (excluding 1843)   6.5   5.7

1845–57   8.7   10.9

1835–57 (excluding 1843)   7.8   9.2

*Figures in brackets are estimates.

Sources for Table C1

Columns (a), (e), (f), and (g) are copied from the columns with the same letters in table 5.1, and the sources for the figures in each of these columns are identified in appendix B. Thus the only new input into table C1 is in columns (b) and (c).

Column (b): Gross Revenues

Although this column is entitled "gross" revenues, the figures refer to the net amount paid by the New Orleans factor after deducting his own commission and freight, storage, insurance fees, and all other charges connected with the sale of the cotton. Nevertheless, the figures are gross in the sense that all expenses connected with raising the crop [column (c)] still remain to be deducted.

My figures are exact for 1839 and for 1844–57 and fairly exact for 1835 and 1836; but they contain estimates for the other years.

1835–38: The figures for these partnership years refer to Polk's half-share of the plantation's revenues.

1835–36: Silas Caldwell to JP, Apr. 28, 1836, May 4, 1837, *Corr.*, III, 609; IV, 109. I estimate that the 1836 crop netted about $43.50 per bale; cf. chapter 4, note 1.

1837: Nearly half (forty-two bales) of the crop was lost when a steamboat sank, but it appears to have been well insured. I estimate that the full crop of eighty-eight bales netted an average of $40 per bale, to which I add $80 realized from the local sale of surplus corn (Bassett, p. 226; *Corr.*, IV, 279, 392, 473).

1838: Bassett, p. 117. The sale of thirty-eight bales netted $1859 (*Corr.*, V, 88, 131), an average of nearly $49 per bale. I estimate that the other thirty-six bales netted $45 per bale. To this I add again an estimate of $80 realized from the local sale of surplus corn.

1839: *Corr.*, V, 372, 441.

1840: I estimate that the crop was about 100 bales (cf. Bassett, p. 152)—well below the 136 bales raised in 1839—and that (as prices were a little above the low prices for the 1839 crop) it netted just below $25 per bale.

1841: I estimate that the crop was about 110 bales and that it netted $25 per bale (i.e., that it netted 6¼ cents a pound for a 400-pound bale; cf. Bassett, pp. 152, 166).

1842: I surmise that the overseer exaggerated the size of the crop (Bassett, p. 172). I estimate that it was only 160 bales and that it netted $24 per bale.

1843: The column remains blank here, as there is no evidence from which to estimate the 1843 crop's size.

1844–57: For each year, exact figures are taken from the letters of the New Orleans factor (W. S. Pickett, or Perkins & Co.) in the Polk MS.

Except for 1845–48, these figures are easily accessible in Bassett (pp. 227–59), but I have corrected Bassett's addition for the 1844 crop, his omission of the last bale of the 1851 crop, and his underreporting of the revenues from the 1854 and 1856 crops. The only (small) estimate in all these figures on cotton revenues is the cost of insuring the 1857 crop at the Troy warehouse (which I infer was $23, as for the 1856 crop).

To these figures I have added revenues derived from selling plantation produce (mainly hogs and corn) in the local market from 1844 through 1847. These were $30 for 1844 and $357 for 1845 (RC to JP, Jan. 22, 1845, Jan. 17, 1846, Polk MS). I estimate them at $200 for 1846 and $100 for 1847.

Column (c): Recurrent Expenses

1835–38: The figures for these partnership years refer to James Polk's half-share of the plantation's expenses.

1835–36: Silas Caldwell to JP, Apr. 28, 1836, May 4, 1837, *Corr.*, III, 609; IV, 109.

1837: To the $1635 expenses reported in WHP to JP, Feb. 5, 1838 (*Corr.*, IV, 356), I add a $31 doctor's bill (JP, 1839 account book, Series 7, Polk MS), $60 for renting the slave Garrison from Jane Polk, and an estimated $50 for "small store accounts," making a total of $1776, of which James Polk's half-share was $888.

1838: The overseer's salary was $500, Garrison's rental was $65, and pork cost $368. I estimate other plantation expenses at $500, of which $115 was paid to a Louisville factor. Of this $1433 total, James Polk's share was $717.

1839–57: Table C2 presents a breakdown of the plantation's expenses. The figures in brackets are my estimates; all other numbers are taken from correspondence in the Polk MS.

Table C2
Recurrent Expenses at the Polk Plantation, 1839–57 (dollars)

Year of Crop	(a) Overseer's Salary and Agent's Expenses	(b) Supplies from New Orleans	(c) Local Supplies and Expenses (excluding pork)	(d) Pork	(e) Animals and Equipment	(f) Rental of Slaves	(g) Rental of Land from WHP	(h) Slaves' Incentive Pay	(j) Total Recurrent Expenses [(a) – (h)]
1835									1100
1836									725
1837									888
1838									717
1839	[500]	[245]	[260]	[240]		65			1444
1840	[400]	[245]	[260]	[200]	[120]	65	134		1424
1841	[400]	[245]	[260]	[150]		65	134		1254
1842	[400]	[245]	[260]	[75]		155	134		1269
1843	[400]	[245]	[260]			140	134		1179
1844	[429]	[245]	[260]			135	134		1332
1845	504	243	262		[120]	135	134	138	1367
1846	604	[280]	[290]			145		103	1456
1847	[560]	[300]	310?		129	75		137	1477
1848	500	[310]	[300]		80	75		103	1392
1849	500	329	291?			75		127	1425
1850	500	[353]	[300]			[75]		230	1441
1851	550	[325]	[300]		[100]	[75]		213	1540
1852	550	297	[300]	98	[65]			190	1552
1853	550	[370]	[300]	[100]				242	1416
1854	[550]	[440]	[300]	[100]				96	1590
1855	[550]	[510]	[300]	[100]	[70]			200	1739
1856	550	580	[300]	[100]				209	1788
1857	550	469	[300]	85				258	1623
1858		378		107				219	

Figures in brackets are estimates. *1835–38*: the figures for these partnership years refer to James Polk's *half*-share of the partnership's expenses. The sources for these four years are specified on the previous page. *1839–57*: notes for each column of this table are on the following pages.

196

Notes to Table C2, Recurrent Expenses

Column (a): Overseer's Salary and Agent's Expenses

Robert Campbell, President Polk's agent from December 1844 until early 1847, charged Polk for his expenses: $29 (1844), $54 (1845), and $154 (1846), and I estimate $60 (1847). John Mairs's annual salary as overseer started at $450 (1845), increased to $500 (1847), and was $550 from 1851 on. Overseer George Bratton was paid $400 in 1837 and $500 in 1838. He died in July 1839. I estimate that Polk paid $500 to Bratton and his successor in 1839 but only $400 to the overseers from 1840 through 1844. The salary of Isaac Dismukes (overseer from 1841 through 1844) seems to have been only $400 in 1844 (RC, accounts, Jan. 22, 1845, Polk MS).

Columns (b) and (c): Supplies and Local Expenses (excluding pork)

My estimates of these expenses are rather larger than those implied in Charles Sydnor's discussion of the Polk plantation (Sydnor, *Slavery in Mississippi*, p. 197).

1839–45: In 1845 supplies sent from New Orleans cost $243 (Bassett, p. 228), and local supplies and expenses (including taxes and medical bills) amounted to about $262 (RC to JP, Jan. 17, 1846, Polk MS). I estimate that from 1839 through 1844 these expenses came to the same total of about $505 annually.

1847 *column (c)*: Polk's 1847 accounts suggest that he had to pay $951 to his Mississippi neighbor J. T. Leigh (who succeeded Robert Campbell in a supervisory role over the overseer). If $500 of this was the overseer's salary (plus $16 interest, because the bulk of that salary was not paid until May 26, 1848) and if $125 was the cost that year in legal fees paid to secure Polk's possession of the forty acres left him by Silas Caldwell (who died in 1846), this implies that $310 covered ordinary local expenses (JP to J. T. Leigh, Jan. 31, May 26, 1848; to JM, Feb. 1, 1848, Letterbook, Polk MS.

1849 *column (c)*: The New Orleans factor paid Leigh $291 on Feb. 7, 1850, presumably to cover the plantation's local expenses incurred in 1849 (Pickett, Perkins to SP, May 9, 1850, Polk MS).

1846–52: Polk imported nineteen slaves between 1845 and 1849 (table A5), and this capital investment will have somewhat increased the plantation's annual recurrent expenses. Based on fragmentary figures (such as those just given for the 1847 and 1849 local expenses), I estimate that the cost of all supplies (including those sent from New Orleans as well as those bought locally) climbed from $505 in 1845 to $570 in 1846, and varied during the next six years between $597 (1852) and $653 (1850). These figures exclude the cost of tools and materials for blacksmith Harry after he was brought to the plantation in 1848, the income from whose lucrative business I also exclude from my calculation of plantation revenues. My figures also exclude the $175 in legal fees—$125 in 1847 and $50 in 1848—that Polk paid to secure possession of the extra forty acres of Silas Caldwell's land, apparently bequeathed to him in 1847. I count these fees instead as part of a $350 addition that year to Polk's capital investment in land (table 5.1).

1853–57: The cost of supplies bought in New Orleans peaked at $580 in 1856 and declined to $469 in 1857 and $378 in 1858. By interpolation, I estimate a steady increase in the cost of New Orleans supplies between 1852 and 1856, but I infer that the cost of local supplies and expenses remained constant at about $300 annually.

Column (d): Pork

William Polk spent $500 for pork in 1837 and $368 in 1838. By 1844 the plantation produced a small surplus for sale in the local market. I infer that the plantation remained (diminishingly) dependent on buying pork locally from 1839 through 1842 but was self-sufficient by 1843, and I guess that it remained self-sufficient through 1851. In 1852, however, overseer Mairs had to pay the New Orleans factor $98 for pork, $85 in 1857, and $107 in 1858. I infer that he also spent for pork an average of $100 each year from 1853 through 1856.

Column (e): Animals and Equipment

I treat the following five figures as recurrent expenses (not as additions to risk capital) on the presumption that, after the initial investments in animals and equipment (in 1834 and 1838) and the increase in animal stock (from 1845 through 1849), any other additions to this form of capital would be offset by depreciation to the existing stock of animals and equipment.

1840: I estimate the cost of the grist mill, including stones and irons, at $120.

1845: In addition to the $50 mule Mairs bought, I estimate the cost of the new cotton press at $70.

1851: I estimate the cost of the new gin at $100.

1852: I estimate the cost of the mule at $65.

1855: I estimate the cost of the mule at $70.

Column (f): Rental of Slaves

These figures include the rental of Garrison from Jane Polk from 1838 through 1846 (after which she sold this slave to James Polk) and the rental of Bob from Marshall Polk, Jr., from about 1842 through 1851, after which Bob was deported to Marshall Polk, Jr.'s, farm in Tennessee. (JP, agreement with Jane Polk, Nov. 3, 1838; JP, accounts as guardian to minor heirs of M. T. Polk, reel 62, Polk MS).

Column (g): Rental of Land from WHP

James Polk rented 230 acres of the plantation from his brother William from 1839 through 1844. The rental for 1843 and 1844 totaled $268 (JP, memo, Dec. 16, 1844, Polk MS).

Column (h): Slaves' Incentive Pay

1844: RC, accounts, Jan. 22, 1845 ("Dec. 28, 1844"); RC to JP, Jan. 9, 1847.

1845: RC to JP, Jan. 17, 1846; RC, accounts, July 22, 1846 ("Oct. 29, 1846").

1846: RC to JP, Jan. 9, 1847.

1847: JP to JM, Mar. 1, Sept. 22, 1848, letterbook; JM to RC, Jan. 27, 1848; Pickett to JP, Jan. 15, 1849, Polk MS. 4 bales ÷ 144 bales × $3707 cotton revenues = $103.

1848: JP to JM, Sept. 22, 1848, letterbook; Pickett to JP, Mar. 21, 1849, Polk MS. 4 bales ÷ 114 bales × $3624 cotton revenues = $127.

1849–53 *and* **1855–57:** I assume that the slaves' produce accounted for 3.5 percent of the plantation's gross revenues (the same ratio as 4/114 bales in 1848). This percentage yields figures consistent with JM to SP, June 17, 1855 (Bassett, p. 210), where Mairs says that the incentive pay was normally about $200; the 1852 figure is consistent with JM to J. W. Childress, June 10, 1853, where Mairs implies that Childress will probably pay more for the slaves' 1852 crop than the $210 that Mairs had already paid.

1854: I assume that SP paid the $200 that Mairs reported as the normal annual payment instead of making the slaves lose the value of the burned cotton, which Mairs had failed to insure at the Yalobusha River warehouse (JM to SP, June 17, 1855, Bassett, p. 210).

Notes

ABBREVIATIONS

Bassett   John Spencer Bassett, *The Southern Plantation Overseer as Revealed in His Letters* (Westport, Conn.: Negro Universities Press, [1925] 1968). ("All the letters in this book . . . are taken from the Correspondence of James Knox Polk.")

Corr.   *Correspondence of James K. Polk*, eds. Herbert Weaver, Wayne Cutler, et al., 9 vols. to date (Nashville, 1969–89; Knoxville, 1993–).

Diary   *The Diary of James K. Polk during His Presidency, 1845 to 1849*, ed. Milo M. Quaife, 4 vols. (New York: Kraus Reprint Co., [1910] 1970).

JM   John Mairs (the Polk overseer from 1845).

JP   James K. Polk.

JP, 1849 inventory   James Polk estate inventory, Dec. 5, 1849, Yalobusha County inventory book E, pp. 31–35, Coffeeville, Mississippi.

Polk MS   James K. Polk Papers, Library of Congress (microfilm, unless otherwise specified).

RC   Robert Campbell (Polk's cousin and agent 1845–47)

Sellers   Charles Grier Sellers, Jr., *James K. Polk*, 2 vols. (Princeton, N.J.: Princeton University Press, 1957–66)

SHC   Southern Historical Collection, University of North Carolina.

SP   Sarah (Childress) Polk (James Polk's wife).

SP, 1860 agreement   Sarah Polk, Sale Agreement, Jan. 25, 1860, James Polk MS, TSA.

TSA   Tennessee State Archives, Nashville.

WHP   William H. Polk (a younger brother of James Polk).

INTRODUCTION

1. On cholera, I am indebted to Dr. John Holtzapple, director of the Polk Ancestral Home in Columbia, Tennessee, who states that on the day after Polk died he was buried with about thirty-two other cholera victims outside the city limits of Nashville.

2. Sellers, *James K. Polk*, 2 vols.; Pletcher, *Diplomacy of Annexation*; McCormac. *James K. Polk*; Bergeron, *Presidency of James K. Polk*.

3. Perhaps the best-known request that historians abandon their overspecialization and try to combine social with political history has been that of Fox-Genovese and Genovese, "Political Crisis of Social History," in their *Fruits of Merchant Capital*, pp. 179–212.

4. Bassett.

5. In posing these questions about benevolence and callousness and about the hybrid nature of the slave system, I seek to extend—and in some degree to modify—my previously published discussion of the nature of the American slave system. That discussion focused wholly on the rice plantations of the southeastern United States; I now want to find how far the regime on American cotton plantations may have resembled or differed from that in the Rice Kingdom. Although I examine here only a single Mississippi cotton plantation, the records on Polk's enterprise are so rich that I believe they can illuminate our view of American slavery in general. Dusinberre, *Them Dark Days*, pp. 21–27, 297–301, 404–10, and esp. pp. 201–6.

CHAPTER 1

1. John C. Calhoun to Richard Pakenham (the British Minister in Washington), Apr. 18, 1844, to Benjamin E. Green, Apr. 19, 1844, U.S. Congress, *Senate Documents*, No. 341, 28 Cong., 1st sess., pp. 52–54.

2. *Nashville Union*, Oct. 1, 3, 1844. *Daily Albany Argus*, Oct. 1–Nov. 2, 1844. *New York Morning News*, n.d. (article dated Oct. 16, 1844), quoted in the *Weekly Herald* (New York), Nov. 16, 1844; *New York Journal of Commerce*, Oct. 29, 1844, quoted in the *New York Morning News*, Oct. 30, 1844, in James Polk MS, TSA.

3. Emphasis added. Francis Pickens to Henry Conner, May 29, 1844, in Cooper, *The South and the Politics of Slavery, 1828–1856*, p, 206. See chapter 12 below.

4. G. J. Pillow to E. Croswell, editor of the *Daily Albany Argus*, Oct. 1, 1844, Polk MS (emphasis in the original). It is unclear to what use Pillow's letter was put. It probably fueled the assertion by Democratic editors that Polk rarely traded in slaves and only to prevent family disruption. It may have been published in the semi-weekly *Albany Argus*. It does not seem to have been printed in the *Daily Albany Argus*, whose editor—thinking of many Northern voters' uneasiness about slavery—apparently preferred to confine discussion of Polk's involvement with the slave market to brief disclaimers and to indignant denunciation of Whig mendacity. Pillow's letter—or a variant of it—was later sent to former President Andrew Jackson, who used it to counter allegations by the Massachusetts businessman Abbott Lawrence (from whom Polk had tried to borrow funds in order to expand his plantation operations) that Polk had purchased a number of slaves for his plantation. *Daily Albany Argus*, Oct. 1–Nov. 2, 1844; Sellers (II), pp. 149–50; R. Armstrong to JP, Nov. 19, 1844, *Corr.*, VIII, 334–35; G. J. Pillow to Andrew Jackson, Nov. 22, 1844, in Hughes and Stonesifer, *Life and Wars of Gideon J. Pillow*, p. 344.

5. Sellers (II), p. 150.

6. Bill of sale, Oct. 8, 1846, Polk MS.

7. The slave Elias was a wedding gift to James Polk in 1824 from his father; Hardy and Little Abe were bequests when his father died in 1827. I infer that James Polk came into possession of Addison and Little Ben after the death of Polk's brother Frank in January 1831. (Evidently Addison was the eldest son of Fanny Lawson, whom Frank had inherited.) I infer that James Polk came into possession of Old Ben and the blacksmith Abraham after the death of Polk's brother John in Sep-

tember 1831. (As James Polk owned no slave named Abe in October 1831, I infer that Little Abe had died before then and that Polk came into possession of the blacksmith Abraham in 1832.) I infer that James Polk came into possession of Pompey and of blacksmith Harry ("Long Harry") after the death of his brother Samuel W. Polk in 1839. I believe James Polk paid cash to his surviving siblings to buy out their shares of the last six-named slaves during the equal divisions of these estates among the siblings. JP, "Division of F. E. Polk's estate" (1831), Reel 3; Samuel Polk, will, Dec. 13, 1826; JP, will, Oct. 24, 1831; JP, list of plantation property, Sept. 26, 1834, Polk MS. Frank Polk, will (recorded June 7, 1831), inventory (recorded June 6, 1831); John L. Polk, inventory (recorded May 21, 1832), Maury County will book, TSA.

From Polk's father-in-law, Joel Childress, the Polks inherited Little Jim, Harbert, Elizabeth, and old Sarah, as well as a minor interest in Matilda. Originally they were also to have received five more slaves, but these were attached to pay debts due from Joel Childress's estate. JP in effect purchased one of these other slaves—Mariah—by paying cash for her when Joel Childress's estate was finally settled, and in 1829 Polk bought from the other legatees full ownership of Matilda. JP and SP, defendants, Aug. 23, 1828; JP, Memo on an agreement among JP, William Rucker, and Andrew Miller, pp. 451–54, Aug. 23, 1828; bill of sale, Oct. 27, 1829, Polk MS.

8. These were Mariah and Matilda (mentioned in note 7); Reuben (bought from JP's mother in 1831); Sylvia and her three young children, Jacob, Alphonso, and Emily (bought in 1832 from Polk's brother-in-law John B. Hays); and eight slaves bought in 1838 from Polk's younger brother William, to be retained on Polk's Mississippi plantation when the brothers dissolved their partnership that year. These eight are named later in this chapter. Bills of sale, Oct. 24, 1831; Aug. 24, 1832; Nov. 3, 1838, Polk MS.

9. These were Peter, Giles, Eve, and Caesar (1831); Dicey, Phil, Henry Carter, and Nancy (1834); Henrietta (1835); Charles (1838); and Allen, Daphney, Matilda, and William (1839). Of these, Henry Carter and Henrietta were the two bought partly to prevent family separations. The circumstances of the 1831, 1834, and 1835 purchases are set forth later in this chapter. Bills of sale, Sept. 21, 19 (two bills), 24, Oct. 6, 1831; Sept. 26, Oct. 10, 13, 18, 1834; Sept. 24, 1839, Polk MS. On Henrietta: bill of sale, Jan. 4, 1835, Polk Correspondence, Tennessee Presidents Center, University of Tennessee at Knoxville; A. O. Harris to JP, Jan. 23, 1835, *Corr.*, III, 60. For Charles's purchase: WHP to JP, Dec. 30, 1839; John Garner to JP, Nov. 3, 1839, *Corr.* V, 358, 285.

10. In addition to forty-four slaves named in his will, Sam Polk owned Fanny Lawson's children and some slaves held by his mother-in-law, Lydia Wallace. I estimate that Fanny Lawson had two surviving children (Addison and one born about 1825). As James Polk's 10 percent share of Lydia Wallace's slaves was valued at $194, I estimate that she held seven slaves (with an average value, including several children, of about $275). Samuel Polk, will, Dec. 13, 1826; JP, accounts for Sam Polk's will, Sept. 1828 (reel 62), Polk MS. *Corr.*, I, 102. Sellers (I), pp. 30, 38, 56–57, 64–65, 67, 114. Abernethy, *From Frontier to Plantation in Tennessee*, pp. 251–53. I believe Sellers (I) p. 63 errs in saying that Sam Polk owned more than 67,000 acres of land since Sellers's source appears to be the same as mine: JP, notes, Apr. 7, 1831, as executor of Sam Polk's estate, Polk MS (Series 7).

11. Sellers (I), pp. 54, 98.

12. His gross income was $2659 during the last nine months of 1824 and per-haps $400 during the first three months of that same year, when he still shared fees (totaling perhaps $800) with a partner. Sellers (I), p. 62.

13. Herbert Biles to JP, Jan. 17, 1833; James Walker to JP, Jan. 24, 1833, *Corr.*, II, 30, 44. Sellers (I), p. 186. Bassett, p. 38.

14. Settlement, Nov. 3, 1836, of WHP's share of Sam Polk's estate (re Chunky Jack); bills of sale, Sept. 21, 19 (two bills), 24, Oct. 6, 24, 1831; JP, will, Oct. 24, 1831, Polk MS.

15. JP to SP, Sept. 26, 1834; Ephraim Beanland to JP, Oct. 4, 10, 1834, *Corr.*, II, 507–9, 514, 519. Sellers (I), p. 249. Bassett, pp. 39–40.

16. Bills of sale, Sept. 26, Oct. 10, 13, 18, 1834; slave list, plantation property, Sept. 26, 1834; slave list, in valuation of JP's and S. M. Caldwell's property, Nov. 2, 1834, Polk MS. Bill of sale, Jan. 4, 1835, Polk Correspondence, University of Tennessee. Nancy, the house servant, sometimes worked at the Mississippi plan-tation, sometimes at Columbia; A. T. McNeal to JP, June 15, 1838, *Corr.*, IV, 479; JP estate inventory 597, Oct. 2, 1849 (recorded May 27, 1851), Davidson County wills, inventories, settlements, XIV, pp. 505–7, TSA.

17. While the first land was being cleared on the Mississippi plantation, Caldwell worked half of the slaves he had assigned to the partnership and half of Polk's, too (and four or five more of Polk's during the 1835 harvest), on Caldwell's own West Tennessee plantation, whose profits heavily subsidized the new Mississippi ven-ture. See chapter 4 below.

18. WHP to JP, Feb. 15, 1837, *Corr.*, IV, 63. William, however, did retain until 1844 ownership of a quarter of the Mississippi plantation land, which he rented to James Polk. WHP to JP, Feb. 5, 1838; JP to WHP, June 25, 1838, *Corr.*, IV, 356–57, 492. Memo between WHP and JP, Dec. 16, 1844, Polk MS.

19. Bill of sale, Nov. 3, 1838; Samuel Polk, will, Dec. 13, 1826, Polk MS.

20. See chapter 3. When Chunky Jack—after he fled in 1833—was recovered in Arkansas, Polk's brother-in-law James Walker already was advising that Jack be sold in order "to reduce the ballance [i.e., the other slaves] to subjection." Jack's next attempt to flee was thwarted when the overseer stabbed him. Finally, a few months later, when Jack was captured (again in Arkansas) after his next flight and incarcerated in Memphis, the overseer strongly urged his sale, declaring that the neighboring planters didn't want Jack back in the Somerville area because he made their slaves unruly. Polk surely reached this same conclusion, for Jack never again appears in the records. Jack was the property of Polk's younger brother William, to whom (beginning in 1832) JP paid an annual rent for Jack's labor on the Somerville plantation, although this rent was terminated on Nov. 1, 1834. (In selling Jack then, JP acted as executor of the estate of Samuel Polk, whose legatee Wil-liam H. Polk was then only nineteen years old.) Ephraim Beanland to JP, Dec. 1, 1833, Apr. 1, Oct. 4, 10, 1834; JP to SP, Sept. 26, 1834; James Walker to JP, Feb. 14, 19, 1834, *Corr.*, II, 144, 315, 331, 378, 508, 514, 519. Settlement, Nov. 3, 1836, of WHP's share of Samuel Polk's estate, Polk MS. See also note 18 in chapter 2.

21. Bill of sale (a family of four slaves, bought for $2110), Sept. 24, 1839, Polk MS. That the fifth slave (Charles, purchased late in 1838) cost Polk about $750 is my inference from the fact that when Polk tried to sell him in 1840—because he had run away—his agent thought he ought to sell for that price. A. T. McNeal to JP, Jan. 15, 1840; *Corr.*, V, 372–73; WHP to JP, Dec. 30, 1839, Bassett, pp. 131–32.

22. He did, however, spend $450 to buy a slave (Caroline Childress) from his mother-in-law in 1845 to help her to punish the slave without selling her out of the family. Bill of sale, Oct. 8, 1845; JP to Robert Campbell, Oct. 11, 1845, Polk MS.

23. JP to S. P. Walker, Sept. 24, 1845, Polk MS. John H. Bills, Diary, July 10, 1845 (marginal notes at end of 1845 volume), John H. Bills MS, TSA. JP to Robert Campbell (emphasis added), Aug. 13, 1846; to Eliza (Polk) Caldwell, Aug. 16, 1846, Letterbook, Polk MS. James Walker to JP, Oct. 15, 1839, *Corr.*, V, 262. Nelson and Nelson, *Memorials of Sarah Childress Polk*, p. 148.

24. For example, Smith, *War with Mexico*, vol. 2, pp. 185–87, 376–77.

25. JP to G. J. Pillow, May 10, June 29, 1846, letterbook, Polk MS.

26. Ibid. JP to Pillow, Apr. 20, 1846; to Robert Campbell, Apr. (misdated "May") 20, May 10, Aug. 13, 1846, letterbook, Polk MS.

27. These campaign debts—all paid by March 1846—had totaled over $16,000:

$9500	to JP's rich uncle, William Wilson Polk
2050	to JP's New Orleans factor
1300	to U. S. Supreme Court Judge John Catron
400	to JP's mother-in-law, Elizabeth Childress
3030	to three other people (David Craighead, William Wood, and Dr. McNeill)

JP, money paid out after Feb. 1845, reel 62, Polk MS. (I omit from the $850 paid to Elizabeth Childress the price—$450—of the slave Polk bought from her in 1845.)

28. I infer Calvin's age from his price of $450, as compared to William's price of $600 and Jim's purchase price of $392. Robert Campbell accounts (filed July 22, 1846): July 22, Aug. 3, 15, Oct. 6, 10, 1846; bills of sale, July 22, Aug. 3, Oct. 8, Nov. 16, 1846; Campbell to JP, Aug. 27, Oct. 9, 23, Nov. 3, 1846, Jan. 9, 1847; JP, note re Calvin (bought Oct. 10), misfiled Aug. 3, 1846, Polk MS.

29. JP to John Childress, June 2, 1846; to RC, Aug. 13, 1846; to J. Knox Walker, Aug. 16, 1846, letterbook, Polk MS. Campbell was Polk's first cousin: *Corr.*, V. 643. Enactment of the proviso was blocked in the Senate. C. W. Morrison, *Democratic Politics and Sectionalism*, pp. 17–20.

30. The three slaves were Joe, Garrison, and Maria Davis. JP to RC, Dec. 12, 1846 and Jan. 23, 1847 (emphasis in the original), letterbook; JP, accounts (Series 7). Jan. 9, 1847; bills of sale, Feb. 1, 2, 1847 (both filed Feb. 2); E. P. McNeal to JP, Feb. 2, 1847, Polk MS.

31. Since Polk's presidential salary was much larger than his expenses in the White House, he had a large cash surplus in 1847–48. He used it to purchase $11,000 of U.S. Treasury certificates because, apparently, he felt uncomfortable about investing money received from government revenues during and shortly after the Mexican War into buying slaves. But he felt no such inhibitions about plowing back the profits of his own plantation enterprise—as soon as they were available— into the expansion of his slave force, JP, list of treasury notes, Dec. 7, 18, 1847; Mar. 1, 1848; June 3, 1848, reel 62, Polk MS. JP estate inventory 597, Oct. 2, 1849 (recorded May 27, 1851), Davidson County wills, inventories, settlements, XIV, pp. 505–7. TSA.

32. The actual purchase of these last half-dozen slaves, authorized by President Polk, was completed soon after he left the White House. In regard to the age of

Jason ("Jacent") I accept the statement on the bill of sale (Mar. 22, 1849), not the later, self-interested claim by Polk's agent—who sought to avoid the appearance of having paid too much for a young child?—that Jason was twelve. Bills of sale, Mar. 20, 1849 (mistakenly written "1848": see last sentences of this note); Mar. 22 (three bills, listing four slaves), Mar 25, 1849; JP to S. P. Walker, Feb. 19, 1849, letterbook; S. P. Walker to JP, Apr. 4, 1849; JM to JP, Apr. 19, 1849; to SP, Mar. 15, 1850, Polk MS. JP, 1849 inventory. Caroline Harris's vendor mistakenly wrote on the Mar. 20 bill of sale that he sold her to S. P. Walker (Polk's agent) on Mar. 20, "1848," and the document is filed accordingly in the Polk MS (reel 52). But Walker wrote unambiguously on the back of this bill that he transferred the slave's ownership to James Polk on March 30, "1849." This was exactly the same day on which Walker transferred to Polk ownership of the five other slaves he had bought for Polk during the preceding ten days, and it is clear proof that Caroline Harris's vendor had inadvertently written the wrong year on her bill of sale.

33. JP to S. P. Walker, Feb. 19, 1849; to E. P. McNeal, Feb. 20, 1849, letterbook, Polk MS, Walker bought the six slaves listed above, but McNeal failed to make an additional purchase that Polk had authorized.

34. Barrow, *Plantation Life*, p. 39.

35. U.S. Congress, House, *Register of Debates*, 19 Cong., 1 sess., 1649–50.

36. See chapter 12.

37. Marsh, "James K. Polk and Slavery," pp. 13–15. J. S. Bassett reported in 1925 that Polk as president had bought six slaves (Harbert, his wife and child, and the three slaves in 1847). But Bassett did not know that the $3000 Polk sent to Robert Campbell in 1846 was for the purchase of six other slaves, nor apparently did Bassett know of Polk's injunctions that these purchases must be kept secret. In addition, Bassett did not know that President Polk had bought another slave in 1845 and, near the end of his term, had authorized the purchase of six more. Bassett, p. 177.

38. Polk used the term "family negroes" to identify a small group of privileged slaves. JP, will, Oct. 24, 1831, Polk MS.

CHAPTER 2

1. JM to SP, Nov. 29, Dec. 15, 1855; cf. JM to SP, Jan. 7, 1856, Polk MS.

2. Anderson Childress to SP, Dec. 21, 1825; John Childress to SP, Jan. 3, 1826, James Polk MS, TSA. Anderson Childress, complainant, Aug. 29, 1823; JP and SP, defendants, Aug. 23, 1828; agreement between W. R. Rucker, JP, and J. W. Childress (Aug. 23, 1828), pp. 451–54, Polk MS.

3. List of plantation property, Sept. 26, 1834; RC to JP, Nov. 3, 1846, Polk MS. *Diary*, IV, 377. See chapters 3 and 6.

4. Six of them were sold in a family group; whether the buyer preserved this family or broke it up by resale is not recorded. M. T. Polk, will, Apr. 12, 1831, Mecklenburg County wills; M. T. Polk estate receipts, 1832–33 (II, 172 on reel C.065.50001), Mecklenburg County estate records, N.C. State Archives, Raleigh.

5. The two preceding paragraphs, and the next one, depend more than usual on inference. The following facts, however, are certain: (1) the seven slaves inherited by Marshall Polk from his father, Sam Polk, included a five-person family and two youths, Wally and Gabriel (who were probably elder sons in this same family); (2) the only slave inherited from Sam Polk by Eliza (Polk) Caldwell—and thus by her husband Silas Caldwell—was the girl Martha, who would have known

Wally before Sam Polk's will was settled in 1828; (3) later (in 1834) when Wally was at James Polk's Somerville plantation, his wife was owned by Silas Caldwell, who offered to buy Wally that January in order to join the two under a single owner; (4) Caldwell bought Wally before March 18, 1834, and less than a fortnight after Marshall Polk's Tennessee executor sold him to someone else; (5) Wally and Martha were among the slaves whom Caldwell sent to his and James Polk's new Mississippi plantation late in 1834; (6) Marshall Polk had removed Wally and Gabriel from Columbia, Tennessee, to Charlotte, North Carolina, sometime between 1828 and May 1830; (7) two of Marshall Polk's slaves fled North Carolina within two months of his death in 1831, and James Polk paid the bills for releasing them from the Knoxville jail. That these two were indeed Wally and Gabriel seems to me almost certain, though they were not named in the jailer's receipts; and that Martha was the slave of Caldwell whom Wally married is my (somewhat less certain) surmise. Apparently Marshall Polk's Tennessee executor, James Walker, bought both Wally and Gabriel from the estate early in 1833. He sold Wally in Tennessee on March 4, 1834, and within a few days Martha's owner, Silas Caldwell, bought Wally. Samuel Polk, will, Dec. 13, 1826, Polk MS. Silas Caldwell to JP, Jan. 22, Mar. 18, 1834, *Corr.*, II, 270–71, 365. Marshall Polk estate records (Series 7), Oct. 20, 1832, Mar. 4, 1834; plantation property, Sept. 26, 1834; valuation of plantation property, Nov. 2, 1834; receipts for two fugitives: Oct. 11, 29, Nov. 3, 4, 1831, Polk MS. M. T. Polk inventory, July 22, 1831; M. T. Polk medical bill, May 7, 1830 (for Wally); M. T. Polk estate receipts, 1832–33 (II, 172), Mecklenburg County estate records, N.C. State Archives. Sellers (I), pp. 115, 184, 186 (quotation).

6. Herbert Biles to JP, Jan. 17, 1833, *Corr.*, II, 31.

7. G. J. Pillow to E. Croswell, Oct. 1, 1844, Polk MS; Adlai Harris to JP, Dec. 30, 1833, *Corr.*, II, 205; Herbert Biles to JP, Feb. 15, 1833 (reporting that Ben and Jim had gotten back to the plantation on Feb. 2), James Polk MS, TSA.

8. Ephraim Beanland to JP, Dec. 1, 22, [Oct.] 30, 1833, *Corr.*, II, 145, 190, 123. In addition to the eight male cotton pickers listed in the October letter, there was a young adult slave at the plantation, named Austin, who soon died of tuberculosis. George Moore to JP, Feb. 2, 1834, Polk MS. WHP to JP, Dec. 2, 1837, *Corr.*, IV, 200.

9. Beanland to JP, Dec. 1, 1833; James Walker to JP, Dec. 14, 1833; Adlai Harris to JP, Dec. 30, 1833, *Corr.*, II, 144, 176, 204.

10. Beanland to JP, Dec. 22, 1833; James Walker to JP, Dec. 20 (1833), Jan. 22, 1834; Adlai Harris to JP, Dec. 30, 1833; Caldwell to JP, Jan. 4, 1834, *Corr.*, II, 190; 187, 274; 205; 219–20.

11. The $63 that James Polk paid Moore, plus the $126 invoice submitted by Beanland, plus imputed interest adds up approximately to the total $194.65 cost recorded by James Polk in his 1834 accounts for Sam Polk's estate. James Polk and his younger brother William shared equally the cost of recovering Jack (as William owned Jack and rented him to James Polk). Samuel Polk, will, Dec. 13, 1826, Polk MS. Caldwell to JP, Jan. 4, 1834; Walker to JP, Jan. 9, 1834; Beanland to JP, Feb. 1, 1834, *Corr.*, II, 219, 235, 285. Mooney, *Slavery in Tennessee*, p. 232, n. 83. Receipt, George Moore to JP, Sept. 24, 1834 (for $63 of the total), reel 65; JP, accounts of Sam Polk's estate, Sept. 26, 1834, Reel 62, Polk MS. Invoice, Beanland to JP, Jan. 3, 1834, Bassett, p. 60. I infer Jack's age from that of his wife, Cloe, who was born about 1788: bill of sale, Nov. 3, 1838, Polk MS.

12. Caldwell to JP, Jan. 4, 1834; Walker to JP, Jan. 9, 1834; Beanland to JP,

Dec. 22, 1833, *Corr.*, II, 219, 235, 190. *Diary*, I, 14 (Sept. 2, 1845). Beanland to Walker, Feb. 6, 1834, Polk MS.

13. JP, will, Oct. 24, 1831, Polk MS. Adlai Harris to JP, Dec. 30, 1833, Jan. 3, 1834; Caldwell to JP, Jan. 4, 22, 1834; Walker to JP, Jan. 22, 1834; Beanland to JP, Mar. 7, 1834; JP to SP, Sept. 26, 1834, *Corr.*, II, 205, 215, 219, 270, 274, 347–48; 509. Beanland to Walker, Feb. 6, 1834; G. J. Pillow to E. Croswell, Oct. 1, 1844, Polk MS.

14. George Moore to JP, Feb. 8, 1834; Beanland to Walker, Feb. 6, 1834, Polk MS. Beanland to JP, Dec. 22, 1833, Feb. 13, 1834; Caldwell to JP, Jan. 2, Feb. 11, 1835, *Corr.*, II, 190, 312; III, 5, 95. Re Austin, see note 8 above.

15. Beanland to JP, Mar. 7, 1834; Caldwell to JP, Jan. 22, Mar. 18, 1834, *Corr.*, II, 347; 270, 365. Marshall Polk estate records, Mar. 4, 1834, Polk MS. M. T. Polk estate receipts, 1832–33, II, 172, Mecklenburg County estate records, N.C. State Archives.

16. Caldwell to JP, Mar. 18, 1834; JP to SP, Sept. 26, 1834, *Corr.*, II, 365, 509. Agreement among W. R. Rucker, JP, and J. W. Childress, Aug. 23, 1828, p. 451; G. J. Pillow to E. Croswell, Oct. 1, 1844, Polk MS. Pillow's letter is quoted in chapter 1 above.

17. George Moore to JP, Feb. 8, 1834, Polk MS. Beanland to JP, Apr. 1, Oct. 4, 10, 1834; JP to SP, Sept. 26, 1834, *Corr.*, II, 378, 514, 519; 508.

18. James Walker to JP, Feb. 19, 1834; Beanland to JP, Mar. 7, 1834, *Corr.*, II, 331, 347. Beanland to JP, Oct. 10, 23, 1834, Polk MS (*Corr.*, II, 520, 539: on p. 539 Jack's name is misprinted as "Dick"). That Jack was sold is the clear implication of James Polk's ceasing to pay rent for him after October 1834: Settlement (of Sam Polk's estate) between JP and WHP, Aug. 3, 1836, Polk Correspondence, University of Tennessee.

CHAPTER 3

1. I omit 1836 and 1837, for which period only a single letter from an overseer has survived. The thirteen certain fugitives were Addison, Alphonso, Billy Nevels, Charles, Gilbert, Harbert, Henry Carter, Joe, Manuel, Perry, Phil, Pompey, and Wilson. The other twelve Polk male slaves old enough to venture flight at some time during these nineteen years were Allen, Andy, Bob, Caesar, Calvin, Charley, Clay, Garrison, Giles, Jim, driver Joe, and Turner. From this list I omit the blacksmith Harry, who, by the time the Polks stopped him from hiring out on his own time in a neighboring county, was over fifty. I also omit "old Ben" (probably too old to flee) and Lewis, Anderson, Jason, Jerry, Davy, and Julius, who—born respectively in 1837, 1838, 1838, 1839, 1845, and 1845—were too young during all or most of this period to have been likely to venture flight. From the figure of forty "non-Beanland" flights I exclude three others (not mentioned in chapter 2) taken when Beanland was Polk's Mississippi overseer in 1835, as well as one in 1857 (a year omitted from my calculation because only three of the overseer's letters have survived). I also exclude from this record of flights by males the only instance noted by an overseer of a female slave's flight: this was Marina in 1839, mentioned later in this chapter. Lists of Polk's slaves are in plantation property, Sept. 26, 1834; RC to JP, Jan. 9, 1847, Polk MS; JP 1849 inventory, Dec. 5, Yalobusha County (MS) inventory book E, pp. 31–33, and SP, bill of sale, Jan. 25, 1860, James Polk MS, TSA.

2. Thus on Jan. 7, 1856, overseer John Mairs acknowledged that Harbert (whose flight he now reported) had fled "wons or twis before" without Mairs's having mentioned it (Re Harbert, see the discussion below). JM to SP, Jan. 7, 1856, Polk MS.

3. I use the male pronoun in this paragraph because all the cases of shooting, stabbing, kidnapping, terrible whippings, and sales of Polk fugitives happened to males. Only one of the nineteen escapees ever named by Polk's overseers was a woman. But on other plantations a higher proportion were females. For example, 23 percent of the fugitives from the Gowrie rice plantation (1851–64) were women; and in 1856 about 30 percent of those escaping permanently to the North via Philadelphia's underground railroad were female. Dusinberre, *Them Dark Days*, p. 144 and notes 63 and 66; Dusinberre, *Civil War Issues in Philadelphia*, p. 55.

4. JP to SP, Sept. 26, 1834, *Corr.*, II, 507–9.

5. Silas Caldwell to JP, Feb. 11, 1835, Jan. 16, 1836, *Corr.*, III, 84–85, 437.

6. A. T. McNeal to JP, June 15, 1838 (misfiled June 13, 1838), Polk MS (two quotations). George Bratton to JP, Sept. 13, 1838, Bassett, p. 114.

7. S. Bell to JP, July 7, 1839, Bassett, p. 121.

8. John Garner to JP, Sept. 10, 1839; the agent was a Mr. Trainum, as reported in WHP to JP, Oct. 28, 1839, *Corr.*, V, 236, 277.

9. Garner to JP, Nov. 3, 1839, *Corr.*, V, 285.

10. Ibid.

11. Garner to JP, Dec. 25, 1839, Polk MS. A. T. McNeal to JP, Jan. 15, 1840, *Corr.*, V, 372.

12. RC to JP, Jan. 9, 1847 (re best worker); bill of sale, Sept. 26, 1834, Polk MS. JP to SP, Sept 26, 1834; Ephraim Beanland to JP, Oct. 26, 1834, *Corr.*, II, 508–9, 540.

13. For example, Lucretia Alexander's enslaved father, a frequent fugitive from previous masters, "never would run away from Miss Susan." Yetman, *Life Under the "Peculiar Institution,"* p. 13.

14. Garner to JP, Nov. 1, 1840 (reporting events of Oct. 10), *Corr.*, V, 573.

15. Ibid.

16. Silas Caldwell to JP, Oct. 20, 1840, Polk MS.

17. The traveler Frederick Olmsted reported that overseers in the Southwest were frequently armed with knives or firearms with which to enforce their authority; for example, Olmsted, *Journey in the Back Country*, pp. 12, 56, 82–83.

18. Isaac Dismukes to JP, Sept. 27, 1841, *Corr.*, V, 762.

19. A. T. McNeal to JP, Jan. 15, 1840; Silas Caldwell to JP, July 23, 1841, *Corr.*, V, 372, 715.

20. Jack Long—probably the brother of Long Harry, James Polk's privileged blacksmith—had been bequeathed by James's father, Sam Polk, to James's younger brother S. W. Polk. Jack Long was to have been sent to James Polk's plantation to replace a slave whom William Polk was removing from that enterprise late in 1838. Samuel Polk, will, Dec. 13, 1826; JP, Memoranda relating to estate of S. W. Polk (Series 7); JP, accounts of S. W. Polk estate, March 1842 (reel 62), Polk MS. WHP to JP, Nov. 25, 1838; James Walker to JP, Dec. 10, 1838, *Corr.*, IV, 619, 642. George Bratton to JP, Dec. 24, 1838, Bassett, p. 116.

21. In the American South, according to the legal historian Thomas Morris, "almost all homicides of slaves . . . ended in acquittals, or at most in verdicts of

manslaughter. . . . There were also killings that never led to criminal actions." T. D. Morris, *Southern Slavery and the Law*, p. 181. The quotation in the text refers to the Tennessee law of 1799, which, in 1821, was in effect adopted by judicial ruling in Mississippi (pp. 172, 175–76).

22. Silas Caldwell to JP, July 23, 1841, *Corr.*, V, 715.

23. Dismukes to JP, Sept. 1, 1841, *Corr.*, V, 746. Mrs. Silas Caldwell to SP, Aug. 23, 1841, Bassett, p. 155. Agreement, Sept. 12, 1836, between Silas Caldwell and WHP; bill of sale, Nov. 3, 1838, from WHP to JP, Polk MS.

24. These are Bobbitt's paraphrases of Polk's and Leigh's words. William Bobbitt to JP, July 16, Aug. 29, 1841, Bassett, pp. 153, 156.

25. Dismukes to JP, Sept. 1, 1841, *Corr.*, V, 746–47.

26. Dismukes to JP, Sept. 27, 1841, *Corr.*, V, 762. Dismukes to JP, Jan. 14, 1843; Aug. 24, Oct. 4, 12, 1842; J. T. Leigh to JP, Sept. 28, 1842, Bassett, pp. 171; 154, 168–69, 170; 168. JP, accounts, Jan. 21, 1845 (reel 62); Silas Caldwell to JP, Jan. 22, 1845; JP to RC, Mar. 18, 1847, Polk MS. S. P. Walker to JP, Jan. 3, 1845, Bassett, p. 174.

27. J. T. Leigh to RC, May 5, 1845; RC to JP, Sept. 24, 1845, Jan. 17, 1846; Daniel Graham to John Catron, Nov. 6, 1849; Pickett, Perkins to SP, Dec. 27, 1852 (also Feb. 27, 1852); JM to SP, Aug. 1, 1855, Polk MS.

28. RC to JP, Jan. 9, Sept. 14, 1847; JM to RC, Aug. 21, 1847, to JP, Feb. 4, May 4, June 6, 1848; JP to JM, May 1, June 5, 1848, to J. T. Leigh, June 17, 1848, Polk MS.

29. I infer that Joe was sold, probably in 1853, because the name of this Joe apparently is absent from the list of slaves at Sarah Polk's plantation in 1860, and because there is no report that Joe had died (or fled yet again) in the meanwhile. Mairs did not whip him for his seventh escape because on that occasion (as explained later in this chapter) Joe voluntarily returned in order to save the life of an ill companion. But Mairs obviously was urging that Joe be sold. JM to SP, Aug. 10, 1850, Mar. 5, 1851, July 9, 1853; to J. W. Childress, June 10, 1853, Bassett, pp. 186, 190, 204–5.

A "Joe" was listed at the plantation in 1860, but apparently this was the Joe owned by Jane Polk until her death in 1852—the "Joe, black boy" (perhaps born in 1820) willed by Sam Polk to his widow in 1827 with the injunction that he was not to be sold out of the family. Jane Polk seems to have rented this Joe to James Polk, beginning in about 1842, and Polk used him as driver on his Mississippi plantation. As this Joe was known by James Polk's executor to be owned by Jane Polk, he was not included in the inventory of Mississippi slaves owned by James Polk in 1849. (The Joe on that list was surely the slave sold to James Polk by Robert Campbell in 1847.) After Jane Polk died in 1852, driver Joe apparently came into the possession of Sarah Polk. I infer that he remained as driver on the Mississippi plantation after Jane Polk's death and that he was the Joe listed among Sarah Polk's slaves in 1860. She may subsequently have sold or given him to her nephew William H. Polk: an 1865 list of slaves who had been owned by W. H. Polk mentions a Joe born in 1820. JP inventory, Dec. 5, 1849, Yalobusha County inventory book E, pp. 31–33. Bill of sale, Jan. 25, 1860, James Polk MS (Mf 805), TSA. List of Negroes belonging to Mrs. W. H. Polk (1865), Lucy Williams Polk Papers, miscellaneous, series PC 75.10, N.C. State Archives.

30. JP to Lydia Eliza Caldwell, Oct. 14, 1848; to JM, Oct. 15, 1848, letterbook, Polk MS.

31. Lydia Caldwell to JP, Nov. 20, 1848, James Polk MS, TSA. S. P. Walker to JP, Nov. 1, 1848; JM to JP, Dec. 2, 1848, Feb. 8, 1849; W. S. Pickett to JP, Jan. 15, 1849, Polk MS. *Organizer* (Oxford), Apr. 7, 1849, in Don H. Doyle, *Faulkner's County*, p. 137.

32. On Sarah's involvement in her husband's political campaigning and in reading newspapers for him and on her trips to the plantations, see Samuel P. Walker to SP, Aug. 26, 1840, Polk MS. SP to JP, June 18, 1841, *Corr.*, V, 700–1. Nelson and Nelson, *Memorials of Sarah Childress Polk*, pp. 51–52, 68, 94, 192. Sellers (I), pp. 372, 460, 474; see also pp. 143, 340, 436, 458. Bassett, p. 181.

33. JM to SP, Jan. 13, Feb. 10, Mar. 5, 18, Apr. 16, 1851, Bassett, pp. 188–92. JM to SP, May 18, 1851, Feb. 28, 1852, Polk MS. I infer that this Pompey was the bondsman bequeathed by Sam Polk to his son S. W. Polk and that, after the latter's death in 1839, the slave came into the possession of James Polk: Sam Polk, will, Dec. 13, 1826, Polk MS. Wilson was born in December 1833 to Maria and Henry Carter: JP inventory, Dec. 5, 1849, Yalobusha County inventory book E, p. 31; list of JP's slaves [1834], Bassett, p. 47; Ephraim Beanland to JP, Dec. 22, 1833, *Corr.*, II, 190.

34. This transaction is described, with references, in chapter 6.

35. JM to SP, Oct. 21, 1852, Polk MS; to J. W. Childress, June 10, 1853, Bassett, p. 204. On Billy's marriage to Barbara, see JM to JP, Apr. 19, 1849, Polk MS. Billy Nevels was still at the Mississippi plantation in 1860, where presumably he had been obliged to find a new wife. Bassett, p. 275.

36. JM to SP, Oct. 15, Aug. 22, 1853, Bassett, pp. 206, 205. Ephraim Beanland to JP, Oct. 10, 1834, *Corr.*, II, 520.

37. Memo of agreement, Aug. 23, 1828, among W. R. Rucker, JP, and J. W. Childress, p. 451; bill of sale (Matilda), Oct. 27, 1829, Polk MS. JP to William Rucker, Sept. 4, 1828, June 24, 1829; Rucker to JP, Jan. 27, 1829, *Corr.*, I, 195, 268, 233.

38. Herbert Biles to JP, Nov. 23, 1832; A. O. Harris to JP, Oct. 31, Nov. 4, 1833, *Corr.*, I, 530; II, 124, 125. JP, accounts, Oct. 30, 1834, Nov. 10, 1836, Polk MS (reel 62).

39. James Walker to JP, Mar. 18, 1836; Silas Caldwell to JP, Feb. 7, 1836, *Corr.*, III, 542–43, 483.

40. JP, Accounts, Nov. 3, 1838, Jan. 20, 1840, reel 62, Polk MS. JP to WHP, Nov. 11, 1840, Lucy Williams Polk MS, N.C. State Archives. WHP to JP, Dec. 4, 1840, *Corr.*, V, 601.

41. G. J. Pillow to E. Croswell, editor of the *Daily Albany Argus*, Oct. 1, 1844; JP, note on RC's receipt, filed July 6, 1846; bill of sale, July 7, 1846, Polk MS.

42. JM to SP, Jan. 7, 1856, Oct. 24 (probably 1856), Polk MS. JM to SP, Feb. 23, Apr. 23, Sept. 13, 14, 1856, May 11, 1857, Bassett, pp. 213–19. Alphonso, who fled at least three times, first did so in autumn 1854. Apparently James Polk (who bought Alphonso from Jane Polk in 1832) had later sold him back to Jane Polk, who let James Polk continue to use Alphonso on his Mississippi plantation. In 1854, when Jane Polk's estate was settled, James Polk's favored nephew, Marshall Polk, Jr., inherited Alphonso. Evidently Marshall sold Alphonso to Sarah Polk sometime before 1860. Cf. chapter 6, note 15. Marshall Polk, Jr. to John H. Bills, Feb. 3, July (n.d.), Oct. 6, Nov. 1, 1854 (typescripts); list of SP's slaves, Jan. 25, 1860, James Polk MS, TSA.

43. Harbert's wife, Mary, and her child, Lewis, were still on the plantation in 1860 but Harbert was not. It is unlikely that Sarah Polk would have brought Harbert

back to central Tennessee without also bringing his wife. Possibly Harbert died before 1860, unrecorded in any of the overseer's extant letters; but it is much more probable that the slave continued to try to escape and that Mairs concluded, as he had done with the inveterate fugitive Joe in 1853, that nothing could break Harbert's spirit and that he must therefore be sold.

44. G. J. Pillow to E. Croswell, editor of the *Daily Albany Argus*, Oct. 1, 1844, Polk MS. Emphasis in the original.

45. Isaac Dismukes to JP, Sept. 27, 1841; Silas Caldwell to JP, Jan. 4, 1834, Mar. 18, 1836; Dismukes to JP, Sept. 1, 1841, *Corr.*, V, 762; II, 219; III, 484; V, 747. Like Polk's Mississippi slaves, bondspeople at the Butler Island (Georgia) rice plantation constructed their own vision of a golden age, twenty years earlier. Dusinberre, *Them Dark Days*, p. 245.

46. Stampp, *Peculiar Institution* (London [1956] 1964), chap. 4, esp. pp. 142, 169–70, 172–75. Jones, *Born a Child of Freedom*, chap. 2 (quotation p. 37).

47. Dismukes to JP, Sept. 1, 1841, *Corr.*, V, 747. JM to J. W. Childress, June 10, 1853, Bassett, p. 204.

48. JP to J. T. Leigh, June 17, 1848, letterbook, Polk MS.

49. Ayers, *Vengeance and Justice*, p. 308, n. 67.

50. Franklin and Schweninger, *Runaway Slaves*, p. 282; also pp. 234–35, 279–82, 290–94 and passim, esp. pp. 97–148.

51. Dusinberre, *Them Dark Days*, pp. 142–58, 162–68, and notes 63 and 110; see also pp. 371–72, 421–22.

52. For example, see Olmsted, *Journey in the Seaboard Slave States*, pp. 159–63; *Journey in the Back Country*, pp. 29–31, 56, 87–88, 476. "Olmsted's impressionistic observation," according to Franklin and Schweninger, "was far more accurate than the 'scientific' data provided in the United States Census." Franklin and Schweninger, *Runaway Slaves*, p. 282; also pp. 295–96, and passim.

CHAPTER 4

1. The partnership's cotton production figures were

	1835 (bales)	1836 (bales)
New Mississippi plantation	20	44
Caldwell's old Tennessee plantation	43	58
Total	63	102
Polk's half-share	31–1/2	51
Caldwell's subsidy to Polk	11–1/2	7

The 1835 crop netted (after deducting for the cost of baling) about $58.70 per bale. I estimate—assuming that the last quarter of the 1836 crop reached the market late—that that year's crop netted only an average of about $43.50 per bale. Silas Caldwell to JP, Jan. 16, Apr. 28, 1836; May 4, 1837, *Corr.*, III, 437, 609; IV, 109. For cotton prices, see Gray, *History of Agriculture*, vol. 2, pp. 1027–28. Since half of each partner's slaves worked in Mississippi (and half in Tennessee) during the two-year duration of the partnership, Caldwell does not appear to have received much compensation for giving this subsidy, except for the use of four or five of Polk's Mississippi slaves at Caldwell's Tennessee plantation during the 1835 harvest and the ownership of a couple of mules, which he extracted from William Polk when they divided the plantation assets in 1836. Caldwell was further disadvantaged by the clause (JP, schedule of slaves [Sept. 5, 1834], Polk MS) that made the partners jointly responsible for the loss of any slave; thus when Polk's twenty-six-year-old Hardy died in 1835 and when his twenty-three-year old blacksmith, Abe, was thrown from a mule and killed in 1836, Caldwell bore half of the $1800 loss. Perhaps Polk, who had cash in hand from selling his own West Tennessee plantation in 1834, had agreed to pay the whole down payment (over $3000) on the new Mississippi plantation, postponing for a year or two the equalization of his and Caldwell's investments in the new land. Caldwell to JP, Sept. 16, 1835; George Bratton to JP, May 13, 1837, *Corr.*, III, 301; IV, 119.

2. Slave prices were higher in Mississippi than in Tennessee, and I estimate that the value of Polk's slaves increased by $500 (i.e., by about 6 percent) when he moved them to Mississippi. I very conservatively estimate that the general inflation of prices added another $750 to the value of his slaves by the end of 1836. This $1250 increase (1835–36) is recorded in column (f) of table 5.1 in chapter 5, and the sources for the estimate are discussed in appendix B, column (f). I have not included in Polk's capital gains the added value of the plantation land cleared by Polk's slaves (they had cleared some 180 acres by planting time in 1837) nor its added value caused by the inflation of the mid-1830s. All of these capital gains on land were soon wiped out by the cotton boom's collapse. As I have no index for the inflation or deflation of northern Mississippi cotton land during the 1830s and 1840s, I have been obliged to ignore these fluctuations in land values. See appendix B, column (e), 1849.

3. Caldwell to JP, Feb. 11, 1835; Apr. 28, 1836, *Corr.*, III, 95, 609.

4. Caldwell to JP, Jan. 31, Nov. 11, Feb. 22, 1836; John Garner to JP, Nov. 23, 1839, Mar. 2, 1840; A. T. McNeal to JP, Jan. 5, 1840, *Corr.*, III, 473, 780, 508–9; V, 312, 399; 373.

5. Caldwell, who paid $4600 for his half-share of 920 acres of plantation land, sold it to W. H. Polk for $7000. The resultant $2400 profit more than doubled Caldwell's total cash return from his two-year partnership with James Polk, bringing Caldwell's average annual profit during 1835–36 to about 16 percent. Indenture, Sept. 4, 1836, between Silas Caldwell and W. H. Polk; agreement, Sept. 12, 1836, between Caldwell and W. H. Polk, Polk MS.

6. In 1837 the plantation's recurrent expenses were about $1776—nearly 30 percent higher than the annual average during the next thirteen years. Table C1, column (c), in Appendix C registers only James Polk's half-share of those expenses during the years 1835–38, when he had only a half-share in the enterprise.

7. WHP to JP, Feb. 5, 1838; Caruthers, Harris & Co. to JP, June 8, 1838; JP to WHP, June 25, 1838, *Corr.*, IV, 356, 473, 492.

8. Dr. J. B. Hays to JP, Dec. 4, 1838, Jan. [9], 11, 13, 1839; James Walker to JP, Dec. 10, 1838, May 25, 1839; S. P. Walker to JP, Dec. 7, 1838; WHP to JP, Jan. 2, 26, 1839, *Corr.*, IV, 627–30, 634–35, 642; V, 3–5, 13, 18, 22, 35–36, 134–35. WHP to JP, Jan. 21, 1839, Polk MS. Sellers (I) p. 331.

9. Although James Polk became sole proprietor of the plantation at the end of 1838, William retained ownership of one-quarter of the land until James finally bought that from him in 1844. Meanwhile, James paid William a fixed rent for William's remaining portion of the land. Indenture, Nov. 3, 1838, between WHP and JP; bill of sale, Nov. 3, 1838 (eight slaves from WHP to JP); bill of sale,

Sept. 24, 1839 (four slaves from West Harris to JP); JP, memo, Dec. 16, 1844, of contract between WHP and JP, Polk MS. The figures for James Polk's cash investment in the plantation in 1834 and in 1838–39 are in columns (b), (c), and (d) of table 5.1 below. On the attempted sale: A. J. Donelson to JP, Oct. 6, 1838, *Corr.*, IV, 573.

10. The figures on the fluctuating value of Polk's slaves are in table 5.1, column (f).

11. Isaac Dismukes to JP, Aug. 16, 1842, Bassett, p. 165. JP to SP, Oct. 26, 1843; Samuel P. Caldwell to JP, Nov. 28, 1843; Nov. 19, 1844; John W. Childress to JP, Dec. 5, 1843, *Corr.*, VI, 353, 665; VIII, 335; VI, 665.

12. On campaign debts, see chapter 1, note 27.

13. JP, Memo, Dec. 16, 1844 . . . W. H. Polk and JP; JP to Samuel Walker, May 24, 1845, Polk MS. Polk learned of his election on November 16, 1844. Sellers (II), p. 157.

14. JP, money account, Feb. 1, 1845, through Apr. 23, 1849, series 7, Polk MS: on campaign debts paid by March 1846, see chapter 1, note 27 above, on Treasury certificates, see chapter 1, note 31; on the Nashville mansion, see Dec. 11, 1846, Apr. 20, June 28, 1847, May 26, 31, June 15, Oct. 2, 11, 1848.

15. JP, money account, Feb. 1, 1845 through Apr. 23, 1849, series 7, Polk MS: thirteen slaves: Oct. 22, 1845, July 20, Aug. 4, 1846, Jan. 1, 7, Feb. 2, 1847. Six slaves: S. P. Walker to JP, Apr. 4, 1849, Polk MS.

16. RC to JP, Jan. 17, 1846; JP to RC, Jan. 30, 1846, letterbook, Polk MS.

17. James Brown to JP, May 7, 1847; also Brown to E. P. McNeal, Oct. 16, 1846, Polk MS.

18. Kotlikoff, "Quantitative Description of the New Orleans Slave Market," p. 35 (I am indebted to Stanley Engerman for this reference). Texas legislature: Bolton, *Poor Whites of the Antebellum South*, p. 82. "Armistice of 1850" is David Potter's term: Potter, *Impending Crisis*, p. 90. Prices of Sarah Polk's cotton are in the reports to her from her New Orleans factor (W. S. Pickett or, in 1857, Perkins & Co.), Polk MS. Most of these reports are easily accessible in Bassett, pp. 229–59.

19. Wright, *Political Economy of the Cotton South*, esp. pp. 144–50, 154.

20. Capital gains are specified in table 5.1, column (f), 1845–59. My estimates of these gains are a little conservative because they posit an increase by 1859 in the value of Polk's slaves (i.e., those not deported between 1851 and 1856) of about 67 percent over their 1849 valuation, whereas the index of New Orleans slave prices was actually, by 1859, 79 percent higher ($1431) than the figure ($800) the Polk assessors had set for the value of a prime male field hand in 1849. This matter is discussed in appendix B, column (f). New Orleans slave prices are from Kotlikoff's article, cited in note 18 above. To the cash profits shown in table C1, column (d), 1845–57, I add for each of the years 1858 and 1859 estimated profits of $4800, this figure being the average annual cash profit during the three years 1855 through 1857.

21. SP, 1860 agreement.

22. Nelson and Nelson, *Memorials of Sarah Childress Polk*, p. 148. The Polks' profit rates are taken from table 4.1, column (c).

CHAPTER 5

1. Genovese, *Political Economy of Slavery*, pp. 19, 23. Fox-Genovese and Genovese, *Fruits of Merchant Capital*, pp. 17, 19. Marx "revealed [capital] as a so-

cial relation . . . the relation between the buyers and sellers of labor-power". *Fruits of Merchant Capital*, p. 20.

2. Kolchin, *American Slavery*, pp. 172–73. See also Kolchin, *Unfree Labor*, pp. 359–60.

3. Of 308,000 slaves sent from the slave-exporting states to the slave-importing states during the 1850s, Michael Tadman estimates that at least 61 percent were sold. Tadman, *Speculators and Slaves*, p. 247; see also pp. 30–31, 211–12, 242.

4. The Genoveses distinguish the Northern "market in labor-power" from what they call the South's "market in labor." Modern plantation economies, they assert, "rested on . . . dependent labor systems that deprived them of the . . . advantages of a market in labor-power, in contradistinction to that market in labor which slavery's capitalization of labor made possible." *Fruits of Merchant Capital*, p. 58.

5. Of course, the buyer of a slave obtained other things besides labor power: the psychological, and sometimes the sexual, satisfactions of dominion. Labor power was nevertheless—in a semicapitalist system like that of the Southern United States, though not in a society with a "traditional" economy like that of nineteenth-century West Africa—the heart of the matter.

6. See the discussion in chapter 6.

7. Patterson, "On Slavery and Slave Formations," pp. 40, 52–55; Patterson, *Slavery and Social Death*, pp. 1–101.

8. The Genoveses agree that "slavery represented a major [economic] advance over quasi-seigneurial alternatives, for it permitted greater economic rationalization and a more flexible labor market" (*Fruits of Merchant Capital*, p. 59).

9. A less unsophisticated definition of capitalism appears in the following paragraph.

10. Peter Kolchin, agreeing with Jerome Blum, points out that Russian landlords had a legal right to buy and sell serfs separate from the land. They argue that therefore Russian serfs were essentially slaves. This legal right was, however, somewhat restricted after the late eighteenth century; I surmise that—at least in long-settled black-earth regions—local custom may have hemmed in the legal right to such an extent that in practice Russia's "market for labor power" approximated more closely the seigniorial than the slave model. Steven Hoch (who has made the most detailed study of an individual Russian estate) reports that the Gagarin family did indeed *transfer* many of their own serfs from long-settled areas of Russia to the newly settled Tambov region when, around 1800, they established their Petrovskoe estate. They may also have moved, subsequently, a few of their Petrovskoe serf families to another Gagarin estate. But Hoch does not once mention the *purchase* by the Gagarins of any serf, and only once a *sale*: in 1840 or 1841 they sold "a number of families to Siberia, a unique event." This sale appears to have been so contrary to custom that it may well have been the cause of the serf revolt at the estate that occurred in June 1841. Thus Hoch's case study suggests that the role of serf trading in Russia was far less significant than the role of slave trading in the American South. This would help to account for the slower rate of economic development in Russia than in the antebellum South. The Russian gentry's "'entrepreneurial' contribution to the economic system," according to Terence Emmons, "was slight, restricted for the most part to their role in putting grain on the market." Kolchin, *Unfree Labor*, pp. 41–46. Blum, *Lord and Peasant in Russia*, esp. pp. 422–36. Hoch, *Serfdom and Social Control in Russia*, pp. 1–2, 12–13, 89, 149, 183 (quotation), and passim.

Emmons, *Russian Landed Gentry and the Peasant Emancipation of 1861*, p. 25; see also pp. 22–23.

11. Although Marta Petrusewicz has shown how far the Barracco family had modernized its management of its huge Calabrian estate by 1850, some historians suggest that most southern Italian and Sicilian landlords had not moved very far in that direction. Petrusewicz, *Latifundium*. Cf., for example, Riall, *Italian Risorgimento*, pp. 58–60; Riall, *Sicily and the Unification of Italy*, pp. 17–21, 42–58; Montroni, *Gli uemini del Re*.

12. This characterization of Southern society differs from, yet draws substantially on and is I believe consonant with, that in Wright, *Old South, New South*, pp. 17–34.

13. Colonel William Polk, ledger, 1833, Polk and Yeatman Family Papers 606 (series 4.1, vol. 8), SHC. JP, notes, Apr. 7, 1831, as executor of Sam Polk's estate, Polk MS (Series 7). Sellers (I), pp. 38, 114.

14. Colonel William Polk to Lucius Polk, Apr. 3, 1827 (emphasis in the original), Polk, Brown, and Ewell family papers #605, SHC. Mooney, *Slavery in Tennessee*, p. 159.

15. Thomas Childress to William Polk, July 17, 1820, May 5, 1822, Polk-Yeatman MS, SHC.

16. Sellers (I), pp. 206–7; see also pp. 208–9, 213, 217–18. Hammond, *Banks and Politics in America*, esp. pp. 328–65.

17. Sellers (I), pp. 209–10. James Walker to JP, Feb. 14, 1836, *Corr.*, III, 499–500.

18. JP to James Walker, Dec. 21, 1838, Lucy Williams Polk Papers, N.C. State Archives. William Polk was cleared of any murder charge (because he acted in self-defense) but was convicted of having assaulted the young lawyer three days before the shooting. He served a six-week term in the Columbia jail. See the discussion in chapter 4 and its note 8.

19. James Walker to JP, Mar. 22, 1836; Jan. 24, 1833, Jan. 22, 1834, *Corr.*, III, 546–47; II, 45, 274–75.

20. Walker to JP, May 2, 10, 29, 1838, *Corr.*, IV, 435, 436n, 442–43, 466; also V, 360, 361n, 407.

21. J. W. Childress to JP, Dec. 5, 1843, Jan. 14, 1844 (emphasis added), Polk MS.

22. RC to JP, Jan. 9, 1847, Polk MS. WHP to JP, Feb. 15, 1837; Silas Caldwell to JP, Jan. 22, 1834; JP to SP, Sept. 26, 1834, *Corr.*, IV, 63; II, 271, 509.

23. JP to WHP, Nov. 29, 1836, Lucy Williams Polk MS, N.C. State Archives.

24. John Garner to JP, June 7, 1840, Bassett, p. 141. William Bobbitt to JP, Apr. 5, 1841, Polk Correspondence, University of Tennessee. JP to JM, Feb. 1, 1848 (letterbook), Polk MS. Beard and Beard, *Rise of American Civilization* vol. 1, pp. 663–68, 672–76. As the Beards acknowledge, "Planting statesmen [were] as eager to make money as cotton spinners" (p. 718).

25. On these first four stages, see John Garner to JP, Mar. 2, June 7, 1840, *Corr.*, V, 399, 483.

26. Caruthers, Harris & Co. to JP, June 8, 1838, Bassett, p. 226. JP to S. P. Walker, Oct. 14, 1848 (letterbook); Pickett, Perkins & Co. to JP, Mar. 25, 1848, Jan. 15, 1849; to S. P. Walker, Feb. 15, 1849, Polk MS. JM to SP, Mar. 5, 1851; Pickett, Perkins to SP, Mar. 24, May, 9, 1851, Polk MS. Pickett, Perkins to SP, Apr. 2, 1852, Bassett, p. 198. Pickett, Perkins to SP, Mar. 25, 1853, Polk MS.

27. Bassett, pp. 240–43; Perkins, Campbell to SP, May 28, 1855, Polk MS. Bassett, pp. 212, 246.

28. JM to SP, Jan. 10, 1854, Bassett, p. 207.

29. Chaplin, *Anxious Pursuit*, pp. 310–17.

30. Ephraim Beanland to JP, Jan. 23, 1836, *Corr.*, III, 456. RC to JP, Sept. 24, 1845, Polk MS. Isaac Dismukes to JP, Sept. 13, 1842; Samuel. P. Caldwell to JP, May 21, 1844, Bassett, pp. 166, 173. On gins, presses, and ginhouses in Mississippi, see J. H. Moore, *Emergence of the Cotton Kingdom*, pp. 10–11, 57–66, 71–72.

31. See appendix B for sources.

32. JP to RC, Jan. 30, 1846 (letterbook), Polk MS.

33. In table 5.1, $15,000 is the sum of columns (c) and (e). See appendix B, column (e), for the reasoning behind these estimates. Of the $4050 that James Polk paid in 1838 for the 230 acres he bought from William Polk, about $2300 was the putative value of the land had it remained uncleared, and about $1750 was the value that had been added by clearing some 140 acres.

34. A prime male field hand who sold for $800 in New Orleans in 1840 would have fetched about one-third less (only $545) during the years 1842 through 1844. Prices climbed as soon as Polk won the 1844 election; and by 1848 they were again about $800. Kotlikoff, "Quantitative Description, p. 35. I am indebted to Stanley Engerman for this reference.

35. Ibid.

36. Silas Caldwell to JP, Jan. 31, 1836, *Corr.*, III, 473. Pickett, Perkins & Co. to SP, Apr. 13, 1852, Polk MS.

37. By 1849 the factor's bill for supplies had grown to $329 (not including materials sent for a separate smithy business run by Polk's slave blacksmith Harry). By the late 1850s the factor's bill often exceeded $500. See, for example, Pickett, Perkins & Co. to JP, Mar. 26, 1849; to SP, Mar. 7, 1850 (misfiled 1851), May 9, 1850 (accounts), Mar.18, 1856, Feb. 3, 1857; Perkins & Co. to SP, Dec. 3, 1857, Polk MS.

38. RC to JP, Jan. 17, 1846, Jan. 9, 1847; RC, accounts, July 22, 1846, Polk MS. Polk's local expenses from 1844 also included payments to his slaves for cotton raised in their own time. The best record of these is in RC to JP, Jan. 9, 1847; see also chapter 9.

39. JP to RC, Jan. 30, 1846 (letterbook), Polk MS. Mairs sold $357 of surplus produce (mainly pork, corn, and oats) in 1845: RC to JP, Jan. 17, 1846, Polk MS.

40. Bassett, p. 237. JM to SP, Apr. 16, 1851. Mairs was probably trying to explain the very low price received for twenty-one bales whose sale had been reported in Pickett, Perkins to SP, Mar. 24, 1851, Polk MS. JM to SP, Apr. 12, May 6, 1850, Bassett, pp. 182–83. Pickett to JP, Jan. 15, 1847, Polk MS.

CHAPTER 6

1. I erred at p. 436 of the hardcover edition of *Them Dark Days* by treating the two terms as antonyms. This embarrassing slip was inconsistent with the use of those terms elsewhere in the book.

2. For example, Eugene Genovese uses "paternalism" to denote a system of dependency, asserting that "paternalism had little to do with Ole Massa's ostensible benevolence." But in alleging that the domestic slave trade was less disruptive to the slaves' family life than had been thought, Genovese also uses

"paternalistic" as a synonym for "humane." Genovese, *Roll, Jordan, Roll*, pp. 4, 453–54.

3. Polk paid his $1294 debt to Catron in March 1846, soon after paying other campaign debts such as his $9500 debt to his rich uncle, William Wilson Polk. JP, money paid out after February 1845, reel 62, Polk MS.

4. John Catron to JP, July 23, 1844, *Corr.*, VII, 384. Fehrenbacher, *Dred Scott Case*, pp. 307, 309, 311–14, 574 (and n. 16), 578–79.

5. These were Henry Carter, Addison (twice), and Gilbert (twice or even three times); see chapter 3.

6. Silas Caldwell to JP, Feb. 11, 1835; Mar. 23, 1836, *Corr.*, III, 95, 547.

7. Jack Long was owned by James Polk's younger brother Samuel W. Polk, who was dying of tuberculosis. The beneficiaries from the $1000 compensation paid by Gee's family for the dead slave would therefore be the legatees of Samuel's will. Thus I refer to the Polks in the plural (of which legatees William Polk was probably prominent). WHP to JP, Nov. 25, 1838; James Walker to JP, Dec. 10, 1838, *Corr.*, IV, 619, 642.

8. WHP to JP, Mar. 7, 1841, Polk MS. In this letter's transcription (in *Corr.*, V, 650) "be" is also underlined—I think mistakenly: the mark under that word is the cross of the "t" from another word ("unthoughtedly") on the next line, which William Polk later scratched out.

9. Chapter 3 above.

10. Sam Polk, will, Dec. 13, 1826, Polk MS. JP estate inventory, Dec. 5, 1849, Yalobusha County inventory book E, pp. 31–33. J. H. Bills to SP, Jan. 28, 1852, Bassett, p. 197. Although Marshall Polk in fact *shared* legal title to these three slaves with his younger stepsiblings and with his stepfather, he appears to have held the controlling interest. M. T. Polk, Sr., will, Apr. 12, 1831, Mecklenburg County estate records (II, 172), N.C. State Archives. J. H. Bills to SP, Apr. 3, 1852, Polk MS. M. T. Polk, Jr., to J. H. Bills, Apr. 7, 1853, James Polk MS (folder 27), TSA.

11. James Walker to JP, June 7, 1849, Polk MS. SP to J. H. Bills, Feb. 21, 1852, JP Papers (reel 2), TSA (underscoring in the original).

12. M. T. Polk, Jr., to J. H. Bills, Mar. 22, 1852 (typescript; emphasis added), JP Papers (folder 27), TSA. J. H. Bills to J. W. Childress, Mar. 13, 1852, Polk MS.

13. At about this time Sarah Polk sent Bob (an unmarried man whom James and later Sarah Polk had rented since 1842 from the estate of Marshall Polk, Sr.) back to West Tennessee.

14. J. H. Bills to J. W. Childress, Mar. 13, 1852; Bills to SP, Apr. 30, 1852, Polk MS. M. T. Polk, Jr., to Bills, Jan. 27, 1853, JP Papers, TSA.

15. M. T. Polk, Jr., to J. H. Bills, Apr. 7, 1853, JP Papers, TSA. Marshall Polk's one concession was that he seems to have sold Alphonso (a slave he inherited in 1854, when Jane Polk's will was finally settled) to Sarah Polk. Thus he forbore from destroying Alphonso's marriage (to Maria Davis) by dragging him off to Tennessee, as he had done to Barbara and to Charles. Alphonso and Maria Davis were both still at Sarah Polk's plantation in 1860.

John S. Bassett's account of these transactions requires amendment. Bassett supposed that the parcel of slaves to which Marshall Polk laid claim included old Charles and Lucy (Barbara's parents); but Lucy had died in 1838, and old Charles had also succumbed before 1849. Bassett did not realize that the Charles whom Marshall claimed was the twenty-six-year-old "Little Charles" (old Charles's son); nor did Bassett know that the younger Charles was married to Rosetta, so that two marriages were split, not one. Bassett, p. 197. George Bratton to JP, Nov. 24, 1838, *Corr.*, IV, 616. JP estate inventory, Dec. 5, 1849, Yalobusha County inventory book E, pp. 31–33. SP, sale agreement, Jan. 25, 1860, JP Papers, TSA.

16. M. T. Polk, Jr., to J. H. Bills, Sept. 10, 1853; Feb. 3 (also Feb. 25), 1854, JP Papers, TSA.

17. Sam Polk, will, Dec. 13, 1826; James Walker to JP, Jan. 1 (1847; filed 1849), Polk MS.

18. Her full name was Jane Maria Walker. I call her Maria here to avoid confusion with her mother, Jane Polk.

19. JP, will signed Feb. 28, 1849, recorded Apr. 2, 1851, Davidson County wills, inventories, settlements, XIV, 585–87, roll 432, TSA. A version that differs only in the name of one of the executors is printed in Collins and Weaver, *Wills of the U.S. Presidents*, pp. 93–95.

20. "I left a written Will with my valuable papers in Tennessee" (in 1845). *Diary*, Feb. 18, 1849, IV, 340–41.

21. Collins and Weaver, *Wills of Presidents*, p. 93.

22. The $11,000 worth of 6 percent U.S. Treasury certificates, which the president bought in 1847–48, would provide Sarah an annual income of $660. By comparison with this modest sum, the Mississippi plantation, from 1849 through 1857, usually yielded annual net cash profits of over $4000—and this did not include capital gains, which made her total profits even higher. See table C1, columns (d) and (h).

23. George Washington, Will, July 1799, in Fitzpatrick, *Writings of George Washington*, vol. 37, pp. 276–77. Martha Washington had no legal power to free her own slaves, for upon her death they "would automatically . . . become the property of her grandchildren [descended from her first husband]." Flexner, *George Washington*, vol. 4, pp. 437, 446, 442 (quotation).

24. I am again indebted here to Dr. John Holtzapple (director of the Polk Ancestral Home in Columbia, Tennessee), who writes that Sarah Polk's "niece Mary . . . married [an] Avent in the 1850's." The niece was Mary Childress, and I infer that the bridegroom was the James M. Avent of Rutherford County, Tennessee, to whom Sarah sold a half-interest in the Yalobusha plantation in 1860. (Avent's surname is misspelled in Bassett, p. 275; see SP, 1860 agreement, p. 1.) Dr. John Holtzapple to author, Dec. 15, 1999. Anson Nelson and Fanny Nelson, *Memorials of Sarah Childress Polk*, p. 176.

25. In the original agreement, Sarah Polk's new business partner was to pay her $30,000 for a half-share in an enterprise valued at $60,000. But as an afterthought, Sarah Polk removed six of the fifty-six slaves from the plantation, reducing the total value of the new partnership by an unspecified amount. I estimate this reduction at $3000 (three of the six slaves then being in their forties, one thirty-five, one twenty, and one only six). Thus the value of the enterprise was reduced to about $57,000, making the new partner's half-share worth some $28,500. (Half of his share was paid in 1860, the other half due in 1862.) SP, 1860 agreement.

26. There is no reason to suppose that Sarah Polk intended to free the half dozen slaves she removed from the plantation; indeed, she seems to have sold or given one of the most valuable of these slaves (driver Joe), as well as Marina, to her nephew William H. Polk. Thus Sarah Polk gave away authority to emancipate these two

slaves; and after William Polk's death in 1862, they remained the property of his widow until—Tennessee having been excluded from Lincoln's Emancipation Proclamation—the Thirteenth Amendment finally freed them in 1865. SP, 1860 agreement. "List of Negroes belonging to Mrs. W. H. Polk [1865]," Lucy Williams Polk Papers, series PC 75.10 ("Miscellaneous"), N.C. State Archives. Cimprich, *Slavery's End in Tennessee*, pp. 101, 116.

27. Sellers (II), pp. 18–19, and its chap. 3, esp. 69, 73–76, 81–84, 92–97.

28. *Diary*, Jan. 5, 1847 (quotation), Feb. 18, 1849, II, 308; IV, 340–41. JP to S. P. Walker, Feb. 19, 1849; also, JP to E. P. McNeal, Feb. 20, 1849, letterbook, Polk MS.

29. Bill of sale ("Jacint"), Mar. 22, 1849, Polk MS. Polk's agent, as instructed on Feb. 19, 1849—the day after Polk drafted his new will—also bought five other slaves in March 1849. Their names, with references, are listed at the end of chapter 1 above.

30. Eventually Polk sold Silvy and her children to Jane Polk, who let James Polk use Silvy's eldest child, Alphonso, as a laborer on his Mississippi plantation. Jane Polk bequeathed Alphonso to her grandson Marshall Polk, Jr., who apparently sold him to Sarah Polk to continue laboring on the Mississippi plantation. Alphonso tried unsuccessfully to flee at least three times during the 1850s. Sam Polk, will, Dec. 13, 1826; bill of sale, Aug. 24, 1832, Polk MS. Ophelia Hays to JP (Dec. 14, 1833), *Corr.*, II, 171–72. Sellers (I), pp. 184–85. RC to JP, Jan. 9, 1847, Polk MS. JM to SP, Sept. 13, 14, 1856, May 11, 1857, Bassett, pp. 216, 218–19. SP, 1860 agreement.

31. See chapter 2.

32. See chapter 3.

33. JP, "Property at the plantation," Sept. 30, 1834, Polk MS. JP to SP, Sept. 26, 1834; Ephraim Beanland to JP, Oct. 14, 26, 1834, *Corr.*, II, 508, 529, 539–40. The maxim is paraphrased from the words of an elderly former slave who, like Caesar's wife, had chosen to stay with her master rather than with her husband. Smedes, *Southern Planter*, p. 9.

34. Bill of sale (Nancy), Oct. 10, 1834, Polk MS. Bill of sale (Henrietta), Jan. 4, 1835, Polk Correspondence, University of Tennessee. A. O. Harris to JP, Jan. 23, 1835, *Corr.*, III, 60 (and 150). JP inventory, recorded May 27, 1851, Davidson County wills, inventories, settlements, XIV, 597 (roll 432), TSA.

35. Sam Polk, will, Dec. 13, 1826; bill of sale, Oct. 24, 1831, Polk MS. Ephraim Beanland to JP, (Oct.) 30, 1833, *Corr.*, II, 123. Silas Caldwell to JP, Jan. 2, 1835, Bassett, p. 44. Caldwell to JP, Feb. 7, 22, 1836; James Walker to JP, Dec. 30, 1839; S. P. Walker to JP, Jan. 7, 1840; WHP to JP, Jan. 3, 1840, *Corr.*, III, 483, 508; V, 359; 370–71, 369. JP, account book, Feb. 24, 1840, Polk MS (Series 7). JP, will, Oct. 24, 1831, Polk MS. JP to WHP, Nov. 29, 1836, Lucy Williams Polk MS, N.C. State Archives.

36. Sam Polk, will, Dec. 13, 1826, Polk MS. James Walker to JP, Dec. 30, 1839; A. T. McNeal to JP, Jan. 15, 1840, *Corr.*, V, 359, 372–73. Re West Tennessee hiring in 1836 and 1838: S. M. Caldwell to JP, Jan. 1, 1844, Polk MS. William Dunaway to JP [Oct. 8, 1840], Polk Correspondence, University of Tennessee. Blacksmith Harry to JP, Nov. 28, 1844, Polk MS (also *Corr.*, VIII, 370). James H. Thomas to JP, Nov. 19, 1845, Polk Correspondence, University of Tennessee. RC to JP, Jan. 17, 1846, Sept. 14, 1847; JP to JM (letterbook) Nov. 24, 1847; JM to JP, Feb. 4, 1848, Polk MS. William Bobbitt to JP, Apr. 5,

1841, Polk Correspondence, University of Tennessee. Isaac Dismukes to JP, Sept. 27, 1841, *Corr.*, V, 762. See also chapter 9.

37. See chapter 3.

38. Bill of sale (E. Childress to JP), Oct. 8, 1845, Polk MS. Mary S. Jetton to SP, Sept. 25, 1845, JP Papers, TSA. RC to JP, Sept. 24, 1845; JM to JP, Sept. 28, 1845; JP to RC, Oct. 11, 1845, Polk MS. SP, 1860 sale agreement.

39. J. T. Leigh to JP, Sept. 17, 1846 (emphasis in the original), Polk MS.

40. JP to Leigh, Oct. 10, 1846 (letterbook) (emphasis in the original); bill of sale, WHP to JP, Nov. 3, 1838, Polk MS.

41. JP to SP, Oct. 26, 1843, *Corr.*, VI, 353.

42. JP to J. T. Leigh, June 17, 1848 (letterbook); Leigh to JP, Sept. 28, 1842, Polk MS. John Garner to JP, Nov. 1, 1840, *Corr.*, V, 573. William Bobbitt to JP, Aug. 29, 1841, Bassett, p. 156.

43. JP to JM, Sept. 3, 1847, in Marsh, "James K. Polk and Slavery," p. 22. Isaac Dismukes to JP, Sept. 1, 1841, *Corr.*, V, 746–47.

44. See chapters 2 and 3.

45. JM to JP, Nov. 8, 1848, and JP's notes on its envelope; JM to JP, July 23, 1848; RC to JP, Aug. 27, 1846, Polk MS.

46. J. T. Leigh to RC, May 5, 1845, Polk MS.

CHAPTER 7

1. Lyell, *Second Visit to the United States*, I, 334.

2. Although many details here and later in this chapter depend on inferences, the overall demographic picture of the Polks' plantation seems clear. The sources on which this chapter is based are discussed at the beginning of appendix A. See table 7.1, and table A4 in appendix A.

3. Of the Polks' twenty-one slave women of childbearing age, at least seven seem to have died young: these were Dicey, Matilda, Eliza, Caroline Henly, Caroline Davis, and Agnes—none of whom was older than twenty-nine when she perished (see notes 5 and 10 and table 7.2)—and almost certainly Mariah Carter, aged about thirty-seven (see note 9). Caroline Johnson probably also died, aged about thirty-nine. The name of neither Mariah Carter nor Caroline Johnson appears in the list of slaves at the plantation in 1860 (the two Carolines listed are Caroline Childress and almost surely the relatively young Caroline Harris, who was certainly still alive in 1855). Although it is conceivable that Sarah Polk removed Mariah and/or Caroline Johnson from the plantation before 1860, there is neither any evidence nor any reason to suppose that she did so; and the much more probable explanation for their absence from the 1860 list is that they had both died. Nevertheless, as the death of neither is absolutely certain, I have preferred to count only one of the two as having died in order to avoid the possibility of overstating the death rate among young women.

4. Of the nineteen babies born by 1849 eight had perished by 1849, and three more (Elizabeth's Fanny, Barbara's Eliza, and Daphney's Frank) died within a few years thereafter—a child mortality rate for these children of 58 percent. See table A1, which lists seventeen of the children born by 1849. I infer that two other children were born (one in 1843 and one in 1844) who died soon thereafter: see the fourth paragraph of appendix A.

5. Bill of sale, Oct. 13, 1834, Polk MS. George Bratton to JP, May 13, 1837; WHP to JP, Dec. 2, 1837, *Corr.*, IV, 119, 279. I infer Dicey's death from the absence of further mention of her in the Polk Papers; for example, she does not appear in the 1849 inventory of Polk's slaves, in Robert Campbell's lists of 1844 and 1846 earners, or in an 1842 list of cotton pickers: JP, 1849 inventory; RC to JP, Jan. 9, 1847; JP, notes on an old envelope, the latter of which is dated May 3, 1842), Polk MS.

6. Bills of sale, A. S. Mayes to H. Turney, Sept. 19, 1831, Series 3; H. Turney to JP, Oct. 6, 1831, Polk MS. When Polk was a partner of his brother-in-law Silas Caldwell (in 1835 and 1836, as explained in chapter 4), Polk let Caldwell use some of his slaves on Caldwell's West Tennessee plantation. Consequently these slaves (including Eve and Mariah) were not sent to Mississippi until after the partnership was dissolved at the end of 1836; by this time, apparently, Eve's second child had been born. See note 7 below.

7. The deaths of four of Eve's children are recorded in JM to JP, Feb. 8, 1849, Polk MS; JM to SP, Nov. 6, 1850 (the twins), and JM to John Childress, July 6, 1854, Bassett, pp. 187, 208 (quotation). Another child of Eve was expected to die from whooping cough in September 1852 (JM to SP, Sept. 20, 1852, Bassett, p. 200): I infer that this was an infant born in 1851. I also infer that Eve was carrying a child in 1836 (WHP to JP, Dec. 17, 1836, *Corr.*, III, 798) who died in about 1841; that this child survived until after 1840 would be consistent with the number of young female slave children counted at Polk's plantation by the U.S. census taker in 1840 (U.S. Manuscript Census of Population, 1840, Yalobusha County, Mississippi, p. 284).

Eve's surviving children in 1860 were apparently Turner (age twenty-six), Angeline (nineteen), Julius (fourteen), and three youngsters: An Marie (seven), Henry Polk (four), and another Ananias (probably an infant). The names of these six slaves are on the 1860 list (SP, 1860 agreement). I infer that Turner was the baby of Eve that was listed in 1834 (Bassett, p. 47) and named as her child "Jim Turner" in JP, 1849 inventory. I infer that Angeline (listed as Eve's child in the 1849 inventory) was the baby girl born in 1840 (*Corr.*, V, 523). Julius was born in 1845 (RC to JP, Sept. 24, 1845, Polk MS). An Marie, born in 1852 (Bassett, p. 201), is recorded as "Any" in the 1860 manuscript list (SP, 1860 agreement); this is mistakenly printed as "Ary" in Bassett, p. 275. I infer that Eve gave her son Henry Polk his second name to distinguish him from Mariah Carter's son Henry and that Ananias was a child of Eve to whom she gave that name because her earlier son, also named Ananias, had died in 1854 (Bassett, p. 208).

8. Silas Caldwell to JP, Jan. 4, 1834, *Corr.*, II, 220. On illnesses, see *Corr.*, II, 190, 458; III, 508; IV, 479; Bassett, p. 150. On abroad marriages, see Herbert Biles to JP, Jan. 17, 1833, *Corr.*, II, 30; JP to RC, Sept. 7, 1846, letterbook, Polk MS. On Davy's birth, see JM to RC, Oct. 28, 1845, Polk MS. The four children still alive in 1860—Malinda, Jim, Andy, and Davy—were listed as Elizabeth's ("Betsy's") in JP, 1849 inventory. Another of her children, Fanny (also listed in that inventory), died in 1850; I infer that this was the child of Elizabeth born in 1847; another of Elizabeth's children had died in 1840. JM to RC, Nov. 18, 1847; to JP, Nov. 5, 1847, Polk MS; to SP, Oct. 8, 1850, Bassett, p. 186. John Garner to JP, Oct. 4, 1840, *Corr.*, V, 564.

9. List of Polk slaves, 1834; William Bobbitt to JP, Aug. 29, 1841; Isaac Dismukes to JP, Feb. 1, 1842, Bassett, pp. 47, 157, 161. RC to JP, Sept. 24, 1845, Polk MS. John Garner to JP, June 1, 7, 1840, *Corr.*, V, 475, 483. Apparently Mariah Carter

died during the early 1850s; the only Mariah still on the 1860 list was surely Mariah Davis, a much younger (by seventeen years) and healthier woman, who was certainly alive in 1856, long after the last reference to Mariah Carter. SP, 1860 agreement; JM to JP, Apr. 19, 1849; to SP, Sept. 10, 1851, Aug. 2, 1856, Polk MS.

10. Bills of sale, Sept. 24, 1839 (Matilda), Nov. 3, 1838 (Eliza), Nov. 16, 1846 (Agnes), Mar. 22, 1849 (Caroline [Davis]), Polk MS. For Matilda, see John Garner to JP, July 5, 1840, Bassett, p. 143; Garner to JP, Aug. 1, Oct. 4, 1840, Corr., V, 522, 564. For Eliza, see RC to JP, Sept. 24, 1845; JM to JP, Sept. 24, 1845, Polk MS. For Caroline Henly, see RC to JP, Aug. 27, Oct. 9, 1846; JM to JP, July 23, Nov. 8, 1848, Polk MS. For Caroline Davis, see JM to JP, Apr. 19, 1849; to SP, Mar. 15, 1850, Polk MS. For Agnes, see JM to SP, Mar. 3, 1853, Bassett, p. 202.

11. Bills of sale, Nov. 3, 1838 (Fan), Sept. 24, 1831 (Caesar), Sept. 26, 1834 (Henry Carter); JP, note about Calvin (bought Oct. 10, 1846), misfiled Aug. 3, 1846; list of plantation property, Sept. 26, 1834 (Abe, Caesar, Henry Carter), Polk MS. For Abe, see S. Caldwell to JP, Jan. 16, 1836, Corr., III, 437. I infer that Fan and Caesar died at the plantation from the absence of their names in the lists of 1844 and 1846 earners (RC to JP, Jan. 9, 1847, Polk MS) and in JP, 1849 inventory. The absence of Caesar's name from an 1842 list of cotton pickers suggests that he died in 1841 (JP, notes on an old envelope, filed May 3, 1842, Polk MS). I suppose Fan to have died in 1843, a year when almost no overseer's reports are extant. For Henry Carter, see JM to SP, Oct. 21, 1852, Polk MS (misdated as Sept. 20, 1852, in Bassett, p. 200). For Calvin, see RC, accounts filed July 22, 1846 ("Oct. 10"); RC to JP, Nov. 3, 1846; JM to SP, Feb. 25, 1854, Polk MS. For Calvin's age, see chapter 1, note 28.

12. These average ages are based on those specified in the two preceding paragraphs. Dicey died at about twenty-four, Mariah at perhaps thirty-seven. I suppose the teenage boy Fan to have died (in 1843) at fifteen. From the calculation of mortality rates I exclude (as explained in note 3 above) the probable death of Caroline Johnson at about age thirty-nine, which, had I included it, would have made the contrast between female and male mortality rates even more striking.

13. Olmsted, *Journey in the Seaboard Slave States*, p. 55n.

14. This calculation is based on the experience of the nearly 800,000 slaves, aged ten to nineteen (slightly over half of them males), who were alive in 1850. If a negligible number of these young slaves were manumitted during the 1850s and if any illegal importations of slaves into the United States were offset by fugitives permanently escaping from the South, any decline by 1860 in the number of these slaves may be presumed to have resulted from their deaths. Evidently, then, some 95,500 of these slaves died during the 1850s but in unequal proportions between the sexes: 42,700 of those who died were males, and 52,800 were females.

From the census figures one can calculate that these dead male slaves made up 10.74 percent of the group who were alive in 1850 but that 13.34 percent of the females had died by 1860. Because 13.34 divided by 10.74 equals 1.24 percent, any female was 24 percent more likely to have died during the decade than was a male:

	Males	Females
Slaves aged 10–19 in 1850	397,700	395,800
Slaves aged 20–29 in 1860	355,000	343,000
Presumed died	42,700	52,800

These figures probably *under*estimate the sex difference in the mortality rates be-cause the number of permanent fugitives during the 1850s surely was substantially larger than the number of slaves illegally imported, and at least 70 percent of the permanent fugitives (many of them in exactly this age cohort) were males. Thus the number of males who died was probably a little smaller than suggested in the table above, and the sex difference in mortality rates may therefore have been substantially greater than the conservative estimate I have made here. U.S. Bureau of the Census, *Statistical View of the United States, . . . [1850] Census*, pp. 88–89 and *Eighth Census, 1860: Population*, pp. 594–95.

15. Two of these three children were, as previously mentioned, Mariah Carter's. The third was a son of Agnes, born prior to the stillbirth that led to Agnes's death. Matilda's son William died of pneumonia at the age of twelve, and her other child lived for only a few hours after its birth: the overseer alleged that Matilda had not told him that the child was on its way soon enough for him to get a midwife. Apparently neither Dicey, Caroline Henly, Caroline Davis, nor Eliza I bore any child who survived for any length of time. For Agnes, see JM to SP, Mar. 3, 1853, Bassett, p. 202. I infer that Agnes's first child, still alive in 1853, probably survived until at least 1860, when it was one of the children then listed (probably George) whose mothers' names are uncertain (SP, 1860 agreement). For Matilda's children, see bill of sale, Sept. 24, 1839, Polk MS; JM to SP, Aug. 3, 1852, Bassett, p. 199; John Garner to JP, May 3, 1840, *Corr.*, V, 437; June 7, 1840, Bassett, p. 141.

16. The infertile woman was Caroline Johnson (J. T. Leigh to JP, Sept.17, 1846, Polk MS). Harbert's wife, Mary (who had had a child by a previous father), had no children after she married Harbert: perhaps he was infertile. And although Charles's wife, Rosetta, was still at the plantation in 1860, she seems never to have had a child: perhaps she never remarried after Marshall Polk, Jr., destroyed her marriage by removing her husband, Charles, in 1852. See chapter 6, where Barbara's removal from the plantation is also recounted.

17. The plantation had fifty-six slaves at the end of 1849, and net exports dur-ing the next decade were probably six, leaving a base population of fifty. Thus the decade's increase (six slaves, bringing the population by 1860 back up to fifty-six) represented a 12 percent natural population growth. See table A5.

18. U.S. Bureau of the Census, *Eighth Census, 1860: Population*, p. 599.

19. For sources, see note 24 and table A1.

20. Of the twenty-one slave families listed in table 7.2, seventeen had in 1860 fewer than three surviving children—often only one surviving child or none at all. But these figures somewhat understate family size because about nine of the women are likely to have borne more children after 1860.

21. Among the thirty-one surviving children [table 7.2, column (d)], I include two no longer at the plantation in 1860: these were Mariah's Henry (whom Presi-dent Polk took as a servant to the White House and who thereafter was kept in Tennessee) and Barbara's Marthy (the infant whom Marshall Polk, Jr., removed to Tennessee with Barbara in 1852) Although this infant may not have even sur-vived until 1860 and although she and her mother, Barbara, were deported in 1852, I include them in this discussion because I have included in my mortality statistics the deaths of Barbara's parents (who died at the plantation before 1849), and it would have been misleading to omit the births of Barbara's two children (and the subsequent death of one of them) from the plantation's vital statistics. The figures

in this paragraph differ slightly from those on plantation birth and death rates, 1835–59, because here—seeking as far as possible to reconstruct whole family histories—I include five children born before 1835 (one of Matilda's, one of Eve's, one of Elizabeth's, and two of Mariah's) and Mary's child (born before she was purchased by Polk in 1846)—of whom four were still alive in 1860.

22. Of the fourteen women still alive in 1860, five were already in their forties and three others were in their thirties.

23. Dusinberre, *Them Dark Days*, p. 416, n. 81 and 82.

24. Of forty-eight children *known* to have been born at the plantation, twenty-one had surely died before 1860 and before reaching age fifteen (see table A1). I conservatively estimate that there were at least seven unrecorded births of children—in 1843–44 and 1857–59, when almost no overseers' letters are extant—who subsequently died unrecorded. Thus, of a total of fifty-five babies, a minimum of twenty-eight children (51 percent) died before age fifteen. For three reasons, however, this figure almost certainly underestimates the child mortality rate: (1) some of the twelve children born *after* 1849 and still alive in January 1860 will have died thereafter, before reaching their fifteenth birthday. (The child mortality rate for those children born *before* 1849 was 58 percent; see note 4 above.) (2) Marthy, Barbara's infant, born in 1851 and removed from the plantation when scarcely a year old, may well have died before her fifteenth birthday. (3) The number of unrecorded births of children who subsequently died unrecorded was probably greater than the seven I have conservatively estimated. (This minimum estimate is discussed in appendix A, fourth paragraph.)

25. James Walker to JP, Jan. 24, 1833, Ephraim Beanland to JP, Oct. 14, 1834; Silas Caldwell to JP, Nov. 27, 1835, Beanland to JP, Jan. 23, 1836, Caldwell to JP, Feb. 22, 1836, *Corr.*, II, 45, 529; III, 379, 456, 508–9. My surmise that it was Elizabeth who had congestive fever in 1834 is based on Beanland to JP, Aug. 24, 1834, *Corr.*, II, 458.

26. A. T. McNeal to JP, June 15, 1838, *Corr.*, IV, 479. Nancy was the house servant whom Polk had bought in 1834, aged about thirty-six and already a grandmother. Although it seems that she was usually employed in Tennessee, Polk had sent her for a spell to the Mississippi plantation—perhaps as punishment for some misdemeanor (such as the one that had led him to deport Silvy to his west Tennessee plantation for the year 1833). As Nancy does not appear to have been kept long in Mississippi, I do not count her among the women discussed in this chapter. She was one of Polk's four house servants in Tennessee when he died there in 1849, and almost certainly she had been kept in Tennessee during most of the previous years. JP estate inventory, Davidson County wills, inventories, settlements, May 27, 1851 (roll 432, XIV, 597), TSA.

27. S. Bell to JP, July 7, 1839, James Cowan to JP, July 2, 1839, Bassett, pp. 120–21. John Garner to JP, Nov. 23, 1839, *Corr.*, V, 312.

28. Garner to JP, Mar. 2, 1840; A. T. McNeal to JP, Aug. 31, 1840, *Corr.*, V, 399, 550. Garner to JP, Sept. 10, 1839, Bassett, p. 126; to JP, May 3, 1840, *Corr.*, V, 437.

29. JM to JP, Apr. 19, May 5, 1849, Polk MS. JM to SP, Aug. 3, 18, 1852, Bassett, p. 199. JM to SP, Sept 20, Oct. 21, 1852, Apr. 18, 1853, Polk MS. (JM's letter of Oct. 21, 1852, is misdated Sept. 20 in Bassett, p. 200. Bassett also miscopied the phrase "of the internal organs" as "of the internal origin.")

30. JM to J. W. Childress, June 10, 1853; to SP, Feb. 25, 1854, Polk MS.

31. RC, accounts filed July 22, 1846, Polk MS. On a slave trader's expectation that slaves deported from Kentucky to the cotton belt would inevitably contract malaria, see Olmsted, *Seaboard Slave States*, p. 647.

32. JP to J. W. Childress, June 2, 1846 (letterbook); JM to SP, Aug. 2, Sept. 13, 1856; bill of sale (Reuben), Oct. 24, 1831; JP, will, Oct. 24, 1831, Polk MS. Silas Caldwell to JP, Feb. 7, 22, Apr. 28, 1836; WHP to JP, Dec. 17, 1836; S. P. Walker to JP, Jan. 7, 1840, *Corr.*, III, 483, 508, 609, 798; V, 370–71. Bill of sale (Eliza), Nov. 3, 1838; RC to JP, Sept. 24, 1845, Polk MS.

33. J. T. Leigh to RC, May 5, 1845; JM to SP, Oct. 21 (misdated Sept. 20 in Bassett, p. 200), Dec. 10, 1852, Polk MS.

34. On the apparent neglect of babies by their minders, see my *Them Dark Days*, pp. 86 (the death by drowning of a toddler) and 262 (citing Kemble, *Journal of a Residence on a Georgian Plantation*, pp. 156, 359–60).

35. JM to SP, Mar. 15, 1850, Bassett, p. 182.

36. The five females were Dicey, Matilda, Caroline Henly, Caroline Davis, and Agnes. The two males were Caesar and Calvin.

37. Of forty-nine young adult slaves who worked at the plantation sometime between 1835 and 1860, twenty-two had been purchased from strangers. Seven of them (i.e., 32 percent) died at age forty or less. Of the twenty-seven young adult workers not purchased from strangers, six (i.e., 22 percent) died at age forty or less. From these calculations of young adult mortality, I exclude all slaves over forty when they first arrived at the plantation (e.g., Allen: WHP to JP, Oct. 28, 1839, Bassett, p. 127) and all under fourteen (e.g., William, who died at twelve, and Mariah's son Henry, who was about twelve when Polk brought him to Tennessee). I also exclude Reuben, who was at the plantation less than two years before Polk removed him, fearing that he would die from malaria.

38. Some 52 percent of Mississippi slaves were supervised by overseers (the proportion being even higher in the counties adjoining the Mississippi River). In Wilkinson County, for example, about 73 percent of the slaves were subject to overseers. In the interior of Mississippi, most overseers were somewhat curbed by the presence of a resident master. But apparently in river areas like Wilkinson County, about one-third of all the slaves lived on absentee plantations, where the overseer's authority was little constrained. Thus absenteeism, although a minority phenomenon, afflicted more Mississippi slaves than historians have recognized; therefore, the Polk plantation was less singular than might at first appear. These figures are my estimates, based on the assumption that Mississippi's 3941 overseers (in 1860) supervised all of the slaves on the 3573 slaveholdings of over 30 slaves each (with more than one overseer working at each of the 316 slaveholdings of over 100 slaves). U.S. Bureau of the Census, *Eighth Census, 1860: Population*, pp. 670–71, and *Agriculture*, pp. 247, 232. Olmsted, *Journey in the Back Country*, p. 119. Cf. Sydnor, *Slavery in Mississippi*, p. 67.

CHAPTER 8

1. Blassingame, *Slave Community*. Genovese, *Roll, Jordan, Roll*. Gutman, *Black Family in Slavery and Freedom*.

2. Johnson's *Soul by Soul* illustrates the new approach. Stevenson's *Life in Black and White* is one of the recent studies suggesting that two-parent nuclear families were not always the norm for slaves. My *Them Dark Days* has some-

times been interpreted—I think erroneously—as tilting too far in the direction of damage.

3. See chapters 3 and 6.

4. See chapter 6. JP, "Property at the plantation to be disposed of," Sept. 30, 1834; list of plantation property, Sept. 26, 1834, Polk MS.

5. See chapters 7 and 3.

6. Bill of sale, Feb. 2, 1847; E. P. McNeal to JP, Feb. 2, 1847; JM to JP, Feb. 16, 1849; to SP, Aug. 18, 1852, Aug. 2, 1856, Polk MS. JM to SP, July 9, 1853, Bassett, p. 204. SP, 1860 agreement. For Alphonso's flights, see chapter 3. For Marshall Polk, see chapter 6, note 15.

7. Maria Davis and Jane were typical in conceiving their first children at what might seem to be early ages. In 1834 Polk's and Silas Caldwell's slaves included eleven women aged fifteen to twenty-eight, of whom seven had children; in each of these seven cases, the first child had been conceived when the mother was aged no more than sixteen to nineteen:

Mother's Age at Conception of Her First Known Child	Number of Mothers
16	2
17	1
18	2
19	2
Total	7

(The other four women on this list—aged fifteen, sixteen, seventeen, and eighteen—did not yet have any living children.) These figures probably overstate the age at which one or two of the mothers conceived their first child because they refer to the age at conception of the first *surviving* child, and one or two infants conceived earlier probably died. Imperfect though they are, these figures strongly support the view that slave women had sex at an early age. The vast majority were denied the economic incentives, available to many free women, to postpone pregnancy. JP and S. Caldwell, plantation property, Sept. 26, 1834, Polk MS, which lists eight Caldwell and three Polk women. In this record Polk's eighteen-year-old slave Elizabeth is not listed with a child, although in fact she had conceived one, in March 1833, who died soon after birth; I therefore count her as one of the two women whose first conception occurred at age sixteen. Corr., II, 30, 190, 220.

8. Bill of sale, Oct. 8, 1846; JM to SP, Apr. 9, 1854, Aug.1, 1855, Polk MS. JM to SP, May 6, 1850, Nov. 12, 1852, June 17, 1855, Sept. 13, 1856, Bassett, pp. 183, 201, 210, 215, 275. I infer that Willis, born probably in 1851 and still alive in 1860, was Jane's child. For Manuel's flights, see chapter 3.

9. See the discussion below.

10. See chapter 3.

11. JP to RC, Sept. 7, 1846, letterbook, Polk MS. See also chapter 3.

12. JP to RC, Sept. 7, 1846, letterbook (emphasis in original); RC to JP, Nov. 3, 1846, Polk MS. The correspondence between Polk and Leigh is discussed in chapter 6. When Polk first mentioned this matter, he also suggested that his agent, Campbell, try to buy some of the children of one of Polk's slaves; but Campbell appears to have totally ignored this suggestion.

13. See chapters 3 and 6.

14. From the following account of the family histories of the slaves at the Polk plantation, I omit four relatively old slaves (old Sarah, old Ben, Pompey, and Allen), young Bob (owned by Marshall Polk, Jr.), and driver Joe (then owned by Jane Polk), whose family histories cannot be reconstructed. These six, plus the twenty-six married slaves and the twenty-four too young to be married, make up the fifty-six slaves at the plantation (i.e., the fifty-five listed in JP, 1849 inventory, plus driver Joe, who—known by the assessors to have been owned by Jane Polk—was not listed in the inventory of slaves supposed to belong to James Polk).

15. See chapters 2 and 7.

16. See chapter 9.

17. See chapters 6 and 3.

18. SP, 1860 agreement. Of the six slaves Sarah Polk took from the Mississippi plantation in 1860, two almost certainly ended up by 1865 in Tennessee, in the possession of William Polk's widow (he died in 1862): these were Marina—whom William Polk had owned in Mississippi before selling her to James Polk in 1838—and driver Joe. List of Negroes belonging to Mrs. W. H. Polk (1865), Lucy Williams Polk Papers, series PC 75.10, "Miscellaneous," N.C. State Archives. As William Polk had also owned Manuel, whom he sold to James Polk in 1838 at the same time he sold Marina, one supposes that William may have persuaded his aunt Sarah Polk to bring Manuel to Tennessee when she brought Marina.

19. See chapter 3.

20. See chapter 3. JM to SP, July 9, 1853, Polk MS.

21. M. T. Polk, Jr., to J. H. Bills, Oct. 6, Nov. 1, Dec. 6, 1854, folder 27, James Polk MS, TSA.

22. See chapter 6.

23. See chapters 1 and 6 (Caroline Childress).

24. See chapter 7 and its note 6. J. T. Leigh, quoted in *DeBow's Review*, vol. 7, p. 381.

25. The three children who died were Eliza 2, William, and Frank. See table A2.

26. JP, 1849 inventory, lists fifty-five slaves; the fifty-sixth was driver Joe, owned by old Jane Polk.

27. On blacksmith Harry, see chapter 9. In addition to Harry, there were (at Polk's death in 1849) seventeen other newly arrived slaves, not the nineteen newly purchased ones identified in chapter 1, because (a) Caroline Henly had died in 1848, and (b) Garrison was not a newcomer to the plantation since Polk had rented him from old Mrs. Polk for many years before finally buying him in 1847.

28. The twenty-one slaves included (a) seventeen of those in "valuation of property," Nov. 2, 1834, Polk MS; (b) Mariah's two young children (Henry and Wilson); (c) Eve's one child (Turner); and (d) the twenty-six-year-old Hardy, who was already mortally ill and who died in 1835. Cf. Bassett, p. 47, a list that omits three older slaves—Lucy, Charles, and Sarah—as well as Garrison, whom Polk rented but did not yet own. These twenty-one slaves included five healthy children, thirteen young adults, and the three older slaves, who seem to have been aged between about 46 and 60.

29. Dicey probably perished around age twenty-four; the blacksmith Abe, twenty-three; Hardy, twenty-six; Caesar, about thirty-five; and Henry Carter, forty.

Lucy died at about fifty and old Charles perhaps at sixty-five, only old Sarah living until the ripe old age of seventy-eight. Birth years were calculated from bills of sale, Sept. 24, 1831 (Caesar), Sept. 26, 1834 (Henry Carter), Oct. 13, 1834 (Dicey); or from "plantation property," Sept. 26, 1834 (Abe, Hardy, old Sarah), Polk MS. *Corr.*, I, 529 and II, 31, suggest that Lucy may have borne her youngest child around 1830. If she was then forty-two, she would have been forty-six when slaves were assigned to the new plantation in 1834. Evidently her husband, then called "olde man Charly" (II, 528), was older. I guess he was then about fifty-five and apparently died some ten years later. For the other deaths, see (for Hardy, Abe, and Lucy), *Corr.*, III, 95, 437; IV, 616. Henry Carter, JM to SP, Oct. 21, 1852, Polk MS. Old Sarah, Bassett, p. 201. For Dicey and Caesar, see chapter 7, including notes 5 and 11.

30. Polk brought the favored mulatto slave, Reuben, back to Tennessee in 1836 because chronic malaria had largely incapacitated him on the cotton plantation. In about 1841 Polk summoned Mariah's son Henry to be a house servant in Tennessee and, later, at the White House. Polk's nephew removed Charles and Barbara (along with Barbara's infant) in 1852. See chapters 2 (Henry) and 6.

31. Sam Polk also bequeathed one slave each to his three married daughters (who no doubt had previously been given other slaves in their marriage dowries). Sam Polk, will, Dec. 13, 1826, Polk MS.

32. These five slaves were Addison (probably a child of Fanny Lawson, from Frank Polk), old Ben and blacksmith Abe (from John Polk), and Pompey and blacksmith Harry (from Samuel W. Polk). A sixth such slave, Little Abe (from Frank Polk), apparently died before October 1831. See chapter 1, note 7.

33. These four slaves were old Charles; his wife, Lucy; and their two surviving children, Barbara and Charles. They did not come into Marshall Polk, Jr.'s, possession until after the death of old Mrs. Polk in 1852 (by which time old Charles and Lucy had died, and Barbara had borne one surviving infant). Sam Polk, will, Dec. 13, 1826, Polk MS. Marshall Polk, will, recorded Sept. 14, 1831, Maury County will book E, p. 382, TSA.

34. These were Cloe and her four children: Caroline Johnson, Manuel, Fan, and Eliza. The other three slaves whom William Polk sold in 1838 to James Polk were not Polk family slaves. Bill of sale (WHP to JP), Nov. 3, 1838, Polk MS.

35. These were Reuben (whom JP bought from old Mrs. Polk); Garrison (whom old Mrs. Polk bought from JP's sister Ophelia), driver Joe (owned by old Mrs. Polk until she bequeathed him to Sarah Polk), and Alphonso (whom JP bought from Ophelia and later sold to old Mrs. Polk, who bequeathed him to Marshall Polk, Jr., who eventually sold him to Sarah Polk). Reuben was only at the Mississippi plantation until 1836. Garrison worked there continuously from 1835 to 1860 (rented to JP by old Mrs. Polk until she sold him to JP in 1847). Joe was there from about 1842 until Sarah Polk removed him in 1860. Alphonso worked there continuously from about 1842 to 1860. Bills of sale, Oct. 24, 1831 (Reuben); Feb. 1 (filed Feb. 2), 1847 (Garrison); Aug. 24, 1832 (Alphonso); Sam Polk, will, Dec. 13, 1826, Polk MS.

36. Joe, old Ben, Pompey, and Long Harry were all named in Sam Polk's will, Dec. 13, 1826, Polk MS. Alphonso, born in 1827 (bill of sale, Aug. 24, 1832, Polk MS) was a child of Sylvia, who is named in Sam Polk's will.

37. Cf. Kolchin, *Unfree Labor*, esp. pp. 195–200, 206–7, 233–36, 330–31.

CHAPTER 9

1. Patterson, *Slavery and Social Death*, pp. 205, 283. Scott, *Slave Emancipation in Cuba*, pp. 13–14. Knight, *Slave Society in Cuba*, p. 61.

2. William Bobbitt to JP, Mar. 19, 1842; JM to JP, Apr. 19, 1849, Polk MS. On the labor shortage: J. W. Childress to JP, Jan. 14, 1844; RC to JP, Feb. 8, 1847, Polk MS.

3. I believe the incentive system depicted on the following pages depended principally on the slaves' working on Sundays, although the article in *DeBow's Review* (vol. 7, p. 381) describing J. T. Leigh's system does not specify when the overtime work was done. Two pages later in *DeBow's Review*, the Northern apologist for slavery who wrote this article asserts that Mississippi slaves often got cash by "doing overwork Saturdays and evenings," but he does not allege that Leigh's incentive scheme was confined to Saturdays and evenings. I infer that the author, seeking to avoid offending Northern sabbatarian readers—who would have disapproved a system based on Sunday work—fudged the matter. Slave narratives (e.g., Ball, *Fifty Years in Chains*, pp. 166, 186–87, 189) make plain that overtime incentive systems usually involved Sunday labor, and I infer that this was the case on the Leigh and Polk plantations.

4. In 1817 the Mississippi legislature made it illegal for planters to let slaves raise their own cotton. Planters sometimes ignored legislation of this sort, and during the 1840s John Leigh and James Polk obviously paid no attention to this law. After Leigh died in 1850, his son—instead of letting his slaves continue to raise cotton on their own patches of land—began to pay them a sort of tiny annual salary, and the historian Charles Sydnor surmises that Sarah Polk similarly amended the system on the Polk plantation. But Sydnor's evidence is unconvincing, confined as it is to three cryptic letters written by overseer John Mairs in 1853 and 1855. Mairs's letters show that in the 1850s, as earlier, the Polk slaves were not paid until after the plantation's cotton was sold in New Orleans; evidently the size of the slaves' payments then depended on the price at which the cotton had been sold. Moreover, the Polk slaves did not finally receive all the money they were due until overseer Mairs was able to lay his hands on enough cash to pay them in full. It is true that when a hundred uninsured bales of the plantation's 1854 crop burned at the Yalobusha River warehouse and when a few weeks later fifty-five insured bales of the same crop burned on a steamboat, Sarah Polk probably paid her slaves about as much as they would have received if the cotton had reached the market safely (i.e., about $200); but this does not indicate that she no longer let the slaves grow their own cotton. Sydnor, *Slavery in Mississippi*, pp. 97, 99–101. *DeBow's Review*, vol. 7, pp. 381, 383. RC, accounts, Dec. 28, 1844 (filed Jan. 22, 1845), Oct. 29, 1846 (filed July 22, 1846); RC to JP, Jan. 17, 1846, Jan. 9, 1847, Polk MS. JM to SP, Apr. 18, 1853; to J. W. Childress, June 10, 1853; to SP, June 17, 1855, Bassett, pp. 203–4, 210–11, 240–43.

5. The median is derived from RC to JP, Jan. 9, 1847. This figure is based on the nineteen individual workers in 1846. If one also included the only slave couple—Phil and Eve—who worked jointly (and apportioned a rather larger share of their payment to Phil than to Eve, who had other Sunday duties besides hoeing cotton), the slaves' median figure would remain unchanged. Mairs's salary: RC to JP, Sept. 24, 1845, Jan. 17, 1846, Polk MS. Polk's *total* profit in 1846 (including

capital gains from clearing land and from the price inflation of the value of his slaves) was actually about $4700. See table C1, column (h).

6. All earnings in the preceding paragraphs are in RC to JP, Jan. 9, 1847, Polk MS.

7. RC to JP, Nov. 3, 1846 (emphasis added), Jan. 9, 1847; RC, accounts, Dec. 28, 1844 (filed Jan. 22, 1845), Polk MS.

8. RC to JP, Jan. 17, 1846; RC, accounts, Oct. 29, 1846 (filed July 22, 1846), Polk MS.

9. RC to JP, Nov. 3, 1846, Jan. 9, 1847; JP to RC, Nov. 14, 1846, letterbook, Polk MS. The plantation's gross revenues are in table C1, column (b).

10. JP to JM, Mar. 1, Sept. 22, 1848, letterbook, Polk MS.

11. RC to JP, Jan. 17, 1846; JP to JM, Sept. 25, 1845, Polk MS.

12. RC to JP, Jan. 9, 1847.

13. See chapter 3.

14. Old Sam Polk bequeathed Harry to James Polk's youngest brother, Samuel W. Polk, who died in 1839. Although Harry remained legally the property of Samuel's estate for several years thereafter, Samuel seems to have bequeathed him to James Polk, who apparently assumed full proprietary rights once the estate had been dissolved. Sam Polk, will, Dec. 13, 1826; S. W. Polk estate (Series 7), Feb. 24, 1839; S. M. Caldwell to JP, Jan. 1, 1844, Polk MS.

15. Blacksmith Harry to JP, May 10, 1842, Nov. 28, 1844, Polk MS. The second of these letters evidently was written on Harry's behalf by a white man; and this may also have been true of the first one. The handwriting of the two is different, the second apparently written by a Democratic Party activist—"one of your best friends" in Carroll County. These two letters are printed in Corr., VI, 59; VIII, 370.

16. See chapter 6.

17. JP to RC, Nov. 14, 1846, letterbook, Polk MS. Harry to JP, May 10, 1842; A. T. McNeal to JP, Jan. 15, 1840, Corr., VI, 59; V, 372–73.

18. William Bobbitt to JP, Apr. 5, 1841, Polk Correspondence, University of Tennessee. S. M. Caldwell to JP, Jan. 1, 1844; RC, accounts, Jan. 22, 1845; RC, receipt, Jan. 25, 1845; RC to JP, Jan. 17, 1846, Jan. 9, 1847, Polk MS.

19. S. M. Caldwell to JP, Jan. 1, 1844, Polk MS. William Bobbitt to JP, Apr. 5, 1841, Jan. 20, 1842, Polk Correspondence, University of Tennessee. JM to JP, Jan. 4, 1848, Feb. 8, 1849; RC to JP, Jan. 22, 1848, Polk MS.

20. RC to JP, Oct. 9, Aug. 27, 1846, Jan. 9, Sept. 14, 1847; JP to RC, Aug. 13, Sept. 7, Nov. 14, 1846, Sept. 2, 1847, Feb. 11, 1848; to JM, Nov. 24, 1847, letterbook; JM to JP, Feb. 4, 1848, Polk MS.

21. For example, the Georgia rice planter Richard Arnold accused his most valuable slave, Amos Morel, of "acquiring dissipated habits" when Morel was allowed to live an independent life in Savannah; Arnold offered this as a reason for obliging this skilled engineer to return to his plantation. Olmsted, Journey in the Seaboard Slave States, p. 427. Hoffmann and Hoffman, North by South, pp. 166–78, esp. 168–69. RC to JP, Aug. 27, 1846, Polk MS.

22. On Sam Polk's death from drink, I am indebted to Professor Wayne Cutler, editor of the Polk Correspondence. On Frank Polk's death, see Sellers (I), p. 184.

23. Blacksmith Harry to JP, Nov. 28, 1844; RC to JP, Jan. 17, Aug. 27, 1846, Polk MS. A parallel case of a Mississippi slave who misled his masters about bad

eyesight is recorded in Smedes, *Southern Planter*, p. 45n. This slave, supposed to be blind, was assigned only light tasks around the master's house; after emancipation it was revealed that the blindness had been faked, and the slave successfully raised eighteen annual crops when farming for himself as a free man.

24. JM to JP, July 6, Sept. 9, 1848, Polk MS. In 1851 Harry's gross earnings were $479; the cost of his materials in a typical year may have been $43, to which must be added interest and depreciation on the Polks' capital investment of $58 in his tools. JM to SP, Jan. 26, 1852; invoice, Mar. 15, 1856, Bassett, pp. 196, 270. W. S. Pickett to JP, Dec. 20, 1847, Polk MS.

25. JM to Daniel Graham, Dec. 6, 1849 (misfiled 1844), Polk MS. On Jack Long, see chapters 3 and 6.

26. Blacksmith Harry to JP, May 10, 1842, Polk MS. Cf. *Corr.*, VI, 59.

27. Harry to JP, Nov. 28, 1844; Thomas Clark to JP (Dec. 19, 1844; misfiled Dec. 19, 1834, on reel 9), Polk MS. The former letter is printed and the latter summarized in *Corr.*, VIII, 370, 553.

28. Harry to JP, Nov. 28, 1844, Polk MS; *Corr.*, VIII, 370. I have slightly emended the editors' readings of this manuscript.

CHAPTER 10

1. U.S. Congress, House, *Register of Debates*, 19 Cong., 1st sess., (1826), 1649–50.

2. Ibid., 21 Cong., 1st sess., (1830), p. 824; see also 822.

3. Mercer's resolution called on President Andrew Jackson to negotiate treaties "for the effectual abolition of the African slave trade, and its ultimate denunciation, as piracy, under the law of nations." The resolution was adopted by a vote of 118 to 32, with Polk, Cave Johnson (whom President Polk later appointed to his cabinet), and two other Tennessee representatives voting in the negative; all five other Tennessee representatives abstained. Ibid., 21 Cong., 2nd sess., Mar. 3, 1831, p. 850.

4. Staudenraus, *African Colonization Movement*, pp. 27–28, 30, 174–75, 185–87.

5. U.S. Congress, House, *Register of Debates*, 22 Cong., 1st sess., Apr. 2, 1832, pp. 2350, 2337, 2333.

6. Ibid., 2333, 2337, 2340; see also 2348. Staudenraus, *African Colonization Movement*, pp. 184–85. W. W. Freehling, *Prelude to Civil War*, pp. 253, 255. When the House voted to reconsider its earlier vote, Mercer withdrew the petition. Egerton, *Charles Fenton Mercer*, pp. 244–45, 286. This episode undercuts, I think, the suggestion that Polk was himself a colonizationist (Marsh, "James K. Polk and Slavery," p. 12). The only evidence I can find to support Marsh's hypothesis is that in 1838 Polk helped one of his Tennessee constituents to transfer local collections to the American Colonization Society in Washington (Thomas J. Hall to JP, Jan. 3, 1838; JP to Joseph Gales, Mar. 5, 1838, *Corr.*, IV, 313–14, 380). This appears to be a sign of a congressman's assiduity in serving constituents, not an indication of Polk's own political stance.

7. Although Speaker Polk excluded virtually any protest against a gag rule, he permitted a long debate—which extended intermittently over a week—between defenders of the Pinckney proposal and those Calhounites who wanted an even more stringent version. An earlier ruling by Polk, in January 1836, had opened the path for Calhounites to move that antislavery petitions be not even received.

U.S. Congress, House, *Register of Debates*, 24 Cong., 1st sess. Jan. 4, May 18, 19, 21, 24, 25, 1836. Richards, *Life and Times of Congressman John Quincy Adams*, pp. 118, 120–21. Adams, *Memoirs*, Jan. 4, May 25, 1836, vol. 9, pp. 266, 286.

8. W. W. Freehling, *Road to Disunion*, pp. 308–36.

9. *Nashville Union*, Oct. 14 [15?], 1839, in Marsh, "James K. Polk and Slavery," p. 55.

10. In November 1838, Polk bought for $11,900 most of his brother William's share in the Mississippi plantation, and in September 1839 he paid another $2,110 for four more slaves. The value of Polk's total previous investment in the plantation (after taking into account the deflation of slave prices during 1839) had been $14,200. See table 5.1 and chapter 4, note 9.

11. Democratic Address to the People of the Slaveholding States, July 20, 1840 (signed by Felix Grundy and Democratic Congressmen from eleven other slave states), reprinted in Tennessee Democratic Central Committee, Address #2, Oct. 1, 1840 (box 5, series 10, Polk MS, Library of Congress), pp. 35, 26–29.

12. JP to Felix Grundy, May 27, 1840 (printed in the *Globe* (Washington), June 6, 1840), *Corr.*, V, 470.

13. Democratic Address, July 20, 1840, pp. 36, 25–26.

14. *Corr.*, V, 560.

15. Sellers (I), p. 420. JP to A. O. P. Nicholson, May 28, 1840, *Corr.*, V, 473. Democratic Address, July 20, 1840, p. 32.

16. Tennessee Democratic Central Committee, Address #2, Oct. 1, 1840, p. 22. This address (quoted here and in the next paragraph) was probably drafted by Polk himself. It surely represented his views. Polk bound it into a leather-covered volume of his own speeches, 1826–41, and he himself signed the inside front cover of the volume. Every pamphlet in this bound volume is either a speech or a public letter of Polk or the report of a committee that he chaired, with the exception of the two addresses issued by the Tennessee Democratic Central Committee during the 1840 presidential campaign. It is, therefore, a fair inference that these two addresses— like the reports of congressional committees that Polk had chaired—were drafted by Polk himself. Box 5, series 10, Polk MS, Library of Congress.

17. For example, Holt, *Political Crisis of the 1850s*, pp. 54–56, 238–45, 252–59.

18. Democratic Address, July 20, 1840, pp. 24–36 (quotation on p. 36).

19. Tennessee Democratic Central Committee, Address #1, July 4, 1840, pp. 2, 20 (box 5, series 10, Polk MS, Library of Congress).

20. Even at the end of the campaign, the Tennessee Democratic Central Committee devoted most of its own address to economic issues. But by appending the long, antiabolitionist address that Felix Grundy and eleven other Southern Democratic congressmen had issued in July (and by adding to it their own threat that abolition would lead to disunion), the Tennessee Democrats gave much more emphasis to antiabolitionism than previously during the campaign.

21. Sellers (I), p. 426; see also, pp. 422–23.

22. I am thinking, for example, of the gradual development and solidification since 1945 of a democratic political culture in Germany and Japan.

CHAPTER 11

1. Cf. Temple, *Notable Men of Tennessee*, p. 255; Holt, *Rise and Fall of the American Whig Party*, pp. 194–206.

2. R. B. Campbell, *Empire for Slavery*, pp. 15–29, 40–49, 54. Sellers (I), p. 337; (II), p. 50.

3. W. W. Freehling, *Road to Disunion*, pp. 356–68, 388–94, 398–410. Tyler had argued in 1820 that extending slavery into Missouri would promote its ultimate extinction, but his employment of this "diffusionist" argument appears to me to have been as cynical as Robert Walker's use in 1844 of the same argument about Texas (pp. 151, 418–23); see esp. Sellers (II), pp. 150–51.

4. These figures for early 1844 are my estimates, based on data in R. B. Campbell, *Empire for Slavery*, p. 55.

5. Sellers (II), pp. 70–98.

6. W. W. Freehling, *Road to Disunion*, pp. 431, 440–49. "Deceived" is my interpretation of the evidence in Sellers (II), pp. 186–89, 205–8, esp. 207n. (John A. Dix to Silas Wright, Feb. 27, 1845), 218–20, and in C. W. Morrison, *Democratic Politics and Sectionalism*, p. 8, n. 24. Sellers is unambiguous: "Clearly Polk deceived. The only doubtful point is how deliberately he deceived"; (II), p. 219.

7. According to Polk's biographer, "The strong position on Oregon [in the 1844 Democratic platform] seems to have been adopted . . . as a means of camouflaging and subordinating the Texas provision." Sellers (II), p. 100; see also pp. 67, 237. W. W. Freehling, *Road to Disunion*, p. 438.

8. Cf. Wright, *Old South, New South*, pp. 25–26, 32.

9. Sellers (I), p. 3 (quotation), 16, 18–20, 28–29, 64–65; 30.

10. Sellers (I), p. 336; (II), pp. 222–23. Late in 1836 Polk wrote that Judge Yell's agent was instructed to "procure for us [Polk and his younger brother William] a first rate cotton plantation in Arkansas this winter. . . . It may be our interest to remove our hands to Arkansas." JP to WHP, Nov. 29, 1836, Lucy Williams Polk Papers, N.C. State Archives. Archibald Yell to JP, Oct. 19, 1836; Aug. 14, Sept. 15, 1839; Jan. 22, 1842, *Corr.*, III, 765–66; VI, 548; V, 242–43; VI, 639.

11. Smith, *War with Mexico*, I, 139n. (p. 449). Merk (with Lois Merk), *Monroe Doctrine*, pp. 133–48 (quotation at p. 134).. Binkley, *Expansionist Movement in Texas*, pp. 6–13, 19–20, 24–29, 129–31.

12. Pletcher, *Diplomacy of Annexation*, pp. 75–79, 113, 117–18, 120, 126, 150–51, 153–56, 165–67, 172–75, 192–93, 201–5.

13. Indeed, the most painstaking historian of these matters, David Pletcher, argues that Polk could have obtained California and New Mexico, as well as Texas, without war had he pursued a more diplomatic course. And, as indicated in note 14, Mexican authorities were even more anxious to avoid war than Pletcher had realized (pp. 576–611).

14. Brack, *Mexico Views Manifest Destiny*, esp. pp. 171–79; see also 135–68.

15. W. W. Freehling, *Road to Disunion*, pp. 427, 435–36. Sellers (II), pp. 146–48.

16. The quotations are from the orders of June 15 and October 16, 1845. Pletcher, *Diplomacy of Annexation*, pp. 255, 283; see also pp. 256, 260, 272, 364–65, 374–76, 407–8. Within three weeks of becoming president, Polk authorized his friend Archibald Yell to promise the Texans that Polk would back their claim to the Rio Grande with military force. On June 15, 1845—even before Texas agreed to annexation—Polk gave General Taylor the order to move his army into Texas (quoted above), declaring that "in the event of annexation, [the Rio Grande] will be our [south]western border." Sellers (II), pp. 222–23; Pletcher, *Diplomacy of Annexation*, p. 255 (quotation).

17. JP, Message to Congress, May 11, 1846, in Richardson, *Messages and Papers of the Presidents*, IV, 442–43.

18. Sellers (II), pp. 416–17.

19. Although Polk's biographer is generally sympathetic to his subject, he alludes here to the president's "gratuitous insistence on an indefensible boundary claim." Ibid., p. 223.

20. The strength of the opposition to the declaration of war was clear from the fact that 35 percent of the congressmen voting (67 out of 190) voted *against* adding the preamble, declaring war, to the appropriation bill. But once the bill had been amended in this way, only 14 congressmen felt they could vote against the combined appropriation bill and declaration of war.

21. On May 30, 1846 (eighteen days after the declaration of war) Polk avowed to the cabinet his purpose to acquire "California, New Mexico, and perhaps some others of the Northern Provinces" of Mexico. A month later the president specified "that I preferred the 26° to any boundary North of it"; on July 7 he defended the twenty-sixth parallel as the most desirable goal, accusing (in his diary) Secretary of State James Buchanan, a Pennsylvanian, of being "sectional" in opposing this goal. Buchanan had objected that Northern, and world, opinion would condemn the introduction of slavery into regions where, under Mexican rule, it did not exist. *Diary*, I, 438, 496; II, 16.

22. JP to WHP, Oct. 2, 1846, letterbook, Polk MS, in Graebner, *Empire on the Pacific*, p. 159.

23. Pletcher, *Diplomacy of Annexation*, pp. 476–80, 491–93. One of the unofficial American agents was Moses Beach (a New York newspaper publisher), who later claimed to have secured agreement of some Mexican clerics and aristocrats to a plan in which Mexico would cede the territory north of 26°. It seems unlikely that the appearance of the twenty-sixth parallel in Beach's proposal—precisely the same boundary that Polk had told his cabinet he hoped to secure—was mere coincidence.

24. Polk did, however, authorize his envoy—in return for Mexico's accepting the loss of all of New Mexico east of the Rio Grande—to promise that the U.S. government would pay various claims by U.S. citizens against the Mexican government. Although these claims were allegedly worth a few million dollars, Polk's offer would have put no cash into Mexican coffers. In making this proposal, Polk implicitly acknowledged (as Buchanan continued explicitly to do) that Texas had no valid claim to the Rio Grande as its border north of El Paso. James Buchanan to John Slidell [the American envoy], Nov. 10, 1845, in J. B. Moore, *Works of James Buchanan*, VI, 302–3. Sellers (II), p. 234.

25. J. B. Moore, *Works of Buchanan*, VI, 305. Pletcher, *Diplomacy of Annexation*, pp. 289–90, 352. Merk (with Lois Merk), *Monroe Doctrine*, p. 158. Sellers (II), p. 265.

26. "Memoir to Accompany the Map of Texas," U.S. Congress, *Senate Documents*, No. 341, 28 Cong., 1 sess., pp. 61, 57, 59.

27. Pletcher, *Diplomacy of Annexation*, pp. 364–65, 369, 374–76, 467–72, 476 (n. 95), 481–83, 494–96.

28. James Buchanan to Nicholas Trist, Apr. 15, 1847, in J. B. Moore, *Works of Buchanan*, VII, 272–74 (quotation at p. 274). Pletcher, *Diplomacy of Annexation*, pp. 498–501. *Diary*, II, 472–73. In January 1847, before Trist's mission had been decided, Polk assured himself in his diary that, although further annexations would

be desirable, California and New Mexico were all that his heart was set upon. *Diary*, II, 308.

29. *Diary*, III, 217 (Nov. 9, 1847). Shenton, *Robert John Walker*, pp. 103–5.

30. *Diary*, III, 189 (quotation, Oct. 12, 1847), 276–77 (Jan. 2, 1848), 347 (quotation, Feb. 21, 1848). JP, Annual Message, Dec. 7, 1847, in Richardson, *Messages and Papers*, IV. 541, 545. Pletcher, *Diplomacy of Annexation*, pp. 511–19, 528–30, 551–55.

31. The total number of American soldiers was 90,000, of whom about 12,850 died. Smith, *War with Mexico*, II, 319.

32. The Whigs gained thirty-four Congressional seats in the 1846–47 midterm elections, increasing their share of House seats from only about 36 percent (after the 1844–45 elections) to almost 50 percent (after the 1846–47 elections). Two-thirds of these Whig gains were concentrated in New York, Pennsylvania, and Ohio, and nearly all of their other gains occurred in the southeastern strip extending from Maryland through Virginia to North Carolina. The results of these congressional elections—scattered from October 1846 through 1847—were almost all known to the president by October 6, 1847, the day Polk ordered Nicholas Trist (as explained in the next paragraph) to return from Mexico. Sellers (II), p. 310. Holt, *American Whig Party*, pp. 238, 244–45, 209. Pletcher, *Diplomacy of Annexation*, p. 529.

33. Pletcher, *Diplomacy of Annexation*, pp. 529, 538, 549, 565.

34. Ibid., pp. 559–60 (including n. 22), 562.

35. I include within the 650,000 square miles the 120,000 square miles acquired in 1850 by the United States from Texas—that is, the land west of present-day Texas that its inflated border claims of 1845 had encompassed. R. B. Morris, *Encyclopedia of American History* (1953), p. 419.

36. Pletcher, *Diplomacy of Annexation*, pp. 560–63. Potter, *Impending Crisis*, p. 3n. Fuller, *Movement for the Acquisition of all Mexico*, pp. 153, 155. Schroeder, *Mr. Polk's War*, p. 158. *Diary*, III, 367–68, 370, 377. Douglas's wife inherited the plantation and its slaves in June 1848. Johannsen, *Stephen A. Douglas*, p. 211.

37. Sellers (I), pp. 40–43; (II), p. 163 (Polk's "whole life had been an unremitting effort to prove himself"). I am indebted to Wayne Cutler, editor of *Correspondence of James K. Polk*, for pointing out that the operation was for a urinary stone, not gallstone. Harris, *Polk's Campaign Biography*, pp. 5–6.

38. Nelson and Nelson, *Memorials of Sarah Childress Polk*, pp. 115–16. *Diary*, for example, Apr. 5, 1847 (II, 456). Sellers (II), pp. 300–6.

39. David Pletcher's scrupulous analysis of Polk's foreign policy concludes that Polk relied far more than was necessary on coercion and coercive threats when subtler diplomacy could have achieved the same goals at less cost and with less risk. These matters are discussed in chapter 13 below. Pletcher, *Diplomacy of Annexation*, esp. pp. 576–611.

CHAPTER 12

1. *Diary*, II, 75–76, 308. Sellers (II). W. W. Freehling, *Road to Disunion*, pp. 430, 437, 448. Pletcher, *Diplomacy of Annexation*, pp. 229, 606. Bergeron, *Presidency of James K. Polk*, pp. 65–68.

2. Watson, *Liberty and Power*, p. 245. W. W. Freehling, *Road to Disunion*, pp. 456–57. Holt, *Rise and Fall of the American Whig Party*, pp. 252–53.

3. Bemis, *John Quincy Adams*, vol. 2, 354–70, 451–55, 462–64. Richards, *Life and Times of Congressman John Quincy Adams*, pp. 146–48, 151–75, esp. 161–62, 165–67, 174–75.

4. C. W. Morrison, *Democratic Politics and Sectionalism*, pp. 5–9, 13–17.

5. *Diary*, I, 496. (Mexican law had banned slavery everywhere in the country except in Texas.) Cf. Sellers (II), p. 424. By 1848 Buchanan had changed his mind about seizing provinces south of New Mexico. Evidently by then he was seeking the support of hungry expansionists in his bid for the Democratic presidential nomination.

6. In January 1847 Buchanan proposed extending the Missouri Compromise line westward to the Pacific Ocean, but Polk was not yet willing to commit himself to 36°30'. Although the president had accepted, by June 1848, that Congress might ban slavery north of that line, he entered a negotiation with John C. Calhoun a few weeks later, implicitly promising that—if legislation favored by Calhoun were to be enacted—Polk would appoint proslavery territorial judges in California and New Mexico. One may infer that such appointees would have legalized slavery in the whole Mexican Cession. See the next paragraph and note 10. Polk's slowness to commit himself to 36°30' has puzzled David Potter and other historians. I infer that the president sought as long as he could to keep open the possibility of legalizing slavery north of 36°30', partly as a bargaining counter against Northern efforts to ban slavery south of that line and partly because he did not like to abandon the chance that slavery might conceivably be legalized even north of that line (e.g., through a ruling by federal judges). He was reluctant to relinquish before he was obliged to do so his Calhounite belief that, as an abstract principle, slavemasters had a right to take their slaves everywhere in the territories. *Diary*, II, 309. Potter, *Impending Crisis*, pp. 68–73, esp. 71. JP, Message to the House of Representatives, Aug. 14, 1848; JP, Annual Message, Dec. 5, 1848, in Richardson, *Messages and Papers*, vol. 4, pp. 608–9, 641–42.

7. See, for example, Sellers (II), p. 483. *Diary*, II, 75.

8. JP to John Childress, June 2, 1846; to RC, Aug. 13, 1846 (quoted in chapter 1 above), letterbook, Polk MS.

9. *Diary*, IV, 72, 206–7 (Aug. 13, Nov. 23, 1848). JP, Annual Message, Dec. 5, 1848, in Richardson, *Messages and Papers*, vol. 4, pp. 641–42.

10. Polk's promise to Calhoun was implicit in his response to the latter's request that the president appoint proslavery territorial judges. Polk, claiming that he was not really making a pledge, told Calhoun that in appointing these judges, "I would do my duty, and jocousely [*sic*] added that my friends . . . must have a 'generous confidence' that I would do so." *Diary*, IV, 21 (July 16, 1848). Brock, *Parties and Political Conscience*, p. 223.

11. See, for example, *Diary*, III, 501–3 (June 24–25, 1848).

12. Ibid., IV, 186–88 (Jan. 16, 1849). James Polk, "Veto to Mr Wilmot with his proviso" (draft), Mar. 3, 1849, Polk MS (reel 61), pp. 9–10.

13. JP to John Leigh, Oct. 10, 1846 (chapter 6 above); to RC, Dec. 12, 1846, Jan. 23, 1847 (emphasis in the original), letterbook; Pickett to JP, Jan. 15, 1847, Polk MS. The 1846 profits are in table C1. In January 1847 Polk countermanded (JP to RC, Jan. 5, 1847, Polk MS) the order to buy several more slaves, probably because he had just committed himself to buying an expensive mansion in Nashville and wanted to pay for it before using large sums to expand his plantation slave force.

14. JP, "Veto to Mr Wilmot with his proviso" (draft), Mar. 3, 1849, Polk MS (reel 61), pp. 8–9. *Diary*, IV, 235, 254, 364–69. C. W. Morrison, *Democratic Politics and Sectionalism*, pp. 19, 34. Sellers (II), pp. 481–83. Richards, *Life and Times of Congressman John Quincy Adams*, p. 200. McCormac, *James K. Polk*, p. 646.

15. Although Benton voted against the Wilmot Proviso on March 2, 1847, he undermined Polk's effort to legalize slavery everywhere south of 36°30' in the Mexican Cession by moving (Aug. 12, 1848) that the Senate retreat from its previous determination to attach a 36°30' clause to the Oregon bill. Chambers, *Old Bullion Benton*, p. 314. Potter, *Impending Crisis*, pp. 75–76.

16. The term is David Potter's, adopted by William Freehling. Potter, *Impending Crisis*, p. 90; W. W. Freehling, *Road to Disunion*, pp. 509–10, 519.

17. This is my reading of the evidence in W. W. Freehling, *Road to Disunion*, 519–23, 528–35, and in Potter, *Impending Crisis*, pp. 122 (quotation), 126–29.

18. A contrary view is argued with great subtlety in Thornton, *Politics and Power in a Slave Society*, pp. 165ff. I remain convinced, nevertheless, that the fundamental reason for the secession of the Deep South in 1860–61 was that affairs had by then (in Thornton's words, p. 165) "taken a more serious turn at Washington" than during the period 1846–50.

19. I believe my view here accords with Thornton's, ibid., p. 475.

20. *Diary*, May 10, 30, June 6, 17, 23, 1848. Pletcher, *Diplomacy of Annexation*, pp. 571–74.

21. W. W. Freehling, *Road to Disunion*, pp. 460, 525.

22. Ibid., pp. 440–48. Sellers (II), 205–8, 215–20.

23. "The central thrust of southern antagonism toward the proviso," according to William Cooper, "concerned theoretical rights, not practical expectations." Cooper, *South and the Politics of Slavery*, p. 243.

24. Potter, *Impending Crisis*, pp. 60–61, 65–66; but cf. p. 73.

25. In his Oregon address, Aug. 14, 1848, Polk expressed his support for the Missouri Compromise line "or some other equitable compromise which would respect the rights of all." Polk's understanding of "some other equitable compromise" is suggested by the sentence in his draft veto of the Wilmot Proviso, where he wrote, "If the inhabitants [of a territory about to become a state] *in forming their State constitutions* either permit or exclude the institution [of slavery], they but exercise the right of Self-Government" (emphasis added). This phraseology indicates that Polk rejected the belief of most Northern Democrats that a territorial legislature could exercise a power to permit or exclude slavery *before* the state constitution was written. Thus Polk's reference to "some other equitable compromise" did not, in fact, represent a retreat from his Southern rights position. Richardson, *Messages and Papers*, vol. 4, p. 609. JP, "Veto to Mr Wilmot with his proviso" (draft), Mar. 3, 1849, Polk MS (reel 61), p. 10.

26. *Diary*, IV, 286–88 (Jan. 16, 1849). JP, "Veto to Mr Wilmot with his proviso" (draft), Mar. 3, 1849, Polk MS (reel 61), p. 9. In his Oregon message to the House of Representatives, Aug. 14, 1848, Polk had already threatened to veto any congressional ban on slavery south of 36°30', implying that secession would be justifiable if free-soilers "pushed [the slavery question] to . . . extremities." And in his annual message to Congress, Dec. 5, 1848, Polk repeated the threat of a veto [it "must be regarded as an original question" (p. 642)—that is, "Congress could not . . . interfere with their relative rights" (p. 641)]. In this annual message (as in his later draft of a message to veto the Wilmot Proviso), Polk seemed also to deny

Northern Democrats' interpretation of the "popular sovereignty" idea, that Congress could grant a territorial legislature the right to ban slavery prior to the writing of the new state's constitution. That right, Polk implied, inhered only in the territory's constitutional convention, at the moment the territory sought entry as a state into the Union. Richardson, *Messages and Papers*, vol. 4, pp. 609, 641–42.

27. JP, Message to the House of Representatives, Aug. 14, 1848, in Richardson, *Messages and Papers*, vol. 4, p. 607. *Diary*, IV, 61–62, 72, 74, 77–78 (Aug. 8, 13–14, 1848). McCormac, *James K. Polk*, p. 642. On Joe, see chapter 3 above.

28. Pletcher, *Diplomacy of Annexation*, pp. 105–6, 216–17, 222–24. Sellers (II), pp. 236–37. Graebner, *Empire on the Pacific*, esp. pp. 7–9, 60–64, 70–72, 87–89, 94–99, 119, 157–58. Weinberg, *Manifest Destiny*, pp. 111–12, 120–21, 129, 144–46.

29. McCormac, *James K. Polk* (1922). Sellers (II), pp. 213–14, 229–34, 264–66. Pletcher, *Diplomacy of Annexation*, p. 606.

30. Pletcher, *Diplomacy of Annexation*, pp. 587–92, 598–600, 602–3, 607–10; see also 222–26, 236–53, 271–72, 296–351, 380–82, 404–17.

31. Ibid., pp. 222–23. Sellers (II), pp. 56–69, 71–72, 78, 82–83, 99–100, 205.

32. JP, "Veto to Mr Wilmot with his proviso" (draft), Mar. 3, 1849, Polk MS (reel 61), pp. 8–10. Richardson, *Messages and Papers*, vol. 4, pp. 608–9. Tennessee Democratic Address #2, Oct. 1, 1840 (Box 5, Series 10, Polk MS, Library of Congress), p. 22.

33. John C. Calhoun to D[avid] Hubbard, Sept. 22, 1844; also, Calhoun to Francis Wharton, 14 July, 1844, in Wilson, *Papers of John C. Calhoun*, vol. 19, pp. 829, 357. Francis Pickens to Henry Conner, May 29, 1844, in Cooper, *South and the Politics of Slavery,* p. 206 (emphasis in the original); see also, p. 118. Wiltse, *John C. Calhoun*, pp. 182, 185, 190.

34. *Diary*, II, 371, 459 (Feb. 8, Apr. 6, 1847); IV, 288, 291 (Jan. 16, 17, 1849). See also Wiltse, *John C. Calhoun*, pp. 382–83, 388–89.

35. Temple, *East Tennessee and the Civil War*, p. 199. The historian Daniel Crofts, working from official figures (which secessionists may have slightly adjusted?), suggests that Unionists got 2.4 percent less of the total vote in East Tennessee than Temple's data indicate. Crofts, *Reluctant Confederates*, p. 342. Temple attributes most of this discrepancy to the omission of Union County—an overwhelmingly Unionist county—from the official figures. Temple, *East Tennessee and the Civil War*, p. 191n.

36. Temple, *East Tennessee and the Civil War*, pp. 219, 221.

37. *Biographical Directory of the American Congress*, p. 1690. M. E. R. Campbell, *Attitude of Tennesseans Toward the Union*, pp. 185, 211. Temple, *East Tennessee and the Civil War*, pp. 227–28. (Mrs. W. H. Polk) to her sister, Mar. 4, 1862; see also Mrs. W. H. Polk to her mother, Dec. 10, 1862, Lucy Williams Polk MS, N.C. State Archives.

38. Catron reached this conclusion by a route different from Taney's. Unlike Taney, Catron averred that the Constitution's territorial clause *did* grant Congress authority to govern the territories. But this grant, Catron argued, did not authorize Congress to ban slavery there because any such ban would deny the constitutionally guaranteed equality of the states and of their citizens (and it would also violate the terms of the Louisiana Purchase). Fehrenbacher, *Dred Scott Case*, pp. 401–4; see also pp. 395, 680 (n. 17).

39. Ibid., pp. 574 (and n. 16), 578–79. Temple, *East Tennessee and the Civil War*, pp. 562, 233.

40. Temple, *East Tennessee and the Civil War*, pp. 220–21. Sellers (II), pp. 4–5, 70–74, 304.

41. Johannsen, *Stephen A. Douglas*, pp. 871, 211, 337, 381.

CHAPTER 13

1. Adams, *Memoirs*, vol. 12, pp. 218–19, 221. Pletcher, *Diplomacy of Annexation*, pp. 329–30. Bemis, *John Quincy Adams*, vol. 1, pp. 321, 332, 332n; see also 309–10, 319–25, 329–31, 339–40; vol. 2, p. 475n. Privately, however, Adams had in 1820 urged a Northern senator to try to amend the Florida treaty in order to ban slavery there. Richards, *Life and Times of Congressman John Quincy Adams*, pp. 101–2.

2. W. W. Freehling, *Road to Disunion*, p. 435.

3. Pletcher, *Diplomacy of Annexation*, pp. 576–611 (quotations on pp. 597, 602, 610–11).

4. Davis, *Slavery and Human Progress*, pp. 192–226 (esp. 192–98, 213), 281–95.

5. Abraham Lincoln, Inaugural Address, Mar. 4, 1861, in Basler, *Collected Works of Abraham Lincoln*, IV, 262–64. Donald, *Lincoln*, pp. 134–37, 165–67, 189–90, 200–2, 238–39, 314–15.

6. Potter, *Impending Crisis*, pp. 57–59, 77.

7. Ibid., pp. 59–61, 276–77, 403–4, 408, 413–15.

8. Fehrenbacher, *Dred Scott Case*, pp. 307, 309, 311–14.

9. Temple, *Notable Men of Tennessee*, p. 329.

10. The proviso did not actually come to a Senate vote in August 1846 because of the filibuster of a free-soil senator over the bill to which the House had attached the proviso. This bill appropriated money to grease the wheels of diplomatic negotiations with Mexico. The filibusterer realized that Southern and Democratic senators had enough votes to remove the proviso from the appropriation bill if there were time to do so before the session expired. Sellers (II), pp. 481–83.

11. W. W. Freehling, *Road to Disunion*, pp. 462, 473–74.

12. Zilversmit, *First Emancipation*, pp. 128, 131, 182, 193. A. G. Freehling, *Drift Toward Dissolution*, pp. 126–69. W. W. Freehling, *Road to Disunion*, p. 126.

13. When Lincoln was a congressman in 1849, he proposed a post-nati scheme of emancipation for the District of Columbia. Donald, *Lincoln*, pp. 136–37; also pp. 165–67, 343–48, 362, 396–97.

14. "This notion, preposterous as it is, of 'getting rid' of nearly three millions of human beings, is almost universal [in Virginia]." Abdy, *Journal of a Residence and Tour, 1833 to . . . 1834*, II, 184. W. W. Freehling, *Road to Disunion*, pp. 127, 157–61, 421–22. Staudenraus, *African Colonization Movement*.

15. Many Northern slaves, however, were sold South after the passage of post-nati laws, and this had the effect that colonization would have had—reducing the number of free blacks within the region. Goldin, "Economics of Emancipation," p. 70.

16. DeBow, "Interest in Slavery," pp. 176–77. Similarly, in 1838 John C. Calhoun told the U.S. Senate, "To destroy [slavery] was to involve a whole region in slaughter, carnage, and desolation." *Congressional Globe*, 25 Cong., 2 Sess., Appendix, pp. 61–62 (Jan. 10, 1838), in McKitrick, *Slavery Defended*, p. 18. Splendid illustrations of demagogic efforts to stir racial anxiety from the *Montgomery*

(Alabama) *Advertiser*, 1849–51, are presented in Thornton, *Politics and Power in a Slave Society*, pp. 205–6, 208.

17. W. W. Freehling, *Road to Disunion*, pp. 472–73.

18. I say nothing here about the long-term interests of the slaves (thousands of whom perished during military service in the Union army or following in the wake of Northern armies) because slavemasters, despite paternalist talk, acted mainly to promote what they supposed were their own interests, not those of their slaves. Nor do I mention how the policy sketched here might have promoted the interests of Americans who lived in the North by saving the lives of the more than 300,000 Northern white men and free blacks who died in the Union army.

19. W. W. Freehling, *Road to Disunion*, pp. 432–33, 446–47. Sellers (II), p. 65.

20. David Potter lucidly explains the significance of Benton's intervention while bewailing it. Potter, *Impending Crisis*, pp. 75–76.

21. W. N. Chambers, *Old Bullion Benton*, pp. 315–16, 328, 341, 344–45.

22. W. W. Freehling, *Road to Disunion*, pp. 435–36, 494.

23. Parks, *John Bell of Tennessee*, pp. 205, 333–34, 398. Temple, *East Tennessee and the Civil War*, pp. 220–21, 230–36.

24. W. W. Freehling, *Road to Disunion*, pp. 356–57, 360, 364, 388–93.

25. Egerton, *Charles Fenton Mercer*, pp. 237–44, 269–70, 275–88. On Berrien, see Brock, *Parties and Political Conscience*, pp. 135–36. Berrien, however, sometimes—for example, in 1849 when he was running for reelection to the Senate— caved in to Democratic pressure and tried to outdo Democrats in his protestations of loyalty to slavery. Holt, *Rise and Fall of the American Whig Party*, pp. 469–70.

26. Polk's biographer Charles Sellers carefully depicts the role of Tennessee's "entrepreneurial Democrats"—such as Polk's brothers-in-law James Walker and Adlai Harris—during the 1830s and earlier. Although Sellers characterizes Polk himself as a "doctrinaire Republican," he shows how Polk compromised his own hard-money stance; by 1843 Polk was personally indebted by over $3000 to the state's new Bank of Tennessee, "whose directors he had appointed." Sellers (I), quotations at pp. 206, viii, 459; see also 170–73, 178, 182, 320–21, 324–25, 345–46, 363–65, 385–98.

27. Sellers (I), p. 149 (quotation). "Outside the ranks of a few ideologues," according to the historian Harry Watson, "many Democratic politicians saw the practical advantages of Whiggish forms of progress and were prepared to welcome them if particular interests got no undue privileges from the state." Watson, *Liberty and Power*, p. 247; see also pp. 236–37. Sellers (II), pp. 14–18. Sellers, *Market Revolution*, pp. 346–47. Cf. Thornton, *Politics and Power in a Slave Society*, pp. 45–57. Neither Sellers, Watson, nor Thornton subscribes exactly to the interpretation suggested here.

28. See, for example, JP, Annual Message to Congress, Dec. 5, 1848, in Richardson, *Messages and Papers*, vol. 4, p. 658.

29. On Polk's relation to the Calhounites and to states' rights doctrines, see Sellers (I), pp. 129, 142, 145–46, 148, 150–52, 160–61. *Diary*, I, 187 (Jan. 23, 1846).

30. Watson, *Liberty and Power*, pp. 212–13, 215–18, 221–24. Holt, *Rise and Fall of the American Whig Party*, pp. 105–7. Sellers, *Market Revolution*, p. 350.

31. Temple, *Notable Men of Tennessee*, pp. 247, 250–53, 257, 259. Sellers (I), pp. 430–34, 437–44, 472–88.

32. Richards, *Life and Times of Congressman John Quincy Adams*, pp. 176–78. Parks, *John Bell of Tennessee*, pp. 171–72. Holt, *Rise and Fall of the American Whig*

Party, pp. 68–69, 117. Howe, *Political Culture of the American Whigs*, pp. 32–42, 124–41.

33. A. G. Freehling, *Drift toward Dissolution*, pp. 162, 272–78.

34. Polk owned thirty-three slaves on his Mississippi plantation at the end of 1844 (table A5); plus blacksmith Harry (rented in Carroll County, Mississippi); plus perhaps four house servants in Tennessee, four being the number of Polk's Tennessee slaves when he died in 1849. JP inventory, May 27, 1851, Davidson County wills, inventories, settlements, XIV, 597 (Roll 432), TSA. Clay apparently possessed just over fifty slaves in 1833. He seems to have sold some of them later, so that he owned thirty-three in 1851. Remini, *Henry Clay*, pp. 205n, 763.

35. Slaves had made up 18 percent of Missouri's population in 1830 but fell to less than 13 percent by 1850. U.S. Bureau of the Census, *Fifth Census, 1830*, p. 151; *Sixth Census, 1840*, p. 418; *Statistical View of the United States*, [1850], p. 133. Chambers, *Old Bullion Benton*, pp. 233, 263–64, 304, 337, 364; see also p. 317. Sellers (II), pp. 320–23. W. W. Freehling, *Road to Disunion*, p. 432. Cf. Benton's defense of the free states from the Calhounite charge that they sought to force emancipation on the slave states: *Thirty Years' View*, vol. 2, pp. 734–35.

36. Remini, *Henry Clay*, pp. 204–5, 437, 611, 772–73.

37. Parks, *John Bell*, p. 361. Bell and his wife apparently held about a three-eighth interest in the Cumberland Iron Works, which in 1852 owned 365 slaves—a number that probably increased by 1856. In 1861 Bell valued his Kentucky coal mines (which he had started buying in 1842) at $150,000 (pp. 115–17, 203, 340–41, 405–6). Cf. Starobin, *Industrial Slavery in the Old South*, p. 15.

38. Sellers (I), p. 374. Watson, *Liberty and Power*, pp. 236–37. Holt, *Rise and Fall of the American Whig Party*, pp. 83–85, 115–17, 178–79, 199–200. Thornton, *Politics and Power*, pp. 40–42, 62.

EPILOGUE

1. W. W. Freehling, *Road to Disunion*, pp. 509–10, 561–62. Potter, *Impending Crisis*, pp. 54–61. Crofts, *Reluctant Confederates*, pp. 195–214, 284–88, 353–60, and passim.

2. Cf. Douglas's speech at Ottawa, Illinois, Aug. 21, 1858, in Angle, *Created Equal?*, esp. pp. 110–12. Other Northern Democratic appeals to racial prejudice are quoted, for example, in Dusinberre, *Civil War Issues in Philadelphia*, pp. 27–28, 109, 136.

3. JP to RC, Aug. 13, 1846, letterbook, Polk MS (quoted in chapter 1).

4. Olmsted, *Journey in the Back Country*, p. 138.

5. JP, Message to the House of Representatives, Aug. 14, 1848, in Richardson, *Messages and Papers*, vol. 4, p. 609.

6. Wyatt-Brown, *Southern Honor*.

7. JP, "Veto to Mr Wilmot with his proviso" (draft), Mar. 3, 1849, Polk MS (reel 61), p. 8.

8. This view is consonant, I think, with that of Bertram Wyatt-Brown, who distinguishes his own understanding of the role of honor during the secession crisis from the revisionist belief that the defense of republican values (and *therefore* of Southern honor) primarily motivated the secessionists. Wyatt-Brown, "Honor and Secession," in his *Yankee Saints and Southern Sinners*, pp. 183–213, esp. 202–4, 198–99.

9. Cf. Thornton, *Politics and Power in a Slave Society*, p. 475.

10. I believe this view accords with important elements of Michael Holt's interpretation: his assessment of Southern Democratic policies, his dissent from determinism, and his emphasis on the far-reaching consequences of Henry Clay's failure to win the presidency in 1844. Holt, *Rise and Fall of the American Whig Party*, esp. pp. 982–83.

11. "Doughfaces" were those Northern Democrats who acceded to most demands of their Southern Democratic associates. Richards, *Slave Power*. Cf., among many others, Baker, *Affairs of Party*, Dusinberre, *Civil War Issues in Philadelphia*, pp. 27–33, 64, 66–80, 84–85, 87–89, 96–98, 102–4, 107–9, 116, 119, 121–22.

12. Cf. Wallace Hettle, *The Peculiar Democracy*.

13. Cf. Ashworth, *Slavery, Capitalism, and Politics*, pp. 323–50.

Select Bibliography

MANUSCRIPTS

The most important sources are in the James K. Polk Papers at the Library of Congress, of which I have used the microfilm version except where otherwise specified. Sources on plantation demography are identified and discussed at the beginning of appendix A. Sources on capital investment and plantation profits appear in appendixes B and C. Supplementary manuscript collections are located as follows:

Mississippi State Archives (Jackson)

> U. S. Bureau of the Census, Manuscript Censuses (Yalobusha County, Miss.), 1840, 1850, 1860

North Carolina Office of Archives and History (Raleigh)

> Mecklenburg County wills, estate records
> Lucy Williams Polk Papers (P.C. 75): [William H. Polk MS]

Southern Historical Collection (Wilson Library, University of North Carolina at Chapel Hill)

> #605 Polk, Brown, and Ewell Family Papers
> #606 Polk and Yeatman Family Papers

Tennessee Presidents Center (University of Tennessee at Knoxville)

> James K. Polk Correspondence

Tennessee State Archives (Nashville)

> Wills, inventories, settlements
> John H. Bills MS
> James Polk MS.

Yalobusha County Courthouse (Coffeeville, Miss.)

> James Polk estate inventory, Dec. 5, 1849: Inventory book E, pp. 31–35.

PRINTED WORKS

Abdy, Edward S. *Journal of a Residence and Tour in the United States of North America from April, 1833 to October, 1834.* 3 vols. London: John Murray, 1835.

Abernethy, Thomas P. *From Frontier to Plantation in Tennessee*. Chapel Hill: University of North Carolina Press, 1932.

Adams, John Quincy, *Memoirs of John Quincy Adams, comprising portions of his Diary from 1795 to 1846*. Edited by C. F. Adams. 12 vols. New York: AMS Press, [1874–77] 1970.

Angle, Paul M., ed. *Created Equal? The Complete Lincoln-Douglas Debates of 1858*. Chicago: University of Chicago Press, 1958.

Ash, Stephen V. *Middle Tennessee Society Transformed, 1860–1870*. Baton Rouge: Louisiana State University Press, 1988.

Ashworth, John. *Slavery, Capitalism, and Politics in the Antebellum Republic. Vol. 1: Commerce and Compromise, 1820–1850*. Cambridge: Cambridge University Press, 1995.

Ayers, Edward L. *Vengeance and Justice: Crime and Punishment in the 19th-Century American South*. New York: Oxford University Press, 1984.

Baker, Jean H. *Affairs of Party: The Political Culture of Northern Democrats in the Mid-Nineteenth Century*. Ithaca, N.Y.: Cornell University Press, 1983.

Ball, Charles. *Fifty Years in Chains*. New York: Dover Publications, [1836] 1970.

Barrow, Bennet H. *Plantation Life in the Florida Parishes of Louisiana, 1836–1846 as Reflected in the Diary of Bennet H. Barrow*. Edited by Edwin Adams Davis. New York: AMS Press, [1943] 1967.

Basler, Roy P., ed. *Collected Works of Abraham Lincoln*. 9 vols. New Brunswick, N.J.: Rutgers University Press, 1953–55.

Bassett, John S., ed. *The Southern Plantation Overseer as Revealed in His Letters*. Westport, Conn.: Negro Universities Press, [1925] 1968.

Bauer, K. Jack. *The Mexican War, 1846–1848*. New York: Macmillan, 1974.

Beard, Charles A., and Mary R. Beard. *The Rise of American Civilization*. 2 vols. London: Jonathan Cape, 1927.

Bemis, Samuel Flagg. *John Quincy Adams*. 2 vols. New York: Knopf, 1949–56.

Benton, Thomas Hart. *Thirty Years' View; or a History of the Working of the American Government for Thirty Years from 1820 to 1850*. 2 vols. New York: D. Appleton, 1854–56.

Bergeron, Paul H. *Antebellum Politics in Tennessee*. Lexington: University Press of Kentucky, 1982.

———. *The Presidency of James K. Polk*. Lawrence: University Press of Kansas, 1987.

Binkley, William C. *The Expansionist Movement in Texas, 1836–1850*. Berkeley: University of California Press, 1925.

Biographical Directory of the American Congress, 1774–1949. Washington, D.C.: U.S. Government Printing Office, 1950.

Blassingame, John W. *The Slave Community: Plantation Life in the Antebellum South*. New York: Oxford University Press, 1972.

Blum, Jerome. *Land and Peasant in Russia from the Ninth to the Nineteenth Century*. Princeton, N.J.: Princeton University Press, 1961.

Bolton, Charles C. *Poor Whites of the Antebellum South: Tenants and Laborers in Central North Carolina and Northeast Mississippi*. Durham: Duke University Press, 1994.

Brack, Gene M. *Mexico Views Manifest Destiny, 1821–1846: An Essay on the Origins of the Mexican War*. Albuquerque: University of New Mexico Press, 1975.

Brock, William R. *Parties and Political Conscience: American Dilemmas, 1840–1850*. Millwood, N.Y.: KTO Press, 1979.

Campbell, Mary E. R. *The Attitude of Tennesseans Toward the Union, 1847–61.* New York: Vantage Press, 1961.

Campbell, Randolph B. *An Empire for Slavery: The Peculiar Institution in Texas, 1821–1861.* Baton Rouge: Louisiana State University Press, 1989.

Chambers, William N. *Old Bullion Benton, Senator from the New West: Thomas Hart Benton, 1782–1858.* New York: Russell & Russell, [1956] 1970.

Chaplin, Joyce E. *An Anxious Pursuit: Agricultural Innovation and Modernity in the Lower South, 1730–1815.* Chapel Hill: University of North Carolina Press, 1993.

Cimprich, John. *Slavery's End in Tennessee, 1861–1865.* Tuscaloosa: University of Alabama Press, 1985.

Collins, Herbert R., and David B. Weaver, eds. *Wills of the U.S. Presidents.* New York: Communications Channels, 1976.

Conrad, Alfred, and John Meyer. "The Economics of Slavery in the Antebellum South." *Journal of Political Economy* 66 (1958): 95–130.

Cooper, William J., Jr. *The South and the Politics of Slavery, 1828–1856.* Baton Rouge: Louisiana State University Press, 1978.

Crofts, Daniel W. *Reluctant Confederates: Upper South Unionists in the Secession Crisis.* Chapel Hill: University of North Carolina Press, 1989.

Cutler, Wayne, John S. D. Eisenhower, Miguel E. Soto, Douglas W. Richmond. *Essays on the Mexican War.* College Station: Texas A & M University Press, 1986.

Davis, David Brion. *Slavery and Human Progress.* New York: Oxford University Press, 1984.

DeBow, J. D. B. "The Interest in Slavery of the Southern Non-Slaveholder." In Eric L. McKitrick (ed.), *Slavery Defended,* pp. 169–77.

DeBow's Review, vol. 7 (1849).

DeVoto, Bernard. *The Year of Decision: 1846.* Boston: Houghton Mifflin, 1943.

Donald, David Herbert. *Lincoln.* London: Pimlico, [1995] 1996.

Doyle, Don H. *Faulkner's County: The Historical Roots of Yoknapatawpha.* Chapel Hill: University of North Carolina Press, 2001.

Dusinberre, William. *Civil War Issues in Philadelphia, 1856–1865.* Philadelphia: University of Pennsylvania Press, 1965.

———. *Them Dark Days: Slavery in the American Rice Swamps.* New York: Oxford University Press, 1996.

Eaton, Clement. *The Freedom-of-Thought Struggle in the Old South.* New York: Harper, 1964.

Egerton, Douglas R. *Charles Fenton Mercer and the Trial of National Conservatism.* Jackson: University Press of Mississippi, 1989.

Emmons, Terence. *The Russian Landed Gentry and the Peasant Emancipation of 1861.* Cambridge: Cambridge University Press, 1968.

Fehrenbacher, Don E. *The Dred Scott Case: Its Significance in American Law and Politics.* New York: Oxford University Press, 1978.

Fitzpatrick, John C., ed. *The Writings of George Washington.* Vol. 37. Washington, D.C.: U.S. Government Printing Office, 1940.

Flexner, James T. *George Washington.* Vol. 4, *Anguish and Farewell, 1793–1799.* Boston: Little, Brown, 1972.

Foner, Eric. "The Wilmot Proviso Revisited." *Journal of American History* 56 (Sept. 1969): 262–79.

Fox-Genovese, Elizabeth, and Eugene Genovese. *Fruits of Merchant Capital: Slavery and Bourgeois Property in the Rise and Expansion of Capitalism.* Oxford: Oxford University Press, 1983.

Franklin, John Hope, and Loren Schweninger. *Runaway Slaves: Rebels on the Plantation.* New York: Oxford University Press, 1999.

Freehling, Alison G. *Drift Toward Dissolution: The Virginia Slavery Debate of 1831–1832.* Baton Rouge: Louisiana State University Press, 1982.

Freehling, William W. *Prelude to Civil War: The Nullification Controversy in South Carolina, 1816–1836.* New York: Harper, 1965.

———. *The Reintegration of American History: Slavery and the Civil War.* New York: Oxford University Press, 1994.

———. *The Road to Disunion. Vol. 1, Secessionists at Bay, 1776–1854.* New York: Oxford University Press, 1990.

Frierson, William L. "John Catron." In *Dictionary of American Biography*, vol. 3, pp. 576–77. New York: Scribner, 1929.

Fuller, John D. P. *The Movement for the Acquisition of All Mexico, 1846–1848.* Baltimore: Johns Hopkins University Press, 1936.

Genovese, Eugene D. *The Political Economy of Slavery: Studies in the Economy & Society of the Slave South.* New York: Vintage, [1965] 1967.

———. *Roll, Jordan, Roll: The World the Slaves Made.* New York: Random House, 1974.

Goldin, Claudia. "The Economics of Emancipation." *Journal of Economic History*, 33 (1973): 66–85.

Graebner, Norman A. *Empire on the Pacific: A Study in American Continental Expansion.* New York: Ronald Press, 1955.

Gray, Lewis Cecil. *History of Agriculture in the Southern United States to 1860.* 2 vols. Washington, D.C.: Carnegie Institution of Washington, 1933.

Gutman, Herbert G. *The Black Family in Slavery and Freedom, 1750–1925.* New York: Random House, 1976.

Hammond, Bray. *Banks and Politics in America, from the Revolution to the Civil War.* Princeton, N.J.: Princeton University Press, 1957.

Harris, J. George. *Polk's Campaign Biography.* Edited by Wayne Cutler. Knoxville: University of Tennessee Press, [1844] 1990.

Hettle, Wallace. *The Peculiar Democracy: Southern Democrats in Peace and Civil War.* Athens: University of Georgia Press, 2001.

Hietala, Thomas R. *Manifest Design: Anxious Aggrandizement in Late Jacksonian America.* Ithaca, N.Y.: Cornell University Press, 1985.

Hoch, Steven L. *Serfdom and Social Control in Russia: Petrovskoe, a Village in Tambov.* Chicago: University of Chicago Press, 1986.

Hoffmann, Charles, and Tess Hoffmann. *North by South: The Two Lives of Richard James Arnold.* Athens: University of Georgia Press, 1988.

Holt, Michael F. *The Political Crisis of the 1850s.* New York: Wiley, 1978.

———. *The Rise and Fall of the American Whig Party.* New York: Oxford University Press, 1999.

Horsman, Reginald. *Race and Manifest Destiny: The Origins of American Racial Anglo-Saxonism.* Cambridge, Mass.: Harvard University Press, 1981.

Howe, Daniel Walker. *The Political Culture of the American Whigs.* Chicago: University of Chicago Press, 1979.

Hughes, Nathaniel C., Jr., and Roy P. Stonesifer, Jr. *The Life and Wars of Gideon J. Pillow*. Chapel Hill: University of North Carolina Press, 1993.

Johannsen, Robert W. *To the Halls of the Montezumas: The Mexican War in the American Imagination*. New York: Oxford University Press, 1985.

———. *Stephen A. Douglas*. New York: Oxford University Press, 1973.

Johnson, Walter. *Soul by Soul: Life Inside the Antebellum Slave Market*. Cambridge, Mass.: Harvard University Press, 1999.

Jones, Norrece T., Jr. *Born a Child of Freedom, Yet a Slave: Mechanisms of Control and Strategies of Resistance in Antebellum South Carolina*. Hanover, N.H.: University Press of New England, 1990.

Kemble, Frances Anne. *Journal of a Residence on a Georgian Plantation in 1838–1839*. Edited by John A. Scott. Athens: University of Georgia Press, [1862] 1984.

Knight, Franklin W. *Slave Society in Cuba during the Nineteenth Century*. Madison: University of Wisconsin Press, 1970.

Kolchin, Peter. *American Slavery, 1619–1877*. London: Penguin, [1993] 1995.

———. *Unfree Labor: American Slavery and Russian Serfdom*. Cambridge, Mass.: Harvard University Press, 1987.

Kotlikoff, Laurence J. "Quantitative Description of the New Orleans Slave Market, 1804 to 1862." In *Without Consent or Contract: Technical Papers,* edited by Robert Fogel and Stanley Engerman, vol. 1, pp. 31–53. New York: Norton, 1992.

Lyell, Charles. *Second Visit to the United States*. 2 vols. London: John Murray, 1849.

McCormac, Eugene I. *James K. Polk: A Political Biography*. Berkeley: University of California Press, 1922.

McKitrick, Eric L., ed. *Slavery Defended: The views of the Old South*. Upper Saddle River, N.J.: Prentice Hall, 1963.

Marsh, Richard Dean. "James K. Polk and Slavery." M.A. thesis, North Texas State University, Denton, 1977.

Merk, Frederick (with Lois Merk). *The Monroe Doctrine and American Expansionism, 1843–1849*. New York: Knopf, 1966.

Merk, Frederick. *Slavery and the Annexation of Texas*. New York: Knopf, 1972.

Montroni, Giovanni. *Gli uemini del re: La nobilita napoletana nell'ottecento*. Rome: Meridiana Libri, 1996.

Mooney, Chase Curran. *Slavery in Tennessee*. Bloomington: University of Indiana Press, 1957.

Moore, John B., ed. *The Works of James Buchanan*. 12 vols. New York: Antiquarian Press, [1908–11] 1960.

Moore, John Hebron. *The Emergence of the Cotton Kingdom in the Old Southwest: Mississippi, 1770–1860*. Baton Rouge: Louisiana State University Press, 1988.

Morris, Christopher. *Becoming Southern: The Evolution of a Way of Life, Warren County and Vicksburg, Mississippi, 1770–1860*. New York: Oxford University Press, 1995.

Morris, Richard B., ed. *Encyclopedia of American History*. New York: Harper, 1953.

Morris, Thomas D. *Southern Slavery and the Law, 1619–1860*. Chapel Hill: University of North Carolina Press, 1996.

Morrison, Chaplain W. *Democratic Politics and Sectionalism: The Wilmot Proviso Controversy*. Chapel Hill: University of North Carolina Press, 1967.

Morrison, Michael. *Slavery and the American West: The Eclipse of Manifest Destiny and the Coming of the Civil War*. Chapel Hill: University of North Carolina Press, 1997.

Nelson, Anson, and Fanny Nelson. *Memorials of Sarah Childress Polk, Wife of the Eleventh President of the United States.* Spartansburg, S.C.: Reprint Co., [1892] 1974.

Oakes, James. *The Ruling Race: A History of American Slaveholders.* New York: Knopf, 1982.

————. *Slavery and Freedom: An Interpretation of the Old South.* New York: Knopf, 1990.

Olmsted, F. L. *A Journey in the Back Country.* London: S. Low & Son, 1860.

————. *A Journey in the Seaboard Slave States.* London: Sampson Low, 1856.

Parks, Joseph Howard. *John Bell of Tennessee.* Baton Rouge: Louisiana State University Press, 1950.

Patterson, Orlando. "On Slavery and Slave Formations." *New Left Review* 117 (1979): 31–67.

————. *Slavery and Social Death: A Comparative Study.* Cambridge, Mass.: Harvard University Press, 1982.

Petrusewicz, Marta. *Latifundium: Moral Economy and Material Life in a European Periphery.* Ann Arbor: University of Michigan Press, 1996.

Pletcher, David M. *The Diplomacy of Annexation: Texas, Oregon, and the Mexican War.* Columbia: University of Missouri Press, 1973.

Polk, James K., *The Diary of James K. Polk during his Presidency, 1845 to 1849.* Edited by Milo M. Quaife. New York: Kraus Reprint Co., [1910] 1970.

Potter, David M. *The Impending Crisis, 1848–1861.* Completed and edited by Don E. Fehrenbacher. New York: Harper, 1976.

Remini, Robert V. *Henry Clay: Statesman for the Union.* New York: Norton, 1991.

Riall, Lucy. *The Italian Risorgimento: State, Society and National Unification.* London: Routledge, 1994.

————. *Sicily and the Unification of Italy: Liberal Policy and Local Power, 1859–1866* Oxford: Clarendon Press, 1998.

Richards, Leonard L. *The Life and Times of Congressman John Quincy Adams.* New York: Oxford University Press, 1986.

————. *The Slave Power: The Free North and Southern Domination, 1780–1860.* Baton Rouge: Louisiana State University Press, 2000.

Richardson, James D., ed. *A Compilation of the Messages and Papers of the Presidents, 1789–1897.* 10 vols. Washington, D.C.: U.S. Government Printing Office, 1896–99.

Scarborough, William K. *The Overseer: Plantation Management in the Old South.* Baton Rouge: Louisiana State University Press, 1966.

Schroeder, John H. *Mr. Polk's War: American Opposition and Dissent, 1846–1848.* Madison: University of Wisconsin Press, 1973.

Scott, Rebecca J. *Slave Emancipation in Cuba: The Transition to Free Labor, 1860–1899.* Princeton, N.J.: Princeton University Press, 1985.

Sellers, Charles Grier, Jr. *James K. Polk: Jacksonian, 1795–1843* (I). Princeton, N.J.: Princeton University Press, 1957

————. *James K. Polk, Continentalist, 1843–1846* (II). Princeton, N.J.: Princeton University Press, 1966.

————. *The Market Revolution.* New York: Oxford University Press, 1991.

Shenton, James Patrick. *Robert John Walker: A Politician from Jackson to Lincoln.* New York: Columbia University Press, 1961.

Smedes, Susan Dabney. [*Memorials of*] *A Southern Planter*. London: John Murray, 1889.

Smith, Justin H. *The War with Mexico*. 2 vols. New York: Macmillan, 1919.

Stampp, Kenneth M. *The Peculiar Institution: Negro Slavery in the American South*. London: Eyre & Spottiswoode, [1956] 1964.

Starobin, Robert S. *Industrial Slavery in the Old South*. New York: Oxford University Press, 1970.

Staudenraus, P. J. *The African Colonization Movement, 1816–1865*. New York: Columbia University Press, 1961.

Stevenson, Brenda. *Life in Black and White: Family and Community in the Slave South*. New York: Oxford University Press, 1996.

Sydnor, Charles S. *Slavery in Mississippi*. New York: Appleton-Century, 1933.

Tadman, Michael. *Speculators and Slaves: Masters, Traders, and Slaves in the Old South*. Madison: University of Wisconsin Press, 1989.

Temple, Oliver P. *East Tennessee and the Civil War*. Freeport, N.Y.: Books for Libraries Press, [1891] 1971.

———. *Notable Men of Tennessee from 1833 to 1875*. New York: Cosmopolitan Press, 1912.

Thornton, J. Mills, III. *Politics and Power in a Slave Society: Alabama, 1800–1860*. Baton Rouge: Louisiana State University Press, 1978.

U.S. Bureau of the Census. *Eighth Census, 1860: Population; Agriculture*. Washington, D.C.: U.S. Government Printing Office, 1864.

———. *Statistical View of the United States, Being a Compendium of the Seventh [1850] Census*. Edited by J. D. B. DeBow. Washington, D.C.: U.S. Government Printing Office, [1854] 1970.

———. *Fifth Census, 1830; Sixth Census, 1840*. Washington, D.C.: U.S. Government Printing Office, [1832, 1841] 1969.

U.S. Congress. House. *Register of Debates*. Washington, D.C.: Gales & Seaton, 1826–37.

———. Senate. *Senate Documents*, 28 Cong., 1 sess. Washington, D.C.: Gales & Seaton, 1844.

Watson, Harry L. *Liberty and Power: The Politics of Jacksonian America*. New York: Noonday Press, 1990.

Wayne, Michael. *The Reshaping of Plantation Society: The Natchez District, 1860–1880*. Baton Rouge: Louisiana State University Press, 1983.

Weaver, Herbert; Wayne Cutler; Paul H. Bergeron, Kermit L. Hall, Earl J. Smith, Carmese M. Paarker, James P. Cooper, Jr., Robert G. Hall, II, Jayne C. DeFiore, eds. *Correspondence of James K. Polk*. 9 vols. to date. Nashville: Vanderbilt University Press, 1969–89; Knoxville: University of Tennessee Press, 1993– .

Weber, David J. *The Mexican Frontier, 1821–1846: The American Southwest Under Mexico*. Albuquerque: University of New Mexico Press, 1982.

———. *The Spanish Frontier in North America*. New Haven, Conn.: Yale University Press, 1992.

Weinberg, Albert K. *Manifest Destiny: A Study of Nationalist Expansionism in American History*. Baltimore: Johns Hopkins University Press, 1935.

Wilson, Clyde N., ed. *The Papers of John C. Calhoun*. Vol. 19. Columbia: University of South Carolina Press, 1990.

Wiltse, Charles M. *John C. Calhoun, Sectionalist, 1840–1850.* Indianapolis: Bobbs-Merrill, 1951.

Wright, Gavin. *Old South, New South: Revolutions in the Southern Economy Since the Civil War.* New York: Basic Books, 1986.

————. *The Political Economy of the Cotton South: Households, Markets, and Wealth in the Nineteenth Century.* New York: Norton, 1978.

Wyatt-Brown, Bertram. *Southern Honor.* New York: Oxford University Press, 1982.

————. *Yankee Saints and Southern Sinners.* Baton Rouge: Louisiana State University Press, 1985.

Yetman, Norman R., ed. *Life Under the "Peculiar Institution": Selections from the Slave Narrative Collection.* New York: Holt, Rinehart and Winston, 1970.

Zilversmit, Arthur. *The First Emancipation: The Abolition of Slavery in the North.* Chicago: University of Chicago Press, 1967.

Index

✦

Numbers in *italics* refer to main discussions. Slaves are alphabetized by first name (e.g., "Caroline Johnson"), even in the few instances when a surname is known.